Pro HTML5 and CSS3 Design Patterns

Michael Bowers

Dionysios Synodinos and

Victor Sumner

Apress®

Pro HTML5 and CSS3 Design Patterns

Copyright © 2011 by Michael Bowers, Dionysios Synodinos, and Victor Sumner

ISBN-13 (pbk): 978-1-4302-3780-8

ISBN-13 (electronic): 978-1-4302-3781-5

President and Publisher: Paul Manning
Lead Editor: Ben Renow-Clarke
Technical Reviewer: Andrew Zack
Editorial Board: Steve Anglin, Mark Beckner, Ewan Buckingham, Gary Cornell, Morgan Ertel, Jonathan Gennick, Jonathan Hassell, Robert Hutchinson, Michelle Lowman, James Markham, Matthew Moodie, Jeff Olson, Jeffrey Pepper, Douglas Pundick, Ben Renow-Clarke, Dominic Shakeshaft, Gwenan Spearing, Matt Wade, Tom Welsh
Coordinating Editor: Jennifer L. Blackwell
Copy Editors: Mary Ann Fugate and Tiffany Taylor
Compositor: Apress Production (Christine Ricketts)
Indexer: BiM Proofreading & Indexing Services
Cover Designer: Anna Ishchenko

Distributed to the book trade worldwide by Springer Science+Business Media NY., 233 Spring Street, 6th Floor, New York, NY 10013. Phone 1-800-SPRINGER, fax (201) 348-4505, e-mail orders-ny@springer-sbm.com, or visit www.springeronline.com.

For information on translations, please e-mail rights@apress.com, or visit www.apress.com.

Apress and friends of ED books may be purchased in bulk for academic, corporate, or promotional use. eBook versions and licenses are also available for most titles. For more information, reference our Special Bulk Sales–eBook Licensing web page at www.apress.com/bulk-sales.

Any source code or other supplementary materials referenced by the author in this text is available to readers at www.apress.com. For detailed information about how to locate your book's source code, go to www.apress.com/source-code/.

I dedicate this book to my wonderful family.
To my loving mother, Aggeliki
To my beautiful wife, Elisa
To my precious daughter, Aggeliki
You make me feel like the luckiest person alive.
—Dionysios Synodinos

This book is dedicated to my wife, Alicia, with love.
—Victor Sumner

Contents at a Glance

Contents at a Glance..iv

Contents..vi

About the Authors..xiv

About the Technical Reviewer xv

Acknowledgments xvi

Introduction xvi

Chapter 1: Design Patterns: Making CSS Easy! 1

Chapter 2: HTML Design Patterns 33

Chapter 3: CSS Selectors and Inheritance 63

Chapter 4: Box Models...81

Chapter 5: Box Model Extents..99

Chapter 6: Box Model Properties..111

Chapter 7: Positioning Models..129

Chapter 8: Positioning: Indented, Offset, and Aligned 153

Chapter 9: Positioning: Advanced 179

Chapter 10: Styling Text 205

Chapter 11: Spacing Content 225

Chapter 12: Aligning Content...247

Chapter 13: Blocks 265

Chapter 14: Images 293

Chapter 15: Tables...327

Chapter 16: Table Column Layout..353

Chapter 17: Layouts...381

Chapter 18: Drop Caps..427

Chapter 19: Callouts and Quotes 447

Chapter 20: Alerts..**465**

Index..**493**

Contents

Contents at a Glance..iv

Contents..vi

About the Authors...xiv

About the Technical Reviewer xv

Acknowledgments xvi

Introduction xvi

Audience xvi

Innovations xvii

Conventions xx

Using This Book xxii

How This Book Is Structured xxiii

Downloading the Code..xxiv

Using the Code... xxv

Contacting the Authors xxv

Chapter 1: Design Patterns: Making CSS Easy! 1

Design Patterns—Structured Recipes..2

Using Design Patterns..2

Using Style Sheets...7

CSS Syntax 8

Using Cascade Order 14

Simplifying the Cascade 17

CSS and HTML Links...18

Common CSS Properties...19

CSS Properties and Values: Common 20

CSS Properties and Values: Content 21

CSS Properties and Values: Layout...22

CSS Properties and Values: Specialized 23

Selectors 23
Media Queries 24
Flexible Units of Measure 25
Fixed Units of Measure 25
Ratios Between Units of Measure at 96 dpi 26
Typical font-size Values at 96 dpi 26
Transitions, Animations, and 2D Transformations 27
Troubleshooting CSS 28
Normalized Style Sheet 30

Chapter 2: HTML Design Patterns 33
Chapter Outline 33
HTML Structure 34
HTML Structure 37
XHTML 42
DOCTYPE 44
Header Elements 46
Conditional Style Sheet 48
Structural Block Elements 50
Terminal Block Elements 52
Multi-purpose Block Elements 54
Inline Elements 56
Class and ID Attributes 58
HTML Whitespace 60

Chapter 3: CSS Selectors and Inheritance 63
Chapter Outline 63
Type, Class, and ID Selectors 64
Position and Group Selectors 66
Attribute Selectors 68
Pseudo-element Selectors 70
Pseudo-class Selectors 72
Subclass Selector 74
Inheritance 76
Visual Inheritance 78

Chapter 4: Box Models 81
Chapter Outline 81
Display 82

Box Model 84
Inline Box 86
Inline-Block Box 88
Block Box 90
Table Box 92
Absolute Box 94
Floated Box 96

Chapter 5: Box Model Extents **99**
Chapter Outline 99
Width 100
Height 102
Sized 104
Shrinkwrapped 106
Stretched 108

Chapter 6: Box Model Properties **111**
Chapter Outline 111
Margin 112
Border 114
Padding 118
Background 120
Overflow 122
Visibility 124
Page Break 126

Chapter 7: Positioning Models **129**
Chapter Outline 129
Positioning Models 130
Positioned 132
Closest Positioned Ancestor 134
Stacking Context 136
Atomic 138
Static 140
Absolute 142
Fixed 144
Relative 146
Float and Clear 148
Relative Float 150

Chapter 8: Positioning: Indented, Offset, and Aligned 153
  Chapter Outline 153
  Indented 154
  Offset Static 156
  Offset or Indented Static Table 158
  Offset Float 160
  Offset Absolute and Offset Fixed 162
  Offset Relative 164
  Aligned Static Inline 166
  Aligned and Offset Static Block 168
  Aligned and Offset Static Table 170
  Aligned and Offset Absolute 172
  Aligned-center Absolute 174
  Aligned Outside 176

Chapter 9: Positioning: Advanced 179
  Chapter Outline 179
  Left Aligned 180
  Left Offset 182
  Right Aligned 184
  Right Offset 186
  Center Aligned 188
  Center Offset 190
  Top Aligned 192
  Top Offset 194
  Bottom Aligned 196
  Bottom Offset 198
  Middle Aligned 200
  Middle Offset 202

Chapter 10: Styling Text 205
  Chapter Outline 205
  Font 206
  Highlight 208
  Text Decoration 210
  Text Shadow 212
  Text Replacement with Image 214
  Text Replacement with Canvas and VML 216

Font Embedding 218
Invisible Text 220
Screenreader-only 222

Chapter 11: Spacing Content **225**

Spacing 226
Blocked 228
Nowrap 230
Preserved 232
Code 234
Padded Content 236
Inline Spacer 238
Inline Decoration 240
Line Break 242
Inline Horizontal Rule 244

Chapter 12: Aligning Content **247**

Text Indent 248
Hanging Indent 250
Horizontal-Aligned Content 252
Vertical-Aligned Content 254
Vertical-Offset Content 256
Subscript and Superscript 258
Nested Alignment 260
Advanced Alignment Example 262

Chapter 13: Blocks **265**

Chapter Outline 265
Structural Meaning 266
Visual Structure 268
Section 270
Lists 272
Background Bulleted 274
Inlined 276
Collapsed Margins 278
Run-In 280
Horizontal Rule 282
Block Spacer 284
Block Space Remover 286

Left Marginal...288
Right Marginal 290
Chapter 14: Images **293**
Chapter Outline..293
Image 294
Image Map 296
Fade-Out 298
Semi-transparent...300
Replaced Text 302
Content over Image...304
Content over Background Image 306
CSS Sprite...308
CSS Sprite cont. 310
Basic Shadowed Image 312
Shadowed Image 314
Shadowed Image cont. 316
Shadowed Image cont. 318
Rounded Corners 320
Rounded Corners cont. 322
Image Example 324
Chapter 15: Tables...**327**
Chapter Outline..327
Table 328
Row and Column Groups 330
Table Selectors 332
Separated Borders..334
Collapsed Borders..336
Styled Collapsed Borders...338
Hidden and Removed Cells 340
Removed and Hidden Rows and Columns 342
Vertical-Aligned Data..344
Striped Tables..346
Tabled, Rowed, and Celled 348
Table Layout 350
Chapter 16: Table Column Layout..**353**
Table Layout Models..353

Using Column Layouts 354
Chapter Outline 354
Column Width 356
Shrinkwrapped Columns.. 358
Sized Columns 360
Content-Proportioned Columns.. 362
Size-Proportioned Columns 364
Percentage-Proportioned Columns.. 366
Inverse-Proportioned Columns 368
Equal Content-Sized Columns 370
Equal-Sized Columns.. 372
Undersized Columns 374
Flex Columns 376
Mixed Column Layouts.. 378

Chapter 17: Layouts..**381**
Chapter Outline 381
Fluid Layout Overview... 382
Outside-in Box 384
Floating Section 388
Float Divider.. 390
Fluid Layout 392
Opposing Floats 394
Event Styling 396
Rollup.. 398
Tab Menu 402
Tabs 406
Flyout Menu 410
Button 414
Layout Links.. 418
Multi-column Layout.. 420
Template Layout 422
Layout Example 424

Chapter 18: Drop Caps..**427**
Chapter Outline 427
Aligned Drop Cap 428
First-Letter Drop Cap 430

Hanging Drop Cap 432
Padded Graphical Drop Cap 434
Floating Drop Cap 436
Floating Graphical Drop Cap 438
Marginal Drop Cap 440
Marginal Graphical Drop Cap 442

Chapter 19: Callouts and Quotes **447**
Chapter Outline 447
Left Floating Callout 448
Right Floating Callout 450
Center Callout 452
Left Marginal Callout..454
Right Marginal Callout 456
Block Quote..458
Inline Block Quote 460
Inline Quote 462

Chapter 20: Alerts..**465**
Chapter Outline 465
JavaScript Alert 466
Tooltip Alert 468
Pop-Up Alert..470
Pop-Up Alert..472
Alert 474
Inline Alert..476
Hanging Alert..478
Graphical Alert 480
Run-In Alert..482
Floating Alert 484
Left Marginal Alert 486
Right Marginal Alert 488
Form Validation 490

Index..**493**

About the Authors

Michael Bowers has been writing software professionally for over 22 years. He taught himself to program when he was 14 and hasn't stopped since.

He is currently a principal engineer and enterprise information architect. He has been a software developer, architect, and modeler for many projects, ranging from web sites to application frameworks to database systems. He has built web applications, integrated enterprise systems, automated factories with robotics, developed a language, interpreter, and compiler, and managed teams. His favorite languages include CSS, HTML, XML, C#, C++, Visual Basic, Java, JavaScript, SQL, and XQuery.

Michael is also an accomplished pianist, with a bachelor's degree in music composition, a master's degree in music theory, and an ABD PhD in music theory. In his spare time, he loves to improvise, arrange, and compose music.

Dionysios Synodinos the research platform team lead at C4Media and a freelance consultant, focusing on rich Internet applications, web application security, mobile web, and web services.

He's also the lead editor for HTML5 and JavaScript for InfoQ, where he also regularly writes about the JVM platform.

Going back and forth between server-side programming and UI design for more than a decade, he has been involved in diverse software projects and contributed to different technical publications.

Victor Sumner is a senior software engineer at LookSmart, LTD. As a self-taught web applications developer, he has had many roles in the web application life cycle, from database administrator to web designer, and all aspects in between. He enjoys working on and solving problems that are outside his comfort zone.

When not at the office, Victor has a number of hobbies, including photography, horseback riding, and gaming. He lives in Ontario, Canada with his wife, Alicia.

About the Technical Reviewer

Andrew Zack is the CEO of ZTMC, Inc. (`ztmc.com`), specializing in search engine optimization (SEO) and Internet marketing strategies. His project background includes almost 20 years of site development and project management experience and over 15 years as an SEO and Internet marketing expert.

He has also been very active in the publishing industry, having co-authored Flash 5 studio and served as a technical reviewer on over ten books and industry publications.

Having started working on the Internet close to its inception, Andrew continually focuses on the cutting edge and beyond, focusing on new platforms and technology to continually stay in the forefront of the industry.

Acknowledgments

I feel blessed having had friends, mentors, and colleagues like Panagiotis Astithas, Christos Stathis, Kostas Troulos, Fotis Stamatelopoulos, Floyd Marinescu, Ryan Slobojan, Werner Schuster, Panagiotis Christias, and Georgia Rouni.

Also I would like to thank the Apress team for all their great work and especially our coordinating editor, Jennifer L. Blackwell, and our editor, Ben Renow-Clarke, for making this a fun experience!

Dionysios Synodinos

Introduction

This is a solutions book for styling HTML5 with CSS3. It contains more than 350 design patterns you can put to use right away. Each design pattern is modular and customizable, and you can combine patterns to create an unlimited number of designs.

Each design pattern has been thoroughly tested and proven to work in all major web browsers including Chrome, Firefox, Internet Explorer, Opera, and Safari. All the content in this book is usable and practical. You won't waste time reading about things that don't work! With this book, you will no longer have to use hacks, tricks, endless testing, and constant tweaking in multiple browsers to get something to work.

Using a design pattern is as easy as copying and pasting it into your code and tweaking a few values. You will immediately see which values you can modify and how they affect the result so you can create the exact style and layout you want—without worrying whether it will work.

This is more than a cookbook. It systematically covers several usable features of CSS and combines these features with HTML to create reusable patterns. Each pattern has an intuitive name to make it easy to find, remember, and talk about. Accessibility and best practices are carefully engineered into each design pattern, example, and source code.

You can read straight through the book, use it as a reference, and use it to find solutions. Each example includes a screenshot and all relevant HTML and CSS code so you can easily see how each design pattern works. The explanation for each design pattern is included alongside, so you can easily study the example while you read about how it works.

Design patterns are organized by topic, and all usable CSS rules are covered in depth and in context like no other book. All design patterns are accessible and follow best practices, making this book a worthwhile read from cover to cover, as well as an excellent reference to keep by your side while you are designing and coding.

This book unleashes your productivity and creativity in web design and development. Design patterns are like Legos—you can combine them in countless ways to create any design. They are like tools in a toolbox, and this book arms you with hundreds of tools you can whip out to solve problems quickly and reliably. Instead of hacking away at a solution, this book shows you how to create designs *predictably*—by combining *predictable patterns*.

Audience

This book is written for those who have some familiarity with CSS and HTML. It is for newcomers who have previously read an introductory book on CSS and HTML. It is for designers and developers who tried CSS at one time and gave up because it never seemed to work right. It is for professionals who want to take their CSS skills to a higher level. It is for all who want to create designs quickly without hacking around until they find something that works in all browsers.

We assume that you know the basics of *coding* CSS and HTML. If you work exclusively in WYSIWYG designers like Dreamweaver or FrontPage and never look at HTML or CSS code, you may find the code in this book overwhelming.

If you like to learn by example, like to see how code works, and have some familiarity with CSS and HTML, you will love this book.

Some design patterns use JavaScript. To fully understand them, you need to understand the basics of JavaScript, but you do not need to know JavaScript to use these patterns. Most importantly, you do not need to know anything about JavaScript to understand and use the remaining 340+ design patterns because they have nothing to do with JavaScript!

Innovations

This book contains several innovative concepts, terms, and approaches. These are not new or radical: the technology is already built into the major browsers, the concepts are implied in the CSS specification, and the terms are commonly used. What makes them innovative is how we define and use them to show what can be done with CSS and HTML. In other words, they are innovative because they simplify learning, understanding, and using CSS and HTML. These ideas change how you think about CSS and HTML, and that makes all the difference. Furthermore, many of the design patterns in the book are innovative because they document combinations of properties and elements to solve difficult problems like never before.

Six Box Models

One innovation in the book is the idea that CSS has *six* box models instead of one. CSS officially has one box model that defines a common set of properties and behaviors. A single box model is a very useful concept, but it is oversimplified. Over the years, we learned the hard way that box model properties work differently depending on the type of box.

This is one reason why so many people struggle with CSS. The box model seems simple, yet when one uses a box model property, such as `width`, it works only some of the time or may work differently than expected. For example, the `width` property sets the interior width of a block box, but on table boxes it sets the outer width of the border, and on inline boxes it does absolutely nothing.

Rather than treating different behaviors as an exception to one very complicated box model, we define six simple box models that specify the behavior for each type of box. Chapter 4 presents the six box models, which are inline, inline-block, block, table, absolute, and float. Since you always know which of these six box models you are using, you always know how each box model property will behave.

Furthermore, each box model defines its own way that it flows or is positioned. For example, inline boxes flow horizontally and wrap across lines. Block boxes flow vertically. Tables flow their cells in columns and rows. Floats flow horizontally, wrap below other floats, and push inline boxes and tables out of the way. Absolute and fixed boxes do not flow; instead, they are removed from the flow and are positioned relative to their closest positioned ancestor.

Box Model Extents

Another innovation in the book is the concept that there are three ways a box can be dimensioned: it can be sized, shrinkwrapped, or stretched (see Chapter 5). Each type of box requires different combinations of properties and property values for it to be sized, shrinkwrapped, or stretched. Various design patterns in Chapters 5 through 9 show how this is done. These three terms are not official CSS terms, but they are implied in the CSS specification in its formulas and where it mentions "size," "shrink-to-fit," and "stretch."[1]

---

[1] In the CSS 2.1 specification, the terms "size" and "sized" occur 15 times in Chapters 8, 9, 10, 11, 17, and 18. These occurrences refer to the general sense that a box has size.

Of course, sizing, shrinkwrapping, and stretching are not new ideas. What is innovative is that this book clearly defines these three terms and shows how they are a foundational feature of CSS and a key *generator* of CSS design patterns.

Box Model Placement

Another innovation is the idea that there are three ways a box can be placed in relation to its container or its siblings: specifically, it can be indented (or outdented), offset from its siblings, or aligned and offset from its container (see Chapter 8). The CSS specification talks much about *offsetting* positioned elements, and it talks a little about *aligning* elements (see Chapter 9 of the CSS 2.1 specification), but it does not discuss how elements can be *indented*, although this behavior is implied in its formulas.

Indenting, offsetting, and aligning are different behaviors. For example, an *indented* box is stretched and its margins shrink its width, whereas an *aligned* box is sized or shrinkwrapped and its margins do not shrink its width. Aligned and indented boxes are aligned to their containers, whereas offset boxes can be offset from their container or offset from their siblings.

Different combinations of properties and property values are needed to indent, offset, and align different types of boxes. The design patterns in Chapters 8 and 9 show how this is done.

Of course, indenting, offsetting, and aligning are not new ideas. What is innovative is that this book clearly defines these three terms and shows how they are a foundational feature of CSS and a key *generator* of CSS design patterns.

Column Layouts

Another innovation is the discovery, naming, and documenting of 12 automated techniques built into browsers for laying out columns in tables (see Chapter 16).

All the major browsers include these powerful column layout features. They are compatible across the major browsers and are very reliable. Even though using tables for page layout is not recommended,[2] *tabular data* still needs to be laid out, and you can take advantage of these column layouts to make tabular data look great.

Fluid Layouts

Another innovation is fluid layouts (see Chapter 17). The concept of fluid layouts is not new, but the process of creating them is commonly one of trial and error. In Chapter 17, we present four simple design patterns you can use to create complex fluid layouts with confidence and predictability in all major browsers.

The terms "shrink" and "shrink-to-fit" occur nine times in Chapters 9 and 10 of the CSS 2.1 specification. The idea that different boxes can shrinkwrap to fit their content is implied in Sections 10.3.5 through 10.3.9 and Section 17.5.2.

The terms "stretch" and "stretched" occur four times in Chapters 9 and 16. The idea of stretching a box to its container is mentioned in passing as shown in the following quote (italics added), "many box positions *and sizes* are calculated with respect to the edges of a rectangular box called a containing block." (See Sections 9.1.2, 9.3.1, and 10.1.)

[2] Using tables for layout creates accessibility issues for nonsighted users. Furthermore, fluid layout techniques (as shown in Chapter 17) are completely accessible and much more adaptable than tables.

These design patterns, Outside-In Box, Floating Section, Float Divider, and Fluid Layout, use floats and percentage widths to make them fluid, but they do so without the problems you normally encounter using these techniques, such as collapsed containers, staggered floats, and percentages that push floats below each other.[3]

The Fluid Layout design pattern creates columnar layouts with the versatility of tables but without using tables. Even better than tables, these layouts automatically adjust their width and reflow from columns into rows as needed to fit into narrow displays.

Event Styling

Another innovation is the Event Styling JavaScript Framework presented in Chapter 17. This is a simple, powerful, open source framework for *dynamically and interactively* styling a document. It uses the latest best practices to ensure that HTML markup is completely free of JavaScript code and completely accessible, and all styling is done with CSS. Furthermore, the framework allows you to select elements in JavaScript using the *same selectors* you use to select elements in CSS. This vastly simplifies and unifies the styling and scripting of a dynamic HTML document!

The book includes this framework to show how to integrate JavaScript, CSS, and HTML so you can use styles interactively. Of course, if you do not want to use JavaScript, you can skip over the five JavaScript design patterns in Chapter 17 and the two JavaScript patterns in Chapter 20—the remaining 343+ design patterns do not use JavaScript.

Combining HTML5 and CSS3 to Create Design Patterns

The final and most pervasive innovation in the book is the idea of combining general *types* of HTML elements with CSS properties to create design patterns. The book defines four major types of HTML elements in Chapter 2 (structural block, terminal block, multi-purpose block, and inline), and Chapter 4 maps them to the six box models (inline, inline-block, block, table, absolute, and float).

Each design pattern specifies how it applies to *types* of HTML elements. In other words, a design pattern is more than a recipe that works only when you use specific elements; it is a pattern that applies to all equivalent *types* of HTML elements.

For example, the Floating Drop Cap design pattern in Chapter 18 specifies a pattern that uses block and inline elements, but it does not specify which block and inline elements you have to use (see Listing 1). For example, you could use a paragraph for the **BLOCK** element and a span for the **INLINE** element (see Listing 2), or you could use a division for the **BLOCK** and a **<strong>** for the **INLINE**, and so forth.

In some exceptional cases, a design pattern may specify an actual element, like a **<span>**. This happens when a specific element is the best solution, the only solution, or an extremely common solution. Even in these cases, you can usually swap out the specified element for another element of the same type.

1. *Listing 1. Floating Drop Cap Design Pattern*

HTML

```
<BLOCK class="hanging-indent">
  <INLINE class="hanging-dropcap"> text </INLINE>
</BLOCK>
```

---

[3] Internet Explorer 6 has a number of *bugs* that may occur when you float elements. Unfortunately, there is no way to create a solution that always bypasses these bugs, although the Fluid Layout design pattern does a good job of avoiding them most of the time. Fortunately, Internet Explorer 7 fixes these bugs.

CSS

```
.hanging-indent { padding-left:+VALUE; text-indent:-VALUE; margin-top:±VALUE; }
.hanging-dropcap { position:relative; top:±VALUE; left:-VALUE; font-size:+SIZE;
  line-height:+SIZE; }
```

2.   **Listing 2.** *Floating Drop Cap Example*

HTML

```
<p class="hanging-indent">
  <span class="hanging-dropcap" >H</span>anging Dropcap.
</p>
```

CSS

```
.hanging-indent { padding-left:50px; text-indent:-50px; margin-top:-25px; }
.hanging-dropcap { position:relative; top:0.55em; left:-3px; font-size:60px;
  line-height:60px; }
```

Conventions

Each design pattern uses the following conventions:

- Uppercase tokens should be replaced with actual values. (Notice how the uppercase tokens in Listing 1 are replaced with values in Listing 2.)

- **Elements** are uppercase when you should replace them with elements of your choice. If an element name is lowercase, it should not be changed unless you ensure the change produces the same box model. The following are typical element placeholders:

    - **ELEMENT** represents any type of element.

    - **INLINE** represents inline elements.

    - **INLINE_TEXT** represents inline elements that contain text such as <span>, <em>, or <code>.

    - **BLOCK** represents block elements.

    - **TERMINAL_BLOCK** represents terminal block elements.

    - **INLINE_BLOCK** represents inline block elements.

    - **HEADING** represents <h1>, <h2>, <h3>, <h4>, <h5>, and <h6>.

    - **PARENT** represents any element that can be a valid parent of its children.

    - **CHILD** represents any element that can be a valid child of its parent.

    - **LIST** represents any list element including <ol>, <ul>, and <dl>.

    - **LIST_ITEM** represent any list item including <li>, <dd>, and <dt>.

- **Selectors** that you should replace are uppercase. If a selector contains lowercase text, that part of the selector should not be changed unless you also modify the HTML pattern, such as changing a class name. The following are typical placeholders:

    - `SELECTOR {}` represents any selector.

    - `INLINE_SELECTOR {}` represents any selector that selects inline elements.

    - `INLINE_BLOCK_SELECTOR {}` represents any selector that selects inline-block elements.

    - `BLOCK_SELECTOR {}` represents any selector that selects block elements.

    - `TERMINAL_BLOCK_SELECTOR {}` represents any selector that selects terminal block elements.

    - `SIZED_BLOCK_SELECTOR {}` represents any selector that selects sized block elements.

    - `TABLE_SELECTOR {}` represents any selector that selects table elements.

    - `CELL_SELECTOR {}` represents any selector that selects table cell elements.

    - `PARENT_SELECTOR {}` represents any selector that selects the parent in the design pattern.

    - `SIBLING_SELECTOR {}` represents any selector that selects the children in the pattern.

    - `TYPE {}` represents a selector that selects elements by a type of your choice such as **h1** or **span**.

    - `*.CLASS {}` represents a selector that selects elements by a class name of your choice.

    - `#ID {}` represents a selector that selects elements by an ID of your choice.

- **Values** that you should replace are represented by uppercase tokens. If a value contains lowercase text, that part of the value should not be changed. The following are typical value tokens:

    - Some values are literal and not meant to be replaced such as **0**, **-9999px**, **1px**, **1em**, **none**, **absolute**, **relative**, and **auto**. These values are always lowercase.

    - **+VALUE** represents a positive measurement greater than or equal to zero, such as **0**, **10px**, or **2em**.

    - **-VALUE** represents a positive measurement less than or equal to zero, such as **0**, **-10px**, or **-2em**.

    - **±VALUE** represents any measurement.

    - **VALUEem** represents an em measurement.

    - **VALUEpx** represents a pixel measurement.

    - **VALUE%** represents a percentage measurement.

- **VALUE_OR_PERCENT** represents a value that can be a measurement or a percentage.

- **WIDTH STYLE COLOR** represents multiple property values, such as those required by **border**. We use an uppercase token for each value.

- **url("FILE.EXT")** represents a background image where you replace **FILE.EXT** with the URL of the image.

- **CONSTANT** represents a valid constant value. For example, **white-space** allows three constant values: **normal**, **pre**, and **nowrap**. For convenience, we often list the valid constant values in uppercase with underscores in between each possible value, such as **NORMAL_PRE_NOWRAP**.

- **ABSOLUTE_FIXED** represents a list of constant values from which you can choose one value. The underscore separates the constant values. The complete list of values for **position** includes **static**, **relative**, **absolute**, and **fixed**. If a design pattern works only for **absolute** and **fixed**, the pattern specifies **position:ABSOLUTE_FIXED**. If it works for all four values, it specifies **position:STATIC_RELATIVE_ABSOLUTE_FIXED** or **position:CONSTANT**.

- **-(TAB_BOTTOM + EXTRA_BORDER + EXTRA_PADDING)** is an example of a formula that you would replace with a calculated value. The uppercase tokens in the formula are tokens that occur elsewhere in the design pattern. For example, if you assigned **TAB_BOTTOM** to **10px**, **EXTRA_BORDER** to **10px**, and **EXTRA_PADDING** to **10px**, you would replace the formula with **-30px**.

Using This Book

You can use the book to master CSS. You can read straight through the book to take your CSS skills to a higher level and to discover the many golden nuggets tucked away inside design patterns. Each chapter is organized so that it builds on design patterns presented earlier in the chapter and presented in previous chapters. On the other hand, since individual chapters and design patterns are self-contained, you can read them one by one in any sequence to master a specific topic or technique.

You can use the book as a reference book. This book explains all of the usable CSS properties and shows how to use them in examples. Even more importantly, many properties behave differently when combined with other properties. Each design pattern identifies and documents the unique combination of properties required to create a specific result. This makes it a reference book not only for how CSS properties work alone, but also for how they work *in combination.*

You can use the book to learn by example. Since all examples in the book follow best practices, you can learn good habits and techniques just by studying them. To make studying the book by example easier, you can use the "See also" sections to look up all related design patterns. This allows you to easily see many examples of how a specific CSS property or feature can be used in a variety of contexts.

You can use the book as a cookbook to help you create designs or to solve problems. Design patterns are organized by topic so you can quickly find related solutions.

We have added extra features to the book to make it easy to find a solution when you need it. You can use the table of contents, the index, thumb tabs, chapter outlines, design pattern names, and the "See also" section of each design pattern to quickly find properties, patterns, answers, and solutions. Since the screenshots in each example are in the same location on every page, you can even thumb through the book while looking at screenshots to find a solution. We find visual scanning a very easy, fast, and effective way to find solutions!

How This Book Is Structured

Chapters 1 through 3 explore the fundamentals of CSS and HTML:

- **Chapter 1 shows how design patterns make CSS easy.** Here we demonstrate how to combine simple design patterns into more complex and powerful patterns. We also review the syntax of CSS and the cascade order. In addition, we present several charts that make using CSS easy: a list of links to useful CSS web sites, a summary of CSS properties; a four-page listing of all usable CSS *properties, values, and selectors* organized by where they can be used; charts on units of measure and font size; two example style sheets for normalizing the styles of elements in all browsers; media queries; transitions, animations and 2D transformations; and a 12-step guide to troubleshooting CSS.

- **Chapter 2 introduces the design patterns that underlie HTML.** In this chapter, we present the best practices of using HTML including coding in XHTML. We also explore the types of structures you can create with HTML including structural blocks, terminal blocks, multi-purpose blocks, and inlines. We also show how to use IDs and attributes for easy selection by CSS selectors.

- **Chapter 3 introduces design patterns for CSS selectors and inheritance.** Here we demonstrate how selectors are the bridge between HTML and CSS. We present design patterns for type, class, ID, position, group, attribute, pseudo-element, pseudo-class, and subclass selectors. We also explore CSS inheritance.

Chapters 4 through 6 explore the six CSS box models. They show how each HTML element is rendered as one of these six types of boxes (or not rendered at all). They demonstrate how the same properties produce different results in each box model, and how each box model flows differently from the other box models.

- **Chapter 4 explores the six box models**: inline, inline-block, block, table, absolute, and float.

- Chapter 5 explores the three ways of dimensioning a box: sized, shrinkwrapped, or stretched.

- **Chapter 6 explores each of the box model properties**: margin, border (radius, shadows, etc.), padding, background, overflow, visibility, and pagebreak.

Chapters 7 through 9 explore how boxes flow or are positioned.

- **Chapter 7 explores the five positioning models** (static, absolute, relative, fixed, and floated) and relates them to the six box models.

- **Chapter 8 explores the three ways a box can be positioned**—for example, a box can be indented or outdented, offset from its siblings, or aligned and offset from its container.

- **Chapter 9 combines the patterns in Chapters 7 and 8**. The combinations result in more than 50 design patterns for positioning elements—with a particular focus on absolute and fixed positioning.

Chapters 10 through 12 explore in detail how inline boxes flow and how to style, space, and align text and objects.

- **Chapter 10 explores the properties that style text** and also contains three design patterns for hiding text while remaining accessible to nonsighted users. It also presents advanced techniques like text replacement with canvas and vml, and CSS3 font-embedding.

- Chapter 11 shows how to *space* inline content horizontally and vertically.

- Chapter 12 shows how to *align* inline content horizontally and vertically.

Chapters 13 and 14 explore in detail how blocks and images flow and how they can be styled.

- **Chapter 13 explores blocks**, starting with a discussion of the structural meaning of blocks and how you can visually display that meaning. It covers lists, inlining blocks, collapsed margins, run-in blocks, block spacing, and marginal blocks.

- **Chapter 14 explores images**, such as image maps, semi-transparent images, replacing text with images, sprites, shadowed images, and rounded corners.

Chapters 15 and 16 explore in detail how to style and lay out tables and cells.

- **Chapter 15 explores tables** including table selectors, collapsed borders, hiding cells, vertically aligning content in cells, and displaying inline and block elements as tables.

- **Chapter 16 explores laying out table columns using 12 patterns**, which automatically shrinkwrap columns, size them, proportionally distribute them, and so forth.

Chapter 17 explores how the flow of floats can be used to create fluid layouts.

- **Chapter 17 shows how to create fluid layouts** that automatically adapt to different devices, fonts, widths, and zoom factors. It also shows how to create interactive layouts using JavaScript.

Chapters 18 through 20 show how to combine design patterns to create a variety of solutions to the same problem. Each solution addresses different needs and has different advantages and disadvantages. Besides being useful solutions in and of themselves, they demonstrate how you can combine patterns to solve any design problem.

- **Chapter 18 explores drop caps.** Here we cover seven types of drop caps using seven different combinations of design patterns.

- **Chapter 19 explores callouts and quotes.** The chapter demonstrates five types of callouts and three types of quotes.

- **Chapter 20 explores alerts.** Here we present three types of interactive alerts and eight types of text alerts (i.e., attention getters). It also explores HTML5 Form Validation and shows how to natively validate HTML5 forms and alert users for wrong input.

Downloading the Code

You can download all the code at `www.apress.com` by searching for and going to the detail page for *Pro HTML5 and CSS3 Design Patterns*. On the book's detail page is a link to the sample code compressed into a ZIP file.

Using the Code

The code is arranged in folders, with a folder for each chapter. To make chapter folders easy to navigate, each folder name includes the chapter number and title. Inside each chapter folder are example folders: one for each design pattern presented in the chapter.

So you can easily find examples, each example folder has the same name as its design pattern. This makes it easy and fast to find design patterns by searching folder names. Since the HTML in each example names and describes its design pattern, you can find a design pattern by searching for words inside HTML files. You could also search inside CSS files for examples that use a particular CSS property, such as **display**.

To make it easy to view examples in multiple browsers, we put a file named **index.html** in the root folder that links to all design pattern folders. In turn, each folder contains a file named **index.html** that links to all the design patterns in that folder. These navigation pages make it quick to find and view each design pattern in each chapter.

Each example folder contains *all* the files needed to make the example work. This makes it a breeze to use the examples in your own work: simply copy a folder and start making changes. You don't have to worry about tracking down and including files from other folders.

The most important files in each example folder are **example.html** and **page.css**. **example.html** contains the HTML code for the example. **page.css** is the main style sheet for the example.

Each example also uses a CSS file named **site.css**. It contains a few nonessential font and heading rules that give all the examples in the book the same basic look and feel.

In a few exceptional cases, we use an additional CSS file to overcome bugs or nonstandard behavior in Internet Explorer and these rules override rules in **page.css**.

The seven JavaScript examples use five JavaScript files. These are explained in the Event Styling design pattern in Chapter 17. **page.js** is the most important file because it contains JavaScript code specific to the example. The remaining JavaScript files are open source libraries.

Lastly, each example folder contains all image files used by that example.

Contacting the Authors

You can contact us at the following addresses:

- Michael Bowers at **mike@cssDesignPatterns.com**
- Dionysios Synodinos at **synodinos@gmail.com**

We look forward to your comments, suggestions, and questions.

CHAPTER 1

Design Patterns: Making CSS Easy!

On the surface, CSS seems easy. It has 45 commonly used properties you can employ to style a document. Below the surface, different combinations of properties and property values trigger completely different results. I call this **CSS polymorphism** because the same property has many meanings. The result of CSS polymorphism is a combinatorial explosion of possibilities.

Learning CSS is more than learning about individual properties. It is about learning the contexts in which properties can be used and how different types of property values work differently in each context. As an example, take the `width` property, which has many different meanings depending on how it is combined with other rules and what values are assigned to it. For instance, `width` has absolutely no effect on inlines. `width:auto` shrinkwraps floats to the width of their content. `width:auto` shrinkwraps absolutes when `left` and `right` are set to `auto`. `width:auto` stretches blocks to the width of their parent element. `width:auto` stretches absolutes to the width of their containing block when `left` and `right` are set to `0`. `width:100%` stretches blocks and floats to the width of their parent element as long as they do not have borders, padding, and margins. `width:100%` stretches tables to the width of their parent even if they do have borders and padding. `width:100%` stretches absolutes to the width of their closest positioned ancestor instead of their parent. `width:100em` sizes an element in relation to the height of its `font-size`, which allows the element to be sized wide enough to contain a certain number of characters. `width:100px` sizes an element to a fixed number of pixels regardless of the `font-size` of its text.

To complicate matters further, not all of the rules are implemented by browsers. For example, over 40 out of 122 properties and over 250 out of 600 CSS rules are not implemented by one or more of the major browsers. CSS combines several specifications that define various levels and profiles. Each level of CSS builds upon the last, typically adding new features and typically denoted as CSS 1, CSS 2, and CSS 3. Profiles are typically a subset of one or more levels of CSS built for a particular device or user interface. Browser support for CSS3 is an important issue for developers, especially since it is still rapidly evolving as a specification.

Trying to learn CSS by memorizing the extraordinary number of exceptions to each rule is extremely frustrating.

To make learning CSS easy, this book documents all *usable* combinations of properties and property values. It puts properties in context and paints a complete picture of how CSS works.

Imagine the time you will save by not having to read about rules that do not work and by not having to test every rule to see whether it works in every browser and in combination with other rules. I have already done this for you. I have run many thousands of tests. I have tested every CSS property and every combination of properties in every major browser, including Internet Explorer 6/7/8/9, Firefox 7, Chrome 12, Opera 9, and Safari 5.

I have boiled down these results into simple design patterns—all the CSS and HTML design patterns you need to create stunning, high-performance, and accessible web sites. This edition of the book (2nd) has been updated to include the latest information and tips about HTML5 and CSS3.

After you learn these design patterns, you'll wonder how you ever developed web sites without them!

1

In this chapter, I discuss the purpose of design patterns and how they work. I give some examples of how to combine design patterns to create new patterns. I also discuss how to use style sheets, CSS syntax, and the cascading order to your advantage.

Next, I present a series of charts that list all the usable CSS properties and units of measure. I then present 12 techniques for troubleshooting CSS quickly. Lastly, I discuss how to standardize the way various browsers style elements—so you can override these default styles with confidence.

Design Patterns—Structured Recipes

Design patterns have been used with great success in software programming. They improve productivity, creativity, and efficiency in web design and development, and they reduce code bloat and complexity. In the context of CSS and HTML, design patterns are sets of common functionality that work across various browsers and screen readers, without sacrificing design values or accessibility or relying on hacks and filters. But until now they have not been applied systematically to HTML and CSS web design and development.

Design patterns underlie all creative activities. We think in terms of patterns when we talk, write, and create. Design patterns are similar to document templates that we can fill in with our own content. In literature, they are like archetypal characters and plots. In music, they are like themes and variations. In programming, they are similar to reusable algorithms that can be systematically varied and combined with each other to produce a desired result.

Once a design pattern is revealed, it greatly increases creativity and productivity. It can be used by itself to create quick results, and it can be easily combined with other patterns to create more complex results. Design patterns simplify and amplify the creative process. They make creation as easy as building with blocks or Legos. You simply choose predesigned patterns, vary them, and combine them to create the result you want. Patterns do not limit creativity—they unleash creativity.

The seminal work *Design Patterns: Elements of Reusable Object-Oriented Software*, by Erich Gamma, Richard Helm, Ralph Johnson, and John Vlissides (Addison-Wesley, 1995), explains that a design pattern consists of four elements: a pattern name, a problem, a solution, and trade-offs. This book follows this approach.

Since this is a practical book, it focuses directly on the concrete patterns designed into CSS and HTML that are actually implemented in the major browsers. This book also creates new design patterns by combining built-in patterns into higher-level patterns.

In a very real sense, this is a book of patterns that you can use to create your designs.

Using Design Patterns

Chapters 1 through 7 present the basic properties and elements for styling layout. Chapters 8 and 9 combine these properties to create all possible block, positioned, and floated layouts. Chapters 10 through 12 present the basic properties for styling text and also present combinations of properties you can use to create inline layouts. Chapters 13 through 16 combine design patterns from previous chapters with specialty properties and elements to style blocks, lists, images, tables, and table columns.

Together, Chapters 1 through 16 present over 300 design patterns created by combining 45 common CSS properties with four types of elements (inline, inline-block, block, and table) and five types of positioning (static, relative, absolute, fixed, and float).

This is the great power of design patterns: it is easy to take basic patterns and combine them to form more complex patterns. This makes learning CSS easy, and it makes using CSS very productive. Chapters 17 through 20 show how to combine these design patterns to create fluid layouts, drop caps, callouts, quotes, and alerts.

To illustrate the simplicity and power of design patterns, the next five examples show how to take a series of basic design patterns and combine them into more complex patterns. You do not need to understand the details of each pattern—just the process of combining patterns.

The first example in this series shows the background property in action. background is a design pattern built into CSS that displays an image behind an element. Example 1-1 shows the background property combined with a division element. The division is sized 250 by 76 pixels so it will reveal the entire background image.[1]

Example 1-1. Background Image

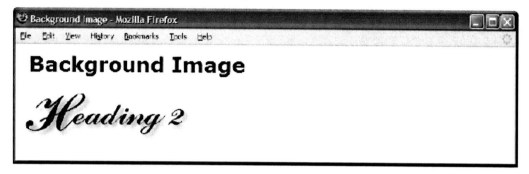

HTML

```
<h1>Background Image</h1>
<div></div>
```

CSS

```
div { background:url("heading2.jpg") no-repeat; width:250px; height:76px; }
```

Example 1-2 demonstrates the Absolute design pattern. The idea behind the Absolute design pattern is to remove an element from the flow and position it relative to another element. CSS provides the position:absolute rule for this purpose. When position:absolute is combined with the top and left properties, you can position an element at an offset from the top left of its closest positioned ancestor. I used position:relative to position the division so it would be the closest positioned ancestor to the span. I then absolutely positioned the span 10 pixels from the top and left sides of the division.[2]

---

[1] This example is simple and yet it combines seven design patterns: the Structural Block Elements design pattern in Chapter 2; the Type Selector pattern in Chapter 3; the Block Box pattern in Chapter 4; the Width, Height, and Sized patterns in Chapter 5; and the Background design pattern in Chapter 6.

[2] This example is simple, and yet it combines seven design patterns: the Inline Elements and Structural Block Elements design patterns in Chapter 2; the Class Selector pattern in Chapter 3; the Absolute Box pattern in Chapter 4; and the Absolute, Relative, and the Closest Positioned Ancestor patterns in Chapter 7.

Example 1-2. Absolute

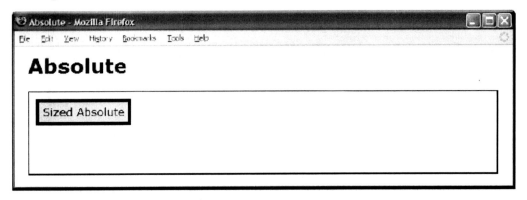

HTML

```
<h1>Absolute</h1>

<div class="positioned">
  <span class="absolute">Sized Absolute</span>
</div>
```

CSS

```
*.positioned { position:relative; }
*.absolute { position:absolute; top:10px; left:10px; }

/* Nonessential styles are not shown */
```

Example 1-3 combines the design patterns in the first two examples to create the Text Replacement design pattern. The idea behind text replacement is to display an image in the place of some text (so you can have more stylistic control over the text because it is embedded in an image). In addition, you want the text to be present behind the image so that it becomes visible if the image fails to download.

I combined the Background and Absolute design patterns to create the Text Replacement pattern. I placed an empty span inside a heading. I relatively positioned the heading so child elements can be absolutely positioned relative to it. I assigned a background image to the span and absolutely positioned it in front of the text in the heading element. I sized the span and the heading to the exact size of the background image.

The end result is that the background image of the span covers the text in the heading, and if the image fails to download, the styled text in the heading is revealed.[3]

---

[3] The Text Replacement example uses the 14 design patterns shown in the previous two examples. It also introduces the ID Selector design pattern in Chapter 3. You can learn more about the Text Replacement design pattern in Chapter 10.

Example 1-3. Text Replacement

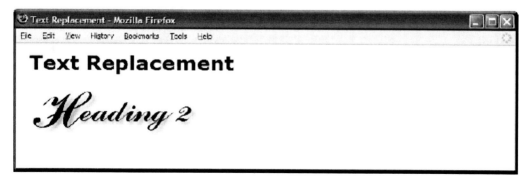

HTML

```
<h1>Text Replacement</h1>
<h2 id="h2" >Heading 2<span></span></h2>
```

CSS

```
#h2 { position:relative; width:250px; height:76px; overflow:hidden; }

#h2 span { position:absolute; width:250px; height:76px; left:0; top:0;
  background:url("heading2.jpg") no-repeat; }
```

Example 1-4 demonstrates the Left Marginal design pattern. The idea behind this pattern is to move one or more elements out of a block into its left margin so you can have headings (or notes, images, etc.) on the left and content on the right.[4]

---

[4] The Left Marginal design pattern combines the Position Selector design pattern in Chapter 3; the Margin pattern in Chapter 6; the Absolute Box pattern in Chapter 4; and the Absolute, Relative, and the Closest Positioned Ancestor patterns in Chapter 7.

Example 1-4. Left Marginal

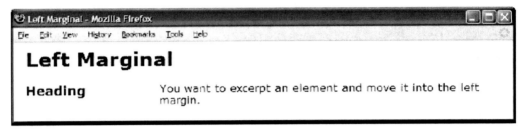

HTML

```
<h1>Left Marginal</h1>

<div class="left-marginal" >
  <h2 class="marginal-heading">Heading</h2>
  You want to excerpt an element and move it into the left margin.</div>
```

CSS

```
*.left-marginal { position:relative; margin-left:200px; }
*.marginal-heading { position:absolute; left:-200px; top:0; margin:0; }
```

Example 1-5 demonstrates the Marginal Graphic Dropcap design pattern. This pattern combines all the design patterns shown in the previous four examples. The idea behind this pattern is to create a graphical drop cap in the left margin of a block with all the advantages of the Text Replacement and Left Marginal design patterns.[5]

To meet these requirements, I used the **indent** class to relatively position the paragraph so that it will be the closest positioned ancestor of the drop cap and to add a 120-pixel left margin to the paragraph to make room for the drop cap. I used the **graphic-dropcap** class to absolutely position the drop cap, to move it into the paragraph's left margin, and to set it to the exact size of the dropcap image. I then absolutely positioned the span inside the graphic drop cap and moved it over the dropcap text so it covers the text with its background image.

Viewed by itself, the Marginal Graphic Dropcap pattern is a somewhat complex combination of 16+ design patterns. On the other hand, when viewed as a combination of the Text Replacement and Left Marginal design patterns, it is quite simple. This is the power of design patterns.

---

[5] The Marginal Graphic Dropcap design pattern is discussed in detail in Chapter 18.

Example 1-5. Marginal Graphic Dropcap

HTML

```
<h1>Marginal Graphic Dropcap</h1>

<p class="indent"><span class="graphic-dropcap" >M<span></span></span>arginal
  Graphic Dropcap. The letter M has been covered by the dropcap image.
  Screen readers read the text and visual users see the image.
  If the browser cannot display the dropcap image,
  the text becomes visible.</p>
```

CSS

```
*.indent { position:relative; margin-left:120px; }

*.graphic-dropcap { position:absolute;
  width:120px; height:90px; left:-120px; top:0; }

*.graphic-dropcap span { position:absolute;
  width:120px; height:90px; margin:0; left:0; top:0;
  background:url("m.jpg") no-repeat; }
```

Using Style Sheets

You can place styles in three locations: style sheets, <style>, and style.

A **style sheet** is an independent file that you can attach to an HTML document using the <link> element or CSS's @import statement. <style> is an HTML element that you can embed within the HTML document itself. style is an attribute that can be embedded within any HTML element.

I recommend putting styles in style sheets. This reduces noncontent in your HTML documents, and it puts all your styles in files that are easily managed.

I recommend naming style sheets using single-word, lowercase names. This keeps style sheet names simple and easy to remember, and works safely in all operating systems. I suggest you use a name that describes the scope and purpose of the style sheet, such as site.css, page.css, handheld.css, print.css, and so forth. The standard extension for a style sheet is .css. The standard Internet media type is text/css.

I recommend using the location of a style sheet to control its scope. If a style sheet is for an entire web site, you could place it in the root directory of the web site. If a style sheet applies only to a document, you could place it in the same directory as the document. Another option, depending on how you organize your site, is to keep all style sheets in one directory.

To link a style sheet to an HTML document, you can include a `<link>` element in the `<head>` section of HTML documents, and you can place the URI of the style sheet within the `href` attribute of the `<link>` element. Listing 1-1 shows the style sheet links that I use in each example in this book. See the Header Elements and Conditional Stylesheet design patterns in Chapter 2 for more information on linking style sheets.

Listing 1-1. *Attaching Style Sheets*

```
<link rel="stylesheet" href="site.css" media="all" type="text/css" />
<link rel="stylesheet" href="page.css" media="all" type="text/css" />
<link rel="stylesheet" href="print.css" media="print" type="text/css" />
<!--[if lte IE 6]>
<link rel="stylesheet" href="ie6.css" media="all" type="text/css" />
<![endif]-->
```

For increased download performance, you may want to include page-specific styles in the `<style>` element instead of in a separate page-specific style sheet. Since these styles are page-specific, there is little disadvantage to putting these styles in the header of the page. On the other hand, I do strongly recommend against using the `style` attribute of HTML elements because this creates very hard-to-maintain code.

CSS Syntax

CSS syntax is easy. A style sheet contains **styles**; a style contains **selectors** and **rules**; and a rule contains a **property** and a **value**. The following is the design pattern for a style:

```
SELECTORS { RULES }
```

The following is the design pattern for a rule:

```
PROPERTY:VALUE;
```

For example, p{margin:0;} is a style. p is the selector, which selects all `<p>` elements in an HTML document. The curly bracket ({}) operators assign the rule, margin:0;, to the selector, p. The colon (:) operator assigns the value 0 to the property, margin. The semicolon (;) operator terminates the rule.

A style may have one or more selectors and one or more rules. For example, p.tip{margin:0; line-height:150%;} is a style. The curly bracket operators group the two rules, margin:0; and line-height:150%;, into a ruleset and assign it to the selector, p.tip, which selects all `<p class="tip">` elements in an HTML document.

CSS Syntax Details

The key points of CSS syntax are as follows:

- **Unicode UTF-8** should be used to encode CSS files—the same way you should encode HTML files.

- **CSS code should be lowercase.** Selectors are *case-sensitive* when referencing element names, classes, attributes, and IDs in XHTML.[6] CSS properties and values

---

[6] In HTML, CSS selectors are case-insensitive.

are *case-insensitive*. For simplicity and consistency, I use lowercase characters for all CSS code including elements, classes, and IDs.

- **Element names, classes, and IDs** are restricted to letters, numbers, underscores (_), hyphens (-), and Unicode characters 161 and higher. The first character of an element, class, or ID must not be a number or a hyphen. A classname and ID must not contain punctuation other than the underscore and hyphen. For example, `my_name2-1` is a valid name for a class or ID, but the following are *invalid*: `1`, `1my_name`, `-my_name`, `my:name`, `my.name`, and `my,name`.

- **Multiple classes** can be assigned to an element by separating each class name with a space, such as `class="class1 class2 class3"`.

- **Constant values** should not be placed in quotes. For example, `color:black;` is correct, but `color:"black";` is not.

- **The backslash** (\) can be used to embed characters in a context where they normally cannot occur; for example, `\26B` embeds `&` in a string or identifier. Anywhere from two to eight hex codes can follow a backslash, or a character can follow a backslash.

- **A string** may contain parentheses, commas, whitespace, single quotes (`'`), and double quotes (`"`) as long as they are escaped with a backslash, such as the following:

```
"embedded left   parentheses \( "
"embedded right  parentheses \) "
"embedded comma \, "
"embedded single quote \' "
"embedded double quote \" "
"embedded single quote  ' in a double-quoted string"
'embedded double quote  " in a single-quoted string'
```

- **A semicolon** should terminate each CSS rule and `@import` statement.

```
color:red;
@import "mystylesheet.css";
```

- **Rulesets** are created by enclosing multiple rules in curly braces, such as `{ color:red; font-size:small; }`.

- **The right curly brace** (}) immediately terminates a set of properties, unless it is embedded within a string, such as `"}"`.

- **A CSS comment** starts with `/*` and ends with `*/`, such as `/* This is a CSS comment */`. Comments cannot be nested. Thus, the first time a browser encounters `*/` in a style sheet, it terminates the comment. If there are subsequent occurrences of `/*`, they are not interpreted as part of the comment—for example:

```
/* This is an incorrect comment
  /* because it tries to nest
    /* several comments. */
      STARTING HERE, THIS TEXT IS OUTSIDE OF ALL COMMENTS! */ */
```

Using Whitespace in CSS

Whitespace in CSS includes only the following characters: space (\20), tab (\09), new line (\0A), return (\0D), and formfeed (\0C). A browser will not interpret other Unicode whitespace characters as whitespace—such as the nonbreaking space (\A0).

You can optionally place whitespace before and after the following: selectors, curly braces, properties, colons, values, and semicolons. For example, all the following statements are correct and produce the exact same result:

```
body{font-size:20px;line-height:150%;}
```

```
body { font-size:20px; line-height:150%; }
```

```
body { font-size : 20px ; line-height : 150% ; }
```

```
body
{
  font-size:  20px;
  line-height: 150%;
}
```

In this book, I use a compact coding style in which I put no whitespace inside rules, and I put one space in between rules and selectors, such as the following:

```
body { font-size:20px; line-height:150%; }
```

Whitespace never occurs within a property name or within a constant property value. Whenever CSS uses multiple words for a property name or constant property value, it uses a hyphen to separate the words, such as font-family and sans-serif. On rare occasions, CSS uses CamelCase to combine multiple words into one constant value, such as ThreeDLightShadow.

Using Property Values

Property values come in the following forms: constant text, constant numbers, lengths, percentages, functions, comma-delimited lists of values, and space-delimited series of values. Each property accepts one or more of these types of values.

I have included all common types of values in Example 1-6. But first, I have listed them here along with an explanation:

- **color:black;** assigns the constant value black to the color property. Most properties have unique constant values. For example, the color property can be assigned to over 170 constants that represent colors ranging from papayawhip to ThreeDDarkShadow.

- **background-color:white;** assigns the constant value white to the background-color property. Notice that the following three rules do the same thing as this rule, but use different types of property values. Hex is also commonly used for color properties in styles, e.g., background-color:#000000;.

- **background-color:rgb(100%,100%,100%);** assigns the CSS function rgb() to background-color. rgb() takes three comma-delimited parameters between its parentheses, which specify the amount of red, green, and blue to use for the color. In this example, percentages are used. One hundred percent of each color makes white.

- **background-color:rgb(255,255,255);** assigns white to the background-color. In this case, values from 0 to 255 are used instead of percentages. The value 0 is no color. The value 255 equals 100% of the color. Using 255 for red, green, and blue makes white.

- **background-color:WindowInfoBackground;** assigns the operating system color WindowInfoBackground to background-color. Notice how operating system color constants are in CamelCase.[7]

- **font-style:italic;** assigns the constant value of italic to font-style. The font-style property also allows two other constant values: normal and oblique.

- **font-size:20px;** assigns a length of 20 pixels to font-size. You can assign a variety of measurements to most properties including px (pixel), em (height of the font or font-size), ex (height of the letter "x"), pt (point, i.e., 1/72 of an inch), in (inch), cm (centimeter), mm (millimeter), and pc (pica, i.e., 12 points, or 1/6 of an inch).

- **font-family:"Century Gothic", verdana, arial, sans-serif;** assigns a comma-delimited list of font names to font-family. If the first font name is unavailable, a browser uses the second, and so forth. The last font name should be one of the generic font names: "serif", "sans-serif", "cursive", "fantasy", "monospace", which work in every browser. Whenever a font name contains a space, it must be enclosed in double quotes, such as "Century Gothic".

- **line-height:150%;** assigns 150% of the font-size to line-height.

- **margin:1em;** assigns the size of the font to margin (i.e., font-size multiplied by 1).

- **border:4px double black;** creates a black, 4-pixel, double-line border. Notice how border takes three space-delimited values that represent the border's width, style, and color. The sequence of the values does not matter. border is a shortcut property for three properties: border-width, border-style, and border-color. There are several other shortcut properties including background, font, list-style, margin, and padding.

- **padding:0.25em;** assigns one-quarter of the font size to padding (i.e., font-size multiplied by 0.25).

- **background-image:url("gradient.jpg");** assigns the gradient.jpg image to background-image using the url function, which takes the URL of a file as its only parameter. I always put a URL in quotes, but you have to only if the URL contains whitespace.

- **background-repeat:repeat-x;** assigns the constant repeat-x to background-repeat. Other background-repeat values include repeat-y, repeat, and no-repeat.

- **margin:0;** assigns zero to margin. Zero is the only length that may be specified without a unit of measurement. All other lengths must be immediately followed by a measurement, such as 1px, -1.5em, 2ex, 14pt, 0.5in, -3cm, 30mm, or 5pc.

- **font-weight:900;** assigns the constant 900 to font-weight. This number is actually a constant. You can use the following constants for font-weight: normal, bold, bolder, lighter, 100, 200, 300, 400, 500, 600, 700, 800, or 900. (Note that browser

---

[7] Each time you assign the same property to the same element, the new rule overrides the previous rule. Since the example contains four background-color rules in a row, the last one is applied.

support is poor for numerical font weights, generally treating 100 through 400 as normal and 500 through 900 as bold. Furthermore, bolder and lighter are rarely supported by browsers and/or operating system fonts. Thus, I rarely use any value for font-weight other than normal or bold.)

Later in the chapter, I present a four-page chart that lists all usable CSS properties and values. color is the only property in the chart that has an incomplete list of usable values. It shows 79 of the 170 color constants. I organized the 79 color constants into three groups that you may find useful: the 16 standard colors organized by hue, 35 common colors organized by hue from light to dark, and the 28 operating system colors. Throughout this book, I often use the color gold. I also use related hues such as wheat, orange, tomato, firebrick, and yellow.

Tip   You can disable a rule by placing the number 1 (or any other character for that matter) immediately in front of a property name—for example, 1background-color:white. This invalidates the rule, but only the one rule. All other valid rules before and after the invalid one are still processed. I often use this technique to invalidate one rule temporarily to disable its effect while testing other rules.

Example 1-6. CSS Syntax Is Easy

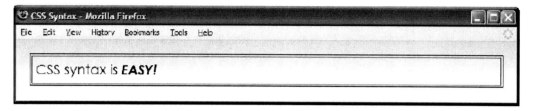

HTML

```
<!DOCTYPE html>

<html lang="en">

<head><title>CSS Syntax</title>
  <meta http-equiv="Content-type" content="text/html; charset=utf-8" />
  <link rel="stylesheet" href="page.css"   media="all"     type="text/css" />

<style><!--
  body { color:black; background-color:white;
    background-color:rgb(100%,100%,100%);
    background-color:rgb(255,255,255);
    background-color:WindowInfoBackground; }
--></style>
</head>

<body>
  <p>CSS syntax is <span style="font-style:italic;">EASY!</span></p>
</body>

</html>
```

CSS

```
body { font-family:"Century Gothic",verdana,arial,sans-serif;
  font-size:20px; line-height:150%;
  margin:1em; border:4px double black; padding:0.25em;
  background-image:url("gradient.gif"); background-repeat:repeat-x; }
p { margin:0; }
span { font-weight:900; }
```

Using Cascade Order

CSS allows you to assign the same rule to the same element multiple times. I call these **competing rules**. Browsers use the cascading order to determine which rule in a set of competing rules gets applied. For example, a browser assigns default rules to each element. When you assign a rule to an element, your rule competes with the default rule, but since it has a higher cascading priority, it overrides the default rule.

The cascading order divides rules into six groups based on the type of selector used in the rule. A rule in a higher-priority group overrides a competing rule in a lower-priority group. Groups are organized by the specificity of their selectors. Selectors in lower-priority groups have less specificity than selectors in higher-priority groups.

The guiding principle behind the cascade order is that *general* selectors set overall styles for a document and *more specific* selectors override the general selectors to apply specific styles.

For example, you may want to style *all elements* in a document with no bottom margin using `*{margin-bottom:0;}`. You may also want to style *all paragraphs* in a document with a bottom margin of 10 pixels using `p{margin-bottom:10px;}`. You may also want to style the *few paragraphs* belonging to the `double-space` class with a bottom margin of 2 ems using `*.double-space{margin-bottom:2em;}`. You may also want to style *one paragraph* with an extra-large bottom margin of 40 pixels using `#paragraph3{margin-bottom:40px;}`. In each of these cases, the cascade order ensures a more specific selector overrides a more general one.

Here are the six selector groups listed from highest to lowest priority:

1. The highest-priority group contains rules with `!important` added to them. They override all non-`!important` rules. For example, `#i100{border:6px solid -black!important;}` takes priority over `#i100{border:6px solid black;}`.

2. The second-highest-priority group contains rules embedded in the `style` attribute. Since using the `style` attribute creates hard-to-maintain code, I do not recommend using it.

3. The third-highest-priority group contains rules that have one or more *ID* selectors. For example, `#i100{border:6px solid black;}` takes priority over `*.c10{border:4px solid black;}`.

4. The fourth-highest-priority group contains rules that have one or more *class*, *attribute*, or *pseudo* selectors. For example, `*.c10{border:4px solid black;}` takes priority over `div{border:2px solid black;}`.

5. The fifth-highest-priority group contains rules that have one or more *element* selectors. For example, `div{border:2px solid black;}` takes priority over `*{border:0px solid black;}`.

6. The lowest-priority group contains rules that have only a *universal* selector— for example, `*{border:0px solid black;}`.

When competing rules belong to the same selector group (such as both rules contain ID selectors), the type and number of selectors prioritize them further. A selector has higher priority when it has *more selectors of a higher priority* than a competing selector. For example, `#i100 *.c20 *.c10{}` has a higher priority than `#i100 *.c10 div p span em{}`. Since both selectors contain an ID selector, they are both in the third-highest-priority group. Since the first has two class selectors and the second has only one class selector, the first has higher priority—even though the second has more selectors.

When competing rules are in the same selector group and have the same number and level of selectors, they are further prioritized by location. Any rule in a higher-priority location overrides a competing rule in a lower-priority location. (Again, this applies only when competing rules are in the same selector group and have the same number and level of selectors. Selector groups always take precedence over location groups.)

The six locations are listed here from highest to lowest priority:

1. The highest-priority location is the `<style>` element in the head of the HTML document. For example, a rule in `<style>` overrides a competing rule in a style sheet imported by an `@import` statement embedded within `<style>`.

2. The second-highest-priority location is a style sheet imported by an `@import` statement embedded within the `<style>` element. For example, a rule in a style sheet imported by an `@import` statement embedded within `<style>` overrides a competing rule in a style sheet attached by a `<link>` element.

3. The third-highest-priority location is a style sheet attached by a `<link>` element. For example, a rule in a style sheet attached by a `<link>` element overrides a competing rule imported by an `@import` statement embedded within the style sheet.

4. The fourth-highest-priority location is a style sheet imported by an `@import` statement embedded within a style sheet attached by a `<link>` element. For example, a rule imported by an `@import` statement embedded within a linked style sheet overrides a competing rule in a style sheet attached by an end user.

5. The fifth-highest-priority location is a style sheet attached by an end user.

    •   An exception is made for `!important` rules in an end-user style sheet. These rules are given *the highest priority*. This allows an end user to create rules to override competing rules in an author's style sheet.

6. The lowest-priority location is the default style sheet supplied by a browser.

When multiple style sheets are attached or imported *at the same location level,* the order in which they are attached determines the priority. Style sheets attached later override style sheets attached previously.

When competing rules are in the same selector group, have the same number and level of selectors, and have the same location level, rules listed later in the code override rules listed earlier.

In Example 1-7, *each* rule in the style sheet is applied to the division element. Each rule applies a different `border-width` to `<div>`. Cascading order determines which rule actually gets applied. I sorted the styles in the style sheet into cascading order from least to most important. As you can see from the screenshot, the browser applies the last rule to the `<div>`, which sets a 14-pixel border around the `<div>`. The browser applies this rule because it has the highest priority in the cascading order—it is an ID selector with `!important` attached to it.

Notice how ID selectors override class selectors, which in turn override element selectors, which in turn override the universal selector. Notice how `!important` gives selectors a whole new magnitude of importance. For example, the `!important` universal selector is more important than the un-`!important` ID selector!

Notice how `border-style:none!important;` is placed in the `body` and `html` selectors to prevent the universal selector * from putting a border around `<body>` and `<html>`. This also illustrates how element selectors override universal selectors.

Example 1-7. Cascade Order

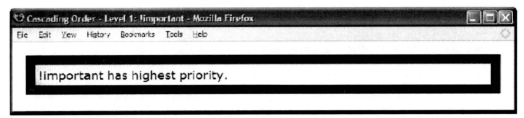

HTML

```
<body>
  <div id="i100" class="c10">!important has highest priority.</div>
</body>
```

CSS

```
html, body { border-style:none!important; }

* { border:0px   solid black; }           /* Universal Selector */
div { border:2px   solid black; }         /* Element Selector */
*.c10 { border:4px   solid black; }       /* Secondary Selector */
#i100 { border:6px   solid black; }       /* ID Selector */

* { border:8px   solid black!important; }     /* !Universal Selector */
div { border:10px solid black!important; }    /* !Element Selector */
*.c10 { border:12px solid black!important; }  /* !Secondary Selector */
#i100 { border:14px solid black!important; }  /* !ID Selector */
```

Simplifying the Cascade

To keep the cascade order as simple as possible, I minimize the number of style sheets that I attach and I do not use @import statements. I also avoid the !important operator. Most importantly, I sort my selectors so they are listed in cascade order in each style sheet.

I organize the style sheet into six groups. I put all universal selectors first, followed by element, class, attribute, pseudo, and ID selectors. If I have any !important selectors, I place them after the ID selectors in another set of groups.

Keeping style sheets sorted in cascade order helps me remember that the ID selectors override *all* class, attribute, pseudo, element, and universal selectors—no matter where they occur in the current style sheet and in all other style sheets. Likewise, it reminds me that class, attribute, and pseudo selectors in each style sheet override all element and universal selectors—no matter where they occur.

Keeping rules sorted in cascading order makes it easy to see the order in which competing rules are applied. This makes it easy to track down which rules are overriding other rules. I keep rules sorted in the cascading order as follows:

```
/* Universal Selectors */
/* Element Selectors */
/* Class, Attribute, and Pseudo Selectors */
/* ID Selectors */

/* !important Universal Selectors */
/* !important Element Selectors */
/* !important Class, Attribute, and Pseudo Selectors */
/* !important ID Selectors */
```

CSS and HTML Links

Description	URL
W3C Homepage for CSS	www.w3.org/Style/CSS
W3C CSS 2.1 Specification	www.w3.org/TR/CSS21
W3C CSS Validator Service	jigsaw.w3.org/css-validator
W3C HTML Validator Service	validator.w3.org
W3C Mobile Web Validator	validator.w3.org/mobile
W3C HTML Home Page	www.w3.org/MarkUp
W3C HTML 4.01 Specification	www.w3.org/TR/html401
W3C XHTML 1.0 Specification	www.w3.org/TR/xhtml1
W3C Mobile Web Best Practices 1.0	www.w3.org/TR/mobile-bp
W3C Accessibility Initiative	www.w3.org/WAI
"HTML 5" Working Group	www.whatwg.org
Mozilla Developer Center	developer.mozilla.org/en/docs
Microsoft Web Workshop	msdn.microsoft.com/workshop/author/css/ css_node_entry.asp
Opera Web Specifications	www.opera.com/docs/specs
Apple Safari Developer Connection	developer.apple.com/internet/safari
Web Design Information	www.welie.com/patterns microformats.org www.alistapart.com www.simplebits.com/notebook www.positioniseverything.net css.maxdesign.com.au csszengarden.com meyerweb.com/eric/css
Web Design Tutorials	www.w3schools.com www.westciv.com/style_master/house
Tools	developer.yahoo.com dean.edwards.name/my/cssQuery addons.mozilla.org/firefox/60 addons.mozilla.org/firefox/179
CSS Mailing Lists	css-discuss.org babblelist.com

Common CSS Properties

```
display margin   text-indent
visibility       margin-left       text-align
        margin-right
float   margin-top        color
clear   margin-bottom
                font
position          border  font-family
z-index border-left       font-size
overflow          border-left-color          font-style
cursor  border-left-width      font-variant
        border-left-style      font-weight


left    border-right     text-decoration
right   border-right-color      text-transform
width   border-right-width
min-width        border-right-style        vertical-align
max-width

        border-top        line-height
top     border-top-color        white-space
bottom  border-top-width        word-spacing
height  border-top-style        etter-spacing
min-height
max-height        border-bottom    direction
        border-bottom-color    unicode-bidi
        border-bottom-width
/* LESS USABLE-------*/ border-bottom-style
/* caption-side          */
/* clip                    */    padding list-style
/* content                  */      padding-left    list-style-type
/* empty-cells            */ padding-right   list-style-position
/* outline                 */    padding-top      list-style-image
/* outline-color         */  padding-bottom
/* outline-style         */  border-collapse
/* outline-width         */  background         table-layout
/* quotes                */ background-color
/* orphans               */ background-image        page-break-after
/* page-break-inside  */    background-repeat       page-break-before
/* widows                */ background-attachment
/*------------------------*/ background-position
```

CSS Properties and Values: Common

This list includes only those CSS properties and values that work in all the major browsers. The letter "i" before a property means it is inherited. The value in *italics* is the default. Some values are symbols representing multiple possibilities for a value. For example, LENGTH represents 0, auto, none, and all measurements (%, px, em, ex, pt, in, cm, mm, and pc).

Common **applies to all elements and box models.**

```
        display:        inline, none, block, inline-block, list-item,
        table-cell, table, table-row

I       visibility:     visible, hidden

        background-color:       transparent, COLOR
        background-image:       none, url("file.jpg")
        background-repeat:      repeat, repeat-x, repeat-y, no-repeat
        background-attachment:  scroll, fixed
        background-position:    0% 0%,   H% V%,   H V,
        left top, left center, left bottom,
        right top, right center, right bottom,
        center top, center center, center bottom

        border: WIDTH    STYLE    COLOR
        border-width:    medium, LENGTH, thin,    thick
        border-style:    none,    hidden, dotted, dashed, solid, double,
        groove, ridge,   inset,   outset
        border-color:    black,   COLOR

        border-left:     WIDTH    STYLE    COLOR
        border-left-width:       same as border-width
        border-left-style:       same as border-style
        border-left-color:       same as border-color
        border-right:    WIDTH    STYLE    COLOR
        border-right-width:      same as border-width
        border-right-style:      same as border-style
        border-right-color:      same as border-color
        border-top:      WIDTH    STYLE    COLOR
        border-top-width:        same as border-width
        border-top-style:        same as border-style
        border-top-color:        same as border-color
        border-bottom:   WIDTH    STYLE    COLOR
        border-bottom-width:     same as border-width
        border-bottom-style:     same as border-style
        border-bottom-color:     same as border-color

I       cursor: auto, default, pointer,
        help, wait, progress, move, crosshair, text,
        n-resize, s-resize, e-resize, w-resize
```

CSS Properties and Values: Content

Content applies to all except for rows.

```
            padding:        0, LENGTH
            padding-left:   0, LENGTH
            padding-right:  0, LENGTH
            padding-top:    0, LENGTH
            padding-bottom: 0, LENGTH
```

```
    i  font:        caption, icon, menu, message-box, small-caption, status-bar
    i  font-family:    serif,  FONTLIST, sans-serif, monospace, fantasy, cursive
    i  font-size: medium, LENGTH, %ParentElementFontSize, xx-small, x-small,
            smaller, small, large, larger, x-large, xx-large
    i  font-style:     normal, italic, oblique
    i  font-variant:   normal, small-caps
    i  font-weight:    normal, lighter, bold, bolder,
            100, 200, 300, 400, 500, 600, 700, 800, 900
```

```
    i  text-decoration:  none, underline, line-through, overline
    i  text-transform:   none, lowercase, uppercase, capitalize
    i  direction:        ltr, rtl
       unicode-bidi:     normal, bidi-override, embed
```

```
    i  line-height:      normal, LENGTH, %FontSize, MULTIPLIER
    i  letter-spacing:   normal, LENGTH
    i  word-spacing:     normal, LENGTH
    i  white-space:      normal, pre, nowrap
```

```
    i  color:    #rrggbb, #rgb, rgb(RED,GREEN,BLUE), rgb(RED%,GREEN%,BLUE%)
        black,   gray,    silver,  white,
        red,     maroon,  purple,  fuchsia,
        lime,    green,   olive,   yellow,
        blue,    navy,    teal,    aqua,
```

```
        violet,      fuschia,     red,         maroon,  black
        wheat,       gold,        orange,      tomato,  firebrick
        lightyellow, yellow,      yellowgreen, olive,   darkolivegreen
        palegreen,   lime,        seagreen,    green,   darkgreen
        lightcyan,   cyan,        turquoise,   teal,    midnightblue
        lightskyblue,deepskyblue,royalblue,    blue,    darkblue
        whitesmoke,  lightgrey, silver, gray, dimgray, darkslategray
```

```
        ActiveBorder, ActiveCaption, AppWorkspace, Background,
        ButtonFace, ButtonHighlight, ButtonShadow, ButtonText,
        CaptionText, GrayText, Highlight, HighlightText,
        InactiveBorder, InactiveCaption, InactiveCaptionText,
        InfoBackground, InfoText, Menu, MenuText, Scrollbar,
        ThreeDDarkShadow, ThreeDFace, ThreeDHighlight,
        ThreeDLightShadow, ThreeDShadow, Window, WindowFrame, WindowText
```

CSS Properties and Values: Layout

Float   **applies to all except cells and rows.**
         float: *none*, left, right

Clear   **applies to all except inlines, inline-blocks, cells, & rows.**
         clear: *none*, left, right, both

Positioned   **applies to all except cells and rows.**
         position: *static*, relative; absolute, fixed
         left: *auto*, LENGTH, %WidthOfContainingBlock
         right: *auto*, LENGTH, %WidthOfContainingBlock
         top: *auto*, LENGTH, %HeightOfContainingBlock
         bottom: *auto*, LENGTH, %HeightOfContainingBlock
         z-index: *auto*, INTEGER

Horizontal Margin   **applies to all except cells and rows.**
         margin: *0*,   LENGTH, %WidthOfContainingBlock, auto
         margin-left: *0*,   LENGTH, %WidthOfContainingBlock, auto
         margin-right: *0*,   LENGTH, %WidthOfContainingBlock, auto

Vertical Margin applies to all except inlines, cells, and rows.
         margin: *0*,   LENGTH, %WidthOfContainingBlock, auto
         margin-top: *0*,   LENGTH, %WidthOfContainingBlock, auto
         margin-bottom: *0*,   LENGTH, %WidthOfContainingBlock, auto

Width   **applies to all except inlines and rows.**
         width: auto, LENGTH, %WidthOfContainingBlock
         min-width: *0*,   LENGTH, %WidthOfContainingBlock
         max-width: *none*, LENGTH, %WidthOfContainingBlock

Height   **applies to all except inlines and tables.**
         height: *auto*, LENGTH, %HeightOfContainingBlock
         min-height: *0*,   LENGTH, %HeightOfContainingBlock
         max-height: *none*, LENGTH, %HeightOfContainingBlock

Content Layout   **applies to all except inlines, tables, and rows.**
     i text-indent: *0*,   LENGTH, %WidthOfContainingBlock
     i text-align: *left*, center, right, justify
        overflow: *visible*, hidden, auto, scroll

CSS Properties and Values: Specialized

List   applies only to lists.
  i list-style: TYPE POSITION IMAGE
  i list-style-type: *disc,* circle, square, none, decimal,
      lower-alpha, upper-alpha, lower-roman, upper-roman
  i list-style-position: *outside,*inside
  i list-style-image: *none,*   url("file.jpg")

Table   applies only to tables.
  i border-collapse: *separate,* collapse
      table-layout: *auto,* fixed

Cell   applies only to cells.
      vertical-align: *baseline,* bottom, middle, top

Inline   applies only to inlines and inline-blocks.
      vertical-align: *baseline,* LENGTH, %LineHeight,
      text-bottom, text-top, middle, top, bottom

Page   applies only to blocks and tables.
      page-break-after: *auto,* always, avoid
      page-break-before: *auto,* always, avoid

Selectors

```
* {}     selects all elements
p  {}     selects all <p> elements
*.c {}    selects all elements where class="c"
p.c {}   selects all <p> elements where class="c"
#main {}          selects one element where id ="main"
a:link  {}       selects all unvisited links
a:visited{}       selects all visited links
a:hover    {}     selects all links being hovered over
a:active   {}     selects the current link being activated
a:focus      {}   selects all links that have the focus
p:first-letter {}        selects first letter of all <p> elements
p:first-line     {}      selects first line   of all <p> elements
p:first-child    {}      selects first child  of all <p> elements
tr:nth-child(even)       selects every even row of a table
tr:nth-child(2n+0)       same as above
tr:nth-child(2n+0)       same as above
tr:nth-child(10n+9)      same as above
#n   *.c   :first-line {}        selects every 9th, 19th, 29th, etc., row
#n > *.c > :first-line {}        child selector example
#n + *.c + :first-line {}        sibling selector example
#n , *.c , :first-line {}        applies independent selectors to same block of properties
*[title]             {}       selects all elements with a title attribute
*[title~="WORD"]         {}       selects all where title attribute contains "WORD"
*[title="EXACT_MATCH_OF_ENTIRE_VALUE"]  {} selects all with exact attribute match
```

Media Queries

CSS has long supported media-dependent style sheets tailored for different media types. For example, a document may use sans-serif fonts when displayed on a screen and serif fonts when printed. "Screen" and "print" are two media types that have been defined.

In the old days of HTML4, this could be written as follows:

```
<link rel="stylesheet" type="text/css" media="screen" href="sans-serif.css">
<link rel="stylesheet" type="text/css" media="print" href="serif.css">
```

With CSS3, media queries extend the functionality of media types by allowing more precise labeling of style sheets. A media query consists of a media type and zero or more expressions that check for the conditions of particular media features. By using media queries, presentations can be tailored to a specific range of output devices without changing the content itself. A media query is a logical expression that is either true or false. A media query is true if the media type of the media query matches the media type of the device where the user agent is running, and all expressions in the media query are true.

Here are a few examples:

```
<--! Applies to devices of a certain media type ('screen') with certain feature (it must be a
color screen)-->
<link rel="stylesheet" media="screen and (color)" href="example.css" />

<!-- The same media query written in an @import-rule in CSS -->
@import url(color.css) screen and (color);
```

A shorthand syntax is offered for media queries that apply to all media types; the keyword "all" can be left out (along with the trailing "and"), i.e., the following are identical:

```
@media (orientation: portrait) { … }
@media all and (orientation: portrait) { … }
```

This way designers and developers can create more complex queries that map their specific needs:

```
@media all and (max-width: 698px) and (min-width: 520px), (min-width: 1150px) {
  body {
    background: #ccc;
  }
}
```

There is a large list of media features, which includes the following:

- width and device-width

- height and device-height

- orientation

- aspect-ratio and device-aspect-ratio

- color and color-index

- monochrome (if not a monochrome device, equals 0)

- resolution

- scan (describes the scanning process of "tv" output devices)

- grid (specifies whether the output device is grid or bitmap)

Flexible Units of Measure

Unit	Description
em	em is the `font-size` assigned to an element. In the case of the `font-size` property, it is the `font-size` assigned to the element's parent. For example, `5em` is five times the `font-size`. Ems are a useful measure when you want to size an element relative to the size of its text. This allows the layout of your documents to flex with the size of the text.
	You can use ems to roughly size the width of an element to fit a certain number of characters. You can do this by multiplying the number of characters by `0.625` to create the em measurement. For example, if you want an element to be 10 characters wide, you can set it to `6.25em`.
	In Internet Explorer 7 and earlier versions, a user can use the View ➤ Text Size menu to enlarge or shrink the overall size of the text. When you assign `font-size:medium` to `<body>` and use ems for all `font-size` properties, Internet Explorer sizes text relative to the text size chosen by the user. This makes your document more usable to users who want to see text larger or smaller than normal. If you assign a fixed measurement to `font-size`, Internet Explorer uses the fixed size and ignores the text size chosen by the user.
ex	ex is the height of the letter "x" of an element's current font. This measurement is related to the em, but is rarely used.

Fixed Units of Measure

Unit	Description
in	in stands for logical inches.
	in is a "logical" inch because the actual physical size depends on the monitor and settings chosen by the operating system and/or user. The dot pitch of a monitor determines the physical size of its pixels, and thus the physical size of the logical inch. Various operating systems have different settings for dpi. Common values are 72 dpi (Macintosh), 75 dpi (Unix), 96 dpi (Windows Normal), 100dpi (Unix Large), and 120 dpi (Windows Large). Since the dots on a monitor do not change size, the logical inch is physically larger at 120 dpi than at 72 dpi because the logical inch contains more dots. Thus, setting the `width` of an element to `96px` is the same as setting it to `1in` on Windows and `1.33in` on a Mac running at 72 dpi.
	The problem with logical inches and all other fixed units of measure is that they do not scale well on systems with different dot-per-inch settings. What may seem just right on Windows at 96 dpi may be too large or too small on other systems. Thus, percentages or ems work best when cross-platform compatibility is desired.
px	px stands for pixels. Pixels are useful when you want to precisely align elements to images because images are measured in pixels.
pt	pt stands for point. A point is 1/72 of a logical inch.
pc	pc stands for picas. A pica is 12 points or 1/6 of a logical inch.
cm	cm stands for logical centimeters. There are 2.54 centimeters per logical inch.
mm	mm stands for millimeters. There are 25.4 millimeters per logical inch.

Ratios Between Units of Measure at 96 dpi

Value	Pixel	Point	Pica	Inch	Millimeter
1 pixel	= 1px	= 0.75pt (3/4)	= 0.063pc (1/16)	= 0.0104in (1/96)	= 0.265mm
1 point	= 1.333px (4/3)	= 1pt	= 0.083pc (1/12)	= 0.0138in (1/72)	= 0.353mm
1 pica	= 16px	= 12pt	= 1pc	= 0.1667in (1/6)	= 4.233mm
1 inch	= 96px	= 72pt	= 6pc	= 1in	= 25.4mm
1 mm	= 3.779px	= 2.835pt	= 4.233pc	= 0.039in	= 1mm

Typical font-size Values at 96 dpi

CSS	Ems	Points	Pixels	Percent	Heading	HTML	Physical Size
xx-small	0.50em	6pt	8px	50%			10 pixels
	0.57em	7pt	9px	57%			12 pixels
x-small	0.63em	7.5pt	10px	63%	h6	1	12 pixels
	0.69em	8pt	11px	69%			13 pixels
	0.75em	9pt	12px	75%		2	14 pixels
small	0.82em	9.75pt	13px	82%	h5		16 pixels
	0.88em	10.5pt	14px	88%			17 pixels
	0.94em	11.25pt	15px	94%			18 pixels
medium	1em	12pt	16px	100%	h4	3	18 pixels
	1.08em	13pt	17px	108%			20 pixels
large	1.13em	13.5pt	18px	113%	h3	4	22 pixels
	1.17em	14pt	19px	117%			23 pixels
	1.25em	15pt	20px	125%			25 pixels
	1.38em	16.5pt	22px	138%			26 pixels
x-large	1.50em	18pt	24px	150%	h2	5	29 pixels
	1.75em	21pt	28px	175%			34 pixels
xx-large	2em	24pt	32px	200%	h1	6	38 pixels

Transitions, Animations, and 2D Transformations

The CSS Transitions spec allows property changes in CSS values to occur smoothly over a specified duration. Normally when the value of a CSS property changes, the rendered result is instantly updated, but with CSS Transitions, the author has the ability to animate smoothly from the old state to the new state over time.

Here is an example:

```
#box {
transition-property: opacity, left;
transition-duration: 3s, 5s;
}
```

The foregoing code will cause the `opacity` property to transition over a period of three seconds and the `left` property to transition over a period of five seconds.

CSS Animations are similar to transitions in that they change the presentational value of CSS properties over time. The key difference is that while transitions trigger implicitly when property values change, animations are explicitly executed when the animation properties are applied. Because of this, animations require explicit values for the properties being animated. These values are specified using keyframes.

The author can specify how many times the animation iterates, whether it alternates between the begin and end values, whether the animation should be running or paused, etc.

Here is an example:

```
#warning {
    animation-name: 'horizontal-slide';
    animation-duration: 5s;
    animation-iteration-count: 10;
}

@keyframes 'horizontal-slide' {

    from {
      left: 0;
    }

    to {
      left: 100px;
    }

}
```

This will produce an animation that moves `#warning` horizontally for 100px over five seconds and repeats itself nine times for a total of ten iterations.

The CSS 2D Transforms spec allows elements rendered by CSS to be transformed in two-dimensional space. Here is an example:

```
#box {
    height: 100px; width: 100px;
    transform: translate(50px, 50px) scale(1.5, 1.5) rotate(90deg);
}
```

The foregoing example moves #box by 50 pixels in both the X and Y directions, scales the element by 150%, and then rotates it 90 degrees clockwise about the z axis.

Troubleshooting CSS

You can use the following steps to troubleshoot a style sheet that is not working. I listed the steps in the order that will most likely help you find the problem quickly.

1. **Validate the HTML document.** This ensures you have no syntax problems that may cause a browser to interpret the structure of the document differently than you expect. Developers can use the W3C Validation Service (`http://validator.w3.org/`), the W3C Unicorn Validator (`http://validator.w3.org/unicorn/`), or one of the various browser plug-ins that provide markup and style validation.

2. **Validate each CSS style sheet.** This ensures you have no syntax problems, which would cause one or more rules to be ignored.

   - **Make sure a proper unit of measure (UOM)** follows nonzero measurements and that no space occurs between the number and its UOM, such as `1em` or `100%`. (`line-height` is an exception; it allows a nonzero measurement without a UOM.)

   - **Make sure only a colon (:)** and optional whitespace occur between a property name and its value, such as `width:100%` or `width : 100%`.

   - **Make sure a semicolon (;)** closes each rule, such as `width:100%;`.

3. **Review the list of CSS parsing errors** using the Error Console in Mozilla browsers. Browsers ignore each rule that has a parsing error, but unlike many other programming languages, they continue parsing and applying the remaining rules.

4. **Verify a selector** is selecting all the elements you think it should be selecting, and only those elements. You can easily see the results of a selector by putting `outline:2px solid invert;` in the selector. (Note that `outline` does not work in Internet Explorer 7, but `border` does.)

5. **Look carefully at the cascade priority** of each rule that fails to be applied. Cascade priority takes precedence over document order. For example, `#myid{color:red;}` takes priority over `*.myclass{color:blue;}`, and `#myid *.myclass{color:green;}` takes priority over both—no matter where they occur in a style sheet and no matter if they occur in a style sheet that was loaded before or after the current style sheet. I find this to be a common cause of trouble because a rule with higher cascade priority can be *anywhere* in *any* style sheet. Assuming you have already validated your style sheet, you can often tell when cascade priority is the problem when some properties in a selector work, but others do not—no matter what values you use. This typically happens when properties are being overridden by another rule with a higher cascade priority. You can usually verify this is the case by adding `!important` after a property. `!important` gives a property a higher priority than all non-`!important` properties. If `!important` makes a property work, you probably have a cascading priority problem.

6. **Verify the case of elements, classes, and IDs** in the style sheet exactly matches their case in the HTML document. This is important because XHTML is case-sensitive. You may want to use lowercase values at all times to avoid accidental mismatches.

7. **Check shorthand properties carefully** to see whether you left out any property values when you created the rule. The problem with shorthand properties is that they assign values to *all* properties for which they are shorthand—even if you set only one value! For example, `background:blue;` sets `background-color` to `blue`, and it also sets `background-image` to `none`, `background-repeat` to `repeat`, `background-attachment` to `scroll`, and `background-position` to `0% 0%`. If a rule containing `background:blue;` has a higher cascading priority than an overlapping rule that assigns `background-image` to `url("image.jpg")`, you will not see the background image because the shorthand property `background:blue;` overrides it and sets `background-image` to none.

   - Shorthand properties include `margin`, `border`, `padding`, `background`, `font`, and `list-style`.

   - `font` is a particularly troublesome shorthand property because it combines so many properties into one, and all these values are inherited! These properties include `font-family`, `font-size`, `font-weight`, `font-variant`, `font-style`, and `line-height`. Remember that assigning even one value to `font`, such as `font:1em;`, causes the browser to set the default values for *all* these properties!

8. **Verify a browser loads all your style sheets**. You can make sure each one is referenced through a `<link>` statement within the `<head>` section of your HTML document, or through `@import` statements in style sheets. If you are not sure a style sheet is being loaded, you can place a unique rule in the style sheet to see whether it gets applied. Such a rule would be something obvious, like `*{border:1px solid black;}`.

9. **Avoid using `@import` statements**. If you use `@import` statements, verify they occur as the first items in the style sheet to ensure they have a lower priority than the rules in the style sheet.

10. **Verify style sheets are loaded in the order you want** by listing `<link>` statements and `@import` statements in order of ascending priority. Rules *at the same level* in the cascading order are overridden by rules in style sheets linked or imported later. But remember that rules with a *higher* cascading priority always override rules with a lower priority no matter in what order the rules occur in a style sheet or whether they occur in style sheets linked or imported later.

11. **Verify the server sends `text/css` as the `Content-Type` header for CSS style sheets**. Mozilla browsers refuse to use a style sheet unless it has a content type of `text/css`. You can view the HTTP headers in Mozilla browsers by using the Web Developer Toolbar and selecting the menu option View Response Headers.

12. **Remove HTML elements that may have been put in a CSS style sheet**, such as `<style>`. Also make sure no child elements have been accidentally placed inside the `<style>` element, which is inside the head of the HTML document.

Normalized Style Sheet

Because each browser has slightly different default settings, you may want to build rules into your style sheets to define baseline settings for each element. For example, different browsers assign the `<h1>` element to different sizes and margins. By assigning your own size and margins to `<h1>`, you can standardize its appearance in all browsers.

The simplest approach (and the easiest approach to maintain) is to create a baseline set of rules for all elements and to load those rules in the first style sheet you attach to a document. You can load a small set of rules that reset all elements to the simplest of styles as shown in Listing 1-2. Or you can load a more extensive set of rules that create a standard style for your site, such as those shown in Listing 1-3. You can find standard sets of baseline rules on the Internet, such as Yahoo's YUI Reset CSS rules (see `http://developer.yahoo.com/yui/reset/`).

Loading a separate baseline style sheet affects the speed at which your page is rendered (see the sidebar "How Fast Will Your Page Load?"). Thus, for performance reasons, you may want to combine style sheets or move styles into the `<style>` section of the HTML document.

Listing 1-2. Simple Baseline Style Sheet (Similar to Yahoo's YUI Reset CSS)

```
body,div,dl,dt,dd,ul,ol,li,h1,h2,h3,h4,h5,h6,pre,form,fieldset,input,p,
blockquote,th,td { margin:0; padding:0; }
table { border-collapse:collapse; border-spacing:0; }
fieldset,img { border:0; }
address,caption,cite,code,dfn,em,strong,th,var
{ font-style:normal; font-weight:normal; }
ol,ul { margin:1em 0; margin-left:40px; padding-left:0; }
ul { list-style-type:disc; }
ol { list-style-type:decimal; }
caption,th { text-align:left; }
h1,h2,h3,h4,h5,h6 { font-size:100%; }
```

HOW FAST WILL YOUR PAGE LOAD?

How fast your document renders is important. A web page that renders within 0.5 seconds is considered instantaneous; 1 second is fast; 2 seconds is normal; more than 2 seconds becomes noticeable; and about 6 seconds is all most broadband users will tolerate. As a rule of thumb, the latency involved in looking up each file typically takes 0.1 to 0.5 seconds—this is on broadband connections and does not include the time it takes to actually download a file. Because of latency, a fast page can typically load three extra files, such as one style sheet, one JavaScript file, and one image, and a normal page can load about seven extra files.

To help with performance, a browser caches files. This may help on subsequent downloads, but it does not help the first time a page downloads. Furthermore, cached files speed performance only when the server sets their expiration date to expire in the future. When the refresh date on a cached file expires, a browser asks the server whether the file has changed. This takes about 0.1 to 0.5 seconds per file—even if the file has not changed and does not need to be downloaded again. Thus, it is important to set the expiration date as far in the future as you dare. How far in the future depends on how often you expect the file to change on the server. The problem is that if you change the file on the server before the expiration date, users will not get the updated file because browsers will not bother asking for it, unless you clear the cache.

Listing 1-3. *Complete Baseline Style Sheet*

```
/* BLOCK ELEMENTS */
html, div, map, dt, form { display:block; }
body       { display:block; margin:8px; font-family:serif; font-size:medium; }
p, dl      { display:block; margin-top:1em; margin-bottom:1em; }
dd         { display:block; margin-left:40px; }
address    { display:block; font-style:italic; }
blockquote { display:block; margin:1em 40px; }
h1 { display:block; font-size:2em;       font-weight:bold;   margin:0.67em 0; }
h2 { display:block; font-size:1.5em;     font-weight:bold;   margin:0.83em 0; }
h3 { display:block; font-size:1.125em;   font-weight:bold;   margin:1em    0; }
h4 { display:block; font-size:1em;       font-weight:bold;   margin:1.33em 0; }
h5 { display:block; font-size:0.75em;    font-weight:bold;   margin:1.67em 0; }
h6 { display:block; font-size:0.5625em;  font-weight:bold;   margin:2.33em 0; }
pre{ display:block; font-family:monospace; white-space:pre; margin:1em    0; }
hr { display:block; height:2px; border:1px; margin:0.5em auto 0.5em auto; }


/* TABLE ELEMENTS */
table   { border-spacing:2px; border-collapse:separate;
          margin-top:0; margin-bottom:0; text-indent:0; }
caption { text-align:center; }
td      { padding:1px; }
th      { font-weight:bold; padding:1px; }
tbody, thead, tfoot { vertical-align:middle; }


/* INLINE ELEMENTS */
strong { font-weight:bold; }
cite, em, var, dfn { font-style:italic; }
code, kbd, samp { font-family:monospace; }
ins { text-decoration:underline; }
del { text-decoration:line-through; }
sub { vertical-align:-0.25em; font-size:smaller; line-height:normal; }
sup { vertical-align: 0.5em;  font-size:smaller; line-height:normal; }
abbr[title], { border-bottom:dotted 1px; }


/* LIST ELEMENTS */
ul { list-style-type:disc;    margin:1em 0; margin-left:40px; padding-left:0;}
ol { list-style-type:decimal; margin:1em 0; margin-left:40px; padding-left:0;}
/* remove top & bottom margins for nested lists */
ul ul, ul ol, ul dl, ol ul, ol ol, ol dl, dl ul, dl ol, dl dl
{ margin-top:0; margin-bottom:0; }
/* use circle when ul nested 2 deep */
ol ul, ul ul { list-style-type:circle; }
/* use square when ul nested 3 deep */
ol ol ul, ol ul ul, ul ol ul, ul ul ul { list-style-type:square; }
```

Tip   You can view Mozilla Firefox's internal default style sheet using `resource://gre-resources/html.css`.

CHAPTER 2

HTML Design Patterns

This chapter explores HTML only as it relates to CSS. It contains design patterns that are essential for styling a document with CSS. It explores HTML at a high level with an eye toward explaining how elements can be put to use structurally and semantically. Each design pattern in this book is created using structural and semantic elements combined with CSS. There are four major types of elements used in design patterns: structural block, terminal block, multi-purpose block, and inline elements. Understanding these types of elements is key to understanding the design patterns in this book and essential to creating your own.

Chapter Outline

- **HTML Structure** shows how HTML elements work together to create a document.

- **XHTML** shows how to mark up a document with valid XHTML. It also points out why using valid XHTML makes styling with CSS more reliable.

- **DOCTYPE** shows how to use document types to validate the way documents are coded, and it explores what document types work best for CSS and HTML.

- **Header Elements** shows how to create metadata about a document and how to link a document to supporting documents and related documents.

- **Conditional Style Sheet** shows how to load a style sheet to fix problems unique to Internet Explorer.

- **Structural Block Elements** shows how to create structural meaning in a document.

- **Terminal Block Elements** shows how certain blocks have semantic meaning because they contain content instead of other blocks.

- **Multi-purpose Block Elements** shows how certain elements can be used for block structure and semantic meaning.

- **Inline Elements** shows how styles can bring out the meaning of semantic markup.

- **Class and ID Attributes** shows how CSS relies on `class` and `id` attributes to select elements. It also shows how the `class` attribute can add meaning to an element.

- **HTML Whitespace** shows how to make whitespace work for you instead of against you.

HTML Structure

Container	Contents
\<html>	**\<head> \<body>**
\<head>	**\<title>** & (**\<meta>** | **\<link>** | **\<object>** | **\<script>** | **\<style>** | **\<base>**)
\<body>	\<noscript> **\<div>**
\<noscript>	inline | block
\<article>	inline | block
\<section>	inline | block
\<nav>	inline | block
\<div>	inline | block
\<h1>	inline
\<p>	inline
\<ol> or **\<ul>**	**\<li>**
\<li>	inline | block
\<dl>	**\<dt> \<dd>**
\<dt>	inline
\<dd>	inline | block
\<table>	**\<caption> \<colgroup> \<thead> \<tfoot> \<tbody>**
\<caption>	inline
\<colgroup>	**\<col>**
\<col>	null
\<thead>	**\<tr>**
\<tfoot>	**\<tr>**
\<tbody>	**\<tr>**
\<tr>	**\<th> \<td>**
\<th>	inline | block
\<td>	inline | block
\<form>	inline | block (excluding **\<form>**)
\<fieldset>	inline | block (excluding **\<form>**)
\<label>	inline (excluding **\<label>**)
\<input>	null
\<textarea>	text
\<select>	**\<optgroup>** | **\<option>**
\<optgroup>	**\<option>**

HTML Structure cont.

Container	Contents
\<option>	text
\<button>	*inline	block (excluding \<a>, \<form>, controls)*
\<address>	inline
\<a>	inline (excluding **\<a>**)
\<img>	null
\<canvas>	null
\<audio>	null
\<video>	null
\<map>	**\<area>**
\<area>	null
\<object>	**\<param>**	inline	block
\<param>	null
**\ **	null
null	No content; single tag with closing slash (e.g., **\ **)
text	Unicode text including HTML entities that are parsed and replaced
block	Includes the following three types of block elements:
structural block	-**\<ol> \<ul> \<dl> \<table> \<tr> \<thead> \<tfoot> \<tbody> \<colgroup> \<col>**
multi-purpose block	**\<div> \<li> \<dd> \<td> \<th> \<form> \<noscript>**
terminal block	**\<h1> \<p> \<dt> \<caption> \<address> \<blockquote>**
inline	Includes the following three major types and six minor types of inline elements:
inline-semantic	*Includes text intermingled with zero or more of the following elements:*
importance	**\<span> \<em> \<strong>**
phrase	**\<a> \<cite> \<code> \<kbd> \<samp> \<var>**
word	**\<abbr> \<dfn> \<cite>**
char	**\<sub> \<sup>**
inline-flow	**\ \<bdo>**
inline-block	Includes replaced elements and form controls:
replaced	**\<img> \<object> \<embed> \<iframe> \<audio> \<video> \<canvas> \<svg>**
controls	**\<input> \<textarea> \<select> \<button> \<label> \<video> (with controls attribute present)**

Additional elements are included in the HTML5 specification, but I did not list them in the preceding table because they have little semantic or structural meaning, are rarely used, or have quirky implementations. The following elements style text: <i>, <b>, <big>, <small>. The <pre> element preserves whitespace, but it cannot contain images, objects, subscripts, or superscripts. The <q> element automatically inserts quotes differently depending on the browser. The <ins> and <del> elements mark elements as inserted or deleted. Frames can cause problems for search engines and users: <iframe>, <frameset>, <frame>, and <noframe>. Internet Explorer 7 will not remove built-in styles from <hr>, <fieldset>, and <legend>, but later versions will. Also from an SEO perspective, traditional frames are not indexed well when displayed since the content is typically indexed outside of the controls that reside in a separate frame. At the same time, traditional framesets are fairly obsolete. Finally, <base> changes the root of all links in your document—use it only if you fully understand it, or it may break all your links. Similarly there are many other elements defined in the HTML5 draft spec that are either not yet implemented in browsers or still undergoing significant revisions.

HTML Structure

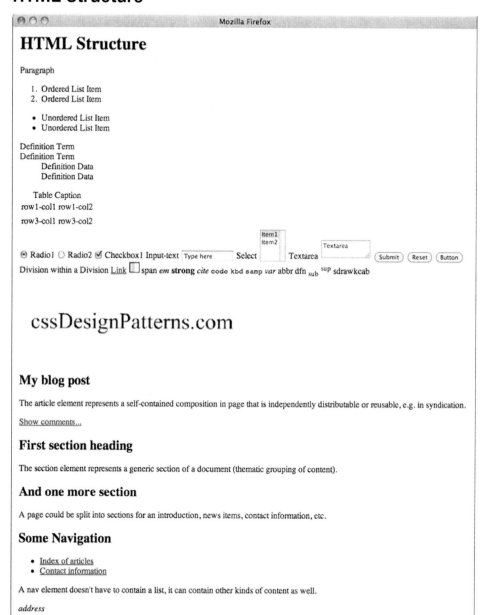

HTML

```
<!DOCTYPE html>

<html lang="en">

<head><title>HTML Structure</title>
  <meta http-equiv="Content-type" content="text/html; charset=utf-8"/>
  <link rel="stylesheet" href="site.css" media="all" type="text/css"/>
  <link rel="stylesheet" href="page.css" media="all" type="text/css"/>
  <link rel="stylesheet" href="print.css" media="print" type="text/css"/>
  <!--[if lte IE 6]>
  <link rel="stylesheet" href="ie6.css" media="all" type="text/css"/>
  <![endif]-->
</head>
<body>
<noscript>Show this when script cannot run.</noscript>
<div>
  <h1>HTML Structure</h1>

  <p>Paragraph</p>

  <ol>
    <li>Ordered List Item</li>
    <li>Ordered List Item</li>
  </ol>
  <ul>
    <li>Unordered List Item</li>
    <li>Unordered List Item</li>
  </ul>
  <dl>
    <dt>Definition Term</dt>
    <dt>Definition Term</dt>
    <dd>Definition Data</dd>
    <dd>Definition Data</dd>
  </dl>

  <table>
    <caption>Table Caption</caption>
    <colgroup>
      <col/>
      <col/>
    </colgroup>
    <thead>
    <tr>
      <td>row1-col1</td>
      <td>row1-col2</td>
    </tr>
    </thead>
    <tfoot>
    <tr>
      <td>row3-col1</td>
      <td>row3-col2</td>
    </tr>
```

```
    </tfoot>
    <tbody>
    </tbody>
</table>

<form id="form1" method="post" action="http://www.tipjar.com/cgi-bin/test">
  <input type="hidden" title="input hidden" name="hidden" value="Secret"/>

  <input id="radio1" name="radios" type="radio" value="radio1" checked="checked"/>
  <label for="radio1">Radio1</label>

  <input id="radio2" name="radios" type="radio" value="radio2-pushed"/>
  <label for="radio2">Radio2</label>

  <input id="xbox1" name="xbox1" type="checkbox" value="xbox1" checked="checked"/>
  <label for="xbox1">Checkbox1</label>

  <label for="inputtext">Input-text</label>
  <input id="inputtext" name="inputtext" type="text" value="Type here" size="14"/>

  <label for="select1">Select</label>
  <select id="select1" name="select" size="2">
    <option selected="selected" value="item1">Item1</option>
    <option value="item2">Item2</option>
  </select>

  <label for="textarea">Textarea</label>
  <textarea id="textarea" name="textarea" rows="2" cols="10">Textarea</textarea>

  <input type="submit" id="submit1" name="submit1" value="Submit"/>
  <input type="reset" id="reset1" name="reset1" value="Reset"/>
  <button type="submit" id="button1" name="button1" value="Button1">Button</button>
</form>

<div>Division within a Division <a id="link1" href="left.html">Link</a>
  <img src="left-right.gif" width="20" height="20" usemap="#map1" alt="alt text"/>
  <map id="map1" name="map1">
    <area href="left.html" alt="left" shape="rect" coords="0,0,10,20"/>
    <area href="right.html" alt="right" shape="rect" coords="10,0,20,20"/>
  </map>

  <span>span</span>
  <em>em</em>
  <strong>strong</strong>
  <cite>cite</cite>
  <code>code</code>
  <kbd>kbd</kbd>
  <samp>samp</samp>
  <var>var</var>
  <abbr>abbr</abbr>
  <dfn>dfn</dfn>
  <sub>sub</sub>
  <sup>sup</sup>
  <bdo dir="rtl">backwards</bdo>
```

```
      <object type="application/x-shockwave-flash">
        <param name="movie" value="http://myserver.com/movie.swf">
        <param name="allowfullscreen" value=true>
      </object>
   </div>
   <article>
     <header>
       <h1>My blog post</h1>

       <p>
         <time pubdate datetime="2011-10-07T10:00-08:00"></time>
       </p>
     </header>
     <p>The article element represents a self-contained composition in page that is
independently distributable or
       reusable, e.g., in syndication.</p>
     <footer>
       <a href="?comments=1">Show comments...</a>
     </footer>
   </article>
   <section>
     <h1>First section heading</h1>

     <p>
       The section element represents a generic section of a document (thematic grouping of
content).
     </p>
   </section>
   <section>
     <h1>And one more section</h1>

     <p>A page could be split into sections for an introduction, news items, contact
information, etc.</p>
   </section>
   <nav>
     <h1>Some Navigation</h1>
     <ul>
       <li><a href="articles.html">Index of articles</a></li>
       <li><a href="contact.html">Contact information</a></li>
     </ul>
     <p>A nav element doesn't have to contain a list; it can contain other kinds of content as
well.</p>
   </nav>
   <address>address</address>
</div>
</body>
</html>
```

CSS

```
/* There are no CSS styles attached to this document. */
```

HTML Structure

Problem	You want to know how HTML elements work together to create an HTML document.
Solution	HTML is a strict hierarchical nesting of elements. Elements may be nested within each other, but they cannot overlap each other. HTML organizes elements into three major categories: structural, block, and inline elements.
	The core **structural elements** are **<html>**, **<head>**, and **<body>**. Information about a document goes in **<head>** and document content goes in **<body>**. Header elements are covered in the Header Elements design pattern discussion.
	There are three types of **block elements**: structural, multi-purpose, and terminal. These are covered in the following design pattern discussions: Structural Block Elements, Terminal Block Elements, and Multi-purpose Block Elements.
	There are three major types of **inline elements**: semantic, flow, and inline-block. These are covered in the Inline Elements design pattern discussion.
Pattern	**HTML Core Structure**
| | ```html
<!DOCTYPE DOCUMENT_TYPE_DEFINITION_USED_FOR_VALIDATION >
<html>
  <head> METADATA </head>
  <body> CONTENT </body>
</html>
``` |
Example	The example contains the simplest expression of each common HTML element.
	The concept behind the **<object>** element is that it represents an external resource, which, depending on the type of the resource, will be treated as an image, as a nested browsing context, or as an external resource to be processed by a plug-in. Different browsers have varying support for this element. The HTML5 specification defines several attributes like **data**, **type**, **name**, etc.
Related to	Header Elements, Structural Block Elements, Terminal Block Elements, Multi-purpose Block Elements, Inline Elements, Structural Meaning, Visual Structure (Chapter 13)
```

XHTML

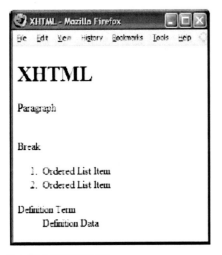 

Valid XHTML

```
<!DOCTYPE html >

<html lang="en">
 <head><title>XHTML</title>
  <meta http-equiv="Content-type" content="text/html; charset=utf-8" />
  <link rel="stylesheet" href="page.css" media="all" type="text/css" />
 </head>
 <body>
  <h1>XHTML</h1> <p>Paragraph</p> <br />Break
  <ol> <li>Ordered List Item</li>    <li>Ordered List Item</li>    </ol>
  <dl> <dt>Definition Term</dt>      <dd>Definition Data</dd>       </dl>
 </body>
</html>
```

Valid HTML

```
<!DOCTYPE html >

<html lang="en" >
 <head><title>HTML</title>
  <meta http-equiv=Content-type content="text/html; charset=utf-8" >
  <link rel=stylesheet href=page.css media=all type="text/css" >
 <body>
  <h1>HTML</h1> <p>Paragraph <br>Break
  <ol> <li>Ordered List Item    <li>Ordered List Item </ol>
  <dl> <dt>Definition Term      <dd>Definition Data   </dl>
```

XHTML

Problem	You want to create a document using XHTML.
Solution	The HTML5 specification defines an abstract language for describing documents and applications, and some APIs for interacting with what is known as the "DOM HTML", or "the DOM" for short. There are various concrete syntaxes for the foregoing language, and two are HTML and XHTML.

HTML (or HTML5) is the format suggested for most authors. It is compatible with most legacy web browsers. If a document is transmitted with an HTML MIME type, such as text/html, then it will be processed as an HTML document by web browsers.

XHTML (or XHTML5) is an application of XML. When a document is transmitted with an XML MIME type, such as application/xhtml+xml, then it is treated as an XML document by web browsers, to be parsed by an XML processor. Authors are reminded that the processing for XML and HTML differs; in particular, even minor syntax errors will prevent a document labeled as XML from being rendered fully, whereas they would be ignored in the HTML syntax.

Essentially an XHTML5 page is a simple HTML5 document that has the following:

HTML doctype/namespace: The `<!DOCTYPE html>` definition is optional, but it would be useful for preventing browser quirks mode.

XHTML well-formed syntax

XML MIME type: application/xhtml+xml; this MIME declaration is not visible in the source code, but it would appear in the HTTP **Content-Type** header that could be configured on the server.

Default XHTML namespace: `<html xmlns="http://www.w3.org/1999/xhtml">`

XHTML is case-sensitive, and HTML is case-insensitive. XHTML requires all tags and attributes to be lowercase (e.g., `<html>` instead of `<HTML>`). CSS selectors are case-sensitive in XHTML! In XHTML, the case of **class** or **id** *values* must match before they will be selected by CSS! For example, the selectors **#test** and ***.test** select `<h1 id="Test" class="TEST">` in HTML, but *not* in XHTML. For this reason, I recommend always using lowercase attribute values and tag names in XHTML and CSS.

XHTML requires the `<html>` tag to include the **xmlns** attribute with the value of `"http://www.w3.org/1999/xhtml"`. XHTML requires the **xml:lang** attribute to be present each time the HTML **lang** attribute is used, such as **xml:lang="en" lang="en"**.

XHTML requires *all* elements to have start and end tags and *all* attributes to be enclosed in quotes and to have a value. HTML does not.

HTML lets you omit the start tags for `<html>`, `<head>`, `<body>`, and `<tbody>`. HTML lets you omit end tags for `<html>`, `<head>`, `<body>`, `<p>`, `<li>`, `<dt>`, `<dd>`, `<tr>`, `<th>`, and `<td>`. A browser implies their presence in HTML. In XHTML, a document will not validate if these tags are omitted.

HTML *prohibits* end tags for elements that must always be empty: `<meta>`, `<link>`, `<base>`, `<br>`, `<hr>`, `<area>`, `<img>`, `<param>`, `<input>`, `<option>`, and `<col>`. XHTML *requires* end tags for *all* elements. Thus, a valid XHTML document containing one of these elements can never be a valid HTML document and vice versa. There is a compromise that works in HTML browsers because they do not require documents to be valid HTML. You can use the XML shorthand notation for an empty element as long as it includes a space before the closing slash and less-than sign. This works as follows: `<meta />`, `<link />`, `<base />`, `<br />`, `<hr />`, `<area />`, `<img />`, `<param />`, `<input />`, `<option />`, and `<col />`. You should use a separate closing tag for all other empty elements, such as `<span></span>`.

Advantages	It has been argued that the strict coding requirements of XHTML identify the structure of a document more clearly than HTML. In HTML, a browser *assumes* the location of a missing end tag to be the start tag of the next block element. In the example, ` ` is rendered after the paragraph in the XHTML document and as part of the paragraph in the HTML document. This is why there is an extra line of whitespace in the XHTML part of the example.

A valid and unambiguous structure is *essential* when you use CSS to style a document because CSS selectors select elements based on their structure. For this reason, some developers might prefer XHTML for their projects.

Related to	DOCTYPE

DOCTYPE

HTML

```
<!-- The following DOCTYPEs place the browser in almost-standards mode.
     The first one is for XHTML, the second one is for HTML 4, and the
        third one for HTML5 (browser support varies).
  -->

<!DOCTYPE html PUBLIC "-//W3C//DTD XHTML 1.0 Transitional//EN"
             "http://www.w3.org/TR/xhtml1/DTD/xhtml1-transitional.dtd">

<!DOCTYPE HTML PUBLIC "-//W3C//DTD HTML 4.01 Transitional//EN"
             "http://www.w3.org/TR/html4/loose.dtd">
<!DOCTYPE html >
```

CONTENT TYPE VS. DOCTYPE

Web servers identify each document they serve with a **MIME content type**. MIME stands for Multipart Internet Mail Extensions. The content type is identified in the HTTP header for the document. A browser determines how to process a document based on its MIME content type. When it gets a document with a content type of `"text/html"`, it renders the document as HTML.

According to the W3C's Note titled "XHTML Media Types" (www.w3.org/TR/xhtml-media-types/), a web server may serve XHTML with one of the following three content types.

- An XHTML document may be served as `"text/html"` as long as you do not want the browser to treat the document as XML and you do not include content from other XML namespaces, such as MathML. A browser receiving an XHTML document with this content type treats the document as HTML.

- XHTML should be served as `"application/xhtml+xml"`. Unfortunately, Internet Explorer 7 and earlier versions refuse to display pages served this way.

- XTHML may be served as `"application/xml"` or `"text/xml"`. Unfortunately, Internet Explorer 7 and earlier versions recognize such a document as generic XML, which means they ignore all XHTML semantics. This means links and forms do not work, and it takes much longer to render the document.

A Gecko browser renders a document served with an XML content type *only* after it has completely downloaded and has absolutely no coding errors. It also renders the document in strict mode regardless of its DOCTYPE (see www.mozilla.org/docs/web-developer/faq.html#accept).

At the current time, the most reliable content type for serving XHTML web pages is `"text/html"`. This tells a browser to render a document as HTML. This approach is supported by the W3C, and it works well in all major browsers. It works because browsers do not validate HTML. They parse web pages in a way that allows them to display any version of HTML and XHTML—including documents containing errors. Contrast this with how a browser processes an XHTML document where the rules of XML prohibit it from rendering an entire XHTML document when it has an error—even the tiniest error created by an accidental typo! Such precision is essential for computer-to-computer transactions, but it is not good for human-generated web pages.

DOCTYPE

Alias	Metadata Declaration
Problem	You want to declare the type of your document so you can validate it against a Document Type Definition (DTD). You want to ensure your document is valid. You want to ensure web browsers follow the same rules in rendering your document.
Solution	The `<!DOCTYPE>` prolog identifies the type and version of HTML or XHTML in which the document is coded. In technical terms, `<!DOCTYPE>` specifies the type of document and the DTD that validates the document. The W3C provides a free online service at `http://validator.w3.org/` that you can use to validate your documents.
	All HTML and XHTML code should be validated. This verifies the code contains no coding errors. If there are errors, CSS selectors may fail to select elements as expected or may even select elements unexpectedly.
	There are benefits to using XHTML. Validated XHTML documents are well formed and have unambiguous structure. You can also use XSLT (Extensible Stylesheet Language) and XQUERY (XML Query Language) processors to extract content and rearrange documents.
	In the HTML4 era, there were two additional varieties of DOCTYPEs: strict and transitional. **Strict** removes all presentational elements and attributes, and **transitional** allows them. I do not recommend presentation elements and attributes, but the strict DOCTYPE may be too strict for some needs. For example, it prohibits the **start** attribute in `<ol>` and the **value** attribute in `<li>`, which are the only available means to control the numbering of an ordered list. The strict DOCTYPE also prohibits `<iframe>`.
	Most important to CSS, browsers use `<!DOCTYPE>` to determine how closely they will follow the CSS standard when they render the document. There are two basic modes: quirks and standards. In **quirks mode**, browsers do not follow the CSS standard, which makes this mode undesirable for styling with CSS. In **standards mode**, they follow the CSS specification.
	To complicate matters, Internet Explorer in strict mode violates a part of the CSS spec by not aligning images in table cells to the baseline. It does this to remove the baseline space below images so that sliced images in tables work as expected. The other major browsers have a third mode called **almost-standards mode** that emulates this nonstandard behavior.
	The standards mode of Internet Explorer and the almost-standards mode of the other major browsers are the most compatible modes. There are two main `<!DOCTYPE>` declarations that trigger this level of compatibility: one for XHTML and one for HTML. They are listed in the DOCTYPE code example. You can find a complete list of DOCTYPEs at `http://hsivonen.iki.fi/doctype/`.
Location	`<!DOCTYPE>` must be the first item in an HTML document. There must be only one `<!DOCTYPE>` per document. You must *not* precede this DOCTYPE with an XML declaration, such as `<?xml version="1.0" ?>`, or Internet Explorer 6 will trigger quirks mode.
Tip	As mentioned earlier, the HTML5 `<!DOCTYPE>` is `<!DOCTYPE html>`. You'll note that it's significantly simpler than earlier DOCTYPEs, and that was intentional. A lot has changed in HTML5 in an attempt to make it even easier to develop a standards-based web page, and it should really pay off in the end. One nice thing about this new DOCTYPE is that all current browsers (IE, FF, Opera, Safari) will look at it and switch the content into standards mode, even if they don't implement HTML5. This means that you could start writing your web pages using HTML5 today, without having to worry about future compatibility.
Related to	XHTML

Header Elements

HTML

```
<!DOCTYPE html PUBLIC "-//W3C//DTD XHTML 1.0 Transitional//EN"
   "http://www.w3.org/TR/xhtml1/DTD/xhtml1-transitional.dtd">

<html xmlns="http://www.w3.org/1999/xhtml" xml:lang="en" lang="en" >

 <head>
   <title>Header Elements</title>

   <meta http-equiv="Content-type" content="text/html; charset=utf-8" />


   <!-- Include links to stylesheets -->
   <link rel="stylesheet" href="site.css"   media="all"   type="text/css" />
   <link rel="stylesheet" href="page.css"   media="all"   type="text/css" />
   <link rel="stylesheet" href="print.css"  media="print" type="text/css" />
   <!--[if lte IE 6]>
   <link rel="stylesheet" href="ie6.css"    media="all"   type="text/css" />
   <![endif]-->


   <!-- Optionally include alternate style sheets that the user can apply. -->
   <link rel="alternate stylesheet" type="text/css" title="cool" href="cool.css" />
   <link rel="alternate stylesheet" type="text/css" title="hot"  href="hot.css"  />


   <!-- Optionally include style rules that apply only to this page. -->
   <style type="text/css" media="all">
    body  { margin:0px; padding:20px; padding-top:0px; width:702px;
            font-family:verdana,arial,sans-serif; font-size:medium; }
    h1    { margin:10px 0 10px 0; font-size:1.9em;  }
   </style>


   <!-- Optionally link to a JavaScript file. -->
   <script type="text/javascript" src="script.js" ></script>


   <!-- Optionally include JavaScript that applies only to this page. -->
   <script type="text/javascript" ><!--
    alert("Hello World!");
   --></script>

 </head>

 <body>  <h1>Header Elements</h1>  </body>
</html>
```

Header Elements

Problem	You want to add metadata to a document. You also want to link the document to style sheets and JavaScript files. You also want to improve performance by embedding CSS rules and JavaScript inside the page.
Solution	You can use **<link rel="stylesheet" type="text/css" />** to link style sheets to a document. You can use **href="URI"** to specify the URI of the style sheet. You can use **media="all"** to apply a style sheet to all devices. You can use **media="print"** to apply a style sheet only when printing. This allows you to hide navigational bars, remove backgrounds, reset inverse color schemes (like white text on a black background) to normal black text on a white background, and so forth. You can use **media="handheld"** to apply a style sheet to handheld devices only. You may find this impractical because styles that work on one handheld device may be ignored or not work at all on another. Few browsers have implemented the following media types: **"tty"**, **"tv"**, **"projection"**, **"braille"**, and **"aural"**.
	You can use **<link rel="alternate stylesheet" />** to provide a user with alternate style sheets. Most browsers put alternate style sheets in a drop-down list and allow users to select and apply one alternate style sheet at a time to a document. Since most web sites do not provide alternate style sheets and since there is no visual indication that they are available, few users look for them or use them. Thus, sites that supply alternate style sheets often put buttons or menus in the document and link them to JavaScript that switches between alternate style sheets.
	You can embed styles in the **<style>** element. These should be styles specific only to the current document. Styles that are used for more than one document should be contained in external style sheets. You may find that putting styles directly in a document greatly speeds the rendering of the document because a browser has fewer files to download. You may also find that this increases the amount of work it takes to maintain a web site.
	Other elements are common in **<head>**, such as **<title>**, **<meta>**, and **<script>**. I have included these elements in the example, but their usage is beyond the scope of this book.

Pattern	HTML
	`<head>`
	`<base href="http://www.example.com/">`
	`<link rel="stylesheet" href="FILE.CSS"`
	`       media="ALL_PRINT_HANDHELD" type="text/css" />`
	`<link rel="alternate stylesheet" type="text/css"`
	`       title="NAME_TO_SHOW_USER" href="FILE.css" />`
	`<style type="text/css" media="all"> STYLES </style>`
	`</head>`

Location	**<link>**, **<style>**, **<title>**, **<meta>**, **<base>** and **<script>** belong in **<head>**.
Related to	HTML Structure, Conditional Style Sheet

Conditional Style Sheet

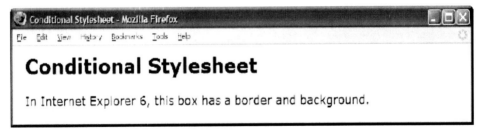

Rendered in Firefox without the conditional style sheet

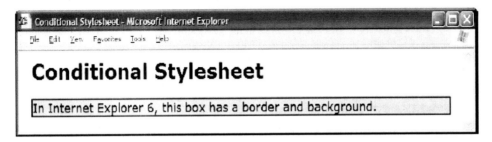

Rendered in Internet Explorer with the conditional style sheet

HTML

```
<html xmlns="http://www.w3.org/1999/xhtml" xml:lang="en" lang="en" >

 <head><title>Conditional Stylesheet</title>
  <meta http-equiv="Content-type" content="text/html; charset=utf-8" />
  <link rel="stylesheet" href="page.css"  media="all"   type="text/css" />
  <!--Embed the following style sheet  only in IE 6 and higher-->
  <!--[if gt IE 5.5]>
   <link rel="stylesheet" href="ie6.css"     media="all"    type="text/css" />
  <![endif]-->
 </head>

 <body>
  <h1>Conditional Stylesheet</h1>
  <p class="test">In Internet Explorer 6, this box has a border and background.</p>
 </body>
</html>
```

CSS page.css

```
*.test  { font-size:18px; }
```

CSS ie6.css

```
*.test  { border:2px solid black; background-color:gold; }
```

Conditional Style Sheet

Problem	You want one set of styles to be applied to Internet Explorer and another set to be applied to other browsers.
Solution	You can use Microsoft Internet Explorer's conditional comments to load a style sheet created exclusively for Internet Explorer. You can place a conditional comment in **\<head>** after all links to other style sheets. Inside the conditional comment, you can place a link to a style sheet. I call this the **conditional style sheet**. Since the conditional style sheet comes last, it overrides previously loaded styles.
	You can create a separate conditional style sheet for Internet Explorer 6, and if necessary you can create one for Internet Explorer 7. You can include styles in this style sheet to compensate for different behaviors and bugs.
	The following pattern loads two conditional style sheets. The first is for Internet Explorer versions 6 and earlier. The second is for Internet Explorer 7 and higher. Internet Explorer 7 fixes most of the bugs in Internet Explorer 6, but there are still a number of CSS features that it does not implement, such as the **content** property.

Pattern

HTML

```
<!--[if lte IE 6]>
    <link rel="stylesheet" href="ie6.css" media="all"
        type="text/css" />
<![endif]-->
<!--[if gt IE 6]>
    <link rel="stylesheet" href="ie.css" media="all"
        type="text/css" />
<![endif]-->
```

Limitations	Conditional style sheets apply only to Internet Explorer. This is unfortunate because they are a good way to work around browser-specific problems. Fortunately, there are few problems in other browsers. I do not recommend CSS hacks because they rely on parsing bugs in a browser's CSS engine. When these bugs get fixed, the hack no longer works. For this reason, I do not use or discuss CSS hacks in this book. In other words, all the design patterns in this book work without hacks.
	Also in Internet Explorer 10, this is considered a legacy feature and will work only in legacy mode.
	`<!--[if IE]> This content is ignored in IE10 and other browsers. <![endif]-->`
Variations	To target different versions of Internet Explorer, you can change the operator and version in the conditional comment. For example, you can use `<!--[if lt IE 5]>` or `<!--[if IE 7]>`.
	The following operators are available: **lte** (less than or equals), **lt** (less than), **gt** (greater than), or **gte** (greater than or equals). You can omit the operator for an equals comparison, such as `<!--[if IE 7]>`.
	If another browser ever implements conditional comments, you can replace **IE** with the constant that identifies that browser.
Related to	Header Elements

Structural Block Elements

HTML Pattern

```
<!-- Ordered List -->
  <ol>
    <li>                            </li>
    <li>  One or more list items... </li>
  </ol>

<!-- Unordered List -->
  <ul>
    <li>                            </li>
    <li>  One or more list items... </li>
  </ul>

<!-- Definition List -->
  <dl>
    <dt>                                </dt>
    <dt>  One or more definition terms... </dt>
    <dd>                                </dd>
    <dd>  One or more definitions...     </dd>
  </dl>

<!-- Table -->
  <table>
   <caption> One optional caption per table. </caption>
   <colgroup> <col /> <col /> </colgroup>
    <thead>
      <tr>
        <th> One or more header cells in a row... </th>
        <td> One or more data cells  in a row...  </td>
      </tr>
    </thead>
    <tfoot>
      <tr>
        <th> One or more rows in a row group...   </th>
        <td>                                      </td>
      </tr>
    </tfoot>
    <tbody>
      <tr>
        <th> Zero or more row groups in a table... </th>
        <td>                                        </td>
      </tr>
    </tbody>
  </table>

<!-- Divisions -->
  <div> <div> <div> ... </div> </div> </div>
```

Structural Block Elements

Problem	You want to structure your document so web browsers can render an enhanced view of the document; search engines can determine important keywords; document processors can use technologies like XSLT to extract content and transform the structure; and JavaScript can navigate the structure to modify content and make a document interactive.
Solution	You can mark up a document with block elements to identify its structure. There is meaning in structure, and HTML markup is most meaningful when its structure reflects the hierarchy and relationships of a document's topics.
	Because a parent element contains child elements, they are related structurally. This implies their content is related. For example, a child's content is typically a subtopic of its parent's topic, and siblings typically have related subtopics. Implicit in the hierarchical nature of HTML is the assumption that document organization is hierarchical.
	Structural blocks may contain block elements only. They have structural meaning, but they have little semantic meaning. In other words, they do not tell you what something is; they tell you how it is organized.
	There are four major structural block elements (**<ol>**, **<ul>**, **<dl>**, and **<table>**) with nine supporting structural elements (**<li>**, **<dt>**, **<dd>**, **<caption>**, **<thead>**, **<tfoot>**, **<tbody>**, **<colgroup>**, and **<col>**).
Details	**<ol>** creates an **ordered list** of one or more list items (**<li>**). Items belong to the same set and are in order. Order implies sequence or ranking.
	<ul> creates an **unordered list** of one or more list items (**<li>**). Items belong to the same set without sequence or ranking.
	<dl> creates a **definition list** of one or more terms (**<dt>**) and definitions (**<dd>**). Structurally, a definition list implies all its terms are synonyms and all its definitions are alternate definitions of its terms. The HTML specification also shows that a definition list can have a broader application, such as listing speakers and their dialog. In generic terms, a definition list is an associative entity that associates keys with values.
	<table> creates a **tabular data structure** in rows (**<tr>**) and cells (**<th>** and **<td>**). It may optionally contain groups of rows: one table header (**<thead>**), one table footer (**<tfoot>**), and one or more table body groups (**<tbody>**). It may optionally contain one or more column groups (**<colgroup>**) containing one or more columns (**<col>**). Column groups and columns are the only structural blocks that are relational instead of hierarchical. In other words, each **<col>** element forms a relationship with cells in a column without actually being their parent. A table may optionally contain a **<caption>**.
	<div> is a **multi-purpose block element**. It can be structural or terminal. I mention it here because it normally creates a **document division**. Document divisions are essential for organizing a document into sections, and sections are the essential building blocks of documents. That is why I list **<div>** as the parent of all structural elements in the HTML Structure design pattern.
	<article> represents a **self-contained composition** in a page that is, in principle, independently distributable or reusable, e.g., via syndication. This could be a forum post, a magazine or newspaper article, a blog entry, etc. When article elements are nested, the inner article elements represent articles that are in principle related to the contents of the outer article. For instance, a blog entry on a site that accepts user-submitted comments could represent the comments as article elements nested within the article element for the blog entry.
	<section> represents a **generic section** of a document and acts as a thematic grouping of content, typically with a heading. Examples of sections would be chapters, the various tabbed pages in a tabbed dialog box, or the numbered sections of a thesis. A web site's home page could be split into sections for an introduction, news items, and contact information. Developers may use **<article>** instead of the section element when it would make sense to syndicate the contents of the element.
	<nav> defines a **section** of a page that links to other pages or to parts within the page—basically a section with navigation links.
Related to	HTML Structure, Terminal Block Elements, Multi-purpose Block Elements

Terminal Block Elements

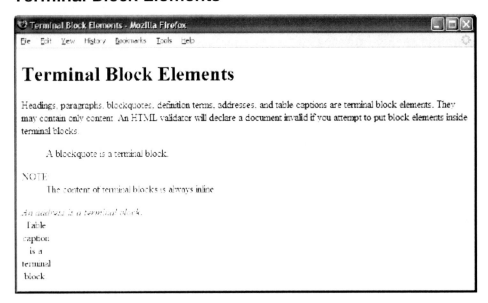

HTML

```
<h1>Terminal Block Elements</h1>

<p>
  Headings, paragraphs, blockquotes, definition terms, addresses,
  and table captions are terminal block elements. They may contain only content.
  An HTML validator will declare a document invalid if you attempt
  to put block elements inside terminal blocks.
</p>

<blockquote>   A blockquote is a terminal block. </blockquote>

<dl>
  <dt>NOTE:</dt>
  <dd>The content of terminal blocks is always inline.</dd>
</dl>

<address>     An address is a terminal block.    </address>

<table>
 <caption>Table caption is a terminal block.</caption>
 <tr><td></td></tr>
</table>
```

Terminal Block Elements

Problem	You want to transition from document structure to content.
Solution	You can use one of the following terminal blocks to terminate document structure so you can insert content: **\<h1>**, **\<p>**, **\<blockquote>**, **\<dt>**, **\<address>**, and **\<caption>**. These elements are the primary containers of content. The multi-purpose block elements discussed in the next design pattern may also contain content. Paragraphs contain most of a document's content followed by headings, blockquotes, list items, and table cells.
	Terminal blocks are terminal nodes in the block structure of a document. They cannot contain blocks. They contain text and inline elements. Structurally, they are siblings to other terminal and structural blocks, which implies they all have subtopics related to their parent block's topic.
	Terminal blocks mainly have semantic meaning. HTML supplies six elements you can use to identify the purpose of content: heading, paragraph, blockquote, definition term, address, and caption.
Details	**\<h1>, \<h2>, \<h3>, \<h4>, \<h5>, and \<h6> create headings** from most important to least. Headings are relational. They imply the following sibling elements (typically paragraphs) have a subtopic that supports the topic of the heading. They also imply a relationship to each other. For example, **\<h2>** implies that it is a subtopic of the previous **\<h1>** element. Headings placed at lower levels of document structure typically have higher heading numbers. You can reinforce the structure of a document by making a heading the first element of each document division.
	\<p> creates a paragraph. Semantically, a paragraph contains one or more sentences. The first sentence defines the topic of the paragraph, and subsequent sentences support that topic. The topic of a paragraph is typically a subtopic of the previous heading and relates to sibling elements.
	\<blockquote> creates a blockquote. Semantically, a blockquote contains a quote from an external source that relates to the topic of its siblings.
	\<dt> creates a definition term. Semantically, a definition term is a term that is being defined directly in the document by one or more definitions. The Structural Block Elements design pattern includes **\<dt>** because it is a part of the **\<dl>** structure. When you use **\<dl>** as an associative entity, **\<dt>** changes its semantic meaning to being a key that is associated with one or more values. Like a term, a key can be looked up to find its associated items.
	\<address> creates a contact record for the document itself. It is not for identifying other types of addresses, such as your favorite restaurants. The HTML specification allows an address to contain any type of content such as a street address, e-mail address, phone number, etc.
	\<caption> creates a table caption. Semantically, it labels a table. **\<caption>** is referred to in the Structural Block Elements design pattern because it is a part of the **\<table>** structure.
Related to	HTML Structure, Structural Block Elements, Multi-purpose Block Elements

Multi-purpose Block Elements

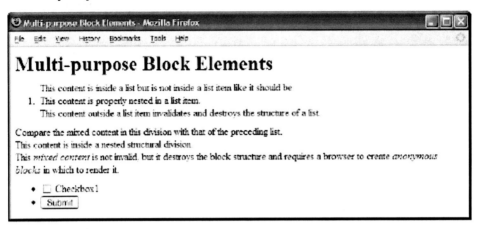

HTML

```
<noscript>Show this text when script cannot run.</noscript>

<div>
 <div>
  <h1>Multi-purpose Block Elements</h1>
 </div>
</div>

<!-- The following code is invalid HTML and broken structure. -->
<ol>
  This content is inside a list but is not inside a list item like it should be.
  <li> This content is properly nested in a list item. </li>
  This content outside a list item invalidates and destroys the structure of a list.
</ol>

<!-- The following code is _valid_ HTML due to a loophole in HTML's DTD,
     but is still broken structure. -->
<div>
  Compare the mixed content in this division with that of the preceding list.
  <div> This content is inside a nested structural division. </div>
  This <em>mixed content</em> is not invalid, but it destroys the block structure
  and requires a browser to create <em>anonymous blocks</em> in which to render it.
</div>

<!-- The following form contains blocks, which in turn contain controls. -->
<form id="form1" method="post" action="http://www.apress.com/cgi-bin/test" >
 <ul>
  <li> <input type="checkbox" id="xbox1" name="xbox1" value="xbox1" />
       <label for="xbox1">Checkbox1</label></li>
  <li> <input type="submit" id="submit1" name="submit1" value="Submit" /> </li>
 </ul>
</form>
```

Multi-purpose Block Elements

Problem	You want the flexibility of extending the document structure by nesting structures within structures or terminating the current structure.
Solution	HTML provides seven elements—**<div>**, **<li>**, **<dd>**, **<td>**, **<th>**, **<form>**, and **<noscript>**— that can extend the structure or terminate it. For this reason, I call them multi-purpose block elements, as they are the most versatile elements. You can use them to identify document divisions, list items, dictionary definitions, table data cells, table header cells, forms, and alternate content to display when scripting is unavailable.
	When a multi-purpose block is used structurally, it has structural meaning. When it is used terminally, it has semantic meaning. For example, when a list item is terminal, it identifies its content as an item in a list. When a list item contains a structural block, such as a table or another list, it functions structurally as a node in a larger nested structure.
	Multi-purpose blocks may contain blocks or content, but not both. Content is defined as text intermingled with inline elements (images, objects, controls, and semantic markup). Block elements should not be siblings with inline elements and text. This is called **mixed content**. Content should always be contained *within* a block—not placed *in between* blocks. Because of limitations in HTML's Document Type Definition language, HTML validators do not always invalidate a document containing mixed content, but this does not mean you should allow it. When a browser encounters mixed content, it wraps the content in an anonymous block. This is because a browser cannot render blocks and content at the same time, as blocks flow down the page and content flows across. CSS selectors cannot select anonymous blocks, which prevents you from being able to style anonymous blocks.
Details	**<div> is a division.** It is normally structural, but it can contain content. As shown in the example, the block structure created by divisions is invisible unless you style each division's margins, border, and/or padding.
	<li> is a list item. Typically, it is a terminal block containing content, but it may contain structural blocks such as tables and lists, or terminal blocks such as headings and paragraphs.
	<dd> is a definition in a definition list. Typically, it is a terminal block containing content, but it may contain structural or terminal blocks.
	<td> and <th> are table cells. **<td>** is a data cell and **<th>** is a header cell. Typically, cells are terminal blocks containing content, but they may contain structural or terminal blocks.
	<form> is a data-entry form. It may contain structural blocks that organize form controls (as shown in this example), or it may directly contain inline form controls (as shown in the HTML Structure example). It may also contain terminal blocks such as headings and paragraphs.
	<noscript> is displayed when a browser does not support scripting. It may contain simple inline content, or it may contain a fully structured document.
Related to	HTML Structure, Structural Block Elements, Terminal Block Elements
See also	**www.cssdesignpatterns.com/multi-purpose-block-elements**

Inline Elements

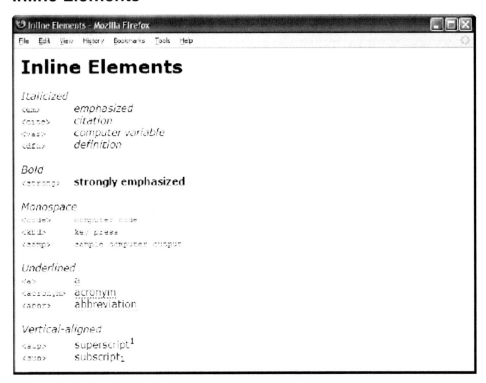

HTML

```
<h1>Inline Elements</h1>
<h2>Italicized</h2>
<code>&lt;em&gt;        </code>    <em>emphasized</em>                         <br />
<code>&lt;cite&gt;      </code>    <cite>citation</cite>                       <br />
<code>&lt;var&gt;       </code>    <var>computer variable</var>                <br />
<code>&lt;dfn&gt;       </code>    <dfn>definition</dfn>                       <br />

<h2>Bold</h2>
<code>&lt;strong&gt;    </code>    <strong>strongly emphasized</strong>        <br />

<h2>Monospace</h2>
<code>&lt;code&gt;      </code>    <code>computer code</code>                   <br />
<code>&lt;kbd&gt;       </code>    <kbd>key press</kbd>                         <br />
<code>&lt;samp&gt;      </code>    <samp>sample computer output</samp>         <br />

<h2>Underlined</h2>
<code>&lt;a&gt;         </code>    <a href="#">a</a>                           <br />
 <code>&lt;abbr&gt;     </code>    <abbr title="a" >abbreviation</abbr>    <br />

<h2>Vertical-aligned</h2>
<code>&lt;sup&gt;       </code>    superscript<sup>1</sup>                     <br />
<code>&lt;sub&gt;       </code>    subscript<sub>1</sub>                       <br />
```

Inline Elements

Problem	You want to add explicit meaning to text, and you want to style text to reflect this meaning.
Solution	HTML provides inline elements to identify the meaning of text, to control the flow of text, and to insert external content into the document, such as images and controls. Inline elements are content.
	Intermingling inline elements and text is desirable. Some call this *mixed content*, but I prefer to define mixed content narrowly as blocks, text, and inlines being mixed together, which is undesirable. I define *content* as text mixed with inline elements, which is desirable. This clearly separates structure from content and emphasizes that inline elements and text should always be contained *within* blocks—not *in between* blocks.
	I organize inline elements into four types: semantic, flow, replaced, and controls. **Semantic elements** identify the meaning of their content. **Flow elements** control the flow, such as inserting a line break. **Replaced elements** are replaced with an object, such as an image. **Controls** are objects used for data entry, such as a text box.
	HTML assigns each semantic inline element to a default style to emphasize that its text has a particular meaning. For example, **`<code>`** is rendered in a monospace font. You can use CSS to override these default styles.
Details	Three semantic inline elements specify the relative *importance* of their content; they are listed in order of increasing importance as follows: **`<span>`**, **`<em>`**, and **`<strong>`**. **`<span>`** is generic and has neutral importance. Search engines use **`<em>`** and **`<strong>`** to rank content.
	I have organized the remaining semantic inline elements by how much content they typically contain, such as a phrase, a word, or a character. Phrase inlines include **`<a>`**, **`<cite>`**, **`<code>`**, **`<kbd>`**, **`<samp>`**, and **`<var>`**. Word inlines include **`<abbr>`**, and **`<dfn>`**. Character inlines include **`<sub>`** and **`<sup>`**.
	Flow-control elements control the flow of content, such as **` `**, which inserts a line break, and **`<bdo>`**, which changes the direction of the flow.
	Replaced elements are replaced by external content, such as **`<img>`**, which is replaced by an image or **`<object>`**, which can be replaced by a video, a Flash movie, a sound file, etc.
	Controls are inline elements used for data entry in forms, such as **`<input>`**, **`<textarea>`**, **`<select>`**, and **`<button>`**.
Default Styles	HTML assigns default styles to each semantic inline element. **`<span>`** has no default style and meaning, so you can use it for any purpose. **`<strong>`** is bold by default. The following are italicized by default: **`<em>`**, **`<dfn>`**, **`<cite>`**, and **`<var>`**. The following are monospace by default: **`<code>`**, **`<kbd>`**, and **`<samp>`**. The following are underlined by default: **`<a>`** and **`<abbr>`**. Internet Explorer 6 does not support **`<abbr>`**.
Related to	HTML Structure; all design patterns in Chapters 10 through 12 and 14
See also	**`www.cssdesignpatterns.com/inline-elements`**

Class and ID Attributes

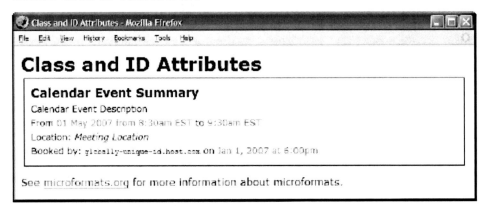

HTML

```
<h1>Class and ID Attributes</h1>

<div id="hcalendar1" class="vevent">
 <h3 class="summary">Calendar Event Summary</h3>

 <p class="description">Calendar Event Description</p>

 <p>From
  <span class="dtstart" title="2007-05-01T08:30:00-05:00"
    >01 May 2007 from 8:30am EST</span> to
  <span class="dtend" title="2007-05-01T09:30:00-05:00"
    >9:30am EST</span></p>

 <p>Location:  <span class="location">Meeting Location</span></p>
 <p>Booked by: <span class="uid">globally-unique-id.host.com</span>
    on <span class="dtstamp" title="20070101T231000Z"
        >Jan 1, 2007 at 6:00pm</span></p>
</div>

<p>See <a href="http://microformats.org/wiki/hcalendar">microformats.org</a>
 for more information about microformats.</p>
```

CSS

```
*.vevent p          { margin:0 0 5px 0; font-size:0.9em; }
*.vevent h3         { margin:0 0 5px 0; }
*.vevent *.location { font-style:italic; }
*.vevent *.uid      { font-family:monospace; }
*.vevent *.dtstart,
*.vevent *.dtend,
*.vevent *.dtstamp  { color:green; }

#hcalendar1 { margin:5px; border:1px solid black; padding:10px; }
```

Class and ID Attributes

Problem	You want to identify some elements as being in the same class as other elements. You want to apply additional semantic and relational meaning to a class of elements. You want to style a class of elements in the same way. You want to identify some elements uniquely in a document so you can style them uniquely and directly access them through JavaScript.
Solution	HTML supplies the **class** and **id** attributes for these purposes. You can assign a **class** and an **id** to any element.
	An ID and class name cannot include a space. It must start with a letter and may contain letters, numbers, the underscore (_), and the dash (-). Since CSS selectors are case-sensitive when using XHTML, it is a common practice to use lowercase class and ID names.
Class	**class** assigns a user-defined semantic meaning to an element. **class** is the primary mechanism for extending the semantic meaning of HTML elements. Elements with the same class are related and can be manipulated as a group. You can use CSS selectors to apply a style to a class of elements. You can use a document processor, such as XSLT, to manipulate a class of elements.
	You can assign multiple classes to an element by putting multiple class names in an element's **class** attribute. A space separates each class name.
	Classes should have semantic names, such as copyright, date, price, back-to-top, example, figure, listing, illustration, note, result, tip, warning, etc.
ID	An ID should be unique within a document. If it is not, a CSS ID selector will match all elements with the same ID—just like the **class** attribute.
	You can use a unique ID as a CSS selector to style one element. You can use it as an anchor that can be targeted by other links. You can use it to access and manipulate a specific element from JavaScript or a document processor.
	IDs should have semantic names, such as skip-to-main-content, page, preheader, header, title, search, postheader, body, nav, site-map, links, main, section1, section2, news, about-us, services, products, etc.
Patterns	
HTML	`<ELEMENT  id="id"  class="class1 class2 etc" ></ELEMENT>`
CSS	`#id     { STYLES }` `*.class { SYTLES }`
Tip	Since **<div>** and **<span>** elements have no semantic meaning, you can assign classes to them without conflicting with any predefined meaning. You can assign classes to **<div>** to create custom document structures with custom semantic meaning. You can assign classes to **<span>** to customize the meaning of text. There are currently no standard class names with precise predefined meanings, although the microformats movement is making progress toward that goal by mapping HTML structure and class names to common standards, such as hCard and hCalendar.
Related to	Type, Class, and ID Selectors, Subclass Selector (Chapter 3)

HTML Whitespace

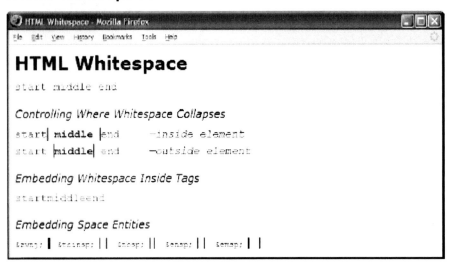

HTML

```
<h1>HTML Whitespace</h1>
<p>      start     middle &#x0020; &#x0009;  <span> </span>     <span></span>
                                    &#x000A; &#x000D;     end        </p>

<h2>Controlling Where Whitespace Collapses</h2>
<p>start<span class="border">  middle </span> end<em>—inside element</em></p>
<p>start <span class="border"> middle</span>  end<em>—outside element</em></p>

<h2>Embedding Whitespace Inside Tags</h2>
 <p>start<span
        class
          =
           "spaced"
            >middle</span
             >end</p>

<h2>Embedding Space Entities</h2>
<code>&amp;zwnj;   </code><span class="border">&zwnj;</span>     
<code>&amp;thinsp; </code><span class="border"> </span>   
<code>    </code><span class="border"> </span>     
<code>&amp;ensp;   </code><span class="border"> </span>     
<code>&amp;emsp;   </code><span class="border"> </span>     
```

CSS

```
em { padding-left:50px; }
p { font-family:monospace; font-size:18px; }

*.border { font-weight:bold;
  border-left:2px solid black; border-right:2px solid black; }
```

HTML Whitespace

Problem	You want to use whitespace in markup to make the code more readable without the whitespace affecting the rendering of the document.
Solution	A browser collapses repeated whitespace into a single space. This allows you to insert extra spaces, tabs, newlines, and returns into the markup to make it more readable without it showing up in the rendered document.
	A browser interprets only the following characters as whitespace: space (** **), tab (**	**), newline (**
), and return (**).
	Empty elements and elements containing only whitespace do not interrupt a contiguous sequence of whitespace. Notice in the first paragraph of the example how a browser renders only one space between the words "start," "middle," and "end"—even though there are many characters between these words including spaces, tabs, newlines, returns, whitespace entities, an empty span, and a span containing whitespace.
	The first whitespace character in a series of contiguous whitespace characters determines the position and style of the collapsed space. In other words, a browser renders collapsed space using the **font-family**, **font-size**, **font-weight**, **line-height**, and **letter-spacing** assigned to the first whitespace character of the series. Larger fonts, wider **letter-spacing**, and taller **line-height** create wider and taller whitespace. Thus, the location of whitespace in an HTML document determines how wide and tall it is.
	The second and third paragraphs of the example show how the location of whitespace determines whether it collapses inside an element or outside. If it collapses inside, it is styled by the element's rules. Since whitespace collapses to the left, you can collapse whitespace in front of an element by simply putting whitespace before it. If you want whitespace to collapse inside an element, you need to remove all whitespace before the element and put at least one whitespace inside it. If you want whitespace to be inside an element and to be placed after its content, simply follow the content with whitespace. If you want whitespace to collapse outside the closing tag of an element, you need to remove all whitespace following the element's content and insert whitespace after the element.
	You can put extra whitespace inside an element's start and end tags without putting undesired whitespace in the content. You can insert extra whitespace between the start tag's name and its attributes; surrounding an attribute's name, equal sign, and value; and before the start tag's greater-than sign. You can insert extra whitespace between the end tag's name and its greater-than sign. The fourth paragraph of the example is an extreme example that has much whitespace inside the tags but none inside the content.
Space Entities	HTML provides five *space* entities that have different widths. These are *not* whitespace! The nonbreaking space, ** **, is the width of a normal space and works in all major browsers; the widths of the other spaces (**‌**, ** **, ** **, and ** **) vary in different browsers.
Preserved	The **<pre>** element preserves all the whitespace that is inside it.
Related to	Spacing, Nowrap, Preserved, Padded Content, Inline Spacer, Linebreak (Chapter 11)

CSS Selectors and Inheritance

This chapter presents design patterns that select elements for styling.

Because selector design patterns are simple, I discuss selector design patterns in groups rather than one at a time. This makes it easy to compare and contrast related forms of selectors. Thus, even though this chapter has only **six** examples, it contains **thirteen** different design patterns.

Inheritance is included in this chapter because it is simply a built-in way to select descendant elements. Inheritance is very closely related to the descendant selector. The Visual Inheritance pattern is included in this chapter because it is a form of inheritance that is visual by nature.

Chapter Outline

- **Type, Class, and ID Selectors** shows how to select elements by tag, class, and ID.

- **Position and Group Selectors** shows how to select elements by how they are nested in the document. It also shows how to apply multiple selectors to the same set of rules.

- **Attribute Selectors** shows how to select elements based on their attributes.

- **Pseudo-element Selectors** shows how to select the first letter or first line of terminal block elements.

- **Pseudo-class Selectors** shows how to style a hyperlink when it is unvisited, visited, being hovered over by the mouse, or has the focus because the user tabbed to it or clicked it with the mouse.

- **Subclass Selector** shows how to apply multiple styles to the same element using classes and subclasses.

- **Inheritance** shows how to style elements through rules assigned to their ancestors.

- **Visual Inheritance** shows how elements visually inherit their parent's background.

Type, Class, and ID Selectors

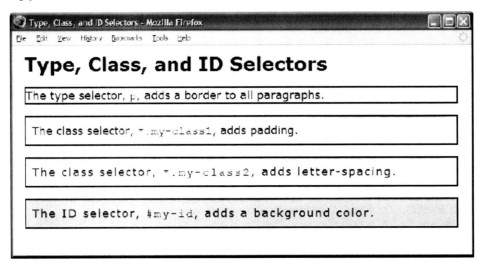

HTML

```
<h1>Type, Class, and ID Selectors</h1>

<p>The type selector, <code>p</code>, adds a border to all paragraphs.</p>

<p class="my-class1">
  The class selector, <code>*.my-class1</code>, adds padding.</p>

<p class="my-class1 my-class2">
  The class selector, <code>*.my-class2</code>, adds letter-spacing.</p>

<p class="my-class1 my-class2" id="my-id">
  The ID selector, <code>#my-id</code>, adds a background color. </p>
```

CSS

```
p { border:2px solid black; }

*.my-class1 { padding:10px; }
*.my-class2 { letter-spacing:0.11em; }

#my-id { background-color:gold; }
```

Type, Class, and ID Selectors

Problem   You want to select elements by type, class, and/or ID so you can style them.

Solution   Apply styles to your chosen class or ID as follows:

Use the type selector to select all elements of a particular type. The type selector is the element's name without the less-than and greater-than signs.

Use the class selector to select all elements that you have assigned to a class. The class selector is the period followed by the name of a class. The class selector is added to the end of a type selector. You can add it onto the end of the universal selector, *****, to select all elements in the document that have a matching class, such as ***.my-class1**. You can also use the class selector all by itself, such as **.my-class1**, which is a shortcut for ***.my-class1**.

Use the ID selector to select all elements in the document assigned to that ID. Each element has one ID, which should be unique in a document.

Patterns   HTML   CSS

```
<ELEMENT>
<ELEMENT class="class class class etc">                type    { STYLES }
<ELEMENT id="id">                                      *.class { STYLES }
<ELEMENT id="id" class="class">                        #id     { STYLES }
```

Location   These design patterns apply to all elements.

Tips   You can assign multiple classes to an element, by separating them with a space. The class operator selects all elements with matching classes. For example, I assigned **my-class1** and **my-class2** to the second and third paragraphs of the example.

Names of classes and IDs are case-sensitive. They must start with a letter and may contain letters, numbers, and the hyphen. I recommend always using lowercase names for classes and IDs because a browser cannot select a class or an element if the case of each letter in the selector does not perfectly match a class name. For example, the browser will not select **<div class="SelectMe">** using **div.selectme**.

If multiple selectors select the same element, each style from each selector is applied to the element. Selectors with higher cascade order override the values applied by selectors with a lower cascade order. IDs override classes, and classes override types. If you apply multiple style sheets to a document, ID selectors override all classes and types in all style sheets.

In CSS3 type selectors are allowed to have an optional namespace prefix that has been previously declared. This may be prepended to the element name separated by the namespace separator with a vertical bar. Here is an example:

```
@namespace foo url(http://www.example.com); /* declaring a namespace */
 foo|h1 { color: blue } /* matches h1 in the "http://www.example.com" namespace */
 foo|* { color: yellow } /* matches all elements in the "http://www.example.com"
namespace */
|h1 { color: red } /* matches all h1 elements, no namespace */
 *|h1 { color: green }  /* matches all h1 elements, with or without a namespace */
 h1 { color: green }  /* similar as above*/
```

CSS3 also specifies a "universal selector" in the form of an asterisk, which represents the qualified name of any element type. It represents any single element in the document tree in any namespace (including those without a namespace) if no default namespace has been specified for selectors. If a universal selector is not the only component of a sequence of simple selectors or is immediately followed by a pseudo-element, then the * may be omitted and the universal selector's presence implied.

```
*[hreflang|=en] and [hreflang|=en] are equivalent,
 *.warning and .warning are equivalent,
 *#myid and #myid are equivalent
```

Type, Class, and ID Selectors cont.

Related to Position and Group Selectors, Pseudo-element Selectors, Pseudo-class Selectors

See also   www.cssdesignpatterns.com/type-selectors
www.cssdesignpatterns.com/class-selectors
www.cssdesignpatterns.com/id-selectors

Position and Group Selectors

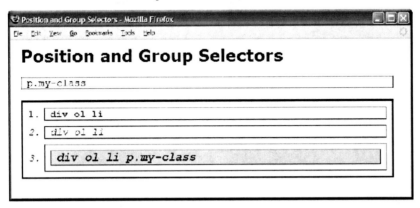

HTML

```
<h1>Position and Group Selectors</h1>

<p class="my-class">p.my-class</p>
<div id="my-id">
 <ol>
  <li>div ol li</li>
  <li>div ol li</li>
  <li>
   <p class="my-class">div ol li p.my-class </p>
  </li>
 </ol>
</div>
CSS
/* Group Selectors */
p,ol,li { border:1px solid black; padding-left:10px; font-family:monospace;
  margin:10px; margin-left:0px; }
ol { margin-left:0px; padding-left:40px; margin-top:20px; }

/* Position Selectors */
div *.my-class { font-size:1.2em; font-weight:bold; }  /* Descendant  Selector */
#my-id   p { background-color:gold; }                   /* Descendant  Selector */
#my-id > * { border:3px solid black; }                  /* Child       Selector */

:root {background: white;} /* Root Selector */
li:nth-child(2n+1) /* Nth-child Selector */
li:nth-last-child(-n+2)     /* Nth-last-child Selector */
li:nth-of-type(2n+1) { float: right; } /* Nth-of-type Selector */

li:nth-last-of-type(2n+1) { float: right; } /* Nth-last-of-type Selector */
```

```
li:first-child { font-weight:bold; color:red; }        /* First-child Selector */
li:last-child { font-weight:bold; color:red; }         /* Last-child Selector */
ul li:first-of-type {color: red} /*  First-of-type Selector */
tr > td:last-of-type   /*  Last-of-type Selector */
li:only-child /* Only-child Selector */
div:only-of-type /* Only-of-type Selector */
p:empty {display: hidden} /* Empty Selector */
li + li { font-style:italic; color:blue; }             /* Sibling     Selector */
```

Position and Group Selectors

Problem	You want to combine selectors to narrow a selection based on element position. In other words, you want to select elements based on whether they are descendants, children, or siblings of other elements. You also want to apply different selectors to the same set of rules.
Solution	Combine selectors as follows: **To apply different selectors to the same group of rules,** chain together multiple selectors using a comma. This is the **group selector**. Each selector in the chain is independently assigned to the same set of styles. **To select descendant elements,** chain together multiple selectors using whitespace. Whitespace is the **descendant selector**. Each descendant selector narrows the selection to descendants of the previous selector. A descendant can be a child, a grandchild, a great-grandchild, and so forth. **To select child elements,** chain together multiple selectors using the greater-than sign. This is the **child selector**. Each child selector narrows the selection to elements that are children of the previous selector. **To select the first child element,** append `:first-child` to any selector. This is the **first-child selector**. This limits the selector only to elements that are the first child of their parents. Similarly you can use rules like :nth-child, :nth-last-child, etc. to specify the exact position of the element. **To select sibling elements,** chain together multiple selectors using the plus sign. This is the **sibling selector**. Each sibling selector narrows the selection to elements that are siblings to the elements chosen by the previous selector.
Patterns	CSS `selector, selector, etc { STYLES }` or `selector   selector   etc { STYLES }` or `selector > selector > etc { STYLES }` or `selector + selector + etc { STYLES }` or `selector:first-child      { STYLES }` Similar with the rest of the pseudo-classes
Location	These design patterns apply to all elements.
Limitations	Only the group and descendant selectors work in Internet Explorer 6. All these selectors work in Internet Explorer 7 and the other major browsers.
Example	The group selector **p,ol,li** applies the same set of styles to all paragraphs, ordered lists, and list items. The selector **div *.my-class** selects all elements assigned to **my-class** that descend from a division. Only the paragraph in the third list item matches this selector. The selector **#my-id p** selects all paragraphs descending from **<div id="my-id">**. Only the paragraph in the third list item matches this selector. The selector **#my-id > p** selects all child elements descending from **<div id="my-id">**. Only the ordered list matches this selector. The selector **li:first-child** selects the first list item in each list. The selector **li + li** selects all list items that are siblings to list items. This selects all but the first list item.
Related to	Inheritance

Attribute Selectors

> **Mozilla Firefox**
>
> # Attribute Selectors
>
> This is a paragraph without the `title` attribute.
>
> ```
> p[title] selects all paragraphs containing a title attribute.
> ```
>
> ```
> p[title~="paragraph"] selects all paragraphs with a title attribute containing the word, paragraph.
> ```
>
> ```
> p[title="#4    paragraph"] selects all paragraphs with a title attribute containing the exact text,
> #4    paragraph. Matches are case sensitive and must match letter-for-letter including whitespace.
> ```
>
> hello

HTML

```
<h1>Attribute Selectors</h1>

<p>This is a paragraph without the <code>title</code> attribute.</p>

<p title="Second">
 <code>p[title]</code> selects all paragraphs containing a title attribute.</p>

<p title="Third paragraph">
 <code>p[title~="paragraph"]</code> selects all paragraphs with a
 title attribute containing the word, <code>paragraph</code>.</p>

<p title="#4    paragraph">
 <code>p[title="#4    paragraph"]</code> selects all paragraphs with a
 title attribute containing the exact text, <code>#4    paragraph</code>. Matches
 are case-sensitive and must match letter-for-letter including whitespace.</p>

<a href="http://www.example.com” target="_blank" hreflang="en-GB">hello</a>
```

CSS

```
code { white-space:pre; }

p[title] { padding:5px 10px; border:1px solid gray; }
p[title~="paragraph"] { background-color:gold; }
p[title="#4    test paragraph"] { font-weight:bold; }
a[href="http://www.example.com"][target="_blank"] { font-weight:bold; }
p[type^="#4"] {color: grey }
a[href$=".com"] { font-weight:bold; }
p[title*="test"] { font-weight:bold; }
```

Attribute Selectors

Problem	You want to select elements depending on whether they contain a specific attribute, contain a specific word within a specific attribute, or contain a specific value within a specific attribute.
Solution	CSS provides three attribute selectors for this purpose. CSS does not name them individually. I call them the Attribute Existence Selector, the Attribute Word Selector, and the Attribute Value Selector. You can append these attribute selectors to the end of any selector. **You can use the Attribute Existence Selector** to select elements that contain a specific attribute. The Attribute Existence Selector is the name of the attribute enclosed in straight brackets. For example, `p[title]` selects all paragraphs containing the title attribute. If an element contains the attribute and the attribute is assigned to a value, the Attribute Existence Selector matches it. The attribute may contain any value, but some browsers will *not* match an empty attribute, such as `<p title="">`. **You can use the Attribute Word Selector** to select elements that contain a specific word within a specific attribute. The Attribute Word Selector is the opening straight bracket, the name of the attribute, a tilde, an equal sign, the word in double quotes, and the closing straight bracket. For example, `p[title~="paragraph"]` selects all paragraphs containing the word **paragraph** inside their title attribute, such as `<p title="Third paragraph">`. The attribute may contain other words in addition to the matching word. A word is separated from other words using spaces. The match is case-sensitive. **You can use the Attribute Value Selector** to select elements that contain a specific value within a specific attribute. The Attribute Value Selector is the opening straight bracket, the name of the attribute, an equal sign, the value in double quotes, and the closing straight bracket. For example, `p[title="#4   paragraph"]` selects all paragraphs containing the exact value **#4 paragraph** inside their title attribute, such as `p[title="#4   paragraph"]`. The match is case-sensitive and must match the entire attribute value including whitespace. You can use any of the substring matching attribute selectors, like `[attr^=val]`, `[attr$=val]`, and `[attr*=val]`, in order to specify an element with the **attr** attribute whose value begins, ends, or just contains "val". You can also use multiple chained attribute selectors, e.g., `a[href="http://www.example.com"][target="_blank"]` to represent several attributes of an element, or several conditions on the same attribute. Similar to type selectors, attribute selectors also support namespacing.

Patterns
 	
CSS
	`SELECTOR[attr] { STYLES }` or `SELECTOR[attr~="WORD"] { STYLES }`
	or
	`SELECTOR[attr="EXACT_MATCH_OF_ENTIRE_VALUE"] { STYLES }`
	or
	`SELECTOR[attr^="ATTRIBUTE_BEGINGS_WITH_VALUE"] { STYLES }`
	or
	`SELECTOR[attr$="ATTRIBUTE_ENDS_WITH_VALUE"] { STYLES }`
	or
	`SELECTOR[attr*="ATTRIBUTE_CONTAINS_VALUE"] { STYLES }`
	or
	`SELECTOR["ATTRIBUTE_SELECTOR_1"]["ATTRIBUTE_SELECTOR_2"] { STYLES }`

Location	These design patterns apply to all elements.
Limitations	Attribute selectors do not work in Internet Explorer 6. They work in Internet Explorer 7 and other major browsers. CSS defines another selector that I call the **Attribute Language Selector** (e.g., `[lang=en]`), but it is not well supported.
Related to	Inheritance

Pseudo-element Selectors

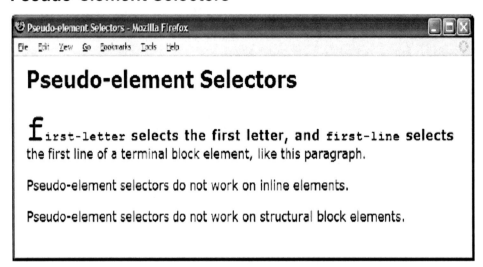

HTML

```
<h1>Pseudo-element Selectors</h1>

<p><code>first-letter</code> selects the first letter, and
    <code>first-line</code> selects the first line of a terminal block element,
    like this paragraph.</p>

<div><span>Pseudo-element selectors do not work on inline elements.</span></div>

<dl>
  <dt>Pseudo-element selectors do not work on structural block elements.</dt>
</dl>
```

CSS

```
p:first-line { font-weight:bold; word-spacing:2px; letter-spacing:1px; }
p:first-letter { font-size:48px; }
span:first-line { font-weight:bold; word-spacing:2px; letter-spacing:1px; }
span:first-letter { font-size:48px; }

dl:first-line { font-weight:bold; word-spacing:2px; letter-spacing:1px; }
dl:first-letter { font-size:48px; }
```

Pseudo-element Selectors

Problem	You want to select the first letter or first line of an element.

Solution	HTML	CSS
	No markup is required.	Combine the **first-letter** and **first-line** pseudo-selector with classes, IDs, and types of your choosing.

Patterns	CSS

```
    ELEMENT:first-letter { STYLES }
or  *.CLASS:first-letter { STYLES }
or  #ID:first-letter { STYLES }
or  ELEMENT:first-line { STYLES }
or  *.CLASS:first-line { STYLES }
or  #ID:first-line { STYLES }
```

Location	**first-letter** and **first-line** work only on terminal block elements. They do not work on inline elements or structural block elements.
Notes	**first-letter** and **first-line** are called pseudo-element selectors because they select a subset of content in an element rather than all the content in an element. In other words, they create a pseudo-element.
Limitations	Internet Explorer 6 ignores a pseudo-element selector unless it is the last selector in a chain of selectors. Newer versions fix this problem.
	The **first-letter** selector works best with font and text properties. Browsers cannot position pseudo-elements and have trouble aligning them. In other words, **position**, **left**, **right**, **top**, and **bottom** have no effect on pseudo-elements. Also, **vertical-align** works inconsistently on pseudo-elements.
	Browsers have exceptional cases where they may not select the first letter or may select more than the first letter. For example, no major browser selects the first letter when an image or object precedes it. For example, Opera 9 does not select the first letter of table cells, and Internet Explorer 6 selects the list marker along with the first letter of a list item, and no matter how much we want them to go away, old browsers are still around to haunt us. Finally, pseudo-element selectors bring out bugs in browsers, so be sure to test your use of them in all major browsers.
Example	In the example, I set three different pseudo-element selectors to the same set of styles. I did not use a grouping selector because Internet Explorer 6 does not recognize pseudo-selectors when they are part of a grouping selector.
Related to	Class Selector, Pseudo-class Selectors

Pseudo-class Selectors

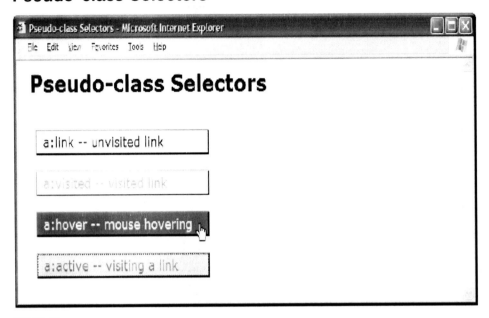

HTML

```
<h1>Pseudo-class Selectors</h1>

<p>
  <a href="http://www.cssdesignpatterns.com">a:link -- unvisited link</a>
  <a href="http://www.htmldesignpatterns.com">a:visited -- visited link</a>
  <a href="http://www.cssdesignpatterns.com">a:hover -- mouse hovering</a>
  <a href="http://www.cssdesignpatterns.com">a:active -- visiting a link</a>
</p>
```

CSS

```
a { padding:3px 10px; margin:20px 10px; text-decoration:none;
  display:block; width:260px;
  border-left:1px solid dimgray; border-right:2px solid black;
  border-top:1px solid dimgray;  border-bottom:2px solid black;  }

a:link { color:black; background-color:white; }
a:visited { color:gray;  background-color:white; }
a:hover { color:white; background-color:green; }
a:active, a:focus { color:green; background-color:gold; }
```

Pseudo-class Selectors

Problem	You want to style a hyperlink depending on whether it is unvisited, visited, being hovered over by the mouse, or in the process of being visited.	
Solution	HTML	CSS
	Insert hyperlinks using **<a>**.	Select hyperlinks based on their state: **Use a:link** to select a hyperlink when it has not been visited. **Use a:visited** to select a hyperlink when it has been visited. **Use a:hover** to select a hyperlink when the mouse hovers over it. **Use a:focus** to select a hyperlink when it receives focus in other browsers. **Use a:active** to select a hyperlink when it receives focus in IE.
Patterns	HTML	CSS

	<a>	`a:link { STYLES }`
		`a:visited { STYLES }`
		`a:hover { STYLES }`
		`a:active, a:focus { STYLES }`

Location	Pseudo-class selectors work on hyperlinks (**<a>**).	
Limitations	Internet Explorer 6 supports the **hover** pseudo-class only on hyperlinks. IE7 and all other major browsers support **hover** on all elements. CSS 2.1 defines two additional pseudo-classes: **first-child** and **lang()**. **first-child** selects an element when it is the first child of another element. **lang()** selects an element when it has been assigned to the specified human language. These pseudo-classes are not supported in Internet Explorer 6. Internet Explorer 7 supports **first-child**, but not **lang**. I do not recommend using them until the majority of users use a browser that supports them.	
Tips	The underline is the standard visual indicator of a hyperlink. If you remove an underline from a hyperlink, you should style it to look like it should be clicked. In the example, I styled the hyperlinks to look like simple buttons. Pseudo-class selectors should be placed in your style sheet in the order listed previously (**link**, **visited**, **hover**, **active**, and **focus**). You can remember the order using the mnemonic Las Vegas Hells Angels Fight. A browser displays the active state when a user tabs to a hyperlink. It is also displayed for less than a second when a user clicks a hyperlink. You can apply a contrasting style to the **active** pseudo-class to make the hyperlink "flash" when the user clicks it. This gives the user immediate feedback that the browser recognized the click.	
Variations	You can use any combination of CSS styles to style hyperlinks.	
Related to	Class Selector, Pseudo-element Selectors	

Subclass Selector

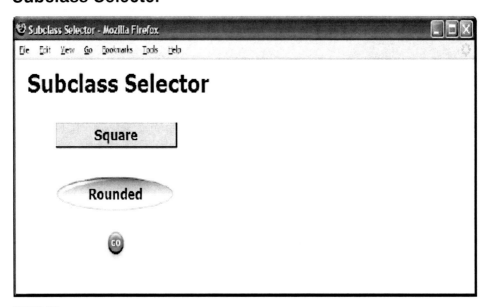

HTML

```
<h1>Subclass Selector</h1>

<div>
  <p class="button square">Square</p>
  <p class="button rounded">Rounded</p>
  <p class="button go">Go</p>
</div>
```

CSS

```
*.button { width:175px; padding:3px 10px; margin:20px 0; text-align:center;
  font-weight:bold; margin-left:50px; line-height:normal; }

*.button.square  { color:darkblue; background-color:gold;
  border-left:1px solid dimgray; border-right:2px solid black;
  border-top:1px solid dimgray;  border-bottom:2px solid black; }

*.button.rounded { color:darkblue; background-color:white;
  line-height:45px; margin-top:30px;
  background:url("oval.gif") no-repeat center center; }

*.button.go { background-color:white; line-height:26px;
  text-indent:-9999px; font-size:10px;
  background: url("go.jpg") no-repeat center center; }
```

Subclass Selector

Problem	You want a class of elements to be styled with common rules. You also want these elements to be divided into subclasses and styled with specialized rules that may override the base rules.	
Solution	HTML	CSS
	You can assign classes to elements in your HTML code using the **class** attribute. A **class** attribute can contain an unlimited number of space-delimited classes. The order of the classes in the attribute is not important. For readability, I recommend listing the base class first followed by its subclasses. The classes assigned to an element do not have to be related, but the code is more logical if you organize them into classes and subclasses.	To select all elements assigned to a base class, use the universal selector followed by the dot operator, followed by the name of the base class, followed by the dot operator, followed by the name of the subclass. I call this chaining together classes. There is no limit to the number of chained classes. The order of the classes in the selector is not important. For readability, I recommend listing the base class first followed by its subclasses. The classes you chain together do not have to be related, but the code is more logical if they are organized into base classes and subclasses.
Pattern	HTML	CSS
	`<ELEMENT class="class subclass etc">`	`*.class { SHARED_BASE_STYLES }` `*.class.subclass.etc { SUBCLASS_STYLES }`
Location	You can apply this design pattern to any element.	
Advantages	You can use this design pattern to build a hierarchy of rules based on classes and subclasses. As in object-oriented programming, subclassed elements "inherit" the rules from their base class and their subclass. CSS cascading order ensures rules from the subclass override the rules in the base class.	
Example	In the example, all paragraphs are assigned to the **button** class. Each one is also assigned to the **square**, **rounded**, and **go** subclasses. All paragraphs assigned to the **button** class share the same base rules assigned by ***.button**, such as **width:175px**. Each subclassed paragraph is assigned to specialized rules through ***.button.square**, ***.button.rounded**, or ***.button.go**. For example, each subclass assigns a different background to its type of button. Some specialized rules, like **margin** and **line-height**, override base rules.	
Related to	Class Selector	

Inheritance

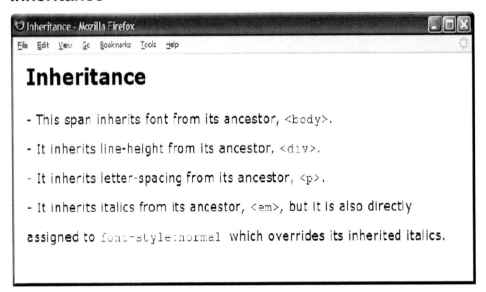

HTML

```
<body>
 <h1>Inheritance</h1>

 <div>
  <p>
   <em>
    <span>
      - This span inherits font from its ancestor, <code>&lt;body&gt;</code>. <br />
      - It inherits line-height from its ancestor, <code>&lt;div&gt;</code>.  <br />
      - It inherits letter-spacing from its ancestor, <code>&lt;p&gt;</code>. <br />
      - It inherits italics from its ancestor, <code>&lt;em&gt;</code>,
        but it is also directly assigned to <code>font-style:normal </code>, which
        overrides its inherited italics.
    </span>
   </em>
  </p>
 </div>
</body>
```

CSS

```
body { font-family:verdana,arial,sans-serif; font-size:18px; }
div { line-height:2em; }
p { letter-spacing:0.8px; }
em { font-style:italic; }
span { font-style:normal; }
```

Inheritance

Problem	You want to style an element and have all its descendants be styled the same.
Solution	CSS is designed so that many properties are inherited by default. This means you can assign one of these inherited properties to any element, and any descendants will inherit the property. Most inline properties are inherited by default. A list of all properties and how they are inherited follows.
Pattern	Inheritance is a type of selector that is built into the CSS language. You do not have to do anything to use inheritance. When a browser encounters an inherited property, it automatically selects descendant inline elements and applies its rule to them. When you assign a property directly to an element, it overrides any inherited value.
Inherited properties	The following properties are inherited by all elements: `visibility` and `cursor` The following properties are inherited by inline elements: `letter-spacing`, `word-spacing`, `white-space`, `line-height`, `color`, `font`, `font-family`, `font-size`, `font-style`, `font-variant`, `font-weight`, `text-decoration`, `text-transform`, and `direction` The following properties are inherited by terminal block elements: `text-indent` and `text-align` The following properties are inherited by list elements: `list-style`, `list-style-type`, `list-style-position`, and `list-style-image` The following property is inherited by table elements: `border-collapse`
Noninherited	The following properties are *not* inherited: `display`, `margin`, `border`, `padding`, `background`, `height`, `min-height`, `max-height`, `width`, `min-width`, `max-width`, `overflow`, `position`, `left`, `right`, `top`, `bottom`, `z-index`, `float`, `clear`, `table-layout`, `vertical-align`, `page-break-after`, `page-break-before`, and `unicode-bidi`
Limitations	CSS provides a constant value named **inherited** that you can assign to any property. When you assign **inherited** to a property, that property inherits its value from its parent element. This allows you to force properties to inherit. Internet Explorer versions 7 and earlier do not implement **inherit**. The following tip shows how you can simulate inheritance for any property.
Tip	You can simulate inheritance for properties that cannot inherit. You first select a starting element using any selector. You then follow the selector by the descendant operator and the universal selector. The pattern is **SELECTOR ***. For example, you can put a border around all elements descended from `<html>` by using `html * { border:1px solid black; }`. I often use this code to see the nesting of all elements in a document.
Related to	Position and Group Selectors

Visual Inheritance

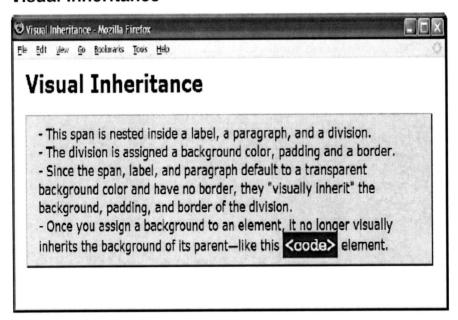

HTML

```
<h1>Visual Inheritance</h1>
<div>
 <p>
  <label>
   <span>
    - This span is nested inside a label, a paragraph, and a division. <br />
    - The division is assigned a background color, padding, and a border. <br />
    - Since the span, label, and paragraph default to a transparent background
      color and have no border, they "visually inherit" the
      background, padding, and border of the division. <br />
    - Once you assign a background to an element, it no longer visually inherits
      the background of its parent—like this <code>&lt;code&gt;</code> element.
   </span>
  </label>
 </p>
</div>
```

CSS

```
div { background-color:gold; color:black; padding:10px 20px;
  border-left:1px solid gray; border-right:2px solid black;
  border-top:1px solid gray; border-bottom:2px solid black; }

p { background-color:transparent; background-image:none; }
label { background-color:transparent; background-image:none; }
span { background-color:transparent; background-image:none; }

code { background-color:firebrick; color:white; }
```

Visual Inheritance

Problem	You want the background of a child element to be the same as its parent.
Solution	CSS automatically layers elements transparently. Child elements are layered on top of parent elements. If margins or positioning cause sibling elements to overlap, following siblings overlap previous siblings. For floated and positioned elements, you can set the layering explicitly using the **z-index** property. This is a design pattern built into CSS. You do not need to do anything to take advantage of it.
	The **background-color** property defaults to transparent, and the **background-image** property defaults to **none**. This allows the background of an element's ancestors to show through. In other words, a browser renders child elements in transparent layers above parent elements unless you set a child's **background-color** to a color, or you set its **background-image** to an image.
	Since child elements are nested within parent elements, each child element *visually* inherits the borders and padding of its parent. In other words, a parent's borders and padding surround its children. If a child has a transparent background and no borders, it appears as if the parent's borders and padding are the child's borders and padding. Without borders around a child, you cannot tell where the parent's padding area ends and the child's padding area begins. Once you add borders to a child element, it no longer visually inherits the borders and padding of its parent because you can see precisely where the parent ends and the child begins.
Pattern	You do not need to do anything to use visual inheritance because **background-color** defaults to **transparent** and **background-image** defaults to **none**. When you want a child element not to visually inherit the background of its parent, you can set the element to its own background color or image as follows:
| | ```
SELECTOR { background-color:COLOR;
    background-image:url("FILE.EXT"); }
``` |
Location	This design pattern applies to all elements.
Example	In the example, the division has a gold background, and all its descendant elements visually inherit the background—except for the code element, which is assigned to the firebrick background color. Notice that I assigned **background-color:transparent** and **background-image:none** to the paragraph, label, and span. I did this to show these rules in action. You do not typically need to assign these rules in your code because **background-color:transparent** and **background-image:none** are the default for all elements. On the other hand, you can use these rules whenever you want to reset an element to a transparent background after another rule assigned it to a background color or image.
Related to	Inheritance
```

Box Models

The fundamental design pattern in CSS is the **Box Model**. The Box Model defines how elements are rendered as boxes. There are six main types of boxes: inline, inline-block, block, table, absolute, and floated. A browser renders each element as one of these boxes. Some elements are rendered in a variation of one of these boxes, such as a list item or table cell. For example, list-item is a block box with an inline marker automatically created by the browser, and table-cell is a block box that does not support margins.

You can use the display property to render an element as a different type of box. You can use position:absolute or position:fixed to render any element as an absolute box. You can use the float:left or float:right rules to render any element as a floated box.

This is the first of three chapters on the Box Model. This chapter explains the six main types of boxes. Chapter 5 introduces extents, which are controlled by width and height. Extents control whether a box is shrinkwrapped to its content, sized, or stretched to the sides of its container. Chapter 6 introduces the Box Model properties: margin, border, padding, background, overflow, visibility, page-break-before, and page-break-after. Background, visibility, and page breaks work the same in all boxes. Borders, padding, and overflow work the same in all boxes except for inline. Width, height, and margins work differently in each type of box.

Chapter Outline

- **Display** shows how to render an element as an inline box, a block box, an inline-block box, a list-item box, a table box, or not at all.

- **Box Model** introduces the general box model underlying all types of boxes.

- **Inline Box** shows how inline boxes work.

- **Inline-Block Box** shows how inline-block and replaced inline boxes work.

- **Block Box** shows how block boxes work.

- **Table Box** shows how table boxes work.

- **Absolute Box** shows how absolute and fixed boxes work.

- **Floated Box** shows how floated boxes work.

Display

HTML

```
<h1>Display</h1>

<code>display:inline</code>
<p>p</p> <p>p</p> <p>p</p>
<ol><li>li</li><li>li</li><li>li</li></ol>
<table><tr><td>td</td><td>td</td></tr><tr><td>td</td><td>td</td></tr></table>

<strong>strong <br /><code>display:inline-block</code></strong>  <br /><br />

<em>em <code>display:block</code></em> <em>em</em> <br />

<div class="ul"><dfn>dfn <code>display:list-item</code></dfn><dfn>dfn</dfn></div>

<br /><img src="star.gif" alt="star" /> <code>display:none</code>
```

CSS

```
p,ol,li,table { display:inline; }
strong { display:inline-block; width:250px; }
em { display:block; }
dfn { display:list-item; list-style-type:square; }
img { display:none; }

*.ul { padding-left:15px; }
```

Display

Problem	You want to fundamentally change how the browser renders an element. For example, you want a block element rendered inline, as a list item, or as a table; or you do not want it to be rendered at all—as if it never existed.
Solution	You can use the **display** property to change how an element is rendered. You can use **display:none** to prevent an element from being rendered. You can use **display:inline** to render an element inline. You can use **display:block** or **display:list-item** to render an element as a block or list item. You can use **display:inline-block** to render an inline element as a block nested in a line.
Pattern	SELECTOR { display:inline; } SELECTOR { display:inline-block; } SELECTOR { display:block; } SELECTOR { display:list-item; } SELECTOR { display:none; }
Location	This design pattern applies to all elements.
Limitations	There are additional display types, but they are not well supported. Internet Explorer 7 does not support **run-in** and **inline-table**. Internet Explorer 7 also does not support **table**, **table-cell**, **table-row**, **table-header-group**, **table-footer-group**, **table-row-group**, **table-column-group**, **table-column**, and **table-caption**.
Tips	When you display an element as a list item, its *parent* needs to be rendered as a block and needs to provide left padding or left margin for the marker. This is required because a list is a two-part structure: an outer block, such as **‹ol›**, **‹ul›**, or **‹dl›**, and an inner block, such as **‹li›**, **‹dd›**, or **‹dt›**. You can assign a marker to it using **list-style-type**. A browser renders a **list-item** as a block with an inline marker. When you want a **list-item** to look like a block, you can simply turn off the marker using **list-style-type:none**—you do not need to change the display type because a list is already a block. You may also want to remove its parent's padding and margin.
Example	The example uses **display:inline** to render the blocks **‹p›** and **‹li›** as inline boxes. It uses **display:inline-block** to render the inline **‹strong›** as an inline block. It uses **display:block** to display the inline **‹em›** as a block. It uses **display:list-item** to render the inline **‹dfn›** elements as list items. It assigns a marker to them using **list-style-type**. It also assigns left padding to their parent to make room for the marker. Lastly, it uses **display:none** to hide an image.
Related to	Visibility (Chapter 6); Blocked (Chapter 11); Inlined, Run-in (Chapter 13); Tabled, Rowed, and Celled (Chapter 15)

Box Model

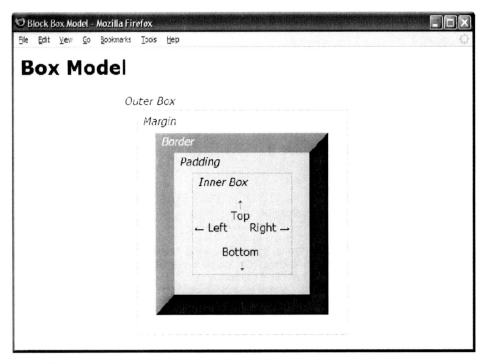

HTML

```
<h1>Box Model</h1>

<div class="box"></div>

<!-- The HTML code that creates the labels and extra borders is not shown. -->
```

CSS

```
*.box { display:static;
  overflow:visible;
  visibility:visible;
  width:160px;
  height:150px;
  padding:30px;
  border-top: 30px solid gray; border-bottom:30px solid black;
  border-left:30px solid gray; border-right: 30px solid black;
  margin-left:230px; margin-top:80px;
  background-color:gold; }


/*  Nonessential rules are not shown. */
```

Box Model

Problem	You want to style the box of an element.
Solution	The Box Model design pattern is built into CSS. This model defines the relationship between the following properties: `display`, `width`, `height`, `padding`, `border`, `margin`, `background`, `overflow`, and `visibility`. **width** normally sets the width of an element's *inner box*. **height** normally sets the height of an element's *inner box*. **padding** sets the size of the padding *surrounding the inner box*. The padding is transparent to the element's background. **border** sets the size, pattern, and color of the border *surrounding the padding*. **margin** sets the size of the margin *surrounding the border*. The margin is transparent to the background of the element's parent. The outside of the margin is the element's *outer box*. **background** assigns the padding area inside the box to a background color and/or image. **overflow** determines what happens when an element's content is larger than its *inner box*. The default is to show the overflowing content. **visibility** can make the element `visible` or `hidden`.

Pattern	```SELECTOR { display:CONSTANT;```
	```overflow:VALUE;```
	```visibility:VALUE;```
	```width:+VALUE;```
	```height:+VALUE;```
	```padding:+VALUE;```
	```border:+WIDTH STYLE COLOR;```
	```margin:±VALUE;```
	```background:VALUES; }```

Location	This design pattern applies to all elements.
Example	The example contains additional HTML markup and CSS rules that are not shown. This extra code renders a label over each part of the box and draws the outer box and inner box borders.
Notes	CSS defines six main types of boxes: inline, inline-block, block, table, absolute, and floated. The type of box is determined by the combination of the following properties: `display`, `position`, and `float`. Box Model properties work differently and produce different layouts depending on the type of box. Certain types of boxes have additional functionality provided by additional properties, such as `line-height`, `border-collapse`, and `table-layout`.
Related to	All Box Model design patterns

Inline Box

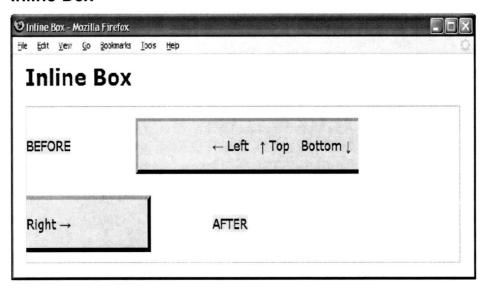

HTML

```
<h1>Inline Box</h1>

<div class="container">
  <span class="default">BEFORE</span>

  <span class="box">&larr; Left   &uarr; Top  
        Bottom &darr;   Right &rarr; </span>

  <span class="default">AFTER</span>
</div>
```

CSS

```
*.box { display:inline; visibility:visible;
  line-height:100px;
  margin:0 100px;
  padding:20px 120px;

  border-top:    5px solid gray;
  border-bottom:5px solid black;
  border-left:   5px solid gray;
  border-right: 5px solid black;

  background-color:gold; }

/*  Nonessential rules are not shown. */
```

Inline Box

Aliases	Inline, inline element, and static inline box are synonyms with inline box.
Problem	You want to style the box of an inline element.
Solution	Inline boxes are rendered in the inline flow. They flow horizontally from left to right (or right to left in some languages) and are wrapped to new lines when they exceed the width of their closest terminal block ancestor. This is called the **inline formatting context**. CSS provides the following properties for styling inline boxes:
	width, height, and **overflow** do *not* work on inline elements, because they always shrinkwrap to fit the width and height of their content.
	margin and **line-height** are applied to inline elements in unique ways. Horizontal margins change the position of inline elements in the flow. A positive value in **margin-left** moves the element away from the previous element, and a negative value moves it closer. A positive value in **margin-right** moves the next element further away, and a negative value moves it closer. **margin-top** and **margin-bottom** are ignored by inline elements. Instead, inline elements use **line-height** to size the height of a line.
	border is applied to inline elements in unique ways. Horizontal borders change the position of inline elements in the flow. The left border moves the element to the left, and the right border moves the next element to the right. The top and bottom borders are rendered above and below the padding area *without* expanding the height of the line or changing the vertical position of the inline element. Because borders do not affect the height of the line, borders can overlap neighboring lines unless you increase **line-height**. When a bordered element is wrapped across lines, the browser does not render the right border at the end of the line, and it does not render the left border at the beginning of the wrapped line. The left and right borders occur only at the beginning and end of the *element*.
	padding is applied to inline elements in exactly the same way as borders.
Pattern	```INLINE_SELECTOR { display:inline; visibility:VALUE;``` ```line-height:+VALUE;``` ```margin:±VALUE;``` ```padding:+VALUE;``` ```border:+WIDTH STYLE COLOR;``` ```background:VALUES; }```
Location	This design pattern applies to inline elements and any element displayed inline.
Related to	Display, Box Model; Shrinkwrapped (Chapter 5); Margin, Border, Padding, Background, Visibility (Chapter 6)

Inline-Block Box

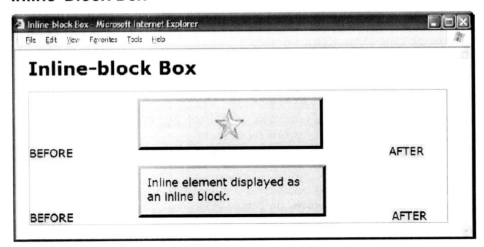

HTML

```
<h1>Inline-block Box</h1>

<div class="container">
  <span class="default">BEFORE</span>
  <img class="replaced-box" src="star.gif" alt="star" />
  <span class="default">AFTER</span>

  <span class="default">BEFORE</span>
  <span class="inline-box">Inline element displayed as an inline block.</span>
  <span class="default">AFTER</span>
</div>
```

CSS

```
*.replaced-box { display:inline-block;
  overflow:visible; visibility:visible;
  width:51px; height:52px;
  margin:10px 100px; padding:10px 120px; }


*.inline-box { display:inline-block;
  overflow:visible; visibility:visible;
  width:275px; height:52px;
  margin:10px 100px; padding:10px 10px; }


/* Nonessential rules are not shown.
  See Inline Box for border and background properties. */
```

Inline-Block Box

Problem	You want to style the box of an inline-block element. Inline-block elements include replaced elements and inline elements displayed as inline blocks. For example, an image is a replaced element because the browser replaces the element with an image. Also, you can use **display:inline-block** to display any *inline* element as a block rendered within an inline context.
Solution	Inline-block boxes participate in the inline flow like inline boxes but have margins, borders, padding, width, and height like block boxes. An inline-block box cannot be wrapped across lines. An inline-block box grows the height of a line to fit its height, padding, borders, and margins. An inline-block box can be shrinkwrapped, sized, or stretched. CSS provides the following properties for styling inline-block boxes:
	width and **height** set the width and height of the element. You can enlarge or shrink a replaced element, such as an image, by setting **width** and/or **height** to a measurement. You can set a replaced element to its natural size using **width:auto** and **height:auto**. You can size an inline-block element, such as a span assigned to **display:inline-block**, by setting **width** and/or **height** to a measurement. You can shrinkwrap an inline-block element using **width:auto** and **height:auto**. You can stretch an inline block using **width:100%**. Note that a stretched inline block is the same as a block.
	margin has unique inline-block features. A positive value in **margin-top** expands the height of the line and a negative value shrinks it. A positive value in **margin-bottom** raises the element and a negative value lowers it. **margin-bottom** may also expand or shrink the height of a line. A positive value in **margin-left** moves the element away from the previous element, and a negative value moves it closer. A positive value in **margin-right** moves the next element further away, and a negative value moves it closer.
	border and **padding** expand the outer size of the inline element. This moves it to the right and moves following content to the right. It also moves it up and increases the height of the line containing it.
| **Pattern** | ```
SELECTOR { display:inline-block; line-height:+VALUE;
overflow:VALUE; visibility:VALUE;
width: +VALUE; height: +VALUE;
margin:±VALUE; padding:+VALUE;
border:+WIDTH STYLE COLOR;  background:VALUES; }
``` |
Location	This design pattern applies to inline elements.
Example	The example shows an image and a span displayed as inline blocks. Note that you do not need to assign **display:inline-block** to *replaced elements* because a browser automatically displays them as inline blocks.
Related to	Display, Box Model; Width, Height, Sized, Shrinkwrapped, Stretched (Chapter 5); Margin, Border, Padding, Background, Overflow, Visibility (Chapter 6)
```

Block Box

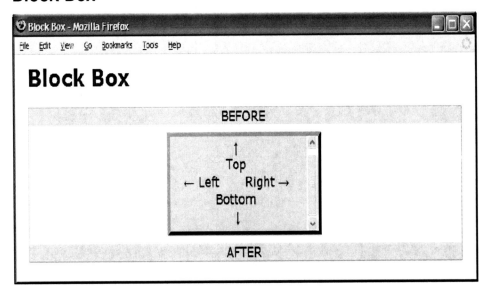

HTML

```
<h1>Block Box</h1>

<div class="container">
  <div class="default">BEFORE</div>

  <div class="box"> &uarr; <br /> Top <br /> &larr; Left      
      Right &rarr; <br /> Bottom <br /> &darr; </div>

  <div class="default">AFTER</div>
</div>
```

CSS

```
*.box { display:block;
  overflow:auto; visibility:visible;
  width:220px; height:100px;
  margin:10px auto; padding:10px; }

/*  Nonessential rules are not shown.
    See Inline Box for border and background properties. */
```

Block Box

Aliases	Block, block element, and static block box are synonyms with block box.
Problem	You want to style the box of a block element.
Solution	Block boxes flow vertically from top to bottom in a block formatting context. This is called the **normal flow** of blocks. Block boxes can contain other block boxes, or they can terminate the block formatting context and start an inline formatting context containing inline boxes. A **terminal block** creates an inline formatting context inside its inner box, but occurs within a block formatting context on the outside of its outer box.
	A block can be stretched to the width and height of its parent or sized smaller or larger than its parent. When sized larger, it *overflows* its parent. The **overflow** property controls how the browser handles overflow.
	width sets the width of the element. **width:auto** is the default value and *stretches* the element to fill the width of its *parent*.
	height sets the height of the element. **height:auto** is the default value and *shrinkwraps* the element to the height of all its child blocks or lines.
	margin-left and **margin-right** indent or outdent the sides of a stretched block, and they offset the sides of a sized block. You cannot *horizontally* shrinkwrap a block box.
	margin-top and **margin-bottom** push blocks further apart with positive values, but negative values bring them closer together, and can even overlap them. A browser collapses top and bottom margins of neighboring blocks.
	margin-left:auto and **margin-right:auto** control the horizontal alignment of a sized block. When you size a block by setting **width** to a measurement, **margin-right:auto** aligns the block to the left side of its parent, and **margin-left:auto** aligns the block to the right side. When you set both **margin-left** and **margin-right** to **auto**, the block is aligned to the center of its parent (as shown in the example).
	border and **padding** expand the outer width and height of the box. This pushes down a block and its following blocks. On stretched blocks, horizontal borders and padding shrink the size of the inner box. On sized blocks, they offset the inner box.
| **Pattern** | ```
SELECTOR { display:block; overflow:VALUE; visibility:VALUE;
width: +VALUE; height: +VALUE;
margin:±VALUE; padding:+VALUE;
border:+WIDTH STYLE COLOR;
background:VALUES; }
``` |
| **Location** | This design pattern applies to block elements. |
| **Related to** | Display, Box Model; Width, Height, Sized, Shrinkwrapped, Stretched (Chapter 5);Margin, Border, Padding, Background, Overflow, Visibility (Chapter 6) |
```

Table Box

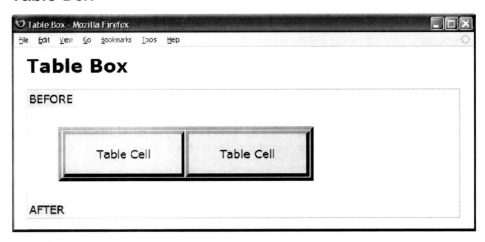

HTML

```
<h1>Table Box Model</h1>
<div class="container">
  <table class="default"><tr><td>BEFORE</td></tr></table>

  <table class="table">
    <tr><td class="cell">Table Cell </td><td class="cell">Table Cell </td></tr>
  </table>

  <table class="default"><tr><td>AFTER</td></tr></table>
</div>
```

CSS

```
*.table {
  border-collapse:separate; table-layout:auto; visibility:visible;
  width:auto; height:auto; margin:30px 50px; }

*.cell { width:auto; height:auto; padding:20px 50px; overflow:hidden; }

/*  Nonessential rules are not shown.
  See Inline Box for border and background properties. */
```

Table Box

Problem	You want to style the box of a table and the boxes of its cells.
Solution	A table is a block box on the outside containing rows of cells on the inside. A table participates in the block flow, and its cells participate in the table flow of rows and columns. A table has margins but does not have padding. A cell has padding but does not have margins. Two additional properties affect the Table Box model: **border-collapse** and **table-layout**. There are many design patterns for laying out cells inside a table. These are found in Chapters 15 and 16, which discuss tables and cells in detail. This design pattern focuses on the outside of the table, and how the table interacts with the position of surrounding elements.

width sets the width of a table. Unlike other boxes, **width** refers to the *outside of the borders* rather than to the inside of its padding.

height sets the height of the table. Unlike other boxes, **height** refers to the *outside of the borders* rather than to the inside of its padding.

margin works differently depending on whether the table is sized, shrink-wrapped, or stretched. When sized or shrinkwrapped, margins offset the table and offset following elements. Negative margins can overlap the table with neighboring elements. When a table is stretched, margins indent the table, which decreases its internal size and shrinks its cells.

border decreases the size of a table's inner box when a table is sized or stretched. No other sized box works like this. This unusual behavior occurs because table borders are *inside* the box specified by **width** and **height**. When the table is shrinkwrapped, **border** works like other boxes and increases the size of a table's outer box.**r**

overflow does not apply to tables because a table cannot overflow. Only a table's cells can overflow. **overflow:hidden** should be applied to cells to ensure consistent behavior in all browsers when fixed cells overflow.

border-collapse determines whether adjacent borders combine into a single border. See Chapters 15 and 16 for details.

table-layout determines whether the table is **fixed** sized or **auto** sized based on its content. See Chapters 15 and 16 for details.

Pattern	```SELECTOR { display:table; visibility:VALUE;```
	 ```width:+VALUE; height:+VALUE;```
	 ```margin:±VALUE; border:+WIDTH STYLE COLOR;```
	 ```background:VALUES;```
	 ```border-collapse:VALUE; table-layout:VALUE; }```

Location	This design pattern applies to table elements.
Related to	Table, Display, Box Model; Width, Height, Sized, Shrinkwrapped, Stretched (Chapter 5); Margin, Border, Padding, Background, Overflow, Visibility (Chapter 6)
See also	Chapter 15 explains tables in much more detail.

Absolute Box

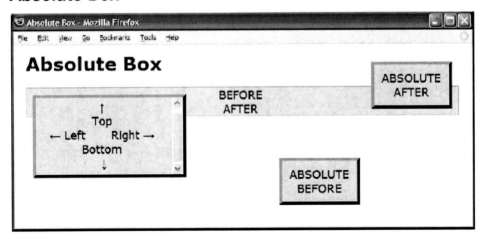

HTML

```
<h1>Absolute Box</h1>

<div class="container" >
  <div class="default">BEFORE</div>
  <div class="box before">ABSOLUTE BEFORE</div>

  <div class="box">&uarr; <br /> Top <br /> &larr; Left    
      Right &rarr; <br /> Bottom <br /> &darr; </div>

  <div class="box after">ABSOLUTE AFTER</div>
  <div class="default">AFTER</div>
</div>
```

CSS

```
*.container { position:relative; }

*.box { position:absolute; overflow:auto; visibility:visible;
  z-index:auto; left:0; right:auto; top:0; bottom:auto;
  width:220px; height:100px;
  margin:10px; padding:10px;}

*.before {width:100px; height:auto; left:400px; right:auto; top:100px; bottom:auto;}
*.after {width:100px; height:auto; left:auto;  right:0px;  top:auto; bottom:0px; }

/*  Nonessential rules are not shown.
  See Inline Box for border and background properties. */
```

Absolute Box

Problem	You want to style the box of an absolute or fixed element.
Solution	An **absolute element** is removed from the normal flow and put in a layer above or below it. It is positioned in relation to its closest positioned ancestor or fixed to the viewport. It can be sized, shrinkwrapped, or stretched to its closest positioned ancestor. *Any* element can be positioned absolutely. Unlike other boxes, the position of an absolute box does *not* affect the position of other boxes. Absolute boxes may overlap freely.

z-index controls the stacking order of positioned elements. A negative value places them below the normal flow, and a positive value places them above the flow. Larger values move them closer to the user in the stacking order.

left, **right**, **top**, and **bottom** apply to absolute boxes. When set to a measurement, **left** aligns the left side of an absolute element to the left side of its container and offsets it by a positive or negative value. **right**, **top**, and **bottom** work analogously. When **left**, **right**, **top**, and **bottom** are all set to **auto**, a browser renders the absolute box in the same position it would have had if it were rendered in the normal flow.

width sets the width of the element. **width:auto** is the default value. When **width** is **auto** and both **left** and **right** are auto, the box is *shrinkwrapped*. When **width** is **auto** and both **left** and **right** are **0** or some other value, the box is *stretched*. When **width** is a value, **left** is a value, and **right** is **auto**, the box is *sized* and offset from the left. When **width** is a value, **left** is **auto**, and **right** is a value, the box is *sized* and offset from the right.

height sets the height of the element. **height**, **top**, and **bottom** work analogously to **width**, **left**, and **right**.

margin assigned to a positive value moves a side of an absolute box toward the center of its container, and a negative value moves it away from center.

border and **padding** shrink the inner box of *stretched* absolute boxes. **border** and **padding** expand the outer box of sized and shrinkwrapped absolute boxes and move them toward the center of their container. |
| **Pattern** | ```
SELECTOR { position:ABSOLUTE_FIXED; z-index:+VALUE;
overflow:VALUE; visibility:VALUE;
left:±VALUE; right:±VALUE; top:±VALUE; bottom:±VALUE;
width: +VALUE; height: +VALUE;
margin:±VALUE; padding:+VALUE;
border:+WIDTH STYLE COLOR; background:VALUES; }
``` |
Location	This design pattern applies to all elements.
Tip	Chapters 7 through 9 show how to position absolute boxes.
Example	Notice how all three absolute boxes are removed from the flow, which brings together the static BEFORE and AFTER blocks.
Related to	Positioned (Chapter 7); Display, Box Model (Chapter 4); Width, Height, Sized, Shrinkwrapped, Stretched (Chapter 5); Margin, Border, Padding, Background, Overflow, Visibility (Chapter 6)
```

Floated Box

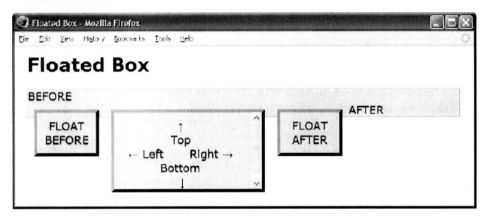

HTML

```
<h1>Floated Box</h1>

<div class="container">
  <div class="default">BEFORE</div>
  <div class="box small">FLOAT BEFORE</div>

  <div class="box">&uarr; <br /> Top <br /> &larr; Left    
      Right &rarr; <br /> Bottom <br /> &darr; </div>

  <div class="box small">FLOAT AFTER</div>
  <div class="default">AFTER</div>
</div>
```

CSS

```
*.box { float:left;  overflow:auto; visibility:visible;
  width:220px; height:100px;
  margin:10px; padding:10px; }

*.small { width:75px; height:auto; }

/*  Nonessential rules are not shown.
    See Inline Box for border and background properties. */
```

Floated Box

Problem	You want to style the box of a float.
Solution	You can float any element using **float:left** or **float:right**. A float is removed from the normal flow and placed above the borders and backgrounds of adjacent blocks. This shrinks the float's parent and collapses it completely when all its children are floated. Even though a float is removed from the flow, it indents adjacent content in the flow. Left floats indent adjacent content to the right, and right floats indent content to the left. A float is positioned vertically at the location in which it would have been rendered in the normal flow. It is positioned horizontally inside its parent's padding area on the left or right. A float stacks next to other floats in the same general vertical location. When a float cannot fit next to another float, it moves down below it. A float's position, size, padding, borders, and margins affect the position of adjacent floats and adjacent inline content. The precise location of a float cannot be predetermined.
	width sets the width of the float. **width:auto** is the default value and *shrinkwraps* the float to fit the width of its widest line.
	height sets the height of the float. **height:auto** is the default value and *shrinkwraps* the float to the height of all its child blocks or lines.
	margin has unique float features. A positive margin pushes the float away from its point of alignment and pushes other floats and inline content away from it. A negative margin pulls the float to the other side of its point of alignment and pulls other floats and inline content closer. Margins around floats do not collapse.
	border and **padding** expand the outer size of a float. The left border and padding of a left float move the float to the right, and its right border and padding move other floats and inline content on the right further to the right. This applies vice versa for right floats. Top border and padding move the float down. The bottom border and padding move down any floats below the float, and extend the float's effect on adjacent content in the normal flow.

Pattern	`SELECTOR { float:LEFT_RIGHT; width:+VALUE; height:+VALUE;`
	`z-index:+VALUE;  margin:±VALUE; padding:+VALUE;`
	`border:+WIDTH STYLE COLOR; background:VALUES;`
	`overflow:VALUE; visibility:VALUE; }`

Location	This design pattern applies to all elements.
Example	The three floats in the example are removed from the flow, which brings together the static BEFORE and AFTER boxes and shrinks the height of the floats' parent. The three floats stack next to each other from left to right. The AFTER text is moved to the right by the last float. Margins, borders, and padding expand the floats' outer boxes and push away other floats.
Related to	Display, Box Model; Width, Height, Sized, Shrinkwrapped, Stretched (Chapter 5); Margin, Border, Padding, Background, Overflow, Visibility (Chapter 6)

Box Model Extents

This is the second of three chapters on the Box Model. It shows how boxes can be sized, shrinkwrapped, and stretched. The previous chapter discusses the six main types of boxes: inline, inline-block, block, table, absolute, and floated. The next chapter discusses properties that style the box.

Each type of box works differently. The design patterns in this chapter show how to apply width and height to each type of box to size, shrinkwrap, or stretch it. Horizontal and vertical dimensions are independent. You can freely combine different vertical and horizontal design patterns. For example, you can stretch horizontally and shrinkwrap vertically.

Chapter Outline

- **Width** contrasts how width can size, shrinkwrap, or stretch each type of box.

- **Height** contrasts how height can size, shrinkwrap, or stretch each type of box.

- **Sized** shows how to set the height or width of an element. An element is sized when you manually assign it a height and/or a width. For example, you can use `height:50%` to size an element's height to 50% of the height of its container.

- **Shrinkwrapped** shows how to shrink the width or height of an element to the size of its content. For example, `height:auto` causes the height of a static block element to expand automatically to fit the total height of its lines, and `width:auto` causes the width of an absolute element to shrink to fit to the width of its widest line.

- **Stretched** shows how to stretch the width or height of an element to the sides of its container. For example, `width:auto` causes the width of a static block element to expand automatically to fit the width of its container. For example, `top:0`, `bottom:0`, and `height:auto` cause an absolute element to expand automatically to fit the height of its container. A stretched element's left side aligns to the left side of its container, and its right side aligns to the right side of the container. Similarly, its top and bottom sides align to the top and bottom sides of its container.

Width

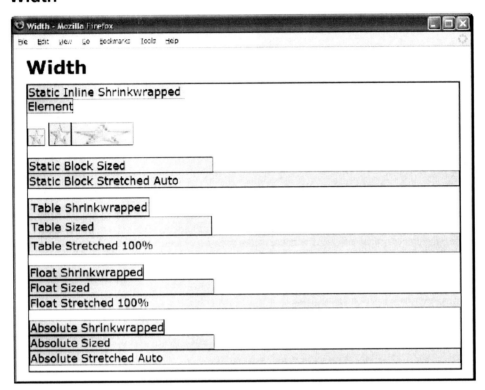

CSS

```
*.static-inline-shrinkwrapped { width:auto; }
*.replaced-inline-shrinkwrapped { width:auto; }
*.replaced-inline-sized { width:35px; }
*.replaced-inline-stretched { width:100%; }

*.static-block-sized { width:300px; }
*.static-block-stretched { width:auto; }

*.table-shrinkwrapped { width:auto; }
*.table-sized { width:300px; }
*.table-stretched { width:100%; }

*.float-shrinkwrapped { width:auto; float:left; }
*.float-sized { width:300px; float:left; clear:both; }
*.float-stretched { width:100%; float:left; clear:both; }

*.absolute-shrinkwrapped { width:auto; left:0; right:auto; position:absolute; }
*.absolute-sized { width:300px; left:0; right:auto; position:absolute; }
*.absolute-stretched { width:auto; left:0; right:0; position:absolute; }
```

Width

Problem	You want to set the width of an element to size it, shrinkwrap it, or stretch it.
Solution	CSS provides the **width** property for this purpose.
	This design pattern is an introduction to the Sized, Shrinkwrapped, and Stretched design patterns. The purpose of this design pattern is to compare how **width** applies to all six main types of boxes: inline, inline-block, block, table, absolute, and floated. This comparison makes it easy to choose the proper combination of width, element, and display box to create the layout you want.
	width works on all types of elements except for inline elements. **width** works differently depending on the type of element and whether it is positioned or floated. **width** is completely independent from **height**. **width:auto** is the default.
width:auto	**width:auto** horizontally *shrinkwraps* the following boxes: inline, inline-block, floated, table, and absolute (when both **left** and **right** are **auto**).
	width:auto horizontally *stretches* block boxes and absolute boxes (when **left** and **right** are both set to a value, such as **0**).
width:+VALUE	You can *size* an element by assigning pixels, ems, a percentage, or another fixed measurement to **width**. Fixed-width elements may not be user-friendly when the viewport is much larger or much smaller than expected. Percentages are more flexible because they can scale to the viewport.
width:100%	**width:100%** stretches an element to the width of its parent, but unlike **auto**, **width:100%** has limitations. A browser does not automatically adjust the width to keep the element stretched. An element's horizontal margins, borders, or padding can expand its width beyond the width of the parent.
Pattern	`SELECTOR { width:+VALUE; }`
Location	**width** applies to all elements except for inline elements.
Tips	A browser ignores **width** on a static inline element because **font** and **font-size** determine the width of its text, which sets the element's width.
	Tables stretched using **width:100%** work almost as well as horizontally stretched absolute elements. When you assign borders or padding to a table, the outer box of a table does not expand, and the table does not overflow its parent. This is because borders and padding are rendered on the inside of the table and do not expand its outer box. On the other hand, a margin assigned to a table will reposition the table, and it will overflow its parent.
Example	The example illustrates all ways of using **width** to create *horizontally* shrinkwrapped, stretched, and sized elements. I omitted nonessential CSS rules and the HTML code to fit the example on one page. The text in the element is the name of its class. The replaced element is an image of a star.
Related to	Sized, Shrinkwrapped, Stretched; Static, Absolute, Float (Chapter 7); Table (Chapter 15)

Height

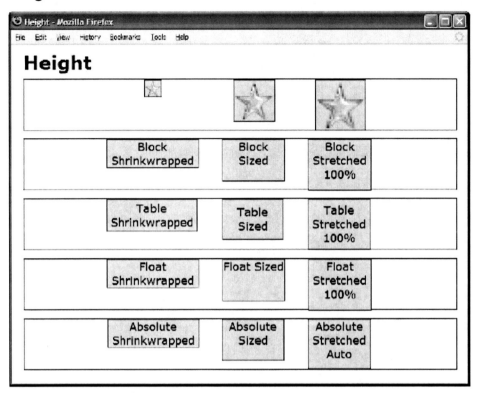

CSS

```
*.replaced-inline-shrinkwrapped { height:auto; }
*.replaced-inline-sized { height:65px; }
*.replaced-inline-stretched { height:100%; }

*.block-shrinkwrapped { height:auto; }
*.block-sized { height:65px; }
*.block-stretched { height:100%; }

*.table-shrinkwrapped { height:auto; }
*.table-sized { height:65px; }
*.table-stretched { height:100%; }

*.float-shrinkwrapped { height:auto; float:left; }
*.float-sized { height:65px; float:left; }
*.float-stretched { height:100%; float:left; }

*.absolute-shrinkwrapped { height:auto; top:0; bottom:auto; position:absolute; }
*.absolute-sized { height:65px; top:0; bottom:auto; position:absolute; }
*.absolute-stretched { height:auto; top:0; bottom:0; position:absolute; }
```

Height

Problem	You want to set the height of an element to size it, shrinkwrap it, or stretch it.
Solution	CSS provides the **height** property for this purpose. This design pattern is an introduction to the Sized, Shrinkwrapped, and Stretched design patterns. The purpose of this design pattern is to compare how **height** applies to all six main types of boxes: inline, inline-block, block, table, absolute, and floated. This comparison makes it easy to choose the proper combination of height, element, and display box to create the layout you want.
	height works on all types of elements except for inline elements. **height** works differently depending on the type of element and whether it is positioned or floated. **height** is completely independent from **width**. **height:auto** is the default.
height:auto	**height:auto** vertically *shrinkwraps* the following boxes: inline, inline-block, block, floated, table, and absolute (when both **top** and **bottom** are **auto**). **height:auto** also vertically *stretches* an absolute box when **top** and **bottom** are both set to a value, such as **0**. This is the best way to vertically stretch a box because **height:100%** has limitations, but it is available only for absolute boxes.
height:+VALUE	You can *size* an element by assigning pixels, ems, a percentage, or another fixed measurement to **height**. Fixed heights may not be user-friendly when the viewport is much larger or much smaller than expected. Percentages are more flexible because they can scale to the viewport.
height:100%	**height:100%** stretches an element to the height of its parent, but unlike **auto**, **height:100%** has limitations. A browser does not automatically adjust the height to keep the element stretched. An element's vertical margins, borders, or padding can expand its height beyond the height of the parent.
Pattern	`SELECTOR { height:+VALUE; }`
Location	**height** applies to all elements except for inline elements.
Tips	A browser ignores **height** on a static inline element because **font** and **font-size** determine the height of its text, which sets the element's height.
	Tables stretched using **height:100%** work almost as well as vertically stretched absolute elements. When you assign borders or padding to a table, the outer box of a table does not expand, and the table does not overflow its parent. This is because borders and padding are rendered on the inside of the table and do not expand its outer box. On the other hand, a margin assigned to a table will reposition the stretched table and overflow its parent.
Example	The example illustrates all ways of using **height** to create *vertically* shrinkwrapped, stretched, and sized elements. I omitted nonessential CSS rules and the HTML code to fit the example on one page. The text in the element is the name of its class. The replaced element is an image of a star.
Related to	Sized, Shrinkwrapped, Stretched; Static, Absolute, Float (Chapter 7); Table (Chapter 15)

Sized

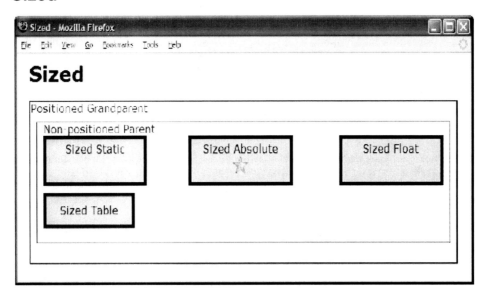

HTML

```
<h1>Sized</h1>
<div class="gp">Positioned Grandparent
  <div class="parent">Non-positioned Parent
    <div id="float" class="z">Sized Float</div>
    <div id="static" class="z">Sized Static</div>
    <table id="table" class="z"><tr><td>Sized Table</td></tr></table>
    <span id="abs" class="z">Sized Absolute
      <img id="star" src="star.gif" alt="star" /></span>
  </div>
</div>
```

CSS

```
*.z { padding:5px; border:5px solid black; }

#float { width:150px; height:50px; }
#static { width:150px; height:50px; }
#table { width:150px; height:50px; }
#abs { width:150px; height:50px; }
#star { width:26px; height:26px; }

/*  Nonessential rules are not shown. */
```

Sized

Problem	You want to set the height and/or width of an element to a *measurement* or a *percentage* of its containing block's height and width.
Solution	Apply styles to your chosen class or ID as follows: Use **height** to set the height of an element to a measurement or a percentage of the height of its container. Use **width** to set the width of an element to a measurement or a percentage of the width of its container. **You can assign width** and **height** independently. In other words, you can size the height only, the width only, or both height and width. **If you do not want to size the height or width,** you can set **width** or **height** to **auto**. **auto** is the default value for width and height.
Pattern	`SELECTOR { width:+VALUE; height:+VALUE; }`
Location	This pattern applies to all elements except for static inline elements.
Explanation	Sized elements require **width** and **height** to be set to a measurement or percentage. A percentage of 100% is used to stretch an element, but any other percentage sizes the element smaller or larger than its container. **height** and **width** specify the *inner box* of an element. Padding surrounds the inner box. Borders surround the padding. Margins surround the borders. The box surrounding the margins is the *outer box*. Padding, borders, and margin expand the outer box and have no effect on the **height** and **width** of the inner box. Negative margins may cause adjacent elements to overlap an element, but they do not change its **height** and **width**. **Tables are an exception** where **height** and **width** specify the outside of the table's *border*. This causes borders and padding to be placed *inside* the specified height and width. This is why the table in the example is smaller than the other elements. **When a float is sized,** it changes the flow. **width** changes the left and right boundaries in which the float's content is flowed, affecting the location of adjacent content and floats. **height** pushes down or pulls up adjacent floats. **When a static block element is sized,** it changes the flow. **height** pushes down or pulls up the following block element. **height** also shrinks or grows the height of its parent (unless the parent is also sized). **width** changes the left and right boundaries in which content is flowed. **When an absolute element is sized,** it does *not* change the flow and it does *not* change the position of other elements. Percentages in width and height refer to its closest positioned ancestor's width and height. **When sizing a replaced element,** such as an image, the browser scales it to the specified size. To use the intrinsic size, set **height** and **width** to **auto**.
Related to	Width, Height, Shrinkwrapped, Stretched; Static, Absolute, Float (Chapter 7)

Shrinkwrapped

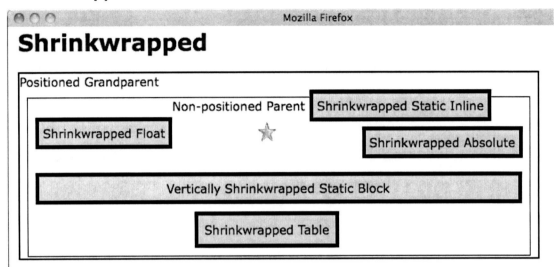

HTML

```
<h1>Shrinkwrapped</h1>

<div class="gp">Positioned Grandparent
  <div class="parent">Non-positioned Parent
    <span id="float" class="z">Shrinkwrapped Float</span>
    <span id="inline" class="z">Shrinkwrapped Static Inline</span><br />
    <img id="star" src="star.gif" alt="star" />
    <div id="block" class="z">Vertically Shrinkwrapped Static Block</div>
    <table id="table" class="z"><tr><td>Shrinkwrapped Table</td></tr></table>
    <span id="abs" class="z">Shrinkwrapped Absolute</span>
  </div>
 </div>
```

CSS

```
#float  { width:auto;  height:auto; float:left; }
#inline { width:auto;  height:auto; }
#star   { width:auto;  height:auto; }
#block  { width:auto;  height:auto; }
#table  { width:auto;  height:auto; }
#abs    { width:auto;  height:auto; left:auto; bottom:auto; position:absolute; }

/*  Nonessential rules are not shown. */
```

Shrinkwrapped

Problem	You want to shrinkwrap the width and/or height of an element to fit the width or height of its content.
Solution	Apply styles to your chosen class or ID as follows: Use **height:auto** to shrink the height to the height of all its lines. Use **width:auto** to shrink the width to the width of its widest line. **width** and **height** are independent. For example, you can shrinkwrap one and size theother.

Patterns	**Shrinkwrapped Float**
	`SELECTOR { width:auto; height:auto;  float:LEFT_RIGHT; }`
	
	Shrinkwrapped Static Inline Element
	`INLINE-SELECTOR { width:auto; height:auto; }`
	
	Shrinkwrapped Static Inline-block Element
	`INLINE-BLOCK-SELECTOR { width:auto; height:auto; }`
	
	Vertically Shrinkwrapped Static Block Element
	`BLOCK-SELECTOR { height:auto;  }`
	
	Shrinkwrapped Table Element
	`TABLE-SELECTOR { width:auto; height:auto; }`
	
	Horizontally Shrinkwrapped Absolute Element
	`SELECTOR { position:absolute; width:auto;`
	`  left:0; right:auto;  }`
	or
	`SELECTOR { position:absolute; width:auto;`
	`  left:auto; right:0; }`
	
	Vertically Shrinkwrapped Absolute Element
	`SELECTOR { position:absolute; height:auto;`
	`  top:0; bottom:auto; }`
	or
	`SELECTOR { position:absolute; height:auto;`
	`  top:auto; bottom:0; }`

Location	This pattern applies to all elements.
Limitations	You cannot horizontally shrinkwrap a static block.
Explanation	Shrinkwrapped elements require **width** and **height** to be set to **auto** so that the browser can automatically size the box based on the width and height of its content. Absolute elements also require **left** or **right**, and **top** or **bottom** to be set to **auto** to prevent them from being stretched.
Tip	Because a shrinkwrapped table is sized based on its content, its behavior is the same as any other shrinkwrapped element. Contrast this to a sized table where the height and width are assigned to the outside of the table's border, causing it to be sized differently from other elements. Another way to constrain the size of a block is using the **max-height** or **max-width** CSS properties.

Shrinkwrapped cont.

Tip cont.	These properties allow authors to constrain content widths and heights to a certain range, which can either be a specific number of pixels, or a percentage of the corresponding dimension of the containing block. Browser support for **max-height** and **max-width** varies—for example, they are not supported in IE6 but are in IE7 and above.
Related to	Width, Height, Sized, Stretched; Static, Absolute, Float (Chapter 7)

Stretched

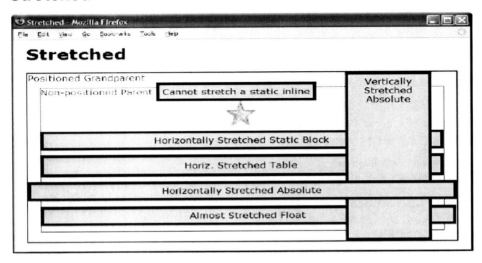

HTML

```
<h1>Stretched</h1>
  <div class="gp">Positioned Grandparent
   <div class="parent">Non-positioned Parent
     <span  id="inline" class="s">Cannot stretch a static inline</span>
     <div   id="sized"><img id="star" src="star.gif" alt="star" /></div>
     <div   id="block" class="s">Horizontally Stretched Static Block</div>
     <table id="table" class="s"><tr><td>Horiz. Stretched Table</td></tr></table>
     <div   id="abs-v" class="s">Vertically Stretched Absolute</div>
     <span  id="abs-h" class="s">Horizontally Stretched Absolute</span>
     <span  id="float" class="s">Almost Stretched Float</span>
   </div>
  </div>
```

CSS

```
#star { width:100%; height:100%; }
#block { width:auto; }
#table { width:100%; }
#abs-v { height:auto; top:0; bottom:0; position:absolute; }
#abs-h { width:auto; left:0; right:0; position:absolute; }
#float { width:100%; float:left; }

/* Nonessential rules are not shown. */
```

Stretched

Problem	You want to stretch the width or height of an element to fill the width or height of its container. In other words, you want to stretch the outer box of an element to the sides of its container.
Solution	You can stretch a box by applying **width:auto**, **width:100%**, **height:auto**, or **height:100%** to different types of boxes.

When using **width:auto** or **height:auto**, a browser calculates the width and height of stretched elements from the *outside in*. A browser starts with the inner box of the parent, and subtracts the stretched element's margins, borders, and padding to calculate its inner box. Contrast this with sized and shrinkwrapped elements, which are sized from the *inside out*.

Use **width:auto** to stretch the width of a block to the sides of its parent.

Use **width:auto**, **left:0**, and **right:0** to stretch an absolute element to the left and right sides of its closest positioned ancestor.

Use **height:auto**, **top:0**, and **bottom:0** to stretch an absolute element to the top and bottom of its closest positioned ancestor.

Use **width:100%** to stretch a table, a float, or an inline block. This works as long as the box does not have horizontal *margins*. Otherwise, it overflows its parent, and the stretch effect is lost. Stretched floats and inline blocks also overflow their parent when they have horizontal *borders* or *padding*.

Use **height:100%** to stretch the height of inline blocks, blocks, tables, and floats to the height of their containers. If the stretched element is *not* the first and only child in its container, this technique will overflow the container.

Patterns	**Stretched Inline-block Element**

```
INLINE-BLOCK-SELECTOR { width:100%; height:100%; }
```

Stretched Static Block Element

```
BLOCK-SELECTOR { width:auto; height:100%; }
```

Stretched Table

```
TABLE-SELECTOR { width:100%; height:100%; }
```

Vertically Stretched Absolute Element

```
SELECTOR { height:auto; top:0; bottom:0; position:absolute; }
```

Horizontally Stretched Absolute Element

```
SELECTOR { width:auto; left:0; right:0; position:absolute; }
```

Stretched Float

```
SELECTOR { width:100%; height:100%; float:LEFT_RIGHT; }
```

Stretched cont.

Location	This pattern works on all elements except for inline elements.
Limitations	Internet Explorer 6 cannot stretch absolute elements, but version 7 can. An absolutely positioned *table* is stretched using `width:100%` and `height:100%`.
Example	The star image is the only child inside a 50-pixel centered division, and is stretched to all four sides of its parent. Notice how the float is not stretched perfectly because its padding and border cause it to overflow its parent.
Tip	Another way to stretch the width or height of an element is using the `min-height` or `min-width` CSS properties. These properties allow authors to constrain content widths and heights to a certain range, which can either be a specific number of pixels, or a percentage of the corresponding dimension of the containing block. Browser support for `min-height` and `min-width` varies—for example, they are not supported in IE6 and buggy in IE7, but fixed in IE8 and above.
Related to	Width, Height, Sized, Shrinkwrapped; Static, Absolute, Float (Chapter 7)

Box Model Properties

This chapter shows how box model properties style the various types of boxes. These are basic design patterns.

The Margin, Border, and Padding design patterns contain examples contrasting how each property works in each type of box. Their main purpose is to contrast in one place how the same property means different things in different contexts. When using this book as a reference, you may also want to refer to the Margin, Border, and Padding design patterns to determine which type of element, box, and property will do what you want.

Chapter Outline

- **Margin** contrasts how margins work differently for different types of boxes. It shows how margins change the position of an element in relation to its container and siblings.

- **Border** contrasts how borders work differently for different types of boxes. It shows how borders change the position of an element in ways similar to margins, and in some ways different from margins.

- **Padding** contrasts how padding works differently for different types of boxes. It shows how padding works almost identically to borders and margins.

- **Background** shows how to assign a color to the background of an element. It also shows how to use a tiled image for the background. You can tile the image across and down, across only, or down only, or show the image only once. You can position the image at a specific location in the background. You can also direct whether the image scrolls with the content or remains in a fixed location.

- **Overflow** shows how to hide overflowing content, display it, or display scrollbars.

- **Visibility** shows how to hide an element while leaving a placeholder for it in the flow.

- **Page Break** shows how to insert a page break into your document before an element or after an element. It also shows how to print blank pages.

Margin

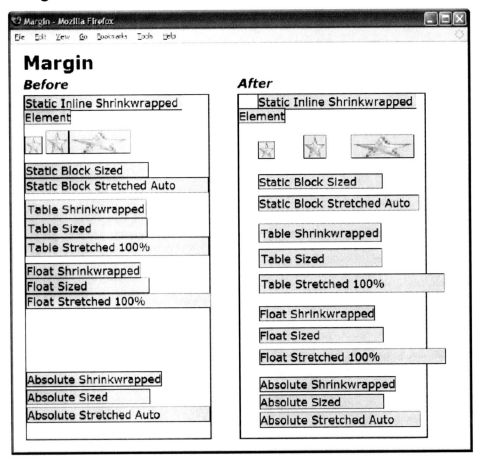

CSS

```
*.before { margin:0; }

*.after { margin-top:10px; margin-bottom:0;
  margin-left:30px; margin-right:10px; }

/* Nonessential rules are not shown.
   HTML code is omitted to allow the example to fit on one page. */
```

Margin

Problem	You want to put a margin on one or more of the sides of an element. You want the margin to be transparent to the background of the element's parent.
Solution	You can use a selector to assign the **margin** property to an element. You can independently set **margin-left**, **margin-right**, **margin-top**, and **margin-bottom**. **Margin** can be positive or negative. Negative values may overlap elements. **margin** works differently depending on the type of element.
margin:±VALUE	You can assign a measurement or percentage to **margin**. A percentage refers to a percentage of the containing block's width. **margin:0** is the default CSS value, but browsers assign different default margins to specific elements.

On an inline element, **margin-top** and **margin-bottom** are ignored.

On an inline or inline-block element, a positive value in **margin-left** moves the element away from the previous element, and a negative value moves it closer. A positive value in **margin-right** moves the next element further away, and a negative value moves it closer.

On an inline-block element, such as an image, a positive value in **margin-top** expands the height of the line, and a negative value shrinks it. A positive value in **margin-bottom** raises the element, and a negative value lowers it.

On a sized block element, a positive or negative value in **margin-left** and **margin-right** offsets it from its point of alignment. A positive value in **margin-top** and **margin-bottom** pushes neighboring blocks further apart, and a negative value brings them closer together. A browser collapses top and bottom margins of neighboring block elements.

On a stretched block or stretched absolute element, a positive margin indents the sides of the element, and a negative value outdents them. Indents shrink an element's inner box, pushing borders and padding inward.

On a table or a sized or shrinkwrapped absolute element, a positive or negative **margin** value offsets it from its point of alignment. Margins on a stretched table don't indent the table but cause it to overflow its container.

On a float, a positive margin pushes the float away from its point of alignment and pushes other floats and inline content away from it. A negative margin pulls the float to the other side of its point of alignment and pulls other floats and inline content closer. Margins on a stretched float don't indent the float but cause it to overflow its container. |
| **margin:auto** | On most elements, **margin:auto** is the same as **margin:0** (that is, no margin).

On a static block element and a stretched absolute element, **auto** automatically expands the margin. For example, **margin-left:auto** and **margin-right:0** align a sized element to the right. |
Pattern	`SELECTOR { margin:±VALUE; }`
Location	**margin** works on most elements. It doesn't work on internal table elements, such as table cells. Vertical margins don't work on inline elements.
Related to	Border, Padding; all patterns in Chapters 4, 7, 8, and 9; Spacing, Inline Spacer, Linebreak, Inline Horizontal Rule (Chapter 11); Text Indent, Hanging Indent (Chapter 12); Lists, Background Bulleted, Collapsed Margins, Horizontal Rule, Block Spacer, Block Spacer Remover, Left Marginal, Right Marginal (Chapter 13); Outside-in Box, Float Divider (Chapter 17)

Border

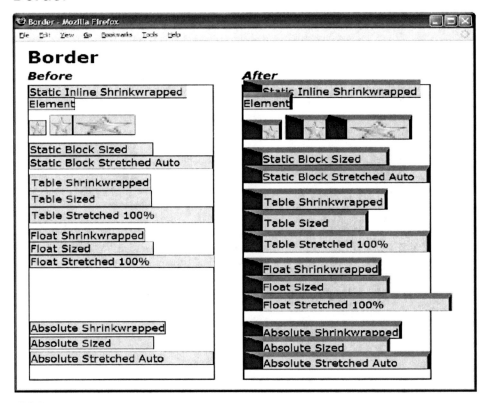

CSS

```
*.before { border:1px solid black; }

*.after { border-top:10px solid dimgray;   border-bottom:1px solid black;
   border-left:30px solid black;    border-right:5px solid black; }

/* Nonessential rules are not shown.
    HTML code is omitted to allow the example to fit on one page. */
```

Border

Problem	You want to put a border on one or more of the sides of an element.
Solution	You can use a selector to assign the **border** property to an element. You can independently set **border-left**, **border-right**, **border-top**, and **border-bottom**. **border** affects an element differently depending on the type of element and its alignment. You can set the style and color of the border. **border:none** is the default.

Borders work almost identically to margins. Borders work like margins in the way they change the position of an element and the position of its neighbors.

The descriptions in the Margin design pattern apply to borders except as follows:

Borders are visible instead of transparent, but you can set the color of a border to transparent if you want. (Note that Internet Explorer 6 doesn't support **transparent** as a color, but all current browsers do.)

Borders can't be negative because they're inside the margin.

Borders between static block elements don't collapse like margins.

Left and right borders around inline text elements are only visible at the start of the element and at the end of the element. Right and left borders aren't drawn where a browser wraps an inline element across lines.

Top and bottom borders on inline elements overlap neighboring lines unless you increase the line height to make room for them. In other words, vertical inline borders don't automatically increase the height of the line. Notice in the example how the border above the text *Static Inline Shrinkwrapped* overlaps the top of its container, and how the word *Element* overlaps the previous line.

Because a table's **width** and **height** refer to the outside of its borders (rather than to the inside of its padding), borders are drawn *inside* the box specified by **width** and **height**. This means borders don't add to the size of shrinkwrapped or sized tables. This also means borders on a stretched table don't cause it to overflow its container; instead, they indent the table like a stretched block or a stretched absolute element. Notice in the example how the width of the sized table's outer box doesn't change when borders are enlarged; instead, the inner box shrinks. Also notice how borders indent the stretched table instead of causing it to overflow its container as it did in the Margin design pattern and as the stretched float does in this example.

Border cont.

Solution cont.

The border can have either a predefined style (solid line, double line, dotted line, pseudo-3D border, and so on) or an image for background. The **border-style** property can have a value of **none**, **hidden**, **dotted**, **dashed**, **solid**, **double**, **groove**, **ridge**, **inset**, or **outset**.

With CSS3, borders can now have rounded corners with the use of the **border-radius** property: for example, **border-top-left-radius: 2em 0.5em**. The two length or percentage values of these properties define the radii of a quarter ellipse that defines the shape of the corner of the outer border edge. The first value is the horizontal radius, and the second is the vertical radius. If the second value is omitted, it's copied from the first. Browser support for these properties varies, and some vendors may support their own prefixes like **-moz-border-radius** or **-webkit-border-radius**.

```
border-top-left-radius: 55pt 25pt
```

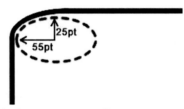

The **box-shadow** property attaches one or more drop-shadows to a box. The property is a comma-separated list of shadows, each specified by two to four length values, an optional color, and an optional **inset** keyword: for example, **box-shadow: rgba(0,0,0,0.4) 10px 10px inset**. The Safari browser requires **-webkit** for **box-shadow**: for example, **-webkit-box-shadow: rgba(0,0,0,0.4) 10px 10px inset**.

The CSS3 spec defines a way to add images to borders and specify their style with properties like **border-image-source**, **border-image-slice**, **border-image-width**, **border-image-outset**, and **border-image-repeat**, but these aren't yet widely supported by major browsers.

Border cont.

Pattern	```SELECTOR { border: WIDTH STYLE COLOR;```
	``` border: none;```
	``` border-left: WIDTH STYLE COLOR;```
	``` border-right: WIDTH STYLE COLOR;```
	``` border-top: WIDTH STYLE COLOR;```
	``` border-bottom: WIDTH STYLE COLOR; }```

Location	This design pattern applies to all elements.
Related to	Margin, Padding; all Box Model patterns in Chapter 4; Absolute (Chapter 7); Text Decoration (Chapter 10); Inline Decoration, Inline Horizontal Rule (Chapter 11); Horizontal Rule (Chapter 13); Table, Separated Borders, Collapsed Borders, Styled Collapsed Borders, Hidden and Removed Cells (Chapter 15); Outside-in Box, Float Divider, Tab Menu (Chapter 17)

Padding

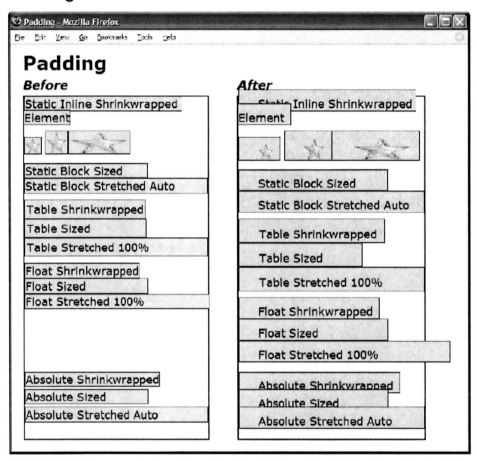

CSS

```
*.before { padding:0; }

*.after { padding-top:10px;   padding-bottom:0;
  padding-left:30px; padding-right:10px; }

/* Nonessential rules are not shown.
   HTML code is omitted to allow the example to fit on one page. */
```

Padding

Problem	You want to use padding on one or more of the sides of an element.
Solution	Use a selector to assign the **padding** property to an element. You can independently set **padding-left**, **padding-right**, **padding-top**, and **padding-bottom**. **padding** affects the position of an element differently depending on the type of element and its alignment. The element's background is displayed in the padding area. **padding:0** is the default.
	Padding works almost identically to borders:
	Padding works like margins and borders in the way it changes the position of an element and the position of its neighbors.
	Like borders, top and bottom padding on inline elements overlap neighboring lines unless you increase the line height to make room for them.
	Like borders, padding doesn't add to the size of *shrinkwrapped* or *sized* tables, and applying padding to the cells of a *stretched* table doesn't cause the table to overflow its container.
	The remaining descriptions in the Border and Margin design patterns apply to Padding except as follows:
	Borders are transparent to the element's background. Contrast this with margins, which are transparent to the parent's background, and borders, which are styled.
	Padding can't be negative because it's inside the border.
	Padding doesn't apply to tables, but it does apply to table cells. The example applies padding to the cells in the table rather than to the table.
	Padding defaults to **0**, which is no padding.
| **Pattern** | ```
-SELECTOR { padding: +WIDTH;
           padding: 0;
           padding: +VERTICAL +HORIZONTAL;
           padding: +TOP +RIGHT +BOTTOM +LEFT;
           padding-left: +WIDTH;
           padding-right: +WIDTH;
           padding-top: +WIDTH;
           padding-bottom: +WIDTH; }
``` |
Location	This design pattern applies to all elements.
Tips	Margins and borders share the same shortcut notation. You can set all four margins and borders using one width; you can set the vertical and horizontal using two widths; or you can set the four individual sides using four widths. The four sides start with the top and move clockwise around the box to the right, bottom, and left.
Related to	Margin, Border; all Box Model patterns in Chapter 4; Highlight, Text Decoration (Chapter 10); Spacing, Padded Content, Inline Decoration (Chapter 11); Hanging Indent (Chapter 12); Lists, Background Bulleted (Chapter 13); Basic Shadowed Image (Chapter 14); Outside-in Box (Chapter 17)
```

Background

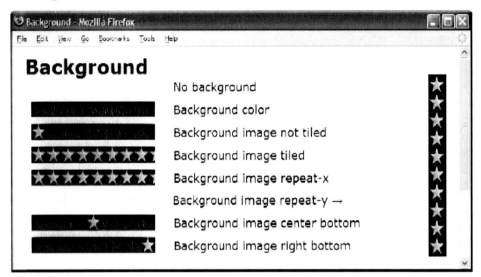

HTML

```
<h1>Background</h1>
<p><span class="no-bg"> </span>No background</p>
<p><span class="bg-color"> </span>Background color</p>
<p><span class="bg-image"> </span>Background image not tiled</p>
<p><span class="bg-repeat"> </span>Background image tiled</p>
<p><span class="bg-rx"> </span>Background image repeat-x</p>
<p><span class="bg-ry"> </span>Background image repeat-y &rarr;</p>
<p><span class="bg-pos-lt"> </span>Background image center bottom</p>
<p><span class="bg-pos-rb"> </span>Background image right bottom</p>
```

CSS

```
p { margin-left:240px; margin-top:0px; margin-bottom:10px; }
span { margin-left:-230px; margin-right:30px; padding-left:195px; font-size:19px;
  background-position:left bottom; background-repeat:no-repeat;
  background-color:black; background-image:url("star.gif"); }

*.no-bg { background-image:none;  background-color:transparent; }
*.bg-color { background-image:none;  background-color:black; }
*.bg-image { background-repeat:no-repeat; }
*.bg-repeat { background-repeat:repeat; }
*.bg-rx { background-repeat:repeat-x; }
*.bg-pos-lt { background-position:center bottom; }
*.bg-pos-rb { background-position:right bottom; }
*.bg-ry { background-repeat:repeat-y; background-position:center top;
  padding-left:22px; float:right; height:263px; margin:0px;
  position:relative; top:-170px; }
```

Background

Problem	You want to put a background color or image behind an element.
Solution	Apply styles as follows:
	Use **background-color** to set the background color of an element.
	Use **background-color:transparent** for a transparent background color.
	Use **background-image:none** to show no background image.
	Use **background-image:url("file.jpg")** to display an image behind the contents of an element. The image fills the padding area of the element.
	Use **background-repeat:repeat** to tile a background image across and down to fill the entire padding area. This is the default value.
	Use **background-repeat:repeat-x** to tile the image across one row.
	Use **background-repeat:repeat-y** to tile the image down one column.
	Use **background-repeat:no-repeat** to not tile the image.
	Use **background-position** to set the horizontal and vertical starting location of the image. This applies whether or not the image is tiled.
	Use **background-attachment:scroll** to scroll a background image when the user scrolls the content. This is the default value.
	Use **background-attachment:fixed** to prevent the image from scrolling.
	The **background** property is a composite of all these properties. The property values can be presented in any order. Each property value is separated by a space. **background:none transparent repeat left top scroll;** is the default.

Pattern	```SELECTOR { background-color: COLOR;```
	 ``` background-image: url("file.jpg");```
	 ``` background-repeat: CONSTANT;```
	 ``` background-position: HORIZONTAL VERTICAL;```
	 ``` background-attachment: SCROLL_FIXED; }```

Location	This design pattern applies to all elements.
Tips	**background-position** requires two values: the first for the horizontal position and the second for vertical. Percentages position an image at a percentage of an element's width and height. Pixels position it at an offset. Ems position it proportional to the element's **font-size**. Whenever you assign a **background-image** to an element, you should also assign a **background-color** and a contrasting **color**. This provides a fallback in case the image doesn't load, and it ensures that text doesn't become invisible or hard to see, such as white text on a white background.
	You can scale a background image with the use of the **background-size** property: for example, **background-size:80px 60px**. The first value gives the width of the corresponding image, and the second value gives its height. If only one value is given, the second is assumed to be **auto**. The **background-size** property is supported in Internet Explorer 9+, Firefox, Opera, Chrome, and Safari.
Example	All the spans in the example are assigned to display a transparent GIF of a star on a black background, starting at lower left in each span. Specific spans override these settings to demonstrate various background settings.
Related to	Box Model (Chapter 4); Stacking Context, Atomic (Chapter 7); Font, Highlight, Text Decoration, Text Replacement, Invisible Text (Chapter 10); Inline Decoration, Inline Horizontal Rule (Chapter 11); Background Bulleted, Horizontal Rule (Chapter 13); Fade-out, Semi-transparent, Replaced Text, Content-over Background Image, CSS Sprite, Shadowed Image, Rounded Corners (Chapter 14); Striped Tables, Table Selectors (Chapter 15); Undersized Columns (Chapter 16); Padded Graphic Dropcap, Floating Graphic Dropcap, Marginal Graphic Dropcap (Chapter 18); Block Quote, Inline Block Quote (Chapter 19); Graphical Alert (Chapter 20)

Overflow

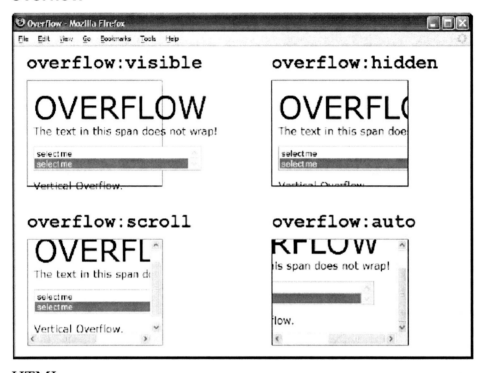

HTML

```
<div id="ex1">
  <h1><code>overflow:visible</code></h1>
  <p class="ex1" >
    <span class="big">OVERFLOW</span> <br />
    <span class="nowrap">The text in this span does not wrap!</span>
    <select size="2">
      <option>select me</option>
      <option selected="selected">select me</option>
    </select><br />
    <span>Vertical Overflow.</span>
  </p>
</div>
```

CSS

```
*.ex1 { overflow:visible; }
*.ex2 { overflow:hidden; }
*.ex3 { overflow:scroll; }
*.ex4 { overflow:auto; }

/*  Nonessential rules are not shown.  */
```

Overflow

Problem	You want to control how a block handles the situation when its content overflows its bounds horizontally and vertically.
Solution	CSS provides the **overflow** property to control how overflowing content is handled. You can set **overflow** to one of four constant values: **visible**, **hidden**, **scroll**, or **auto**. The default value is **visible**. **visible** allows overflowing content to be rendered outside the containing block. **hidden** hides the overflowing content and does *not* provide scrollbars. This prevents a user from scrolling overflowed content into view. **scroll** clips the overflowing content and provides scrollbars so the user can scroll the overflowed content into view. **auto** works like **scroll** except that it shows scrollbars only as needed.

Pattern	`SIZED_BLOCK_SELECTOR { overflow:visible; }`
	or
	`SIZED_BLOCK_SELECTOR { overflow:hidden; }`
	or
	`SIZED_BLOCK_SELECTOR { overflow:scroll; }`
	or
	`SIZED_BLOCK_SELECTOR { overflow:auto; }`

Location	This design pattern applies to sized block elements that have **width** and/or **height** set to a measurement or percentage.
Exceptions	Internet Explorer 6 implements **overflow:visible** incorrectly. Instead of allowing content to overflow the block, it expands the width and/or height of the block to accommodate the content. Internet Explorer 7 fixes this flaw.
Tips	It's usually best to avoid using **overflow:hidden**, **overflow:scroll**, or **overflow:auto** because users get frustrated when you truncate content or require them to scroll. This property is needed only when you size a block smaller than its content. If you use shrinkwrapped and stretched blocks, you don't need to use this property, and your layouts will dynamically expand as needed to display their content. CSS 3 defines two properties, **overflow-x** and **overflow-y**, that can be used in place of **overflow**. They separately direct how horizontal and vertical overflow should be handled. All major browsers support them. For example, you can always display one scrollbar and let the other scrollbar appear as needed using **overflow-x:scroll** and **overflow-y:auto**. You can also hide overflow in one dimension and scroll overflow in the other using **overflow-x:hidden** and **overflow-y:scroll**.
Example	To fit the example on one page, some code is omitted. The example shows enough HTML to create one of the overflow divisions, and it contains the four CSS overflow rules.
Related to	Box Model, Inline Box, Table Box (Chapter 4); Width, Height, Stretched (Chapter 5); Atomic (Chapter 6); Screenreader Only (Chapter 10); Nowrap (Chapter 11); Replaced Text (Chapter 14); Sized Columns, Undersized Columns (Chapter 16); Tabs (Chapter 17)

Visibility

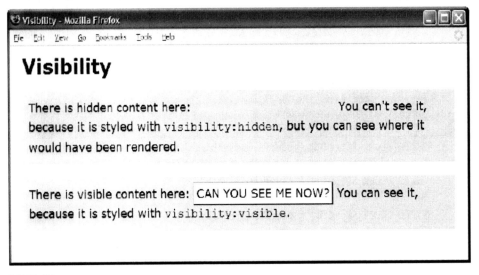

HTML

```
<h1>Visibility</h1>

<p>There is hidden content here: <span class="hidden">CAN YOU SEE ME NOW?</span>
   You can't see it, because it's styled with <code>visibility:hidden</code>,
   but you can see where it would have been rendered. </p>

<p>There is visible content here: <span class="visible">CAN YOU SEE ME NOW?</span> You can see
it, because it's styled with <code>visibility:visible</code>. </p>
```

CSS

```
span { padding:4px; background-color:white;
  border-left:1px solid gray; border-right:2px solid black;
  border-top:1px solid gray; border-bottom:2px solid black; }
p { background-color:gold; padding:10px; line-height:1.5em; }

*.hidden { visibility:hidden; }
*.visible { visibility:visible; }

span:hover { visibility:hidden; }
```

Visibility

Problem	You want to hide an element and leave a blank spot where the element would have been rendered.
Solution	CSS provides the **visibility** property for hiding an element without affecting the position of other elements in the inline flow, block flow, or float flow. Contrast this with **display:none**, which doesn't render an element by completely removing it from all flows—as if it never existed. Because absolute elements are already removed from all flows, there is no functional difference in applying **visibility:hidden** and **display:none** to absolute elements. Apply styles to your chosen class or ID as follows: Use **visibility:hidden** to hide an element without removing it. Use **visibility:visible** to show an element. This is the default.

Pattern	**CSS**
	
	`SELECTOR { visibility:hidden; }`
	`SELECTOR { visibility:visible; }`

Location	This design pattern applies to all elements. **visibility** is inherited by all elements.
Tips	The main advantage of **visibility:hidden** is that you can hide content using JavaScript without forcing the browser to reflow the entire page. This could be useful when you want to hide selected content while the user drags and drops it to a new location. Note that **hover** is not supported by mobile devices and can be an issue when you're doing web development for iOS or Android devices. A document-management system can mark text for removal and let the user toggle the display of such text between **visibility:visible**, **visibility:hidden**, **display:none**, and **text-decoration:line-through**. This toggles through showing the text, hiding it, removing it, and running a line through it. You can create an unpleasant flickering effect when a user mouses over an element by selecting an element using the **hover** pseudo class and styling it with **visibility:hidden** as shown in the example. **display:none** is more commonly used than **visibility:hidden** because it not only hides an element—it completely removes it from the flow.
Related to	Page Break; Box Model, Display (Chapter 4); Row and Column Groups, Hidden and Removed Cells, Removed and Hidden Rows and Columns (Chapter 15); Popup Alert (Chapter 20)

Page Break

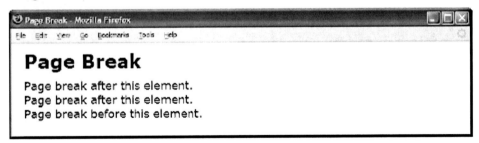

HTML

```
<div class="page-break-after">Page break after this element. </div>
<div class="page-break-after">Page break after this element. </div>
<div class="page-break-before">Page break before this element.</div>
```

CSS

```
*.page-break-before { page-break-before:always; }
*.page-break-after { page-break-after:always; }
```

Print Preview

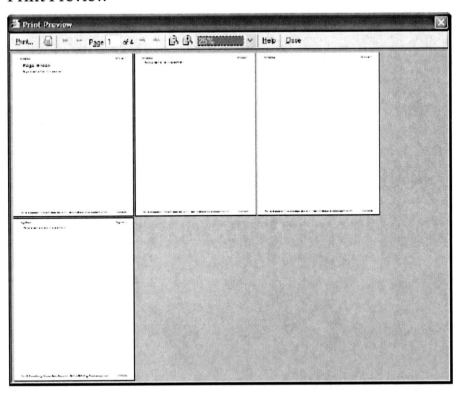

Page Break

Problem	You want to insert a page break in the document for printing purposes.
Solution	CSS provides two properties for inserting page breaks: **page-break-before** and **page-break-after**. You can insert a page break before an element by using **page-break-before:always**. You can insert a page break after an element by using **page-break-after:always**. The default values are **page-break-before:auto** and **page-break-after:auto**. These default values direct the browser to use its default algorithm to automatically determine the location of page breaks. You can override a previously set page break using **page-break-before:auto** and **page-break-after:auto**.
Pattern	-SELECTOR { page-break-before:always; } *or* SELECTOR { page-break-after:always; } *or* SELECTOR { page-break-before:auto; } *or* SELECTOR { page-break-after:auto; }
Location	This design pattern applies to all elements.
Limitations	Internet Explorer 6 and Opera 9 always insert a page break whenever they encounter an element set to **page-break-before:always** or **page-break-after:always**. This inserts an extra blank page whenever one element is set to **page-break-after:always** and the next element is set to **page-break-before:always**. The example demonstrates this "feature": it shows a screenshot of print preview in Internet Explorer 6 containing four printed pages. The third printed page is blank. Firefox 2 doesn't insert this extra blank page. An easy way to avoid inserting blank pages is not to use both **page-break-after** and **page-break-before** in the same document.
Tips	If you want to print a blank page, insert an element into the document and style it with **page-break-before** and **visibility:hidden**. CSS provides other values for these properties and other page-break properties, but only **page-break-before:always** and **page-break-after:always** work reliably in the major browsers.

CHAPTER 7

Positioning Models

This is the first of three chapters on positioning. This chapter presents the CSS positioning models. Chapter 8 shows how to indent, offset, and align elements. Chapter 9 combines these techniques to create advanced positioning design patterns.

Chapter Outline

- **Positioning Models** introduces and demonstrates the six positioning models.

- **Positioned** explains, demonstrates, and contrasts the four values of the **position** property: **static**, **absolute**, **fixed**, and **relative**.

- **Closest Positioned Ancestor** shows how absolute boxes can be positioned relative to any ancestor element rather than just the element's parent.

- **Stacking Context** shows how positioned boxes can be stacked behind or in front of static elements and each other.

- **Atomic** explains how to render inline content *in* a block rather than *on* a block.

- **Static** explains the basics of normal flow.

- **Absolute** shows how to remove any element from the normal flow and position it absolutely with respect to the *inside of the border* of its *closest positioned ancestor*.

- **Fixed** shows how to remove any element from the normal flow and position it absolutely with respect to the *viewport*.

- **Relative** shows how to use relative positioning to control stacking order, or offset an element without affecting its shape or the position of other elements.

- **Float and Clear** shows how you can remove an element from the normal flow and float it to the left or right side of its parent. It also shows how to clear elements so that they're positioned below floats on the left, right, or both sides.

- **Relative Float** shows how you can relatively position a float.

Positioning Models

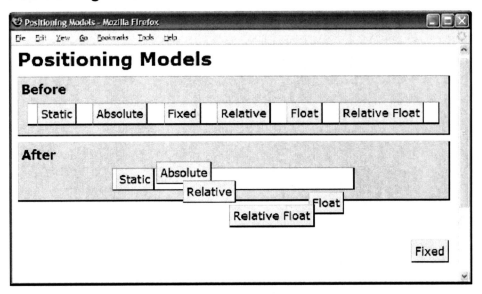

HTML

```
<h1>Positioning Models</h1>
<div class="section"><h2>Before</h2>
  <p><span>Static</span><span>Absolute</span>
    <span>Fixed</span><span>Relative</span>
    <span>Float</span><span>Relative Float</span></p></div>

 <div class="section"><h2>After</h2>
  <p class="static centered" >
    <span class="static centered">Static</span>
    <span class="absolute">Absolute</span>
    <span class="fixed">Fixed</span>
    <span class="relative">Relative</span>
    <span class="float">Float</span>
    <span class="relative float">Relative Float</span></p></div>
```

CSS

```
*.centered { width:380px; margin-left:auto; margin-right:auto; }
*.static { position:static; }
*.absolute { position:absolute; top:20px; left:215px; }
*.fixed { position:fixed; bottom:20px; right:5px; }
*.relative { position:relative; top:20px; left:30px; }
*.float { float:right; }
```

Positioning Models

Introduction

This isn't a design pattern, but an introduction to positioning.

CSS provides six positioning models for positioning an element: static, absolute, fixed, relative, float, and relative float. The six positioning models are related to the six box models, but they aren't the same. The **static positioning model** can position inline, inline-block, block, and table boxes. The **absolute and fixed positioning models** can position absolute boxes, which can be any type of element. The **float positioning model** can position float boxes, which can be any type of element. The **relative positioning model** can relatively position any type of box except for absolute boxes. The **relative-float positioning model** can relatively position float boxes.

Each positioning model controls positioning using the same basic properties of `display`, `width`, `height`, and `margin`. Even though these properties are the same, their values have different functions in each model. For example, `width:auto` stretches a static block, whereas `width:auto` shrinkwraps an absolute element. You can see this in the example where the first paragraph is stretched and the absolute span is shrinkwrapped.

Positioning models also use additional properties in ways that are unique to the model. Absolute and fixed positioning use `left`, `right`, `top`, `bottom`, and `z-index` to control the alignment of the absolute box. Relative positioning uses `left`, `top`, and `z-index` to control the offset of the box. Float positioning uses `float` and `clear`.

Because these models use the same basic properties, different positioning layouts are triggered using unique combinations of element type, display box, and property *values*. Each design pattern exposes the exact combination of rules and elements that triggers each type of layout. For example, setting `width` to a value, `margin-left` to `auto`, and `margin-right` to `auto` centers a static block, but it doesn't center a static inline. For example, to center an absolute element, you must also set `left` and `right` to `0`.

There are over 50 combinations of design patterns that produce unique layouts. These patterns are presented in these three chapters on positioning (Chapters 7 through 9). These patterns are easy to learn because they're combinations of box models, extents, margins, and positioning. In other words, the six box models (inline, inline-block, block, table, absolute, and float) can be combined with the three extents (sized, shrinkwrapped, and stretched) and the three types of margins (indented, offset, and aligned). In addition, any type of box except absolute can be relatively positioned.

Box models, extents, and margins are discussed in Chapters 4 through 6. The positioning models are discussed in this chapter. Indents, offsets, and alignment are discussed in Chapter 8. Chapter 9 systematically combines the design patterns in these chapters to create over 50 unique layouts.

Related to

Positioned, Static, Absolute, Fixed, Relative, Float and Clear, Relative Float

Positioned

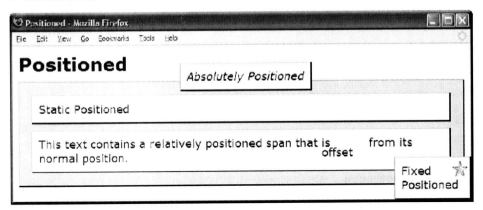

HTML

```
<h1>Positioned</h1>
<div class="relative" id="canvas">
 <p class="static">Static Positioned</p>
 <p class="static">This text contains a relatively positioned span that is
   <span class="relative offset">offset</span> from its normal position.</p>
 <em  class="absolute">Absolutely Positioned</em>
 <img class="fixed1" src="star.gif" alt="star" />
 <p   class="fixed2">Fixed Positioned</p>
</div>
```

CSS

```
div,p,em { margin:10px; padding:10px; background-color:white;
  border-left:1px solid gray; border-right:2px solid black;
  border-top:1px solid gray; border-bottom:2px solid black; }

*.static { position:static; }
*.relative { position:relative; left:auto; top:auto; bottom:auto; right:auto; }
*.absolute { position:absolute; left:35%; top:-40px; }
*.fixed1 { position:fixed; z-index:20; right:5px; bottom:35px; }
*.fixed2 { position:fixed; z-index:10; right:0px; bottom:0;
  width:100px; margin:0;}

*.offset  { bottom:-15px; left:-20px; }

#canvas { background-color:gold; }

/*  Nonessential rules are not shown. */
```

Positioned

Problem	You want to turn an element into a positioned element so that its descendants can be positioned relative to it. You may also want to offset the element from its current location, its nearest positioned ancestor, or the viewport; move the element into its own layer; remove the element from the flow; or change the stacking order of the element to control when it overlaps other elements or is overlapped.
Solution	You can use **position:static** to *unposition an element* so that it's rendered normally in the flow. **static** is the default value for **position**. You can use **position:relative** to position an element at an offset from its location in the normal flow. You can use **position:absolute** to position an element at an offset from its location in the normal flow or from its nearest positioned ancestor. You can use **position:fixed** to position an element at an offset from the viewport.
	You can use **left** to offset the left side of an element from the left side of its reference position. Positive values offset to the right and negative to the left. You can use **right** to offset the right side of an element from the right side of its reference position. Positive values offset to the left and negative to the right. You can use **top** to offset the top of an element from the top of its reference position. Positive values offset down and negative offset up. You can use **bottom** to offset the bottom of an element from the bottom of its reference position. Positive values offset up and negative offset down. You can use **z-index** to position an element in a specific layer of the stacking order. Larger numbers bring the item closer to the front. You can use **marg**in to offset elements from their position.

Pattern	SELECTOR { position:ABSOLUTE_FIXED_RELATIVE;
	  z-index:+VALUE;
	  left:±VALUE; right:±VALUE;
	  margin-left:±VALUE; margin-right:±VALUE;
	  top:±VALUE; bottom:±VALUE;
	  margin-top:±VALUE; margin-bottom:±VALUE; }

Location	This design pattern applies to all elements.
Limitations	*Fixed* position doesn't work in Internet Explorer 6, but it works fine in all newer versions.
Example	I assigned **position:relative** to the division to make it *positioned*.
	An element is positioned when it has been assigned to **position:relative**, **position:absolute**, or **position:fixed**. Floats can be positioned using **position:relative**. Being positioned makes an element the *reference point* to which its closest absolutely positioned descendants are positioned.
	The image of the star comes before the final paragraph in document order. This would normally cause the final paragraph to be rendered on top of the star, but I assigned a higher **z-index** to the image to place it on top.
Related to	Closest Positioned Ancestor, Static, Absolute, Fixed, Relative, Float and Clear

Closest Positioned Ancestor

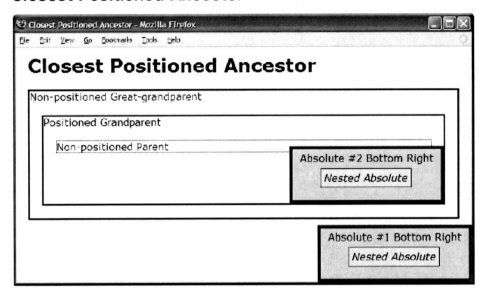

HTML

```
<body>
<h1>Closest Positioned Ancestor</h1>

<div class="static ggp">Non-positioned Great-grandparent
  <div class="absolute sized bottom-right box1">Absolute #1 Bottom Right
    <em class="absolute offset box2">Nested Absolute</em></div>
  <div class="relative gp">Positioned Grandparent
    <div class="static parent">Non-positioned Parent
      <span class="absolute sized bottom-right box1">Absolute #2 Bottom Right
        <em class="absolute offset box2">Nested Absolute</em></span>
    </div></div></div>
</body>
```

CSS

```
*.static { position:static; }
*.relative { position:relative; }
*.absolute { position:absolute; }

*.sized { width:230px; height:70px; }
*.bottom-right { bottom:0; right:0; }
*.offset { left:45px; top:30px; }

/*  Nonessential rules are not shown. */
```

Closest Positioned Ancestor

Problem	You want to position an element so you can position other elements in relation to it. Such an element is the closest positioned ancestor to its descendants.
Solution	You can position an element by assigning **position:relative**, **position:absolute**, or **position:fixed** to it. Positioned elements are positioned relative to their closest positioned ancestor. This allows you to remove elements from the normal flow and position them far away from their original position in the flow. Notice in the example how the absolute span (Absolute #2) is removed from its non-positioned parent and aligned to the bottom right of its positioned grandparent, which is its closest positioned ancestor.
	When a positioned element has no positioned ancestor, **<body>** is the positioned ancestor. In other words, **<body>** is positioned by default. Notice in the example how the absolute division (Absolute #1) is removed from its non-positioned parent and aligned to the bottom right of **<body>**.
	The main purpose for aligning positioned elements to their closest positioned ancestors is to create self-contained layouts. You can reposition a self-contained layout, and all its descendants will move along with it—both positioned and non-positioned. Notice in the example how the absolute **<em>** elements are positioned relative to their closest positioned ancestors, as these ancestors are moved to the bottom right of their closest positioned ancestors.
Pattern	SELECTOR { **position:relative;** }
	or
	SELECTOR { position:absolute; }
	or
	SELECTOR { position:fixed; }
Location	This pattern applies to all elements.
Limitations	A closest positioned ancestor has to be an actual ancestor. CSS doesn't provide a way to position elements relative to any element in a document. That would be a very welcome feature, but as it is, you must choose an ancestor to be the reference for positioned elements.
Advantages	There is no limit on how deep you can nest self-contained positioned layouts. This is a very powerful feature for creating reusable layouts.
Disadvantages	Positioning is very powerful, but its biggest weakness is that it ultimately requires elements to be sized, and sized layouts don't scale well on devices with displays or fonts that are smaller or larger than designed for.
Tip	**position:relative** is a great way to create a positioned ancestor because it doesn't remove it from the normal flow. This allows you to create layouts that combine normal flow and absolute position.
Related to	Positioned, Stacking Context, Atomic, Absolute, Fixed, Relative, Relative Float

Stacking Context

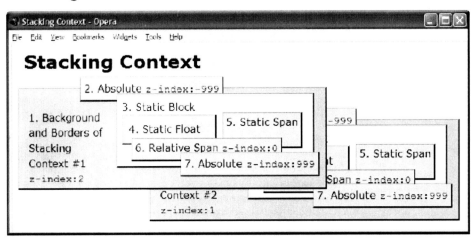

HTML

```
<h1>Stacking Context</h1>
<div class="stacking-context1 box">
  <div class="caption">1. Background and Borders of Stacking Context #1
    <br /><code>z-index:2</code></div>
  <span class="level2 box">2. Absolute <code>z-index:-999</code></span>
  <div class="level3 box">3. Static Block<br />
    <span class="level4 box">4. Static Float</span>
    <span class="level5 box">5. Static Span</span><br /><br /><p class="clear"></p>
    <span class="level6 box">6. Relative Span <code>z-index:0</code></span>
    <span class="level7 box">7. Absolute <code>z-index:999</code></span>
  </div>
</div>
<div class="stacking-context2 box"><!-- ...Same exact code as previous... --></div>
```

CSS

```
*.stacking-context1 { z-index:2; position:absolute; left:10px;  top:70px;  }
*.stacking-context2 { z-index:1; position:absolute; left:223px; top:120px; }

*.level2 { z-index:-999; position:absolute; }
*.level3 { position:static; }
*.level4 { float:left; }
*.level5 { position:static; }
*.level6 { z-index:0; position:relative; }
*.level7 { z-index:999; position:absolute; }

/*  Nonessential rules are not shown. */
```

Stacking Context

Aliases	Stacking Order, Stacking Level, Z-index, Layering, Painting Order
Problem	You want to control how positioned elements are stacked from front to back.
Solution	CSS provides **z-order** to control the stacking of elements. *Static* elements are stacked from back to front in document order. *Positioned* elements are stacked from back to front from smallest to largest **z-index** with document order breaking ties. Positioned elements with a negative **z-index** are placed behind static elements and non-positioned floats. **z-index** values don't have to be contiguous. The default value for **z-index** is **auto**.
	A *positioned* element with a numeric **z-index** creates a local, self-contained, *stacking context*, in which *all* its descendants are rendered—static, float, and positioned. A stacking context is *not* created when **z-index** is set to **auto** or when **z-index** is assigned to a non-positioned element. The following values create stacking contexts: **z-index:0**, **z-index:-1**, and **z-index:9999**.
	Each stacking context is atomic and doesn't allow *ancestors or siblings* to be layered in between its children. Each local stacking context is assigned to an *internal* stacking level of **0**, and its descendants are stacked *relative to it*. This is an important point. **z-index** isn't global. It's *relative* to the closest positioned ancestor that has been assigned to a numeric **z-index**. The root element, **<html>**, creates the root stacking context.
	A stacking context is rendered in layers from back to front as follows:
	1. Background color, image, and borders of the stacking context element
	2. Descendant positioned elements with a negative **z-index**
	3. Descendant non-positioned block elements
	4. Descendant non-positioned floats
	5. Descendant non-positioned inline elements
	6. Descendant positioned elements with **z-index:auto** and **z-index:0**
	7. Descendant positioned elements with a positive **z-index**
	Steps 2, 6, and 7 each recursively render stacking contexts because each positioned element with a numeric **z-index** creates a local stacking context.
	Before a browser renders an element's content, it renders its box starting with its background color, then its background image, and then its borders. A browser then renders a box's contents on top of the box.
Pattern	`SELECTOR { z-index:±VALUE;  position:ABSOLUTE_FIXED_RELATIVE; }`
Location	This pattern applies to all elements.
Limitations	Firefox 2 incorrectly switches steps 1 and 2, which puts negative child-stacking contexts behind the background and borders of the parent context! This has been fixed in newer versions of Firefox.
Example	The example shows all seven stacking levels repeated in two stacking contexts. Notice how stacking levels are relative to each stacking context.
Related to	Positioned, Closest Positioned Ancestor, Absolute, Relative, Relative Float

Atomic

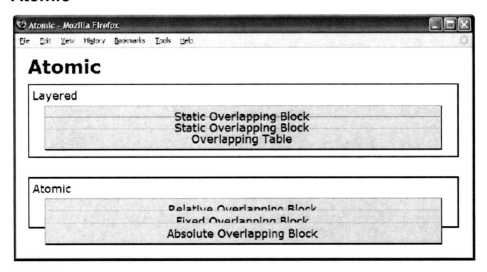

HTML

```
<h1>Atomic</h1>
<div>Layered
  <p class="static">Static Overlapping Block</p>
  <p class="static overlap">Static Overlapping Block</p>
  <table class="static overlap"><tr><td>Overlapping Table</td></tr></table></div>

<div>Atomic
  <p class="relative">Relative Overlapping Block</p>
  <p class="fixed">Fixed Overlapping Block</p>
  <p class="absolute">Absolute Overlapping Block</p></div>
```

CSS

```
*.static { position:static; }
*.overlap { margin-top:-22px; }

*.relative { position:relative; }
*.fixed { position:fixed; margin-top:-16px; }
*.absolute { position:absolute; top:65px; }

/*  Nonessential rules are not shown. */
```

Atomic

Aliases	hasLayout, Grouped
Problem	You want content to be rendered *in* a block, not *on* it. In other words, you want text and inline content to be rendered atomically with its block so that when the block is overlapped by another block, its content is overlapped too.
	The problem is that a browser renders static *inline* content in a separate layer above the backgrounds of static *blocks*. When static blocks overlap each other, their backgrounds overlap, but their inline content doesn't! Notice in the example how the borders and backgrounds of the blocks in the first division overlap, but their text doesn't. All the major browsers work this way because a stacking context renders *all* block backgrounds and borders first, then all floats, and then all inline elements and content. This places the backgrounds and borders of blocks in a layer below floats and inline content.
	This may seem unusual because you tend to think of inline content as being *in* the blocks that contain them, not *on* them. But it makes sense that inline elements are rendered *on* blocks because inline content overflows by default.
Solution	A positioned element is atomic, which means no external elements can be layered in between its static descendants, its inline content, and its background. Notice in the second division of the example how neighboring blocks overlap each other, including their inline text. This is because they're positioned, and the stacking context requires positioned elements to be rendered atomically. You can use relative, absolute, and fixed positioning to make an element atomic. Blocks set to **overflow:scroll** are also atomic because their content is literally contained in the block's scrollable area.
Pattern	`SELECTOR { position:RELATIVE_ABSOLUTE_FIXED; }`
Location	This pattern applies to all elements.
Limitations	**overflow** doesn't consistently create atomicity in older browsers. Blocks set to **overflow:hidden** are atomic in Firefox 2.0 and Internet Explorer 7, but not in Internet Explorer 6 and other major browsers. Blocks set to **overflow:scroll** are atomic except for in Internet Explorer 6. **overflow** consistently creates atomicity in newer browsers.
	All tables and sized blocks are atomic in Internet Explorer 7, but not in other major browsers. This is because Internet Explorer 7 and earlier versions use an internal feature and a proprietary DOM property called **hasLayout**, which is true when an element has layout. When an element has layout, it's rendered in its own window with its own layout context. All of its children are rendered atomically inside its rectangular box. It can't shrinkwrap, and external floats don't affect the position of its inline content.
Tip	Internet Explorer 6 has bugs that are sometimes fixed by triggering **hasLayout**. You can use its proprietary property **zoom:1** to trigger layout, but be aware that **zoom** causes your style sheet not to validate.
Related to	Positioned, Static, Absolute, Fixed, Relative, Float and Clear

Static

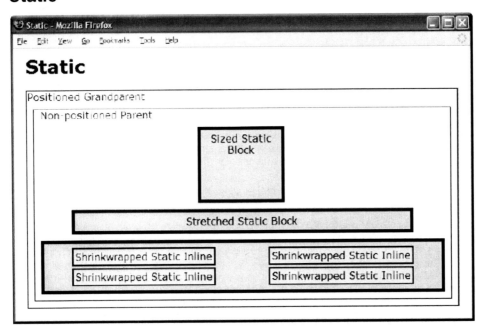

HTML

```
<h1>Static</h1>
<div class="gp">Positioned Grandparent
   <div class="parent">Non-positioned Parent
     <div id="zs" class="box">Sized Static Block </div>
     <div id="ss" class="box">Stretched Static Block</div>
     <div class="box"> <span>Shrinkwrapped Static Inline</span>
                       <span>Shrinkwrapped Static Inline</span>
                       <span>Shrinkwrapped Static Inline</span>
                       <span>Shrinkwrapped Static Inline</span>
     </div></div></div>
```

CSS

```
span { position:static; margin:40px; line-height:32px;
  padding:3px; border:2px solid black; background-color:yellow; }

#zs { position:static;  width:120px; height:100px; margin:10px auto; }

#ss { position:static;  width:auto;  height:auto; margin:10px 50px; }
```

Static

Problem	You want elements to flow automatically one after the other in lines and blocks so they fluidly adapt to the size of the user's display.
Solution	You can apply **position:static** to an element to position an element in the normal flow. Because this is the default, elements are automatically rendered in the normal flow. The *normal flow* consists of nested blocks rendered vertically down the viewport. Inside a block, one or more blocks or lines are rendered vertically down the block. Inside a line, text and objects are rendered horizontally across the line. The starting position of a static element is determined by the previous static element. The size, padding, borders, and margins of a static element determine the starting position of the next element.
Patterns	**Inline Static Element** INLINE-SELECTOR { position:static; line-height:±VALUE; margin-left:±VALUE; margin-right:±VALUE; } **Block Static Element** BLOCK-SELECTOR { position:static; width:+VALUE; height:+VALUE; margin-left:±VALUE; margin-right:±VALUE; margin-top:±VALUE; margin-bottom:±VALUE; }
Location	This pattern applies to all elements.
Example	All elements in the example are static. Block elements are rendered in blocks that flow down from the top. Each block, except for the sized block, is automatically stretched to the width of its container minus its left and right margins and the parent's padding. The top margin pushes the selected static block element down, and the bottom margin pushes down the following static block element. Adjacent vertical margins collapse into each other. The resulting margin is the larger of the two adjacent margins. In the example, each block has a top and bottom margin of 10 pixels. These margins collapse so that only a 10-pixel margin exists between them. You can assign **height** and **width** to a static block to create a sized block. Left and/or right margins assigned to **auto** expand to compensate for the specified width. You can center a sized static block element by setting both left and right margins to **auto**, as shown in the first block in the example. The static *inline* elements in the example have left and right margins of 40 pixels. Left and right margins push inline elements apart, and they don't collapse. When the content of an inline element exceeds the width of its container, a browser wraps it into a new line. Top and bottom margins are ignored on inline elements because **line-height** directs the height of lines.
Related to	Absolute, Fixed, Relative; Sized, Stretched, Shrinkwrapped (Chapter 5)

Absolute

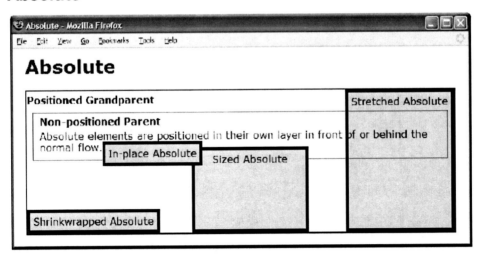

HTML

```
<h1>Absolute</h1>
<div class="gp"><h2>Positioned Grandparent</h2>
  <div class="parent"><h2>Non-positioned Parent</h2>
    Absolute elements are positioned in their own layer in front of or behind the
    normal flow.
    <span id="in-place" class="box">In-place Absolute</span>
    <span id="sized" class="box">Sized Absolute</span>
    <p id="stretched" class="box">Stretched Absolute</p>
    <p id="shrinkwrapped" class="box">Shrinkwrapped Absolute</p></div></div>
```

CSS

```
#in-place  { position:absolute; z-index:1; }

#shrinkwrapped { position:absolute; z-index:0;
  width:auto; left:0; bottom:0; margin:0; }

#sized { position:absolute; z-index:auto;
  width:170px; height:115px; bottom:0; left:270px; margin:0; }

#stretched { position:absolute; z-index:-1;
  height:auto; right:0; top:0; bottom:0; margin:0; }

/*  Nonessential rules are not shown. */
```

142

Absolute

Problem	You want to remove an element from the normal flow and move it into its own layer. You also want to position it relative to the inner border of its closest positioned ancestor, or you want it to be positioned at the same position it would have had in the normal flow. You don't want its position to have any effect on the position of other elements.
Solution	You can use **position:absolute** to render *any* element as an absolute box. You can use **width** and **height** to size it. Percentages refer to its closest positioned ancestor rather than its parent. You can assign a value, such as **0**, to **left**, **right**, **top**, and **bottom** to *align* it to the sides of its closest position ancestor. Or you can assign **auto** to **left**, **right**, **top**, and **bottom** to render it at the same position it would have had in the normal flow. You can use **margin-left**, **margin-right**, **margin-top**, and **margin-bottom** to *offset* its sides from the sides of its closest positioned ancestor. You can use **z-index** to control the stacking order of the element. Elements with a larger **z-index** are rendered in a layer closer to the user. You can assign **position:relative**, **position:absolute**, or **position:fixed** to an ancestor element to make it positioned. If you don't have any positioned ancestors, a browser uses **<body>** as the closest positioned ancestor.

Patterns	SELECTOR { **position:absolute;** z-index:VALUE;
	  width:+VALUE; left:±VALUE; margin-left:±VALUE;
	  right:±VALUE; margin-right:±VALUE;
	  height:+VALUE; top:±VALUE; margin-top:±VALUE;
	  bottom:±VALUE; margin-bottom:±VALUE; }
	
	plus
	
	  ANCESTOR-SELECTOR { position:relative; }
	
	or ANCESTOR-SELECTOR { position:absolute; }
	
	or ANCESTOR-SELECTOR { position:fixed; }

Location	You can absolutely position any type of element.
Limitations	Internet Explorer 6 shrinkwraps stretched absolute elements. Internet Explorer 7 and earlier versions can't center absolute elements.
Advantages	Absolute elements give you precise control over their placement in relation to their closest positioned ancestor. Absolute elements can be sized, shrinkwrapped, and stretched. An absolute element is rendered in a layer above the normal flow as an absolute box, which is much like a block box. Unlike floats, absolutes don't flow. Their position is unaffected by and doesn't affect the position of other elements and content. This may cause them to overlap or be overlapped. If all children are positioned absolutely, the parent collapses to a height of zero (unless you set the height to a value) because its children have been removed from the normal flow.
Disadvantages	Layouts created using absolute positioning don't scale well on devices with displays or fonts that are much smaller or larger than you designed for.
Related to	Offset Absolute (Chapter 8); Fixed; Sized, Shrinkwrapped, Stretched (Chapter 5)

Fixed

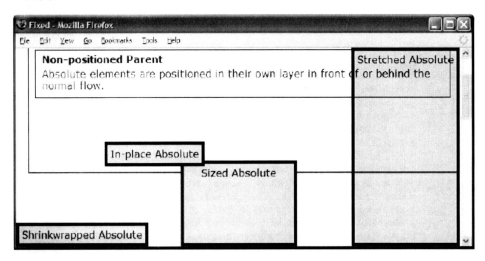

HTML

```
<h1>Fixed</h1>
<div class="gp"><h2>Positioned Grandparent</h2>
  <div class="parent"><h2>Non-positioned Parent</h2>
    Absolute elements are positioned in their own layer in front of or behind the
    normal flow.
    <span id="in-place" class="box">In-place Absolute</span>
    <span id="sized" class="box">Sized Absolute</span>
    <p id="stretched" class="box">Stretched Absolute</p>
    <p id="shrinkwrapped" class="box">Shrinkwrapped Absolute</p></div></div>
```

CSS

```
*.gp { position:relative; z-index:1; }

#in-place { position:fixed; z-index:1; }

#shrinkwrapped { position:fixed; z-index:0;
  width:auto; left:0; bottom:0; margin:0; }

#sized { position:fixed; z-index:auto;
  width:170px; height:115px; bottom:0; left:270px; margin:0; }

#stretched { position:fixed; z-index:-1;
  height:auto; right:0; top:0; bottom:0; margin:0; }

/*  Nonessential rules are not shown. */
```

Fixed

Problem	You want to move an element into its own layer and fix its position to the viewport, or you want it to be positioned at the same position it would have had in the normal flow. You also don't want the element to scroll when the viewport scrolls. This is called a **fixed-position element** or a **fixed element**.
Solution	You can use **position:fixed** to turn any element into a fixed-positioned element. Fixed works identically to Absolute except that an element is positioned relative to the viewport rather than its closest positioned ancestor, and the element doesn't scroll when the viewport scrolls. If you have positioned the fixed element at the same position it would have had in the normal flow, it still doesn't scroll when the viewport scrolls.

Pattern	SELECTOR { position:fixed; z-index:VALUE;
	  width:+VALUE; left:±VALUE; margin-left:±VALUE;
	  right:±VALUE; margin-right:±VALUE;
	  height:+VALUE; top:±VALUE; margin-top:±VALUE;
	  bottom:±VALUE; margin-bottom:VALUE; }

Location	This pattern applies to all elements.
Limitations	Internet Explorer 6 renders fixed-position elements as absolute. Internet Explorer 7 and above render fixed elements properly.
Advantages	Fixed elements give you precise control over their placement in relation to the viewport. They don't scroll with the viewport. They're well suited for holding controls, such as menus, toolbars, buttons, and so on.
Disadvantages	Layouts created using fixed positioning don't scale well on devices with displays or fonts that are much smaller than you designed for.
Example	This example contains the same positioned elements as the Absolute design pattern example. The only difference is the elements are fixed instead of absolute. Notice how the browser window is scrolled down in the example, and the position of the fixed elements remains the same. Notice how the fixed elements are positioned relative to the viewport instead of their grandparent, which is the closest positioned ancestor. Notice how the in-place absolute is initially positioned where it would have been in the normal flow but remains fixed at that position and doesn't scroll when the viewport scrolls. If the in-place absolute is initially rendered offscreen, it won't be visible even when the viewport is scrolled.
	Notice how the fixed elements in the example are layered exactly the same as the absolute elements in the Absolute design pattern example. The in-place absolute is in front of the sized absolute because it has a **z-index** of **1** and the sized absolute has a **z-index** of **auto**. The stretched absolute is layered behind the positioned grandparent because it has a **z-index** of **-1** and the positioned grandparent has a **z-index** of **1**. Because the positioned grandparent has a transparent background, you can see the stretched absolute element behind it.
Related to	Absolute; Sized, Shrinkwrapped, Stretched (Chapter 5)

Relative

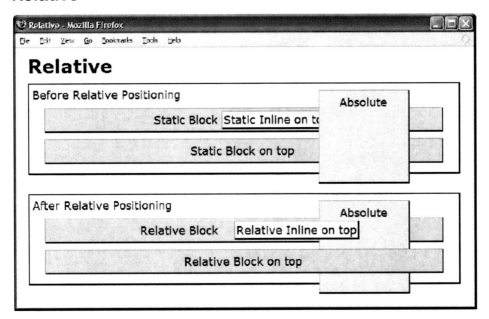

HTML

```
<h1>Relative</h1>
<div class="relative">Before Relative Positioning
  <p class="static">Static Block
   <span class="static ontop">Static Inline on top</span></p>
  <p class="static ontop">Static Block on top</p>
  <p class="absolute">Absolute</p></div>

<div class="relative">After Relative Positioning
  <p class="relative">Relative Block
  <span class="relative ontop offset">Relative Inline on top</span></p>
  <p class="relative ontop">Relative Block on top</p>
  <p class="absolute">Absolute</p></div>
```

CSS

```
*.ontop    { z-index:1; }
*.static   { position:static; }
*.relative { position:relative; }
*.absolute { position:absolute; z-index:auto; }
*.offset   { left:20px; top:auto; }

/*  Nonessential rules are not shown. */
```

Relative

Problems	You want to control the stacking order of a float or an element in the normal flow. The problem is that **z-index** doesn't apply to floats or static-positioned elements. Controlling the stacking order is important when you have positioned elements overlapping floats and static elements.
	You want to position an element so it can be a closest positioned ancestor.
	You want to offset an element without removing its place in the normal flow. You don't want to change the shape it has in the normal flow. And you don't want the offset to change the position of other elements.
Solutions	To control the stacking order of an element in the normal flow, you can position it relatively using **position:relative**. You can use **z-index** to set its stacking order in relation to other positioned elements.
	A relative element is positioned without leaving the normal flow and without changing the shape that it has in the normal flow. For example, if an inline element is wrapped across one or more lines, it retains this unique layout when relatively positioned. Contrast this with absolute positioning, which changes an inline element into an absolute box and reflows the content into the absolute block box, which may change its layout.
	You can optionally offset a relatively positioned element from its position in the flow using **left** and **top**. This doesn't change the position of other elements in the flow. **left** and **top** default to **auto**, and **auto** keeps relatively positioned elements in their normal position in the normal flow.
	You can assign **position:relative** to any element so that absolute descendants can be positioned relative to it—for details, see **Closest Positioned Ancestor** in this chapter. You can use **position:relative**, **left**, and **top** to offset any element—for details, see **Offset Relative** in Chapter 8. You can use **position: relative** to offset and control the stacking order of floats—for details, see **Relative Float** in this chapter.
Pattern	SELECTOR { position:relative; z-index:+VALUE; left:auto; top:auto; }
Location	This pattern applies to all elements.
Limitations	Because of the way Internet Explorer 7 and earlier versions implement **hasLayout**, relative *inline* elements in a *positioned block* can't be stacked on top of elements outside the block. Because of this, Internet Explorer 7 can't render the relative inline span in the example in front of the absolute paragraph. This happens because the inline span is literally contained within the paragraph because the paragraph has layout. This problem doesn't occur in other major browsers, and it doesn't occur in Internet Explorer when the parent block doesn't have layout, such as when it's a static block. This problem has been resolved in Internet Explorer 8 and 9.
Related to	Positioned, Closest Positioned Ancestor, Stacking Context, Atomic, Relative Float; Offset Relative (Chapter 8)

Float and Clear

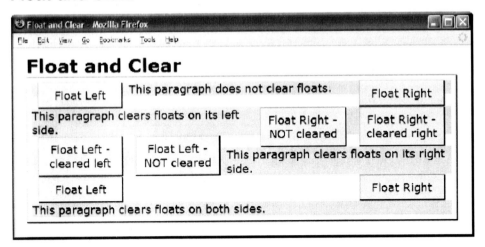

HTML

```
<h1>Float</h1>
<div>
  <div class="float left  clear-left" >Float Left </div>
  <div class="float right clear-right">Float Right</div>
  <p class="clear-none">This paragraph does not clear floats.
    <span class="float right clear-right">Float Right - cleared right</span>
    <span class="float ight  clear-none" >Float Right - NOT cleared</span></p>

  <p class="clear-left">This paragraph clears floats on its left side.</p>
  <div class="float left clear-left">Float Left - cleared left</div>
  <div class="float left clear-none">Float Left - NOT cleared</div>

  <p class="clear-right">This paragraph clears floats on its right side.
    <span class="float left  clear-left">Float Left </span>
    <span class="float right clear-right">Float Right</span></p>

  <p class="clear-both">This paragraph clears floats on both sides.</p> </div>
```

CSS

```
*.float { margin:0px 10px;  width:120px; background-color:yellow; color:black; }
*.left { float:left; }
*.right { float:right; }
*.clear-left { clear:left; }
*.clear-right { clear:right; }
*.clear-both { clear:both; }
*.clear-none { clear:none;  }

/*  Nonessential rules are not shown. */
```

Float and Clear

Problem	You want to remove an element from the normal flow and display it on the left or right side of its parent. You want it rendered as a block aligned to the inside of its parent's padding. You also want its top to align with the line from which it was extracted. You also want to control when other floats and nonfloated content flows next to floats or is moved below them on one or both sides.
Solution	You can use **float:left** or **float:right** to remove an element from the normal flow and place it on the left or right inner edge of its parent's padding area. You can use **float:none** to override another rule that floats an element. Floats exist in their own layer above the backgrounds of block elements and next to inline content in the normal flow. A left float indents content on its right side, and a right float indents content on its left. A float doesn't affect the position of *block* boxes—just their inline content. Floats affect the position of other floats and may be stacked next to each other on the left or right. Floats also may push down other floats and inline content. A float's vertical and horizontal margins offset it from its parent and from other floats. Floats don't overlap other floats or content (unless a float has a negative margin).
	You can use **clear:left** to move a block or float below any floats on its left side. You can use **clear:right** to move a block or float below any floats on its right side. You can use **clear:both** to move a block or float below floats on its right or left.
Patterns	SELECTOR { float:none; } SELECTOR { float:left; } SELECTOR { float:right; } SELECTOR { clear:none; } SELECTOR { clear:left; } SELECTOR { clear:right; } SELECTOR { clear:both; }
Location	*Any* element can be floated. **clear** works on tables, blocks, and floats. **clear** has *no* effect on inline, absolutely positioned, or fixed-position elements.
Tips	When you need to predict the vertical location of a float, it's best to float a *block* element. A browser places the top of a floated *block* exactly where it would have been rendered if it were not floated. A browser places the top of a floated *inline* element depending on where it would have been rendered in a *line* if it were not floated. If at the beginning of a line, its top is aligned to the *top* of the line; otherwise, its top is aligned to the *bottom* of the line.
Example	The example contains eight floats: four spans and four divisions. The four paragraphs demonstrate each setting of **clear**. When a float isn't cleared on the side that it's floated, it stacks next to other floats on that side. When cleared on a side, a float or block element moves below floats on that side.
Related to	Static, Absolute, Fixed

Relative Float

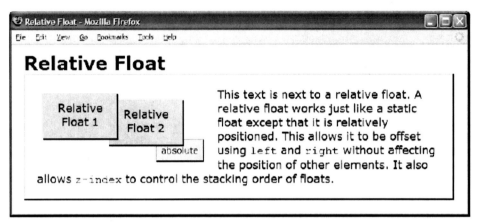

HTML

```
<h1>Relative Float</h1>

<div class="parent">
  <div class="relative1 float">Relative Float 1</div>
  <div class="relative2 float">Relative Float 2</div>

  <p>This text is next to a relative float. A relative float works just like a
  static float except that it is relatively positioned. This allows it to be
  offset using <code>left</code> and <code>right</code> without affecting
  the position of other elements. It also allows <code>z-index</code> to
  control the stacking order of floats.

  <span class="absolute">absolute</span></p></div>
```

CSS

```
*.parent { position:relative; padding:20px; }

*.relative1 { position:relative; z-index:3; top:10px; left:10px; }
*.relative2 { position:relative; z-index:2; top:20px; left:-30px; }

*.float { float:left; width:100px; height:50px;
  margin-right:25px; margin-bottom:40px; }

*.absolute { position:absolute; z-index:1; top:102px; left:215px; }

/*  Nonessential rules are not shown. */
```

Relative Float

Problem	You want to offset a float from its current position without affecting the position of any other element, including other floats and inline content. You also want to control the stacking order of floats in relation to each other and in relation to positioned elements.
Solution	You can use **position:relative** to relatively position a float. A relative float remains in the normal flow of floats and can be offset from its position in the flow using **left** and **top**. A relative float is rendered in a positioned layer, which allows you to use **z-index** to control its stacking order in relation to floats and other positioned elements. Because a relative float is positioned, absolute descendants can be positioned relative to it.

Pattern	SELECTOR { position:relative;
	  left:±VALUE;
	  right:±VALUE;
	  z-index:±VALUE;
	  float:LEFT_RIGHT;
	  width:+VALUE;
	  height:+VALUE;
	  margin:±VALUE; }

Location	This pattern applies to all elements.
Advantages	This design pattern allows you to use **margin** to adjust the position of inline content in relation to the float. You can then use **left** and **top** to adjust the position of the float without changing the location of the inline content. This gives you great flexibility in positioning floats. Without this design pattern, you could not control the stacking order of floats and other positioned elements—other than controlling their order in the document.
Tip	Only **position:relative** and **position:static** are compatible with floats. If you assign **position:absolute** or **position:fixed** to a float, the results are undefined, and each browser handles the situation differently. For example, some versions of Firefox set **float** to **none** and render the element as an absolute element, and Internet Explorer 7 partly floats and partly positions it.
Example	The example contains two relative floats, a static paragraph, and an absolutely positioned span. Using **left** and **top**, you relatively offset each float from its floated position without affecting the location of the neighboring inline content in the paragraph. Using **z-index**, you stack each float and the absolute element in reverse order in comparison to document order.
Related to	Positioned, Static, Absolute, Fixed, Relative, Float and Clear

Positioning:
Indented, Offset, and Aligned

This chapter shows how margins can offset and align elements.

A stretched element is *indented* or *outdented* when one or more of its sides is displaced into or out of its container, changing the width or height of the element.

A sized or shrinkwrapped element is *offset* when the entire element is shifted from its normal position without changing the height or width of the element.

A sized or shrinkwrapped element is *aligned* when it's relocated to one of the sides of its container without changing its size and optionally offset from that side.

Chapter Outline

- **Indented** shows how to indent an element from the sides of its container.

- **Offset Static** shows how to offset an element from surrounding elements.

- **Offset or Indented Static Table** shows how to offset a table from its container.

- **Offset Float** shows how to offset a float from surrounding floats and content.

- **Offset Absolute and Offset Fixed** shows how to offset an absolute element from the position it would have had in the normal flow.

- **Offset Relative** shows how to offset *any* element without affecting other elements.

- **Aligned Static Inline** shows how to align inline elements horizontally and vertically.

- **Aligned and Offset Static Block** shows how to align and offset static block elements.

- **Aligned and Offset Static Table** shows how to align and offset tables.

- **Aligned and Offset Absolute** shows how to align and offset absolute elements.

- **Aligned-center Absolute** shows how to center absolute elements.

- **Aligned Outside** shows how to align elements to the outside of their container.

Indented

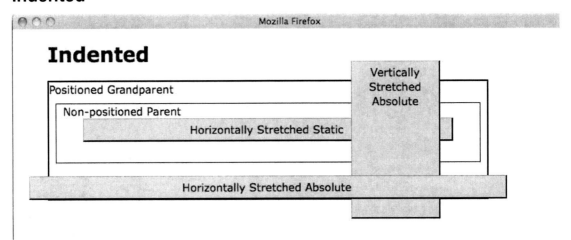

HTML

```
<h1>Indented</h1>
<div class="gp">Positioned Grandparent
  <div class="parent">Non-positioned Parent
    <div id="hss" class="s">Horizontally Stretched Static</div>
    <div id="vsa" class="s">Vertically Stretched Absolute</div>
    <span id="hsa" class="s">Horizontally Stretched Absolute</span>
  </div>
</div>
```

CSS

```
.gp { position:relative; z-index:10; }

#hss { position:static;
    width:auto; margin-left:30px; margin-right:30px;
    height:auto; margin-top:auto; margin-bottom:20px; }

#vsa { position:absolute;
    width:120px; left:auto; margin-left:auto; right:0; margin-right:70px;
    height:auto; top:0; margin-top:-30px; bottom:0; margin-bottom:-30px; }

#hsa { position:absolute;
    width:auto; left:0; margin-left:-30px; right:0; margin-right:-30px;
    height:auto; top:auto; margin-top:30px; bottom:auto; margin-bottom:auto; }

/* Nonessential rules are not shown. */
```

Indented

Problem	You want to indent the left and right sides of a static element, or you want to indent the left, right, top, and bottom sides of a *stretched absolute* element. You also want to outdent these elements.
Solution	Indenting is a combination of stretching an element to the sides of its container and then offsetting its sides. Indenting to the inside shrinks the size of an element. Indenting to the outside (or outdenting) expands the size of an element. Each side may be indented or outdented independently. Margins expand or shrink the height and width of a stretched element. Contrast this with the offset design patterns, where margins move a sized or shrinkwrapped element without changing its size.
	Positive margins indent, and negative margins outdent. In other words, positive margins move sides toward the center, and negative margins move them away from the center. You can use left:0, right:0, top:0, and bottom:0 to align the sides of the absolute element to the sides of its closest positioned ancestor. Once opposite sides of an element are aligned to its container (in other words, the element is stretched), margins can indent or outdent each side independently.
Patterns	**Horizontally Indented Static Block Element**

```
BLOCK-SELECTOR { position:static; width:auto; margin-left:±VALUE;
margin-right:±VALUE; }
```

Horizontally Indented Absolute Element

```
SELECTOR { position:absolute; width:auto; left:0; margin-left:±VALUE;
right:0; margin-right:±VALUE; }
```

Vertically Indented Absolute Element

```
SELECTOR { position:absolute; height:auto; top:0; margin-top:±VALUE;
bottom:0; margin-bottom:±VALUE; }
```

Location	This pattern works on static block elements and absolute elements.
Limitations	You can't vertically stretch and indent a static element. You can't stretch and indent a float. You can't stretch and indent an inline-text element. You can't indent or outdent an element that is stretched using width:100% or height:100%.
Related to	Sized, Shrinkwrapped (Chapter 5); Margin (Chapter 6); Static, Absolute (Chapter 7); Text Indent, Hanging Indent (Chapter 12); Lists, Left Marginal, Right Marginal (Chapter 13); Padded Graphic Dropcap, Floating Dropcap, Floating Graphic Dropcap, Marginal Dropcap, Marginal Graphic Dropcap (Chapter 18); Left Marginal Callout, Right Marginal Callout (Chapter 19); Hanging Alert, Left Marginal Alert, Right Marginal Alert (Chapter 20)

Offset Static

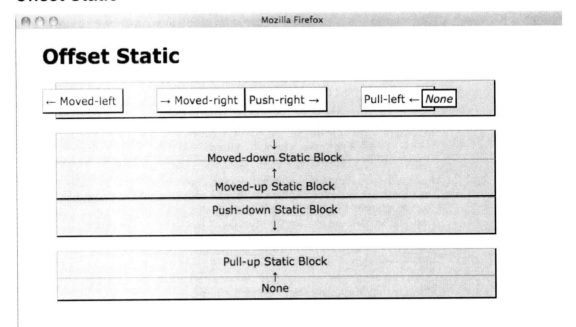

HTML

```
<h1>Offset Static</h1>
<div>
   <span class="moved-left">&larr; Moved-left </span>
   <span class="moved-right">&rarr; Moved-right </span>
   <span class="push-right">Push-right &rarr; </span>
   <span class="pull-left">Pull-left &larr;   </span>
   <em>None</em>
</div>
<div class="moved-down center">&darr;<br />Moved-down Static Block </div>
<div class="moved-up center">&uarr;<br />Moved-up Static Block</div>
<div class="push-down center">Push-down Static Block<br />&darr;</div>
<div class="pull-up center">Pull-up Static Block<br />&uarr;</div>
<div class="center">None</div>
```

CSS

```
.moved-left { margin-left:-26px; } .push-right { margin-right:50px; } .moved-right { margin-
left:50px; } .pull-left { margin-right:-20px; } .moved-down { margin-top:20px; } .push-down {
margin-bottom:20px; } .moved-up { margin-top:-13px; } .pull-up { margin-bottom:-16px; }

/* Nonessential rules are not shown. */
```

Offset Static

Problem	You want to control the spacing between static elements in the normal flow by moving them closer together or further apart.
Solution	Margins offset sized and shrinkwrapped elements. Left and top margins offset an element from the ending position set by the previous element. Right and bottom margins define the starting position of the following element. Negative margins move an element closer to surrounding elements, and positive margins move an element farther away. In other words, margins extend or retract the starting and ending positions of sized and shrinkwrapped elements.
	For example, you can use a positive value in `margin-left` to move an *inline* element to the right, and a negative value to move it to the left. A negative left margin can cause an inline element to overlap or precede the previous inline element, or overlap the left side of its containing block. `margin-right` doesn't affect an inline element's position; it affects the *following* element's position. A positive value in `margin-right` pushes the next element to the right, and a negative value pulls it to the left. A negative right margin can cause the following inline element to overlap or precede an element.
	`margin-top` and `margin-bottom` work similarly with *block* elements except that they pull and push blocks up and down. `margin-top` moves a block up or down, and `margin-bottom` moves the following block up or down. Negative margins can move blocks on top of neighboring blocks.
Inline Patterns	**Left-extended Static Inline Element (Moved-right)**
	`INLINE-SELECTOR { position:static; margin-left:+VALUE; }`
	Left-retracted Static Inline Element (Moved-left)
	`INLINE-SELECTOR { position:static; margin-left:-VALUE; }`
	Right-extended Static Inline Element (Push-right)
	`INLINE-SELECTOR { position:static; margin-right:+VALUE; }`
	Right-retracted Static Inline Element (Pull-left)
	`INLINE-SELECTOR { position:static; margin-right:-VALUE; }`
Block Patterns	**Top-extended Static Block Element (Moved-down)**
	`BLOCK-SELECTOR { position:static; margin-top:+VALUE; }`
	Top-retracted Static Block Element (Moved-up)
	`BLOCK-SELECTOR { position:static; margin-top:-VALUE; }`
	Bottom-extended Static Block Element (Push-down)
	`BLOCK-SELECTOR { position:static; margin-bottom:+VALUE; }`
	Bottom-retracted Static Block Element (Pull-up)
	`BLOCK-SELECTOR { position:static; margin-bottom:-VALUE; }`

OffsetStatic cont.

Location	This pattern applies to all static elements.
Related to	Offset Relative, Aligned Static Inline, Aligned and Offset Static Block; Sized, Shrinkwrapped (Chapter 5); Static (Chapter 7); all offset design patterns in Chapter 9; Spacing, Inline Spacer, Inline Decoration, Linebreak, Inline Horizontal Rule (Chapter 11); Vertical-offset Content (Chapter 12); Block Horizontal Rule, Block Spacer, Block Space Remover (Chapter 13)

Offset or Indented Static Table

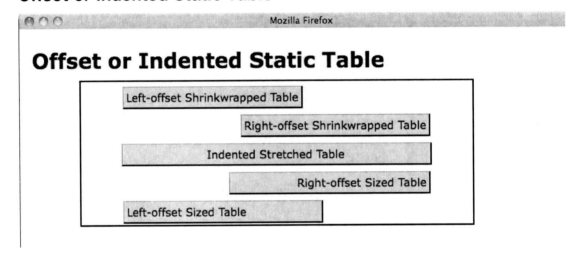

HTML

```
<h1>Offset or Indented Static Table</h1>
<div class="parent">
  <table class="l-wrap"><tr><td>Left-offset Shrinkwrapped Table</td></tr></table>
  <table class="r-wrap"><tr><td>Right-offset Shrinkwrapped Table</td></tr></table>
  <table class="stretched"><tr><td>Indented Stretched Table</td></tr></table>
  <table class="r-sized"><tr><td>Right-offset Sized Table</td></tr></table>
  <table class="l-sized"><tr><td>Left-offset Sized Table</td></tr></table>
</div>
```

CSS

```
.l-wrap { width:auto; margin-left:60px; margin-right:auto; } .r-wrap { width:auto; margin-
left:auto; margin-right:60px;}

.stretched { width:80%; margin-left:auto; margin-right:auto; }

.r-sized { width:300px; margin-left:auto; margin-right:60px; text-align:right; } .l-sized {
width:300px; margin-left:60px; margin-right:auto; text-align:left; }

/* Nonessential rules are not shown. */
```

Offset or Indented Static Table

Problem	You want to offset a shrinkwrapped or sized table in the normal flow, or you want to indent a stretched table in the normal flow.
Solution	You can offset a sized or shrinkwrapped table using left and right margins. You can use a negative margin to move the table away from the center of its container, and you can use a positive margin to move the table toward the center of its container. When you assign a value to `margin-left`, you need to assign `margin-right` to auto, and vice versa.
	You can indent a stretched table equally on both sides by reducing its width to a percentage less than 100% and setting the left and right margins to auto. This creates a centered effect where both sides are indented equally. Because of browser incompatibilities, and because you have to use `width:100%` to stretch a table to the width of its container, there is no *automatic* way to indent left and right sides *unequally* and keep the table stretched. On the other hand, because block elements stretch automatically to the width of their container, you can indent the left and right sides of a block unequally.
	Unlike positioned elements, you can't center a table and then offset it.
HTML Pattern	`<table><tr><td>CONTENT</td></tr> </table>`
CSS Patterns	**Left-offset Shrinkwrapped Static Table**
	`SELECTOR { position:static; width:auto; margin-left:±VALUE; margin-right:auto; }`
	Right-offset Shrinkwrapped Static Table
	`SELECTOR { position:static; width:auto; margin-left:auto; margin-right:±VALUE; }`
	Offset Stretched Static Table
	`SELECTOR { position:static; width:100%; margin-left:auto; margin-right:auto; }`
	Left-offset Sized Static Table
	`SELECTOR { position:static; width:+VALUE; margin-left:±VALUE; margin-right:auto; }`
	Right-offset Sized Static Table
	`SELECTOR { position:static; width:+VALUE; margin-left:auto; margin-right:±VALUE; }`
Location	This pattern applies to table elements.
Limitations	Internet Explorer versions 6 and 7 have a bug that ignores `margin-left` when a *shrinkwrapped* table is a child of any element besides `<body>`.
Tips	Margins apply to the table element, but they do *not* apply to cells, rows, row groups, columns, or column groups.
Related to	Sized, Shrinkwrapped, Stretched (Chapter 5); Left Aligned, Right Aligned, Centered Aligned (Chapter 9); Table (Chapter 15)

Offset Float

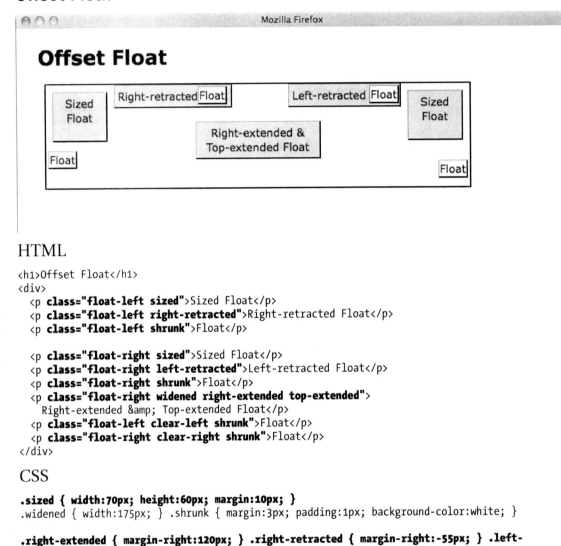

HTML

```
<h1>Offset Float</h1>
<div>
  <p class="float-left sized">Sized Float</p>
  <p class="float-left right-retracted">Right-retracted Float</p>
  <p class="float-left shrunk">Float</p>

  <p class="float-right sized">Sized Float</p>
  <p class="float-right left-retracted">Left-retracted Float</p>
  <p class="float-right shrunk">Float</p>
  <p class="float-right widened right-extended top-extended">
    Right-extended &amp; Top-extended Float</p>
  <p class="float-left clear-left shrunk">Float</p>
  <p class="float-right clear-right shrunk">Float</p>
</div>
```

CSS

```
.sized { width:70px; height:60px; margin:10px; }
.widened { width:175px; } .shrunk { margin:3px; padding:1px; background-color:white; }

.right-extended { margin-right:120px; } .right-retracted { margin-right:-55px; } .left-
retracted { margin-left:-185px; } .top-extended { margin-top:20px; }

.float-left { float:left; } .float-right { float:right; }
.clear-left { clear:left; } .clear-right { clear:right; }

/* Nonessential rules are not shown. */
```

Offset Float

Problem	You want to control the spacing between floats by moving them closer together or further apart.
Solution	A float's margins work just like static inline elements and blocks. Positive margins push content and other floats away, and negative margins bring them closer. Large enough negative margins can cause floats to overlap with each other and with neighboring inline content.
	Thus, floats exist in their own flow where the position of one float affects the position of neighboring floats and inline content. Contrast this with absolute and fixed elements, where each one is positioned independently.
	Margins *offset* floats rather than *indent* them because they don't change their size, they change their position.

Horizontal Patterns	**Left-extended Float**
	`SELECTOR { float:LEFT_OR_RIGHT; `**`margin-left:+VALUE;`**` }`
	
	Left-retracted Float
	`SELECTOR { float:LEFT_OR_RIGHT; `**`margin-left:-VALUE;`**` }`
	
	Right-extended Float
	`SELECTOR { float:LEFT_OR_RIGHT; `**`margin-right:+VALUE;`**` }`
	
	Right-retracted Float
	`SELECTOR { float:LEFT_OR_RIGHT; `**`margin-right:-VALUE;`**` }`

Vertical Patterns	**Top-extended Float**
	`SELECTOR { float:LEFT_OR_RIGHT; `**`margin-top:+VALUE;`**` }`
	
	Top-retracted Float
	`SELECTOR { float:LEFT_OR_RIGHT; `**`margin-top:-VALUE;`**` }`
	
	Bottom-extended Float
	`SELECTOR { float:LEFT_OR_RIGHT; `**`margin-bottom:+VALUE;`**` }`
	
	Bottom-retracted Float
	`SELECTOR { float:LEFT_OR_RIGHT; `**`margin-bottom:-VALUE;`**` }`

Location	This pattern applies to all elements.
Advantages	Floats can create versatile layouts. These layouts easily reflow to fit displays of all sizes.
Disadvantages	Floats tend to trigger browser bugs in all browsers.
Tips	Stacking floats to the left or right aligns floats, and extending or retracting margins fine-tunes their position.
Related to	Float and Clear (Chapter 7); Outside-in Box, Floating Section, Float Divider, Fluid Layout, Opposing Floats (Chapter 17); Floating Dropcap, Floating Graphic Dropcap (Chapter 18); Left Floating Callout, Right Floating Callout (Chapter 19); Floating Alert (Chapter 20)

Offset Absolute and Offset Fixed

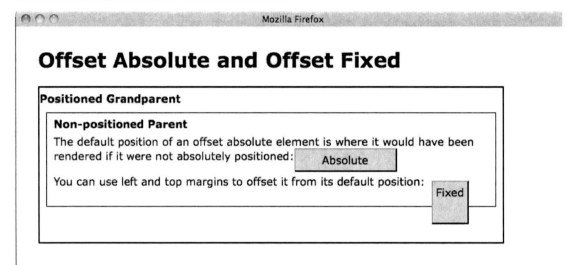

HTML

```
<h1>Offset Absolute and Offset Fixed</h1>

<div class="gp"><h2>Positioned Grandparent</h2>
  <div class="parent"><h2>Non-positioned Parent</h2>
    The default position of an offset absolute element is where it would have
    been rendered if it were not absolutely positioned:
    <span id="absolute" class="border">Absolute</span>

    <p>You can use left and top margins to offset it from its
    default position: <span id="fixed" class="border">Fixed</span></p>
  </div>
</div>
```

CSS

```
#absolute { position:absolute; width:140px; height:auto; }

#fixed { position:fixed;
  height:50px; margin-top:10px;
  width:auto; margin-left:10px; }

/* Nonessential rules are not shown. */
```

Offset Absolute and Offset Fixed

Problem	You want to remove an element from the normal flow and offset it from the position it would have had in the flow. Unlike the Offset Relative design pattern, you don't want the element to retain the exact shape it would have had in the normal flow. Instead, you want it to be rendered as a block that can be sized or shrinkwrapped. You optionally want the element to be fixed to the viewport so it doesn't scroll when the document scrolls.
Solution	**Use `position:absolute`** to position the element absolutely or **`position:fixed`** to lock its position so it doesn't scroll with the document. Don't set left, right, top, or bottom to a value other than auto, or you'll align the element to its closest positioned ancestor. Because auto is their default value, you can omit left, right, top, and bottom.
	Use `margin-top` and `margin-left` to offset the element from the position it would have had in the normal flow. Positive values move it down and right, and negative values move it up and left. You can use width:auto or height:auto to shrinkwrap the element, or you can use width:+VALUE or height:+VALUE to size it.
Patterns	**Shrinkwrapped-offset Absolute Element**
| | ```
SELECTOR { position:ABSOLUTE_FIXED;
    height:auto; width:auto;
    margin-top:±VALUE; margin-left:±VALUE; }
``` |
| | **Sized-offset Absolute Element** |
| | ```
SELECTOR { position:ABSOLUTE_FIXED;
    height:+VALUE; width:+VALUE;
    margin-top:±VALUE; margin-left:±VALUE; }
``` |
Location	This pattern applies to all elements.
Advantages	This pattern allows you to remove an element from the normal flow, shrinkwrap or size it, and then offset it *from the position it would have had in the normal flow*. Contrast this with the Aligned and Offset Absolute design pattern, where an absolute element is aligned and offset from an edge of its closest positioned ancestor.
Tips	The horizontal and vertical dimensions are independent. You can shrinkwrap one dimension and size the other. You can also align one dimension to an edge of the closest positioned ancestor and offset the other dimension from the position it would have had in the normal flow.
Example	Notice how both the absolute and the fixed spans are located in the flow where they would have been located if they were not positioned. Margins vertically and horizontally offset the fixed span by 10 pixels.
Related to	Aligned and Offset Absolute; Sized, Shrinkwrapped (Chapter 5); Margin (Chapter 6); Positioned, Closest Positioned Ancestor, Absolute, Fixed (Chapter 7)

Offset Relative

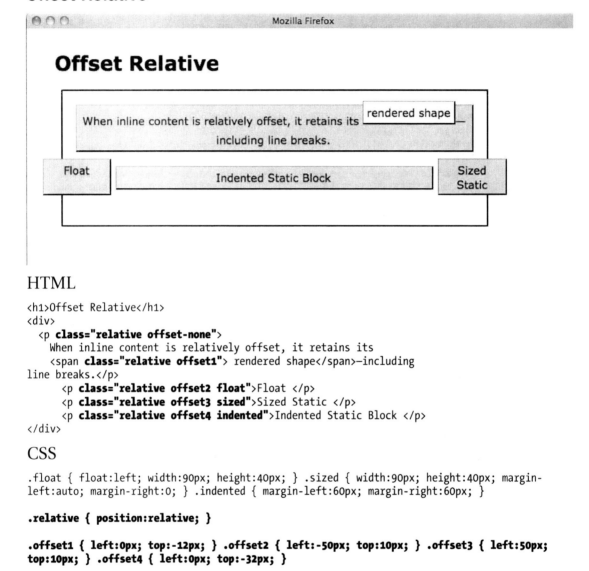

HTML

```
<h1>Offset Relative</h1>
<div>
  <p class="relative offset-none">
    When inline content is relatively offset, it retains its
    <span class="relative offset1"> rendered shape</span>—including
line breaks.</p>
      <p class="relative offset2 float">Float </p>
      <p class="relative offset3 sized">Sized Static </p>
      <p class="relative offset4 indented">Indented Static Block </p>
</div>
```

CSS

```
.float { float:left; width:90px; height:40px; } .sized { width:90px; height:40px; margin-
left:auto; margin-right:0; } .indented { margin-left:60px; margin-right:60px; }

.relative { position:relative; }

.offset1 { left:0px; top:-12px; } .offset2 { left:-50px; top:10px; } .offset3 { left:50px;
top:10px; } .offset4 { left:0px; top:-32px; }

/* Nonessential rules are not shown. */
```

Offset Relative

Problem	You want to offset an element up, down, left, or right from its position in the normal flow or floating flow. You want the offset to have no effect on the position of other elements. And unlike the Offset Absolute and Offset Fixed design patterns, you want the element to retain the exact shape (size, line breaks, line spacing, and so on) that it would have had in the normal flow.
Solution	A *relative element* is a float or static element that is set to `position:relative`. It's initially positioned by the normal or floating flow.
	You can use `top` and `left` to offset it from this position. Positive values move it down and right, and negative values move it up and left. Unlike an element's margins, *relative offsets* have absolutely no effect on the position of other elements.
	A relative element is rendered in a layer without leaving the flow. This allows you to overlap elements and control their stacking order using `z-index`. A relative element is positioned, which allows absolute descendants to be positioned relative to it. A relative element is *atomic*, which means external elements can't be layered in between its static descendants, inline content, and its background. If `z-index` is set to a nonzero value, a relative element creates its own stacking context, which means no external elements can be layered between any of its descendants even if they're positioned.
Patterns	`SELECTOR { position:relative; top:±VALUE; left:±VALUE; z-index:+VALUE }`
Location	This pattern applies to all elements.
Limitations	A relative element can't be absolute or fixed at the same time.
Example	Notice in the example how the inline span retains its shape when offset relatively. Also notice how the left float is relatively offset to the left by 50 pixels, the sized static block is offset to the right by 50 pixels, and both are lowered 10 pixels. The indented static block is raised 32 pixels to fit between the float and the sized static block.
Related to	Positioned, Closest Positioned Ancestor, Static, Absolute, Fixed, Relative, Relative Float (Chapter 7); Nested Alignment (Chapter 12); Floating Dropcap, Floating Graphic Dropcap (Chapter 18); Left Floating Callout, Right Floating Callout, Center Callout, Block Quote (Chapter 19)

Aligned Static Inline

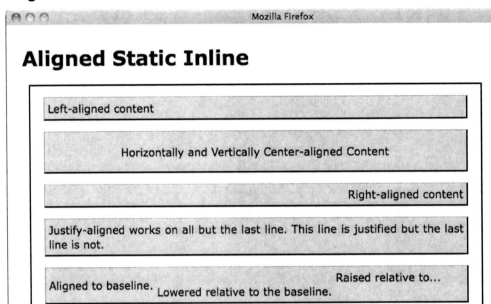

HTML

```
<h1>Aligned Static Inline</h1>
<div>
  <p id="l">Left-aligned content</p>
  <p id="c">Horizontally and Vertically Center-aligned Content</p>
  <p id="r">Right-aligned content</p>
  <p id="j">Justify-aligned works on all but the last line. This line is
    justified but the last line is not.</p>
    <p><span class="baseline">Aligned to baseline.</span>
      <span class="lowered">Lowered relative to the baseline.</span>
      <span class="raised">Raised relative to... </span></p></div>
```

CSS

```
.baseline { vertical-align:baseline; } .raised { vertical-align:10px; } .lowered { vertical-
align:-10px; }

#l { position:static; text-align:left; } #c { position:static; text-align:center; line-
height:48px; } #r { position:static; text-align:right; } #j { position:static; text-
align:justify; }

/* Nonessential rules are not shown. */
```

Aligned Static Inline

Problem	You want to align static inline elements horizontally and/or vertically, and you want to offset them from their alignment.
Solution	**To horizontally align content to the sides of its terminal block container,** you can use text-align. text-align:left aligns content to the left side. text-align:right aligns content to the right side. text-align:center centers content. text-align:justify aligns content to the left and right sides of its container. For content to be justified, there must be more than one line, because the browser doesn't justify the last line.
	To align inline content to the vertical center of a line, you can set line-height to a value larger than the height of the content. This works because a browser vertically centers the content of each line. This effect doesn't work when you have more than one line.
	To align inline content vertically, you can use vertical-align:CONSTANT or vertical-align:±VALUE. The only time you can see the vertical alignment is when items in the same line have different heights or different vertical alignment. Vertical alignment doesn't persist between lines because a browser shrinkwraps and vertically centers the content of each line. Thus, inline vertical alignment is relative to the content actually present in a line.

Horizontal Patterns	**Left-aligned Static Inline Element**
	`TERMINAL-BLOCK-SELECTOR { position:static; text-align:left; }`
	
	Center-aligned Static Inline Element
	`TERMINAL-BLOCK-SELECTOR { position:static; text-align:center; }`
	
	Right-aligned Static Inline Element
	`TERMINAL-BLOCK-SELECTOR { position:static; text-align:right; }`
	
	Justified Static Inline Element
	`TERMINAL-BLOCK-SELECTOR { position:static; text-align:justify; }`

Vertical Patterns	**Middle-aligned Static Inline Element**
	`SELECTOR { position:static; line-height:+VALUE; }`
	
	Relative-aligned Static Inline Element
	`SELECTOR { position:static; vertical-align:±VALUE; }`

Location	These patterns work on inline elements.
Related to	Aligned and Offset Static Block; Left Aligned, Left Offset, Right Aligned, Right Offset, Center Aligned, Center Offset (Chapter 9); Invisible Text (Chapter 10); Spacing, Blocked (Chapter 11); Horizontal-aligned Content (Chapter 12); Table (Chapter 15)

Aligned and Offset Static Block

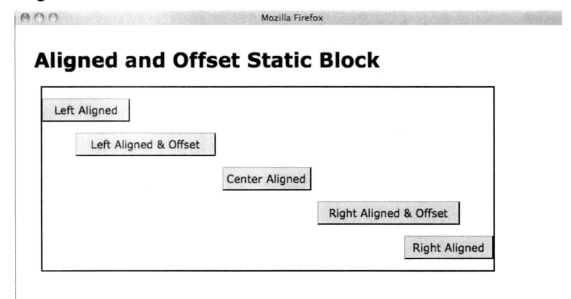

HTML

```
<h1>Aligned and Offset Static Block</h1>
<div class="gp">
  <p id="left">Left Aligned</p>
  <p id="left-off">Left Aligned &amp; Offset</p>
  <p id="center">Center Aligned</p>
  <p id="right-off">Right Aligned &amp; Offset</p>
  <p id="right">Right Aligned</p>
</div>
```

CSS

```
#left { position:static; width:120px; margin-left:0; margin-right:auto; }
#left-off { position:static; width:200px; margin-left:50px; margin-right:auto; }
#center { position:static; width:120px; margin-left:auto; margin-right:auto; }
#right { position:static; width:120px; margin-left:auto; margin-right:0; }
#right-off { position:static; width:200px; margin-left:auto; margin-right:50px; }

/* Nonessential rules are not shown. */
```

Aligned and Offset Static Block

Problem	You want to align a static block element to the left side, right side, or center of its parent, and you want to offset it from its alignment.
Solution	*Sized* blocks can be aligned and offset from their container. Static blocks can't be horizontally shrinkwrapped, and thus are either sized or stretched. If a block is stretched, it can't be aligned and offset because it's indented. Use `width:+VALUE` to specify an element's width. You can't align a static block unless you set its width to a measurement or percentage.
	To align to the left side, use `margin-right:auto` to align the element to the left side. Use `margin-left:+VALUE` to offset the element to the right of the left side. Use `margin-left:-VALUE` to offset the element to the left of the left side.
	To align to the center, use both `margin-left:auto` and `margin-right:auto` to horizontally center the element within its container.
	To align to the right side, use `margin-left:auto` to align the element to the right side. Use `margin-right:+VALUE` to offset the element to the right of the right side. Use `margin-right:-VALUE` to offset the element to the left of the right side.

Patterns	**Left-aligned Sized Static Block Element**
	`BLOCK-SELECTOR { position:static; width:+VALUE;`
	`    margin-left:±VALUE; margin-right:auto; }`
	Center-aligned Sized Static Block Element
	`BLOCK-SELECTOR { position:static; width:+VALUE;`
	`    margin-left:auto; margin-right:auto; }`
	Right-aligned Sized Static Block Element
	`BLOCK-SELECTOR { position:static; width:+VALUE;`
	`    margin-left:auto; margin-right:±VALUE; }`

Location	This pattern works on static block elements.
Explanation	A static element expands to fill the width of its container. When you set the width of a static element, its width no longer fills the container. Instead, its margins expand to fill the container. You can use the `auto` value to control which margins expand. `margin-left:auto` automatically expands the left margin to let the element align to the right. Conversely, `margin-right:auto` expands the right margin to let the element align to the left. `margin-left:auto` and `margin-right:auto` automatically expand both margins equally to center the element.
Limitations	You can't vertically align a static block element because it's always aligned to the top of its parent block or below its previous sibling.
Related to	Aligned Static Inline; Sized (Chapter 5); Left Aligned, Left Offset, Right Aligned, Right Offset, Center Aligned, Center Offset (Chapter 9); Left Marginal, Right Marginal (Chapter 13); Marginal Dropcap, Marginal Graphic Dropcap (Chapter 18); Left Marginal Callout, Right Marginal Callout (Chapter 19); Left Marginal Alert, Right Marginal Alert (Chapter 20)

Aligned and Offset Static Table

HTML

```
<h1>Aligned Static Table</h1>
<div class="parent">
  <table class="l-wrap"><tr><td>Left-aligned Shrinkwrapped Table</td></tr></table>
  <table class="c-wrap"><tr><td>Centered Shrinkwrapped Table</td></tr></table>
  <table class="r-wrap"><tr><td>Right-offset Shrinkwrapped Table</td></tr></table>
  <table class="stretched"><tr><td>Stretched Table</td></tr></table>
  <table class="r-sized"><tr><td>Right-aligned Sized Table</td></tr></table>
  <table class="c-sized"><tr><td>Centered Sized Table</td></tr></table>
  <table class="l-sized"><tr><td>Left-offset Sized Table</td></tr></table>
</div>
```

CSS

```
.l-wrap { width:auto; margin-left:0; margin-right:auto; } .c-wrap { width:auto; margin-
left:auto; margin-right:auto;} .r-wrap { width:auto; margin-left:auto; margin-right:20px; }

.stretched { width:100%; margin-left:0; margin-right:0; }

.r-sized { width:350px; margin-left:auto; margin-right:0; text-align:right; } .c-sized {
width:350px; margin-left:auto; margin-right:auto; text-align:center; } .l-sized { width:350px;
margin-left:20px; margin-right:auto; text-align:left; }

/* Nonessential rules are not shown. */
```

Aligned and Offset Static Table

Problem	You want to align a shrinkwrapped, stretched, or sized table *without* removing it from the normal flow.
Solution	The table is the only element in the normal flow that can shrinkwrap to fit the width of its content or be sized to a specific width. Block elements can't be shrinkwrapped to their width unless they're positioned or floated. Inline elements can't be sized unless they're positioned or floated.
	Because a table can be shrinkwrapped, sized, and stretched, it's the most versatile element. It can also be aligned to the left, right, or center while it's shrinkwrapped or sized.
	To align a table to the left, use margin-left:0 and margin-right:auto.
	To align a table to the right, use margin-left:auto and margin-right:0.
	To align a table to the center, use margin-left:auto and margin-right:auto.
	To offset a table, change the margin to a nonzero value. A positive value offsets toward the center, and a negative offsets away from the center.
HTML Pattern	`<table><tr><td>CONTENT</td></tr></table>`

CSS Patterns	**Left-aligned Shrinkwrapped Static Table**
	`SELECTOR { position:static; width:auto; margin-left:0; margin-right:auto; }`
	
	Centered Shrinkwrapped Static Table
	`SELECTOR { position:static; width:auto; margin-left:auto; margin-right:auto; }`
	
	Right-aligned Shrinkwrapped Static Table
	`SELECTOR { position:static; width:auto; margin-left:auto; margin-right:0; }`
	
	Stretched Static Table
	`SELECTOR { position:static; width:100%; margin-left:0; margin-right:0; }`
	
	Left-aligned Sized Static Table
	`SELECTOR { position:static; width:+VALUE; margin-left:0; margin-right:auto; }`
	
	Centered Sized Static Table
	`SELECTOR { position:static; width:+VALUE; margin-left:auto; margin-right:auto; }`
	
	Right-aligned Sized Static Table
	`SELECTOR { position:static; width:+VALUE; margin-left:auto; margin-right:0; }`

Location	This pattern applies to table elements.
Related to	Sized, Shrinkwrapped, Stretched (Chapter 5); Left Aligned, Left Offset, Right Aligned, Right Offset, Center Aligned, Center Offset (Chapter 9); Table (Chapter 15)

Aligned and Offset Absolute

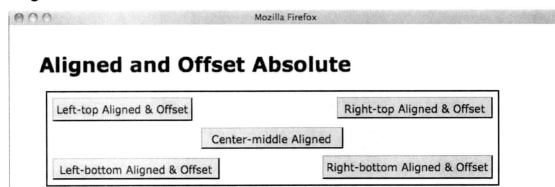

HTML

```
<h1>Aligned and Offset Absolute</h1>
<div>
  <p id="lt">Left-top Aligned &amp; Offset</p>
  <p id="lb">Left-bottom Aligned &amp; Offset</p>
  <p id="cm">Center-middle Aligned</p>
  <p id="rt">Right-top Aligned &amp; Offset</p>
  <p id="rb">Right-bottom Aligned &amp; Offset</p>
</div>
```

CSS

```
div { position:relative; }

#lt { position:absolute;
  width:auto; left:0; margin-left:8px; right:auto; margin-right:auto;
  height:auto; top:0; margin-top:8px; bottom:auto; margin-bottom:auto; }
#lb { position:absolute;
  width:240px; left:0; margin-left:8px; right:auto; margin-right:auto;
  height:18px; top:auto; margin-top:auto; bottom:0; margin-bottom:8px; }
#cm { position:absolute;
  width:200px; left:0; margin-left:auto; right:0; margin-right:auto;
  height:18px; top:0; margin-top:auto; bottom:0; margin-bottom:auto; }
#rt { position:absolute;
  width:220px; left:auto; margin-left:auto; right:0; margin-right:8px;
  height:18px; top:0; margin-top:8px; bottom:auto; margin-bottom:auto; }
#rb { position:absolute;
  width:auto; left:auto; margin-left:auto; right:0; margin-right:8px;
  height:auto; top:auto; margin-top:auto; bottom:0; margin-bottom:8px; }

/* Nonessential rules are not shown. */
```

Aligned and Offset Absolute

Problem	You want to align an absolutely positioned element to the left, right, top, or bottom of its closest positioned ancestor. You also want to offset it from its alignment. You also want to size or shrinkwrap the element.
Solution	Apply styles to your chosen class or ID as follows:

Use **width:+VALUE and height:+VALUE** to size the element.
Use **width:auto and height:auto** to shrinkwrap the element.

To offset from the left side:
Use **left:0 and right:auto** to align an element to the left.
Use **margin-left:+VALUE** to offset the element to the right of the left side.
Use **margin-left:-VALUE** to offset the element to the left of the left side.

To offset from the right side:
Use **right:0 and left:auto** to align an element to the right.
Use **margin-right:+VALUE** to offset the element to the left of the right side.
Use **margin-right:-VALUE** to offset the element to the right of the right side.

To offset from the top:
Use **top:0 and bottom:auto** to align an element to the top.
Use **margin-top:+VALUE** to offset the element below the top.
Use **margin-top:-VALUE** to offset the element above the top.

To offset from the bottom:
Use **bottom:0 and top:auto** to align an element to the bottom.
Use **margin-bottom:+VALUE** to offset the element above the bottom.
Use **margin-bottom:-VALUE** to offset the element below the bottom.

Patterns	**Left-offset Absolute Element**

```
SELECTOR { position:absolute; left:0; right:auto;
  margin-left:±VALUE; margin-right:auto; }
```

Right-offset Absolute Element

```
SELECTOR { position:absolute; left:auto; right:0;
  margin-left:auto; margin-right:±VALUE; }
```

Top-offset Absolute Element

```
SELECTOR { position:absolute; top:0; bottom:auto;
  margin-top:±VALUE; margin-bottom:auto; }
```

Bottom-offset Absolute Element

```
SELECTOR { position:absolute; top:auto; bottom:0;
  margin-top:auto; margin-bottom:±VALUE; }
```

Location	This pattern applies to all elements.

Aligned and OffsetAbsolute cont.

Example	Each absolute element in the example is shrinkwrapped. Each could be sized without affecting the alignment or the offset. The centered element is discussed in the next design pattern—Aligned-center Absolute. I included it in the example because it's a combination of all four of these design patterns.
Related to	Sized, Shrinkwrapped (Chapter 5); Margin (Chapter 6); Positioned, Closest Positioned Ancestor, Absolute, Fixed (Chapter 7); all design patterns in Chapter 9; Text Replacement, Screenreader Only (Chapter 10); Left Marginal, Right Marginal (Chapter 13); Content-over Image, Content-over Background Image (Chapter 14); Flyout Menu (Chapter 17); Marginal Dropcap, Marginal Graphic Dropcap (Chapter 18); Left Marginal Callout, Right Marginal Callout (Chapter 19); Popup Alert, Graphical Alert, Left Marginal Alert, Right Marginal Alert (Chapter 20)

Aligned-center Absolute

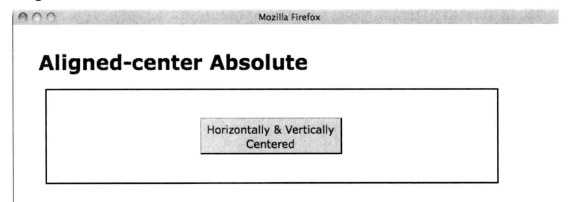

HTML

```
<h1>Aligned-center Absolute</h1>
<div>
  <p id="cm" class="hc vc">Horizontally &amp; Vertically Centered</p>
</div>
```

CSS

```
div { position:relative; }
#cm { position:absolute; }

.hc { width:200px; left:0; margin-left:auto; right:0; margin-right:auto; } .vc { height:40px;
top:0; margin-top:auto; bottom:0; margin-bottom:auto; }

/* Nonessential rules are not shown. */
```

Aligned-center Absolute

Problem	You want to align an absolutely positioned element to the horizontal and/or vertical center of its closest positioned ancestor.
Solution	Apply styles to your chosen class or ID as follows:
	To horizontally center:
	Use **width:+VALUE** to specify the element's width.
	Use **left:0 and right:0** to align the element to the left and right sides.
	Use **margin-left:auto and margin-right:auto** to center the element.
	To vertically center:
	Use **height:+VALUE** to specify the element's height.
	Use **top:0 and bottom:0** to align the element to the top and bottom.
	Use **margin-top:auto and margin-bottom:auto** to center the element.
Patterns	**Vertically Aligned-center Absolute Element**
	`SELECTOR { position:absolute; left:0; right:0;` `    margin-left:auto; margin-right:auto; }`
	Horizontally Aligned-center Absolute Element
	`SELECTOR { position:absolute; left:0; right:0;` `    margin-left:auto; margin-right:auto; }`
Location	This pattern applies to all elements.
Limitations	This pattern doesn't work in Internet Explorer 7 (and earlier versions) because it doesn't support aligning to the left and right sides at the same time, and it doesn't support aligning to the top and bottom sides at the same time.
Explanation	This is an extension of the Aligned and Offset Absolute design pattern. It aligns an element to the sides of its closest positioned ancestor and then uses automatic margins to center it. The element must be sized for automatic margins to work.
Related to	Indented; Positioned, Closest Positioned Ancestor, Absolute, Fixed (Chapter 7); Center Aligned, Center Offset, Middle Aligned, Middle Offset (Chapter 9)

Aligned Outside

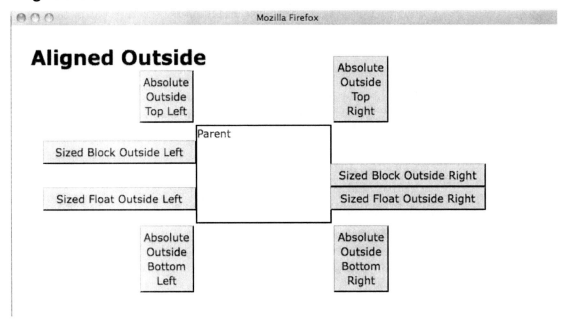

HTML

```
<h1>Aligned Outside</h1>
<div class="parent">Parent
  <p class="sized-block-outside-left">Sized Block Outside Left</p>
  <p class="sized-block-outside-right">Sized Block Outside Right</p>
  <p class="sized-float-outside-left">Sized Float Outside Left</p>
  <p class="sized-float-outside-right">Sized Float Outside Right</p>
  <p class="top left">Absolute Outside Top Left</p>
  <p class="top right">Absolute Outside Top Right</p>
  <p class="bottom left">Absolute Outside Bottom Left</p>
  <p class="bottom right">Absolute Outside Bottom Right</p>
</div>
```

CSS

```
.parent { position:relative; height:140px; width:200px; }

.sized-block-outside-left { width:220px; margin-left:-234px; } .sized-block-outside-right {
width:220px; margin-left:100%; } .sized-float-outside-left { width:220px; margin-left:-234px;
float:left; } .sized-float-outside-right { width:220px; margin-left:100%; float:left; }

.left { position:absolute; right:100%; margin-right:5px; } .right { position:absolute;
left:100%; margin-left:5px; } .top { position:absolute; bottom:100%; margin-bottom:5px; }
.bottom { position:absolute; top:100%; margin-top:5px; }

/* Nonessential rules are not shown. */
```

Aligned Outside

Problem	You want to align an element to the *outside* of its container. For example, you want to align the left side of an element to the right side of its container, or vice versa. Or you want to align the bottom of an element to the top of its container, or vice versa.
Solution	You can align an *absolute* element to the outside of any of the four sides of its closest positioned ancestor. Because 100% is the width of an element's container, offsetting an element 100% from one side aligns it to the outside of the other side. In addition, you can use margin to offset the element further. An aligned-outside absolute element can be sized or shrinkwrapped.
	You can align static blocks and floats to the outside left or right sides of their parent, but not to the top or bottom. They must be sized. The technique described previously can align blocks and floats to the outside right, but not to the outside left. To align blocks and floats to the outside left, you need to put the negative of the element's outer width in margin-left. The outer width is the inner width plus left and right padding and borders.

Patterns	**Sized Block Aligned Outside Left**
	
	`SELECTOR { width:INNER; margin-left:-OUTER; }`
	
	Sized Block Aligned Outside Right
	
	`SELECTOR { width:INNER; margin-left:100%; }`
	
	Sized Float Aligned Outside Left
	
	`SELECTOR { width:INNER; margin-left:-OUTER; float:left; }`
	
	Sized Float Aligned Outside Right
	
	`SELECTOR { width:INNER; margin-left:100%; float:left; }`
	
	Absolute Aligned Outside Left
	
	`SELECTOR { right:100%; margin-right:±OFFSET; position:absolute; }`
	
	Absolute Aligned Outside Right
	
	`SELECTOR { left:100%; margin-left:±OFFSET; position:absolute; }`
	
	Absolute Aligned Outside Top
	
	`SELECTOR { bottom:100%; margin-bottom:±OFFSET; position:absolute; }`
	
	Absolute Aligned Outside Bottom
	
	`SELECTOR { top:100%; margin-top:±OFFSET; position:absolute; }`

Location	This pattern applies to all elements when positioned absolutely.
Limitations	You can't align inline elements to the outside of their containers. You can't align static blocks or floats to the outside top or bottom of their containers. Internet Explorer 6 can't outside-align static blocks and floats, but later versions can.
Related to	Aligned and Offset Absolute; Sized, Shrinkwrapped (Chapter 5); Flyout Menu (Chapter 17)

CHAPTER 9

Positioning: Advanced

This is the third of three chapters on positioning. It combines the positioning techniques of the previous 2 chapters into 12 design patterns that align and offset static and positioned elements to the left, center, right, top, middle, or bottom of their container while stretching, sizing, or shrinkwrapping them. This chapter focuses on static and absolute positioned elements.

This chapter combines design patterns from Chapter 8 to align and offset elements from their containers. It also introduces new patterns to align and offset elements from the top, middle, and bottom of their containers. If you aren't already familiar with the design patterns in Chapters 5–8, you may want to review them. Because aligning and offsetting from the left and right sides are similar, you may want to skim over Right Aligned and Right Offset.

Chapter Outline

- **Left Aligned** shows how to align an element to the left side of its container.
- **Left Offset** shows how to offset a left-aligned element.
- **Right Aligned** shows how to align an element to the right side of its container.
- **Right Offset** shows how to offset a right-aligned element.
- **Center Aligned** shows how to align an element to the center of its container.
- **Center Offset** shows how to offset a center-aligned element.
- **Top Aligned** shows how to align an element to the top of its container.
- **Top Offset** shows how to offset a top-aligned element.
- **Bottom Aligned** shows how to align an element to the bottom of its container.
- **Bottom Offset** shows how to offset a bottom-aligned element.
- **Middle Aligned** shows how to align an element to the middle of its container.
- **Middle Offset** shows how to offset a middle-aligned element.

Left Aligned

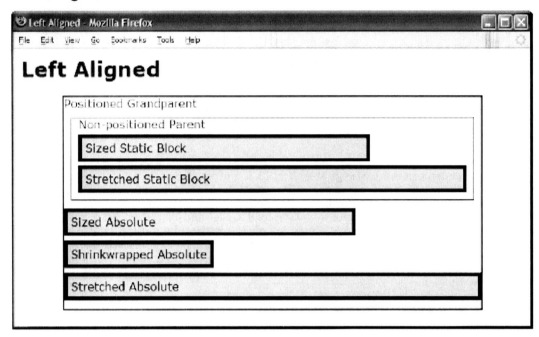

HTML

```
<h1>Left Aligned</h1>
<div class="gp">Positioned Grandparent
  <div class="parent">Non-positioned Parent
    <div  id="zs" class="example">Sized Static Block </div>
    <div  id="ss" class="example">Stretched Static Block</div>
    <span id="za" class="example">Sized Absolute</span>
    <span id="wa" class="example">Shrinkwrapped Absolute</span>
    <span id="sa" class="example">Stretched Absolute</span></div></div>
```

CSS

```
.gp { position:relative; height:295px; width:600px; border:2px solid black;  }
.parent  { margin:10px; padding:10px; padding-top:0; border:1px solid black; }
.example { padding:5px;  border:5px solid black;  background-color:gold;      }

#zs { position:static;          text-align:left;                    margin-top:5px;
width:400px;                    margin-left:0;        margin-right:auto; }
#ss { position:static;          text-align:left;                    margin-top:5px;
width:auto;                     margin-left:0;        margin-right:0;    }
#za { position:absolute;        text-align:left;            top:0; margin-top:155px;
width:400px;  left:0;           margin-left:0; right:auto; margin-right:auto; }
#wa { position:absolute;        text-align:left;             top:0; margin-top:200px;
width:auto;    left:0;          margin-left:0; right:auto; margin-right:auto; }
#sa { position:absolute;        text-align:left;            top:0; margin-top:245px;
width:auto;left:0;              margin-left:0; right:0;    margin-right:0;    }
```

Left Aligned

Problem	You want to align an element and its content to the left side of its parent or closest positioned ancestor.
Solution	**To left-align content**, assign `text-align:left` to the containing block.
	To create a left-aligned *sized* **element**, you can use `width:+VALUE` to size it. You can use `margin-left:0` to align it to the left side. You can use `margin-right:auto` to prevent it from aligning to the right side. For an absolute element, you can also use `left:0` to align the element to the left side and `right:auto` to prevent it from aligning to the right side.
	To create a left-aligned *stretched* **element**, you can use `width:auto`, `margin-left:0`, and `margin-right:0` to stretch its width to the sides of its container. For an absolute element, you can also use `left:0` and `right:0` to stretch it to the left and right sides.
	To create a left-aligned *shrinkwrapped* **element**, you can use `width:auto`, `right:auto`, and `margin-right:auto` to shrinkwrap the width. You can use `left:0` and `margin-left:0` to align it to the left side.
Patterns	**Left-aligned sized static block**

```
BLOCK-SELECTOR { position:static;      text-align:left;
                 width:+VALUE;         margin-left:0;
                                       margin-right:auto; }
```

Left-aligned stretched static block

```
BLOCK-SELECTOR { position:static;      text-align:left;
                 width:auto;           margin-left:0;
                                       margin-right:0;    }
```

Left-aligned sized absolute element

```
SELECTOR { position:absolute;          text-align:left;
           width:+VALUE;  left:0;      margin-left:0;
                          right:auto;  margin-right:auto; }
```

Left-aligned shrinkwrapped absolute element

```
SELECTOR { position:absolute;          text-align:left;
           width:auto;    left:0;      margin-left:0;
                          right:auto;  margin-right:auto; }
```

Left-aligned stretched absolute element

```
SELECTOR { position:absolute;          text-align:left;
           width:auto;    left:0;      margin-left:0;
                          right:0;     margin-right:0;    }
```

Location	This pattern applies to all elements.
Limitations	Stretched Absolute patterns don't work in Internet Explorer prior to version 7.
Related to	Left Offset, Right Aligned, Center Aligned; Static, Absolute (Chapter 7); Sized, Shrinkwrapped, Stretched (Chapter 5); Aligned design patterns in Chapter 8

Left Offset

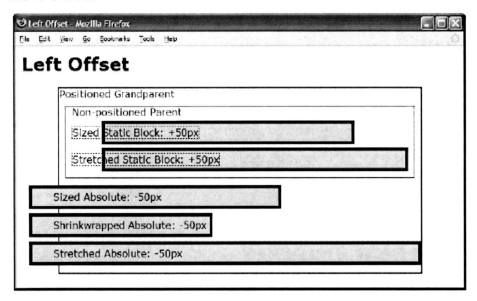

HTML

```
<h1>Left Offset</h1>
<div class="gp">Positioned Grandparent
 <div class="parent">Non-positioned Parent
  <div  id="zs" class="ex"><span>Sized Static Block: +50px</span></div>
  <div  id="ss" class="ex"><span>Stretched Static Block: +50px</span></div>
  <span id="za" class="ex"><span>Sized Absolute: -50px</span></span>
  <span id="wa" class="ex"><span>Shrinkwrapped Absolute: -50px</span></span>
  <span id="sa" class="ex"><span>Stretched Absolute:-50px</span></span></div></div>
```

CSS

```
.gp { position:relative; height:295px; width:600px; border:2px solid black;  }
.parent   { margin:10px; padding:10px; padding-top:0; border:1px solid black; }
.ex       { padding:5px;  border:5px solid black;  background-color:gold;        }
div.ex  span { margin-left:-60px; border:1px dotted black; }
span.ex span { margin-left:30px;  border:none;            }

#zs { position:static;        text-align:left;                    margin-top:5px;
       width:400px;           margin-left:50px;        margin-right:auto; }
#ss { position:static;        text-align:left;                    margin-top:5px;
       width:auto;            margin-left:50px;        margin-right:0;    }
#za { position:absolute;      text-align:left;         top:0; margin-top:155px;
       width:400px;  left:0;  margin-left:-50px;  right:auto;  margin-right:auto;}
#wa { position:absolute;      text-align:left;         top:0; margin-top:200px;
       width:auto;   left:0;  margin-left:-50px;  right:auto; margin-right:auto;}
#sa { position:absolute;      text-align:left;         top:0; margin-top:245px;
       width:auto;   left:0;  margin-left:-50px;  right:0;    margin-right:0    }
```

Left Offset

Problem	You want to offset an element and its content from the left side of its parent or closest positioned ancestor.
Solution	To offset a left-aligned element from its left side, you can assign a value other than zero to `margin-left`. A positive value in `margin-left` offsets to the right (toward the inside), and a negative value offsets to the left (toward the outside). This design pattern is symmetrical to the Right Offset pattern in every way. See the Left Aligned design pattern for details on how to left-align an element.

Patterns

Left-offset sized static block

```
BLOCK-SELECTOR { position:static;          text-align:left;
   width:+VALUE; margin-left:±VALUE;        margin-right:auto; }
```

Left-offset stretched static block

```
BLOCK-SELECTOR { position:static;          text-align:left;
   width:auto;    margin-left:±VALUE;       margin-right:0;     }
```

Left-offset sized absolute element

```
SELECTOR { position:absolute;              text-align:left;
           width:+VALUE;  left:0;          margin-left:±VALUE;
                          right:auto;       margin-right:auto; }
```

Left-offset shrinkwrapped absolute element

```
SELECTOR { position:absolute;              text-align:left;
           width:auto;    left:0;          margin-left:±VALUE;
                          right:auto;       margin-right:auto; }
```

Left-offset stretched absolute element

```
SELECTOR { position:absolute;              text-align:left;
           width:auto;    left:0;          margin-left:±VALUE;
                          right:0;          margin-right:0;     }
```

Location	This pattern applies to all elements.
Limitations	Stretched Absolute patterns don't work in Internet Explorer for versions prior to 7. Inline text can't extend outside a *sized* block in Internet Explorer version 6 or 7.
Related to	Left Aligned, Right Offset, Center Offset; Offset and Aligned design patterns in Chapter 8

Right Aligned

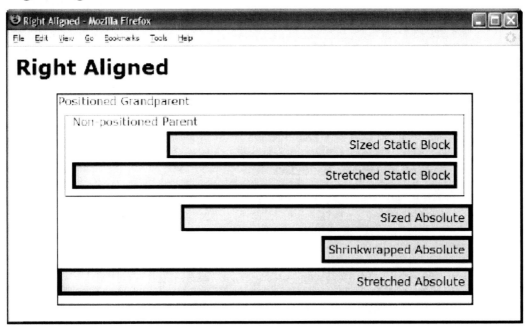

HTML

```
<h1>Right Aligned</h1>
<div class="gp">Positioned Grandparent
  <div class="parent">Non-positioned Parent
    <div  id="zs" class="example">Sized Static Block </div>
    <div  id="ss" class="example">Stretched Static Block</div>
    <span id="za" class="example">Sized Absolute</span>
    <span id="wa" class="example">Shrinkwrapped Absolute</span>
    <span id="sa" class="example">Stretched Absolute</span></div></div>
```

CSS

```
.gp { position:relative; height:295px; width:600px; border:2px solid black;  }
.parent  { margin:10px; padding:10px; padding-top:0; border:1px solid black; }
.example { padding:5px;  border:5px solid black;  background-color:gold;      }

#zs { position:static;        text-align:right;                    margin-top:5px;
        width:400px;          margin-left:auto;     margin-right:0;            }
#ss { position:static;        text-align:right;                    margin-top:5px;
        width:auto;           margin-left:0;        margin-right:0;            }
#za { position:absolute;      text-align:right;         top:0; margin-top:155px;
        width:400px;  left:auto; margin-left:auto; right:0; margin-right:0;    }
#wa { position:absolute;      text-align:right;         top:0; margin-top:200px;
        width:auto;   left:auto; margin-left:auto; right:0; margin-right:0;    }
#sa { position:absolute;      text-align:right;                top:0; margin-top:245px;
        width:auto;   left:0;   margin-left:0;     right:0; margin-right:0;    }
```

Right Aligned

Problem	You want to align an element and its content to the right side of its parent or closest positioned ancestor.
Solution	This design pattern is symmetrical to Left Aligned in every way. To **right-align content**, assign `text-align:right` to the containing block. To create a **right-aligned** *sized* element, you can use `width:+VALUE` to size it. You can use `margin-right:0` to align it to the right side. You can use `margin-left:auto` to prevent it from aligning to the left side. For an absolute element, you can also use `right:0` to align the element to the right side and `left:auto` to prevent it from aligning to the left side. To create a **right-aligned** *stretched* element, you can use `width:auto`, `margin-left:0`, and `margin-right:0` to stretch its width to the sides of its container. For an absolute element, you can also use `left:0` and `right:0` to stretch it to the left and right sides. To create a **right-aligned** *shrinkwrapped* element, you can use `width:auto`, `left:auto`, and `margin-left:auto` to shrinkwrap the width. You can use `right:0` and `margin-right:0` to align it to the right side.
| **Patterns** | **Right-aligned sized static block**<br><br>```
BLOCK-SELECTOR { position:static;      text-align:right;
                width:+VALUE;          margin-left:auto;
                                       margin-right:0; }
```<br>**Right-aligned stretched static block**<br><br>```
BLOCK-SELECTOR { position:static;      text-align:right;
                width:auto;            margin-left:0;
                                       margin-right:0; }
```<br>**Right-aligned sized absolute element**<br><br>```
SELECTOR { position:absolute;          text-align:right;
           width:+VALUE;  left:auto;   margin-left:auto;
                          right:0;      margin-right:0; }
```<br>**Right-aligned shrinkwrapped absolute element**<br><br>```
SELECTOR { position:absolute;          text-align:right;
           width:auto;    left:auto;   margin-left:auto;
                          right:0;      margin-right:0; }
```<br>**Right-aligned stretched absolute element**<br><br>```
SELECTOR { position:absolute;          text-align:right;
           width:auto;    left:0;      margin-left:0;
                          right:0;      margin-right:0; }
``` |
Location	This pattern applies to all elements.
Limitations	Stretched Absolute doesn't work in Internet Explorer 6, but it does work in version 7.
Related to	Left Aligned, Right Offset, Center Aligned; Static, Absolute (Chapter 7); Sized, Shrinkwrapped, Stretched (Chapter 5); Aligned design patterns in Chapter 8
```

Right Offset

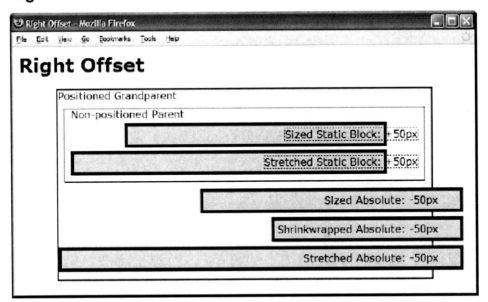

HTML

```
<h1>Right Offset</h1>
<div class="gp">Positioned Grandparent
 <div class="parent">Non-positioned Parent
  <div  id="zs" class="ex"><span>Sized Static Block: +50px</span></div>
  <div  id="ss" class="ex"><span>Stretched Static Block: +50px</span></div>
  <span id="za" class="ex"><span>Sized Absolute: -50px</span></span>
  <span id="wa" class="ex"><span>Shrinkwrapped Absolute: -50px</span></span>
  <span id="sa" class="ex"><span>Stretched Absolute:-50px</span></span></div></div>
```

CSS

```
.gp { position:relative; height:295px; width:600px; border:2px solid black;  }
.parent  { margin:10px; padding:10px; padding-top:0; border:1px solid black; }
.ex      { padding:5px;  border:5px solid black;  background-color:gold;       }
div.ex  span { margin-right:-60px; border:1px dotted black; }
span.ex span { margin-right:30px;  border:none;                }

#zs { position:static;          text-align:right;                     margin-top:5px;
          width:400px;          margin-left:auto;         margin-right:50px;       }
#ss { position:static;          text-align:right;                     margin-top:5px;
          width:auto;           margin-left:0;            margin-right:50px;       }
#za { position:absolute;        text-align:right;         top:0; margin-top:155px;
          width:400px; left:auto; margin-left:auto; right:0;  margin-right:-50px;  }
#wa { position:absolute;        text-align:right;         top:0; margin-top:200px;
          width:auto;  left:auto; margin-left:auto; right:0;  margin-right:-50px;  }
#sa { position:absolute;        text-align:right;         top:0; margin-top:245px;
          width:auto;  left:0;   margin-left:0;    right:0;   margin-right:-50px;  }
```

Right Offset

Problem	You want to align an element and its content to the right side of its parent or closest positioned ancestor.
Solution	To offset a right-aligned element from its right side, you can assign a value other than zero to `margin-right`. A positive value in `margin-right` offsets to the left (toward the inside), and a negative value offsets to the right (toward the outside). This design pattern is symmetrical to the Left Offset pattern in every way. See the Right Aligned design pattern for details on how to right-align an element.
| **Patterns** | **Right-offset sized static block**<br><br>```
BLOCK-SELECTOR { position:static;      text-align:right;
                width:+VALUE;          margin-left:auto;
                                       margin-right:±VALUE; }
```<br>**Right-offset stretched static block**<br><br>```
BLOCK-SELECTOR { position:static;      text-align:right;
                width:auto;            margin-left:0;
                                       margin-right:±VALUE; }
```<br>**Right-offset sized absolute element**<br><br>```
SELECTOR { position:absolute;          text-align:right;
           width:+VALUE;  left:auto;   margin-left:auto;
                          right:0;      margin-right:±VALUE; }
```<br>**Right-offset shrinkwrapped absolute element**<br><br>```
SELECTOR { position:absolute;          text-align:right;
           width:auto;   left:auto;    margin-left:auto;
                         right:0;       margin-right:±VALUE; }
```<br>**Right-offset stretched absolute element**<br><br>```
SELECTOR { position:absolute;          text-align:right;
           width:auto;   left:0;       margin-left:0;
                         right:0;       margin-right:±VALUE; }
``` |
Location	This pattern applies to all elements.
Limitations	Stretched Absolute doesn't work in Internet Explorer for versions prior to 7.
Related to	Left Offset, Right Aligned, Center Offset; Offset and Aligned design patterns in (Chapter 8)
```

Center Aligned

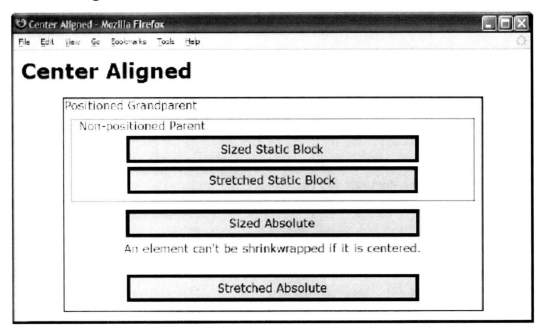

HTML

```
<h1>Center Aligned</h1>
<div class="gp">Positioned Grandparent
  <div class="parent">Non-positioned Parent
    <div  id="zs" class="example">Sized Static Block </div>
    <div  id="ss" class="example">Stretched Static Block</div>
    <span id="za" class="example">Sized Absolute</span>
    <span id="wa">An element can't be shrinkwrapped if it is centered.</span>
    <span id="sa" class="example">Stretched Absolute</span></div></div>
```

CSS

```
.gp { position:relative; height:295px; width:600px; border:2px solid black;  }
.parent  { margin:10px; padding:10px; padding-top:0; border:1px solid black; }
.example { padding:5px;  border:5px solid black;  background-color:gold;      }

#zs { position:static;       text-align:center;                  margin-top:5px;
      width:400px;           margin-left:auto;       margin-right:auto;  }
#ss { position:static;       text-align:center;                  margin-top:5px;
      width:auto;            margin-left:70px;        margin-right:70px;      }
#za { position:absolute;     text-align:center;    top:0; margin-top:155px;
       width:67%;  left:0;   margin-left:auto; right:0;  margin-right:auto;  }
#wa { position:absolute;     text-align:center;           top:0; margin-top:200px;
      width:auto;  left:0;   margin-left:0;    right:0;     margin-right:0;       }
#sa { position:absolute;     text-align:center;           top:0; margin-top:245px;
      width:auto;  left:0;   margin-left:15%;  right:0;     margin-right:15%;    }
```

Center Aligned

Problem	You want to align an element and its content to the horizontal center of its parent or closest positioned ancestor.
Solution	To **center-align content**, assign `text-align:center` to its containing block.
	To **create a center-aligned *sized* element**, you can use `margin-left:auto;` and `margin-right:auto;` and set `width:+VALUE` to size it. For absolute elements, you can also use `right:0` and `left:0` to align the element to the left and right sides.
	To **create a center-aligned *stretched* element**, set `margin-left` and `margin-right` to the same value. A larger value shrinks the element, and a smaller value grows it. For absolute stretched elements, you can also use `left:0` and `right:0`.

Patterns

Center-aligned sized static block

```
BLOCK-SELECTOR { position:static;      text-align:center;
                 width:+VALUE;          margin-left:auto;
                                        margin-right:auto;    }
```

Center-aligned stretched static block

```
BLOCK-SELECTOR { position:static;      text-align:center;
                 width:auto;            margin-left:+VALUE;
                                        margin-right:+VALUE; }
```

Center-aligned sized absolute element

```
SELECTOR { position:absolute;          text-align:center;
           width:+VALUE;  left:0;      margin-left:auto;
                          right:0;      margin-right:auto;    }
```

Center-aligned stretched absolute element

```
SELECTOR { position:absolute;          text-align:center;
           width:auto;   left:0;       margin-left:+VALUE;
                         right:0;       margin-right:+VALUE; }
```

Location	This pattern applies to all elements.
Limitations	A horizontally shrinkwrapped element can't be center aligned.
	Internet Explorer 6 can't center *absolute* elements; version 7 can center *stretched* absolute elements but still can't center *sized* absolute elements. Versions 8 and forward do center *sized* absolute elements.
Tips	A center-aligned sized pattern keeps the width constant and grows the margins dynamically. A center-aligned stretched pattern grows the width dynamically and keeps the margins constant. You can use percentages for widths and margins. A percentage sizes the width or margin proportional to the width of the containing block.
Related to	Left Aligned, Right Aligned, Center Offset; Static, Absolute (Chapter 7); Sized, Shrinkwrapped, Stretched (Chapter 5); Aligned design patterns in Chapter 8

Center Offset

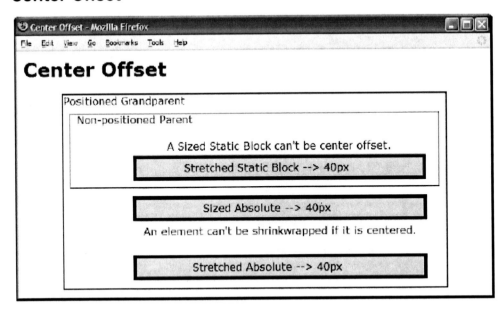

HTML

```
<h1>Center Offset</h1>
<div class="gp">Positioned Grandparent
  <div class="parent">Non-positioned Parent
    <div  id="zs" ><br />A sized static block can't be center offset.</div>
    <div  id="ss" class="ex"><span>Stretched Static Block &rarr; 40px</span></div>
    <span id="za" class="ex"><span>Sized Absolute &rarr; 40px</span></span>
    <span id="wa" >An element can't be shrinkwrapped if it is centered.</span>
    <span id="sa" class="ex"><span>Stretched Absolute &rarr; 40px</span></span>
</div></div>
```

CSS

```
.gp { position:relative; height:295px; width:600px; border:2px solid black;     }
.parent { margin:10px; padding:10px; padding-top:0; border:1px solid black;     }
.ex     { padding:5px;  border:5px solid black;  background-color:gold;         }
.ex span { margin-left:-40px; }

#zs { position:static;         text-align:center;                  margin-top:5px;
      width:auto;              margin-left:90px;             margin-right:10px;     }
#ss { position:static;         text-align:center;                  margin-top:5px;
      width:auto;              margin-left:90px;        margin-right:10px;     }
#za { position:absolute;       text-align:center;         top:0; margin-top:155px;
      width:440px; left:80px;  margin-left:auto; right:0; margin-right:auto;     }
#wa { position:absolute;       text-align:center;         top:0; margin-top:200px;
      width:auto;  left:0;     margin-left:110px; right:0;  margin-right:30px;     }
#sa { position:absolute;       text-align:center;         top:0; margin-top:245px;
      width:auto;  left:0;     margin-left:110px; right:0;  margin-right:30px;     }
```

Center Offset

Problem	You want to align an element and its content to the center of its parent or closest positioned ancestor and then offset it from the center.
Solution	**To create a center-offset *inline* element**, you can use `margin-left:+VALUE` to offset the element to the right and `margin-left:-VALUE` to offset it to the left. Also assign `text-align:center` to the containing block element.
	To create a center-offset *sized* absolute element, you can use a positive value in `left` to offset to the right and a negative value to offset to the left. You can also assign the following to the element: `margin-left:auto;`, `margin-right:auto;`, and `right:0;`, and set `width:+VALUE` to size the element.
	To create a center-offset *stretched* element, set `margin-left` and `margin-right` to the same value. A larger value shrinks the element, and a smaller value grows it. To offset it to the left, subtract the desired offset from `margin-left` and add it to `margin-right`. To offset it to the right, add the desired offset to `margin-left` and subtract it from `margin-right`. For absolute stretched elements, you can also use `left:0` and `right:0`.
	A sized static block element can't be center offset.
	A shrinkwrapped absolute element can't be center offset.
Patterns	**Center-offset inline element**

```
INLINE-SELECTOR { margin-left:±VALUE; }
BLOCK-SELECTOR  { text-align:center;  }
```

Center-offset stretched static block

```
BLOCK-SELECTOR { position:static;     text-align:center;
                 width:auto;          margin-left:±VALUE;
                                      margin-right:±VALUE; }
```

Center-offset sized absolute element

```
SELECTOR { position:absolute;         text-align:center;
           width:+VALUE;  left:±VALUE; margin-left:auto;
                          right:0;     margin-right:0;        }
```

Center-offset stretched absolute element

```
SELECTOR { position:absolute;         text-align:center;
           width:auto;    left:0;     margin-left:±VALUE;
                          right:0;     margin-right:±VALUE; }
```

Location	This pattern applies to all elements.
Limitations	Same as Center Aligned.
Example	Notice how each block is centered and then offset to the right by 80 pixels. Also notice how the text in each block is centered and then offset to the left by 40 pixels.
Related to	Left Offset, Right Offset, Center Aligned; Static, Absolute (Chapter 7); Sized, Shrinkwrapped, Stretched (Chapter 5); Offset and Aligned design patterns in Chapter 8

Top Aligned

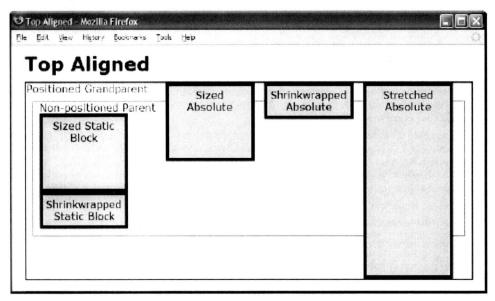

HTML

```
<h1>Top Aligned</h1>
<div class="gp">Positioned Grandparent
  <div class="parent">Non-positioned Parent
    <div  id="zs" class="ex"><span>Sized Static Block</span></div>
    <div  id="ws" class="ex"><span>Shrinkwrapped Static Block</span></div>
    <span id="za" class="ex"><span>Sized Absolute</span></span>
    <div  id="wa" class="ex"><span>Shrinkwrapped Absolute</span></div>
    <span id="sa" class="ex"><span>Stretched Absolute</span></span></div></div>
```

CSS

```
.gp { position:relative; height:300px; width:700px; border:2px solid black;  }
.parent  { margin:10px; padding:10px; padding-top:0; border:1px solid black; }
.ex      { padding:5px;  border:5px solid black;  background-color:gold;
           width:120px; text-align:center; position:relative;       }
.ex span { left:0; width:130px; height:auto; }

#zs { height:100px;            margin-top:0;              margin-bottom:auto;
      position:static;                                                       }
#ws { height:auto;            margin-top:0;              margin-bottom:auto;
      position:static;                                                       }
#za { height:100px;     top:0; margin-top:0;  bottom:auto; margin-bottom:auto;
      position:absolute;                               margin-left:200px; }
#wa { height:auto;      top:0; margin-top:0;  bottom:auto; margin-bottom:auto;
      position:absolute;                               margin-left:355px; }
#sa { height:auto;      top:0; margin-top:0;  bottom:0;   margin-bottom:0;
      position:absolute;                               margin-left:510px; }
```

Top Aligned

Problem	You want to align an element and its content to the top of its parent or closest positioned ancestor.
Solution	**To create a top-aligned *sized* element**, you can use `height:+VALUE` to size it. You can use `margin-top:0` to align it to the top. You can use `margin-bottom:auto` to prevent it from aligning to the bottom. For an absolute element, you can also use `top:0` to align the element to the top and `bottom:auto` to prevent it from aligning to the bottom.
	To create a top-aligned *shrinkwrapped* element, you can use `height:auto`, `bottom:auto`, and `margin-bottom:auto` to shrinkwrap the height. You can use `top:0` and `margin-top:0` to align it to the top.
	To create a top-aligned *stretched* element, you can use `height:auto`, `margin-top:0`, and `margin-bottom:0` to stretch its height to the top and bottom of its container. For an absolute element, you can also use `top:0` and `bottom:0` to stretch it to the top and bottom.
Patterns	**Top-aligned sized static block**
	``` BLOCK-SELECTOR { position:static; height:+VALUE; margin-top:0; margin-bottom:auto; } ```
	Top-aligned shrinkwrapped static block
	``` BLOCK-SELECTOR { position:static; height:auto; margin-top:0; margin-bottom:0; } ```
	Top-aligned sized absolute element
	``` SELECTOR { position:absolute; height:+VALUE; margin-top:0; margin-bottom:auto; top:0; bottom:auto; } ```
	Top-aligned shrinkwrapped absolute element
	``` SELECTOR { position:absolute; height:auto; margin-top:0; margin-bottom:auto; top:0; bottom:auto; } ```
	Top-aligned stretched absolute element
	``` SELECTOR { position:absolute; height:auto; margin-top:0; margin-bottom:0; top:0; bottom:0; } ```
Location	This pattern applies to all elements.
Limitations	Stretched Absolute doesn't work in Internet Explorer 6, but it does work in more recent versions.
Tip	A browser renders blocks and content starting at the top of their containers and flows them down. This automatically aligns the first item to the top of its container and the top of the next item to the bottom of the previous item.
Related to	Top Offset, Bottom Aligned, Middle Aligned; Static, Absolute (Chapter 7); Sized, Shrinkwrapped, Stretched (Chapter 5)

Top Offset

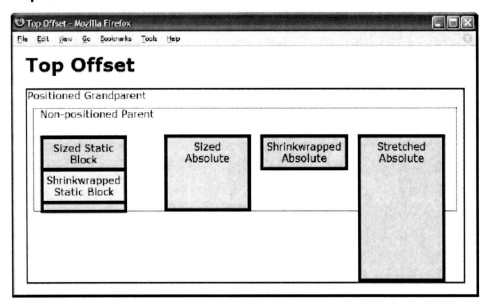

HTML

```
<h1>Top Offset</h1>
<div class="gp">Positioned Grandparent
  <div class="parent">Non-positioned Parent
    <div id="zs" class="ex"><span>Sized Static Block</span></div>
    <div id="ws" class="ex"><span>Shrinkwrapped Static Block</span></div>
    <span id="za" class="ex"><span>Sized Absolute</span></span>
    <div id="wa" class="ex"><span>Shrinkwrapped Absolute</span></div>
    <span id="sa" class="ex"><span>Stretched Absolute</span></span></div></div>
```

CSS

```
.gp { position:relative; height:300px; width:700px; border:2px solid black;  }
.parent  { margin:10px; padding:10px; padding-top:0; border:1px solid black; }
.ex      { padding:5px;  border:5px solid black;  background-color:gold;
           width:120px; text-align:center; position:relative;        }
.ex span { left:0; width:130px; height:auto; }

#zs { height:100px;                 margin-top:25px;                      margin-bottom:0;
position:static;                                                                    }
#ws { height:auto;                  margin-top:-70px;                     margin-bottom:0;
position:static;                                                  background-color:yellow; }
#za { height:100px,      top:0;     margin-top:70px;   bottom:auto;       margin-bottom:auto;
position:absolute;                                                margin-left:200px; }
#wa { height:auto;       top:0;     margin-top:70px;   bottom:auto;       margin-bottom:0;
position:absolute;                                                margin-left:355px; }
#sa { height:auto;       top:0;     margin-top:70px;   bottom:0;          margin-bottom:0;
position:absolute;                                                margin-left:510px; }
```

Top Offset

Problem	You want to offset an element and its content from the top of its parent or closest positioned ancestor.
Solution	**To offset a top-aligned element from the top,** you can assign a value other than zero to `margin-top`. A positive value in `margin-top` offsets down (toward the inside), and a negative value offsets up (toward the outside).
	This design pattern is symmetrical to the Bottom Offset pattern, except content inside bottom-offset elements can't be automatically aligned to the bottom.
	See the Top Aligned design pattern for details on how to top-align an element.
Patterns	**Top-offset sized static block**

```
BLOCK-SELECTOR { position:static;      height:+VALUE;
                 margin-top:±VALUE;     margin-bottom:auto; }
```

Top-offset shrinkwrapped static block

```
BLOCK-SELECTOR { position:static;      height:auto;
                 margin-top:±VALUE;     margin-bottom:0;    }
```

Top-offset sized absolute element

```
SELECTOR { position:absolute;      height:+VALUE;
           margin-top:±VALUE;       margin-bottom:auto;
           top:0;                       bottom:auto;  }
```

Top-offset shrinkwrapped absolute element

```
SELECTOR { position:absolute;      height:auto;
           margin-top:±VALUE;       margin-bottom:auto;
           top:0;                       bottom:auto;  }
```

Top-offset stretched absolute element

```
SELECTOR { position:absolute;      height:auto;
           margin-top:±VALUE;       margin-bottom:0;
           top:0;                       bottom:0;     }
```

Location	This pattern applies to all elements.
Limitations	Stretched Absolute doesn't work in Internet Explorer 6, but it does work in all newer versions.
Example	The shrinkwrapped static block has a negative top margin that moves it up and over the previous sized static block.
Related to	Top Aligned, Bottom Offset, Middle Offset

Bottom Aligned

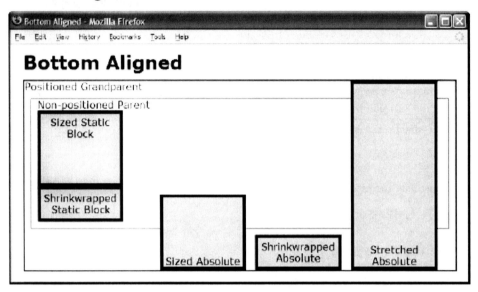

HTML

```
<h1>Bottom Aligned</h1>
<div class="gp">Positioned Grandparent
 <div class="parent">Non-positioned Parent
   <div  id="zs" class="ex"><span>Sized Static Block</span></div>
   <div  id="ws" class="ex"><span>Shrinkwrapped Static Block</span></div>
   <span id="za" class="ex"><span>Sized Absolute</span></span>
   <div  id="wa" class="ex"><span>Shrinkwrapped Absolute</span></div>
   <span id="sa" class="ex"><span>Stretched Absolute</span></span></div></div>
```

CSS

```
.gp { position:relative; height:300px; width:700px; border:2px solid black;  }
.parent  { margin:10px; padding:10px; padding-top:0; border:1px solid black; }
.ex      { padding:5px;  border:5px solid black;  background-color:gold;
           width:120px; text-align:center; position:relative;  }
.ex span { height:auto; left:0; width:130px; }
```

```
span.ex span {position:absolute;top:auto;margin-top:auto;bottom:0;margin-bottom:0; }
#zs { height:100px;            margin-top:auto;            margin-bottom:0;
      position:static;                                    margin-left:0px;   }
#ws { height:auto;            margin-top:auto;            margin-bottom:0;
position:static;                                                            }
#za { height:100px; top:auto; margin-top:auto; bottom:0; margin-bottom:0;
position:absolute;                                       margin-left:200px; }
#wa { height:auto;  top:auto; margin-top:auto; bottom:0; margin-bottom:0;
      position:absolute;                                 margin-left:355px; }
#sa { height:auto;  top:0;    margin-top:0;    bottom:0; margin-bottom:0;
      position:absolute;                                 margin-left:510px; }
```

Bottom Aligned

Problem	You want to align an element and its content to the bottom of its parent or closest positioned ancestor.
Solution	This design pattern is symmetrical to Top Aligned except that it applies this pattern twice: once to the element and once to the element's content.
	To create a bottom-aligned *sized* element, you can use `height:+VALUE` to size it. You can use `margin-bottom:0` to align it to the bottom. You can use `margin-top:auto` to prevent it from aligning to the top. For an absolute element, you can also use `bottom:0` to align the element to the bottom and `top:auto` to prevent it from aligning to the top.
	You can't bottom-align a static shrinkwrapped element because normal flow determines its position.
	To create a bottom-aligned *shrinkwrapped* absolute element, you can use `bottom:0` and `margin-bottom:0` to align it to the bottom. You can use `height:auto`, `top:auto`, and `margin-top:auto` to shrinkwrap the height.
	To create a bottom-aligned *stretched* element, you can use `height:auto`, `margin-bottom:0`, and `margin-top:0` to stretch its height to the bottom and top of its container. For an absolute element, you can also use `bottom:0` and `top:0` to stretch it.

Patterns	**Bottom-aligned sized static block**
	
	`BLOCK-SELECTOR { position:static;      height:+VALUE;`
	`                margin-top:auto;     margin-bottom:0; }`
	
	Bottom-aligned sized absolute element
	
	`SELECTOR { position:absolute;      height:+VALUE;`
	`           margin-top:auto;      margin-bottom:0;`
	`                top:auto;              bottom:0; }`
	
	Bottom-aligned shrinkwrapped absolute element
	
	`SELECTOR { position:absolute;      height:auto;`
	`           margin-top:auto;      margin-bottom:0;`
	`                top:auto;              bottom:0; }`
	
	Bottom-aligned stretched absolute element
	
	`SELECTOR { position:absolute;      height:auto;`
	`           margin-top:0;         margin-bottom:0;`
	`                top:0;                 bottom:0; }`

Location	This pattern applies to all elements.
Limitations	Stretched Absolute doesn't work in Internet Explorer 6, but it does work in newer versions.
Tip	There is no property to align *content* to the bottom of its container. Instead, you need to use this design pattern to align content to the bottom of its parent. See the absolutely positioned spans in the example. Note that when a parent is shrinkwrapped, positioning its content collapses its height.
Related to	Top Aligned, Bottom Offset, Middle Aligned; Static, Absolute (Chapter 7); Sized, Shrinkwrapped, Stretched (Chapter 5)

Bottom Offset

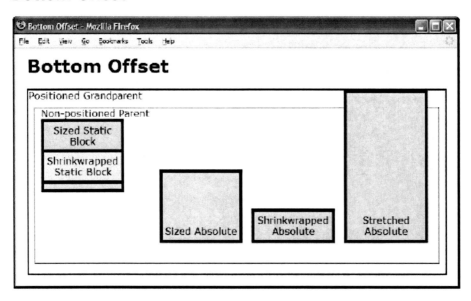

HTML

```
<h1>Bottom Offset</h1>
<div class="gp">Positioned Grandparent
 <div class="parent">Non-positioned Parent
  <div  id="zs" class="ex"><span>Sized Static Block</span></div>
  <div  id="ws" class="ex"><span>Shrinkwrapped Static Block</span></div>
  <span id="za" class="ex"><span>Sized Absolute</span></span>
  <div  id="wa" class="ex"><span>Shrinkwrapped Absolute</span></div>
  <span id="sa" class="ex"><span>Stretched Absolute</span></span></div></div>
```

CSS

```
.gp { position:relative; height:300px; width:700px; border:2px solid black;  }
.parent  { margin:10px; padding:10px; padding-top:0; border:1px solid black; }
.ex      { padding:5px;  border:5px solid black;  background-color:gold;
           width:120px; text-align:center; position:relative;  }
.ex span { height:auto; left:0; width:130px; }
span.ex span{position:absolute;top:auto;margin-top:auto;bottom:5px;margin-bottom:0;}

#zs { height:100px;            margin-top:auto;            margin-bottom:-70px;
      position:static;                                                        }
#ws { height:auto;            margin-top:auto;            margin-bottom:120px;
      position:static;                                    background-color:yellow;  }
#za { height:100px; top:auto; margin-top:auto; bottom:0; margin-bottom:50px;
      position:absolute;                                 margin-left:200px; }
#wa { height:auto;  top:auto; margin-top:auto; bottom:0; margin-bottom:50px;
      position:absolute;                                 margin-left:355px; }
#sa { height:auto;  top:0;    margin-top:auto; bottom:0; margin-bottom:50px;
      position:absolute;                                 margin-left:510px; }
```

198

Bottom Offset

Problem	You want to offset an element and its content from the bottom of its parent or closest positioned ancestor.
Solution	**To offset a bottom-aligned element from the bottom,** you can assign a value other than zero to `margin-bottom`. A positive value in `margin-bottom` offsets up (toward the inside), and a negative value offsets down (toward the outside). This design pattern is symmetrical to Top Offset except that it applies this pattern twice: once to the element and once to the element's content. See the Bottom Aligned design pattern for details on how to top-align an element.

Patterns	**Bottom-offset sized static block**
	
	`BLOCK-SELECTOR { position:static;    height:+VALUE;`
	`                margin-top:auto;    margin-bottom:±VALUE; }`
	
	Bottom-offset sized absolute element
	
	`SELECTOR { position:absolute;    height:+VALUE;`
	`          margin-top:auto;    margin-bottom:±VALUE;`
	`          top:auto;               bottom:0; }`
	
	Bottom-offset shrinkwrapped absolute element
	
	`SELECTOR { position:absolute;    height:auto;`
	`          margin-top:auto;    margin-bottom:±VALUE;`
	`          top:auto;               bottom:0; }`
	
	Bottom-offset stretched absolute element
	
	`SELECTOR { position:absolute;    height:auto;`
	`          margin-top:0;       margin-bottom:±VALUE;`
	`          top:0;                  bottom:0; }`

Location	This pattern applies to all elements.
Limitations	Stretched Absolute doesn't work in Internet Explorer 6, but it does work in newer versions.
Tip	There is no property to align *content* to the bottom of its container. Instead, you need to apply this design pattern to the content to align it to the bottom of its parent. See the absolutely positioned spans in the example. Note that when a parent is shrinkwrapped, positioning its content collapses its height.
Example	The sized static block has a negative bottom margin that moves the shrinkwrapped static block up and over it. The shrinkwrapped static block has a large bottom margin that lowers the bottom of its parent. Notice how the example applies this pattern to the sized and stretched absolute elements and to the spans within them.
Related to	Top Offset, Bottom Aligned, Middle Offset

Middle Aligned

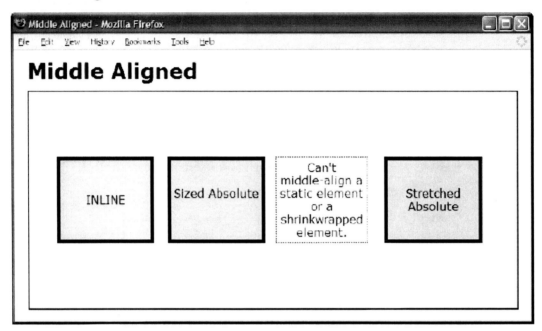

HTML

```
<h1>Middle Aligned</h1>
<div class="gp">
 <div id="ia" class="ex1 ex2">INLINE</div>
 <div id="za" class="ex1 ex2"><span>Sized Absolute</span></div>
 <div id="wa" class="ex1">Can't middle-align a static element
                         or a shrinkwrapped element.</div>
 <div id="sa" class="ex1 ex2"><span>Stretched Absolute</span></div></div>
```

CSS

```
.gp { position:relative; height:300px; width:700px; border:2px solid black;        }
.ex1 { width:120px; padding:5px; text-align:center; border:1px dotted black;        }
.ex2 { position:relative; border:5px solid black;  background-color:gold; left:0; }
.ex1 span  { height:36px; left:0; width:130px;
      position:absolute; top:0; margin-top:auto; bottom:0; margin-bottom:auto;      }

#ia    { height:100px;  top:0; margin-top:auto; bottom:0; margin-bottom:auto;
      position:absolute;      line-height:100px;                 margin-left:40px; }
#za    { height:100px;  top:0; margin-top:auto; bottom:0; margin-bottom:auto;
      position:absolute;                                        margin-left:200px; }
#wa    { height:auto;   top:0; margin-top:90px; bottom:0; margin-bottom:90px;
      position:absolute;                                        margin-left:355px; }
#sa    { height:auto;   top:0; margin-top:90px; bottom:0; margin-bottom:90px;
      position:absolute;                                        margin-left:510px; }
```

Middle Aligned

Problem	You want to align an element and its content to the vertical middle of its closest positioned ancestor.
Solution	**To create a middle-aligned *inline* element**, assign line-height:+VALUE to the same measurement or percentage assigned to the height of its parent. This pattern requires the element's parent to be sized.
	To create a middle-aligned *sized* absolute element, set height to size it. You can use top:0 and bottom:0 to align the element to the top and bottom. You can use margin-top:auto and margin-bottom:auto to realign the element to the middle.
	To create a middle-aligned *stretched* absolute element, set margin-top and margin-bottom to the same value. A larger value shrinks the element, and a smaller value grows it. A negative value expands the element beyond the height of its container. You can use top:0 and bottom:0 to align the element to the top and bottom.
	A static element can't be middle aligned.
	A shrinkwrapped element can't be middle aligned.
Patterns	**Middle-aligned inline element**
| | ```
SELECTOR { line-height:+VALUE; }
``` |
| | **Middle-aligned sized absolute element** |
| | ```
SELECTOR { position:absolute;          height:+VALUE;
           margin-top:auto;            margin-bottom:0;
                  top:0;                    bottom:0;  }
``` |
| | **Middle-aligned stretched absolute element** |
| | ```
SELECTOR { position:absolute;          height:auto;
           margin-top:±VALUE;          margin-bottom:±VALUE;
                  top:0;                    bottom:0;  }
``` |
Location	This pattern works only on absolute elements.
Limitations	Internet Explorer 6 can't middle-align *absolute* elements. Version 7 can middle-align *stretched* absolute elements but not *sized* absolute elements. These problems are resolved in versions 8 and 9.
Tip	There is no text-align property to align *content* to the middle. Instead, you need to wrap content in an inline element, absolutely position it, and align it to the middle. This technique only works with elements that are inside stretched or sized absolute elements.
Example	In the example, this pattern aligns the content in each division to the middle of its parent division. The inline content is middle aligned. The <span> elements are middle aligned. The divisions are middle aligned.
Related to	Center Offset, Top Aligned, Bottom Aligned; Static, Absolute (Chapter 7); Sized, Shrinkwrapped, Stretched (Chapter 5)
```

Middle Offset

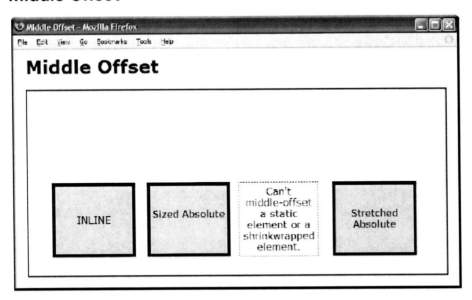

HTML

```
<h1>Middle Offset</h1>
<div class="gp">

 <div id="ia" class="ex1 ex2">INLINE</div>
 <div id="za" class="ex1 ex2"><span>Sized Absolute</span></div>
 <div id="wa" class="ex1">Can't middle-offset a static element
                        or a shrinkwrapped element.</div>
 <div id="sa" class="ex1 ex2"><span>Stretched Absolute</span></div></div>
```

CSS

```
.gp { position:relative; height:300px; width:700px; border:2px solid black;           }
.ex1 { width:120px; padding:5px; text-align:center; border:1px dotted black;      }
.ex2 { position:relative; border:5px solid black;  background-color:gold; left:0; }
.ex1 span { height:36px; left:0; width:130px;
       position:absolute; top:0; margin-top:auto; bottom:0; margin-bottom:auto;      }

#ia    { height:100px; top:60px; margin-top:auto; bottom:-60px; margin-bottom:auto;
         position:absolute;       line-height:100px;        margin-left:40px; }
#za    { height:100px; top:60px; margin-top:auto; bottom:-60px; margin-bottom:auto;
         position:absolute;                            margin-left:200px; }
#wa    { height:auto;  top:0;    margin-top:150px; bottom:0;    margin-bottom:30px;
         position:absolute;                            margin-left:355px; }
#sa    { height:auto;  top:0;    margin-top:150px; bottom:0;    margin-bottom:30px;
         position:absolute;                            margin-left:510px; }
```

Middle Offset

Problem	You want to align an element and its content to an offset from the vertical middle of its closest positioned ancestor.
Solution	**To create a middle-offset *sized* absolute element**, you can use the Middle-aligned Sized Absolute Element pattern and set `top` to the desired offset and set `bottom` to the inverse of the desired offset. **To create a middle-offset *stretched* absolute element**, you can use the Middle-aligned Stretched Absolute Element pattern and add the desired offset to `margin-top` and subtract the desired offset from `margin-bottom`. An inline element can't be middle-offset. A static element can't be middle-offset. A shrinkwrapped element can't be middle-offset.
| **Patterns** | **Middle-offset sized absolute element**<br><br>```
SELECTOR { position:absolute;      height:+VALUE;
           margin-top:auto;        margin-bottom:0;
                  top:±VALUE;       bottom:±VALUE; }
```<br>*where* `top` = `top` + *OFFSET and* `bottom` = `bottom` – *OFFSET*<br><br>**Middle-offset stretched absolute element**<br><br>```
SELECTOR { position:absolute;      height:auto;
           margin-top:±VALUE;      margin-bottom:±VALUE;
                  top:0;            bottom:0; }
```<br>*where* `margin-top` = `margin-top` + *OFFSET*<br>*and* `margin-bottom` = `margin-bottom` – *OFFSET* |
Location	This pattern works only on absolute elements.
Limitations	Internet Explorer 6 can't middle-align *absolute* elements. Version 7 can middle-align *stretched* absolute elements but not *sized* absolute elements. Both issues have been resolved in versions 8 and 9.
Example	This example is the same as the middle-aligned example, except it's offset by 60 pixels. The first two divisions are sized absolute elements. I offset them from the middle by setting `top` to an offset of 60 pixels and `bottom` to the inverse offset of –60 pixels. The last two divisions are stretched absolute elements. I vertically centered them by assigning them to a `margin-top` and `margin-bottom` of 90 pixels. I then offset them from the middle by adding 60 pixels to `margin-top` to create a value of `150px`, and subtracting 60 pixels from `margin-bottom` to create a value of `30px`.
Related to	Center Offset, Top Aligned, Bottom Aligned; Static, Absolute (Chapter 7); Sized, Shrinkwrapped, Stretched (Chapter 5)

Styling Text

This is the first of three chapters containing design patterns that style text. The next chapter discusses how to put space around text. Chapter 12 discusses how to align text. Strictly speaking, this is the only chapter that actually styles *text*. The following two chapters style *inline elements*, which can contain text or be replaced by images, objects, controls, movies, and so on.

Chapter Outline

- **Font** shows how to style text using fonts.

- **Highlight** shows how to highlight text using color and tiled background images.

- **Text Decoration** shows how to create custom styles for underlines, overlines, and line-throughs.

- **Text Shadow** shows how to automatically generate shadows behind text in Internet Explorer 6 and Safari.

- **Text Replacement with Image** shows how to replace text with an image. The text is readable by screen readers and degrades nicely when the image is unavailable. This is an essential tool for making sites beautiful and accessible.

- **Text Replacement with canvas and VML** (Vector Markup Language) consists of two separate parts: a font generator, which converts fonts to a proprietary format using VML, and a rendering engine. An advantage of this technique is that users can select and copy the text, whereas this is impossible with the image-replacement method.

- **Font Embedding** is a CSS3 alternative to the text-replacement techniques, which uses the `@font-face` attribute to directly download a font file from the server before applying it to an element.

- **Invisible Text** shows how to hide text without adding markup. It isn't as useful as Text Replacement but requires no additional markup.

- **Screenreader-only** shows how to make text readable by screen readers while completely hiding it from sighted users. This is an essential tool for making sites accessible for nonsighted users while keeping them uncluttered for sighted users.

Font

HTML

```
<h1>Font</h1>

<p><code>font-family:</code><span class="family1" >sans serif</span>
 <span class="family2">serif</span> <span class="family3" >monospace</span></p>

<p><code>font-size:</code><span class="size1">small</span>
 <span class="size2">medium</span><span class="size3">large</span></p>

<p><code>color:</code><span class="color1">black</span>
 <span class="color2">gold</span></p>
<p><code>font-style:</code><span class="style1">normal</span>
 <span class="style2">italic</span></p>
<p><code>font-weight:</code><span class="weight1">normal</span>
 <span class="weight2">bold</span></p>
<p><code>font-variant:</code><span class="variant1">normal</span>
 <span class="variant2">smallcaps</span></p>
<p><code>text-transform:</code><span class="trans1">none</span>
 <span class="trans2">lowercase</span><span class="trans3">uppercase</span>
 <span class="trans4">capitalize</span></p>
```

CSS

```
.family1 { font-family:sans-serif; }      .family2 { font-family:serif; }
.family3 { font-family:monospace; }
.size1 { font-size:small; }               .size2 { font-size:medium; }
.size3 { font-size:large; }
.style1 { font-style:normal; }            .style2 { font-style:italic; }
.weight1 { font-weight:normal; }          .weight2 { font-weight:bold; }
.variant1 { font-variant:normal; }        .variant2 { font-variant:small-caps; }
.color1 { color:black; }                  .color2 { color:gold; }
.trans1 { text-transform:none; }          .trans2 { text-transform:lowercase; }
.trans3 { text-transform:uppercase; }     .trans4 { text-transform:capitalize; }
```

Font

Problem	You want to style text using a font and various font attributes.
Solution	What we call a "font" is actually a set of fonts designed to work together to create normal, bold, italic, and small-cap effects. CSS calls this a *font family*. When you set font properties, the browser and the operating system choose a font from the font family that most closely matches your request. If your requested font is unavailable, such as a small-cap serif font, the operating system chooses the closest font and simulates the requested font.
	A font has two other important attributes: color and case. A font can be rendered in any color, but some fonts can't render certain cases. For example, some fonts have only uppercase characters, and most fonts don't have small-cap characters, which are small uppercase characters.
	CSS has seven properties that style the font in which text is rendered.
	Use `font-family` to direct the browser to select a font from a comma-delimited list of fonts. If a browser can't find your first choice, it attempts to find your second choice, and so forth. The last font in the list should be one of the standard font-name constants: **sans-serif**, **serif**, or **monospace**. You should place the font name in quotes if it contains spaces.
	Use `font-size` to size a font. You can use ems or a percentage when you want a size relative to the font size of an element's parent. You can use one of the built-in constants such as **xx-small**, **x-small**, **small**, **medium**, **large**, **x-large**, or **xx-large**. You can use pixels when you want a specific size, but you can't count on this size in your layouts because a browser increases or decreases font sizes when zooming in or out for a user. Also be aware that Internet Explorer 6 can't enlarge fixed-size fonts when zooming in, which causes accessibility problems.
	Use `color` to set the color of the font, which should contrast with the **background-color**; otherwise, text will be hard to read or invisible. You can use **font-style:italic** to make the text italic. You can use **font-weight:bold** to make the text bold. You can use **text-transform** to change the text's case to **lowercase**, **uppercase**, or **capitalize**. You can use **font-variant:smallcaps** to render the text in small caps. You can simulate small caps by shrinking the font size to **0.8em** and using **text-transform:uppercase**.
Pattern	`SELECTOR { font-family:FONT,FONT,etc; color:COLOR; font-size:+VALUE; font-style:NORMAL_ITALIC; font-weight:NORMAL_BOLD; font-variant:NORMAL_SMALLCAPS; font-transform:LOWERCASE_UPPERCASE_CAPITALIZE; }`
Location	This pattern applies to any type of element.
Tip	Because **font-size** is inherited, you can assign **font-size:small** to **<body>** and use percents or ems to scale the **font-size** as needed.
Related to	Inline Decoration (Chapter 11); Vertical-aligned Content, Subscript and Superscript, Nested Alignment (Chapter 12); Dropcap design patterns (Chapter 18)

Highlight

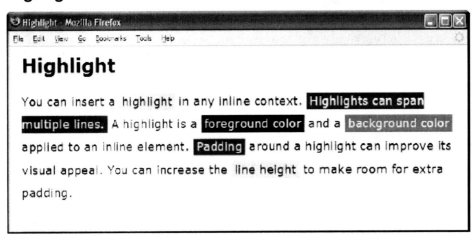

HTML

```
<p>You can insert a
  <span class="highlight black-on-gold">highlight</span>
  in any inline context.
  <span class="highlight white-on-firebrick">Highlights can span multiple
  lines.</span> A highlight is a
  <span class="highlight">foreground color</span> and a
  <span class="highlight cyan-on-royalblue">background color</span>
  applied to an inline element.
  <span class="highlight palegreen-on-darkgreen">Padding</span>
  around a highlight can improve its visual appeal. You can increase the
  <span class="highlight textured">line height</span>
  to make room for extra padding.
</p>
```

CSS

```
p { margin-top:20px; letter-spacing:0.5px; line-height:1.9em; }

.highlight { color:white; background-color:black;
  padding-left:0.25em; padding-right:0.25em;
  padding-top:0.05em;  padding-bottom:0.13em;
  background-image:none; }

.black-on-gold { color:black; background-color:gold; }
.white-on-firebrick { color:white; background-color:firebrick; }
.cyan-on-royalblue { color:lightcyan; background-color:royalblue; }
.palegreen-on-darkgreen { color:palegreen; background-color:darkgreen; }
.textured { color:black; background-color:white;
  background-image:url("paper.jpg"); }
```

Highlight

Problem	You want to highlight text with a background color and a forecolor. You optionally want to highlight text with a background image.
Solution	A highlight is colored text superimposed on a contrasting background color or tiled image. To create a highlight, apply the following styles: **color** sets the foreground color of the text. **background-color** sets the background color of the text. **padding-left:+VALUE** sets the padding distance on the left side. **padding-right:+VALUE** sets the padding distance on the right side. **padding-top:+VALUE** sets the padding distance on the top. **padding-bottom:+VALUE** sets the padding distance on the bottom. **background-image** uses a tiled image as the highlight. This can be omitted or set to **none** if you don't want to use a background image. **background-position** sets the location of the highlight. This can be omitted if the default value of **left top** is what you want. **background-repeat:repeat** tiles the image. This can be omitted because it's the default value.
Pattern	INLINE-SELECTOR { color:COLOR; background-color:COLOR; padding-left:+VALUE; padding-right:+VALUE; padding-top:+VALUE; padding-bottom:+VALUE; background-image:url("FILE.EXT"); } BLOCK-SELECTOR { line-height:+VALUE; }
Location	This pattern applies to any type of element.
Tips	You can use **em** measurements to scale the padding to match the size of the font. I find that **0.25em** on the left and right, **0.05em** on the top, and **0.13em** on the bottom creates a well-proportioned box around text of all sizes. A browser doesn't expand the height of a line to fit the vertical padding of its content. Thus, vertical padding overlaps content in neighboring lines unless you increase the height of a line using **line-height**. Use contrasting colors for **color** and **background-color** to ensure the text is readable. When using background images, be sure to assign contrasting background and foreground colors in case the browser can't load the background image.
Example	In the example, I named classes *descriptively* to make it easier to match the code to the screenshot. In a real document, I would name classes *functionally* because that makes it easier to restyle the document later. For example, the class **highlight white-on-firebrick** is better named **highlight-alert**. Functional classes enhance the meaning of a document and don't require changes to the HTML markup when you change style rules.
Related to	Background (Chapter 6)

Text Decoration

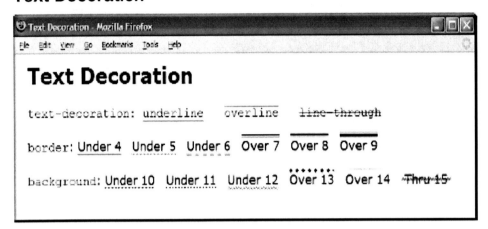

HTML

```
<h1>Text Decoration</h1>

<p>
  <code>text-decoration:
  <span class="t1">underline</span>  <span class="t2">overline</span>  
  <span class="t3">line-through</span></code>

  <br /><br /><code>border</code>:
  <span class="t4">Under 4</span>   <span class="t5">Under 5</span>  
  <span class="t6">Under 6</span>   <span class="t7">Over 7</span>  
  <span class="t8">Over 8</span>   <span class="t9">Over 9</span>  

  <br /><br /><code>background</code>:
  <span class="t10">Under 10</span>   <span class="t11">Under 11</span>  
  <span class="t12">Under 12</span>   <span class="t13">Over 13</span>  
  <span class="t14">Over 14</span>   <span class="t15">Thru 15</span>  
</p>
```

CSS

```
.t1 { text-decoration:underline; }        *.t2 { text-decoration:overline; }
.t3 { text-decoration:line-through; }

.t4 { border-bottom:1px solid black; }    *.t5 { border-bottom:1px dotted black; }
.t6 { border-bottom:2px dashed gray; }    *.t7 { border-top:3px double red; }
.t8 { border-top:4px groove blue; }       *.t9 { border-top:6px ridge green; }

.t10 { background:repeat-x left bottom url("tight-dot.gif"); padding-bottom:0px; }
.t11 { background:repeat-x left bottom url("dotted.gif"); padding-bottom:0px; }
.t12 { background:repeat-x left bottom url("wavy-green.gif"); padding-bottom:2px; }
.t13 { background:repeat-x left top url("diamond-blue.gif"); padding-top:3px; }
.t14 { background:repeat-x left top url("gradient3.gif"); padding-top:2px; }
.t15 { background:repeat-x left center url("wavy-red3.gif"); padding:5px; }
```

Text Decoration

Problem	You want to use a custom style for underlines, overlines, and line-throughs.
Solution	Use **text-decoration** to put a line under, over, or through text. The line's color is the text's color, and the browser determines its thickness.
	You can also use the **border** property to create an underline or an overline.
	Use **border** to control the thickness, style, and color of the line.
	You can also use the **background-image** property to create an unlimited variety of underlines, overlines, and line-throughs. By tiling images, you can create any pattern in any thickness in multiple colors.
	Use **background-image** to specify an image for the text decoration.
	Use **background-position** to set the location of the text decoration.
	Use **background-repeat:repeat-x** to tile the image horizontally.
	Use **padding-top** or **padding-bottom** to insert vertical space between the text decoration and the text.
Patterns	**Text Decoration**
	`INLINE-SELECTOR { text-decoration:underline; }INLINE-SELECTOR { text-decoration:overline; }INLINE-SELECTOR { text-decoration:line-through; }`
	Border Underline
	`INLINE-SELECTOR { border-bottom:WIDTH STYLE COLOR; }`
	Border Overline
	`INLINE-SELECTOR { border-top:WIDTH STYLE COLOR; }`
	Background Underline
	`INLINE-SELECTOR { background-repeat:repeat-x;  background-position:left bottom;  background-image:url("FILE.EXT");  padding-bottom:+VALUE; }`
	Background Overline
	`INLINE-SELECTOR { background-repeat:repeat-x;  background-position:left top; background-image:url("FILE.EXT");  padding-top:+VALUE; }`
	Background Line-through
	`INLINE-SELECTOR { background-repeat:repeat-x;  background-position:left center;  background-image:url("FILE.EXT");  padding-bottom:+VALUE; }`
Location	This pattern applies to inline elements.
Tip	Transparent GIFs as background images integrate well with different background colors.
Related to	Border, Background (Chapter 6)

Text Shadow

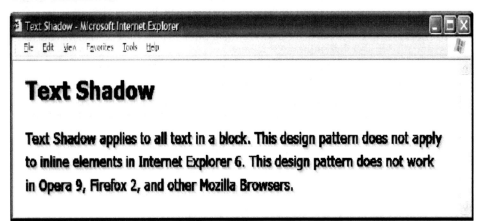

HTML

```
<h1 class="shadow">Text Shadow</h1>

<p class="shadow">Text Shadow applies to all text in a block.
   This design pattern does not apply to inline elements in Internet Explorer 6.
   This design pattern does not work in Opera 9, Firefox 2,
   and other Mozilla Browsers</p>
```

CSS All Browsers

```
.shadow { text-shadow:#999999 5px 5px 5px; }
```

CSS Internet Explorer 6

```
.shadow { filter:shadow(color=#999999, direction=135, strength=4); zoom:1; }
```

Text Shadow

Problem	You want to place a shadow behind text.
Solution	All major browsers support the CSS property **text-shadow**, except Internet Explorer, which provides a proprietary property called **filter:shadow** that causes your CSS not to validate.
	In Safari, use `text-shadow` to add a shadow to text: **COLOR** is the color of the shadow. **X-OFFSET** is the horizontal offset of the shadow. **Y-OFFSET** is the vertical offset of the shadow. **DIFFUSION** is the amount of blur. Greater values make greater blur.
	In Internet Explorer 6, use `filter:shadow` to add a shadow to text: **COLOR** is the color of the shadow. **DIRECTION** is the direction of the shadow: 0 = top, 45 = top right, 90 = right, 135 = bottom right, 180 = bottom, 225 = bottom left, 270 = left, 315 = top left. **SIZE** is the size of the shadow in pixels. Use **zoom:1** to trigger the shadow effect in Internet Explorer. Internet Explorer 6 requires a block to have layout before it applies filter effects to it. **zoom:1** triggers layout. Layout is a proprietary feature specific to Internet Explorer. Layout is discussed in the Atomic design pattern in Chapter 7.

Pattern	`SELECTOR { text-shadow:COLOR X-OFFSET Y-OFFSET DIFFUSION;`
	`filter:shadow(color=COLOR,         direction=DIRECTION,`
	`strength=SIZE);     zoom:1; }`

Location	This pattern applies to block elements. Specifically, **text-shadow** applies to all elements, and **filter:shadow** applies only to block elements.
Limitations	With both **text-shadow** and **filter:shadow**, this pattern works in all recent browser versions. I include this design pattern because it doesn't hurt to use text shadows when a browser doesn't support it. The shadow effect is nonessential. Avoid using shadows to create special effects (such as an eclipse) where **color** and **background-color** are the same, because this makes for invisible text in browsers that don't support shadows. If you assign a border to the shadowed block element, Internet Explorer 6 puts a shadow around the border and the text inside it.
Tips	A shadow effect around text makes the text bolder and causes it to stand out from its background. Shadows work best for headings and for text overlaying background images. A subtle shadow enhances readability, and a strong shadow makes text harder to read.
Related to	Font

Text Replacement with Image

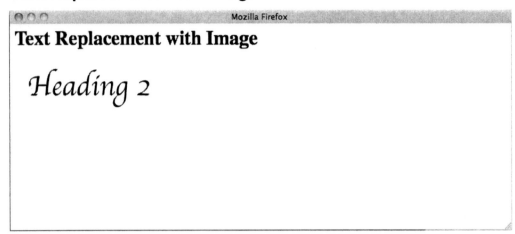

Example shown with text replaced by an image

Example shown when browser could not display the image

HTML

```
<h1>Text Replacement with Image</h1>

<h2 id="h2">Heading 2<span></span></h2>
```

CSS

```
#h2 { position:relative; width:250px; height:76px; padding:0; overflow:hidden; }

#h2 span { position:absolute; width:250px; height:76px; left:0; top:0; margin:0;
   background-image:url("heading2.jpg"); background-repeat:no-repeat; }
```

Text Replacement with Image

Problem	You want to replace text with an image, and you want the text to be read by a screen reader. You also want the text to be visible when the image is unavailable.
Solution	Insert an empty **\<span\>** into the block element that contains the text you want to replace with an image. Assign the image as the span's background image. Relatively position the block, and absolutely position the span. This displays the span in front of the block. Size both the block and the span to fit the image. Because the block and the span are the same size and the span is in front of the block, the span's background image covers the text in the block. If the image is unavailable, the browser renders the span's background as transparent, and this lets the text show through.

Assign a unique ID to the block containing the text you want to replace, and style it as follows:

position:relative; positions the block so the background image of the **\<span\>** can be positioned on top of the text.

width and height size the block to fit the image.

padding:0; removes padding that could allow text to show through.

overflow:hidden; ensures that long text doesn't show through, but be aware that if the image isn't displayed, long text could be truncated.

Insert an empty **\<span\>** into the block, and style it as follows:

position:absolute;, left:0;, and top:0; position the image over the text in the block.

width and height size the **\<span\>** to fit the image.

margin:0; removes margins that could allow text to show through.

background-image:url("FILE.EXT") loads the image.

background-repeat:no-repeat ensures that the image doesn't repeat.

Pattern	
HTML	```<BLOCK id="UNIQUE-ID"> TEXT <span></span></BLOCK>```

CSS	```#UNIQUE-ID { position:relative; padding:0; overflow:hidden;```
	``` width:IMAGE_WIDTH;```
	``` height:IMAGE_HEIGHT; }```
	```#UNIQUE-ID span { position:absolute; left:0; top:0; margin:0;```
	``` width:IMAGE_WIDTH;```
	``` height:IMAGE_HEIGHT;```
	``` background-image:url("FILE.EXT");```
	``` background-repeat:no-repeat; }```

Location	This pattern applies to any block, float, absolute, or fixed element.
Tip	Text replacement works well with links and buttons that use rollover effects.
Related to	Text Replacement with canvas and VML, Invisible Text, Screenreader-only; Background (Chapter 6); Marginal Graphic Dropcap (Chapter 18)

Text Replacement with Canvas and VML

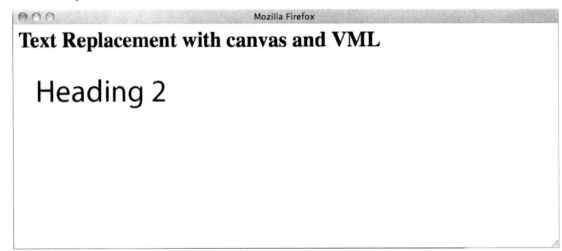

Example shown with text replaced

HTML

```
<!doctype html>
<html>
  <head>
    <meta http-equiv="Content-Type" content="text/html; charset=utf-8">
    <script src="cufon-yui.js" type="text/javascript"></script>
    <script src="Myriad_Pro_400.font.js" type="text/javascript"></script>
    <script type="text/javascript">
      Cufon.replace('h2', { fontFamily: 'Myriad Pro' });
    </script>
  </head>
  <body>
    <h1>Test Replacement with VML and canvas</h1>
    <h2>Heading 2</h2>
  </body>
</html>
```

Text Replacement with Canvas and VML

Problem	You want to replace text with canvas and VML.
Solution	This technique, also know as Cufón, converts font paths to vector graphics stored in JSON data format and then renders the fonts to canvas elements or VML (depending on availability) using a JavaScript rendering engine.

The example uses **https://github.com/sorccu/cufon**.

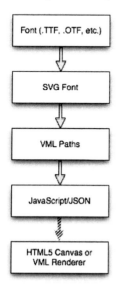

Follow these setup steps:

1. Download **cufon-yui.js** from the Cufón web site (**http://cufon.shoqolate.com/generate/**) and upload it to your own server.

2. Use the font converter (**http://cufon.shoqolate.com/generate/**) to generate your **.font.js** file, which you also have to upload to your server.

3. Include **cufon-yui.js** and **.font.js** in your HTML code.

4. Set the element to be replaced: for example, **Cufon.replace('#content > h1:first-child');**.

Pattern	JavaScript
	`<script type="text/javascript">    Cufon.replace('ELEMENT', { fontFamily: 'FONT_FAMILY' });</script>`
Location	This pattern applies to any block, float, absolute, or fixed element.
Tips	This technique works well even with large amounts of text.
	Text can be selected and copied, unlike the case of Text Replacement with Image.
	All Cufón-enabled pages must be UTF-8 encoded. Compatible encodings, such as US-ASCII, should work fine.
	A significant disadvantage of using Cufón is the requirement that the embedded font's license allow its distribution in unencrypted form, which many commercial fonts expressly forbid.
Related to	Text Replacement with Image

Font Embedding

Mozilla Firefox

Embedding Font

Heading 2

Example shown with font rendered

HTML

```
<h1>Embedding Font</h1>

<h2 id="h2">Heading 2<span></span></h2>
```

CSS

```
@font-face {
font-family: Chunkfive;
src: url('chunkfive.otf') format ("opentype");
}

#h2 {
    font-family: Chunkfive, Arial, sans-serif;
}
```

Font Embedding

Problem	You want the web page to directly download a font file from the server to the user's computer and use it to render some text.
Solution	Upload your font file to your server, assign a unique ID to the block containing the text you want to style, and use the **@font-face** attribute:
	position:relative; positions the block so the background image of the **<span>** can be positioned on top of the text.
	width and height size the block to fit the image.
	padding:0; removes padding that could allow text to show through.
	overflow:hidden; ensures that long text doesn't show through, but be aware that if the image isn't displayed, long text could be truncated.
	Insert an empty **<span>** into the block, and style it as follows:
	position:absolute;, **left:0;**, and **top:0;** position the image over the text in the block.
	width and height size the **<span>** to fit the image.
	margin:0; removes margins that could allow text to show through.
	background-image:url("FILE.EXT") loads the image.
	background-repeat:no-repeat ensures that the image doesn't repeat.
Pattern	
HTML	`<BLOCK id="ID"> TEXT </BLOCK>`
CSS	`@font-face {  font-family: FONT-NAME;  src: url(URL) format (FORMAT);}` `#ID { font-family: FONT-NAME }`
Location	This pattern applies to any block, float, absolute, or fixed element.
Tips	The embedded font's license must allow it to be embedded using **@font-face**.
Limitations	Internet Explorer only works with EOT font files.
Related to	Text Replacement with Image, Text Replacement with canvas and VML

Invisible Text

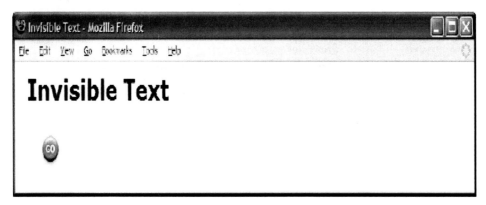

HTML

```
<h1>Invisible Text</h1>

<p class="invisible-text">Invisible Text</p>
```

CSS

```
.invisible-text {
  text-indent:-9999px;
  text-align:left;
  width:75px;
  height:35px;
  background-image:url("go.jpg");
  background-repeat:no-repeat;
  background-position:center center; }
```

Invisible Text

Problem	You want to hide the text in a terminal block element without hiding the element itself. You don't want to insert any extra markup into the document. You want the text to be read by a screen reader. You want to set the height and width so you can display a background image instead of the text.
Solution	Use `text-indent:-9999px` to move the text off the screen so it isn't visible.
	Use `text-align:left` to ensure that the block doesn't inherit another value for **text-align**. This is important because **text-indent** works properly only when text is aligned to the left.
	Use **width** and **height** to size the element to display the background image.
	Use **text-align** to move the text to the left or right side—further out of the way of a background image.
Pattern	`TERMINAL_BLOCK_SELECTOR { text-indent:-9999px; text-align:left; width:+VALUE; height:+VALUE; background-image:url("FILE.EXT"); background-repeat:VALUE; background-position:H V; }`
Location	This pattern applies to any terminal block element.
Limitations	This design pattern *only* works on terminal block elements, like the paragraph. It doesn't work on inline elements. If the browser can't display the background image, the user doesn't see anything.
Tip	If you can insert a tiny bit of extra markup, the Text Replacement design pattern is much better.
Related to	Text Replacement; Text Indent, Hanging Indent (Chapter 12)

Screenreader-only

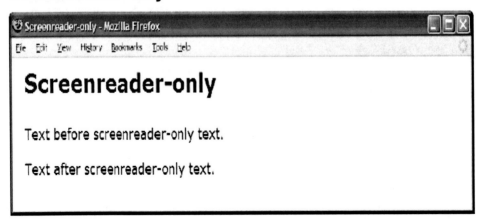

HTML

```
<h1>Screenreader-only</h1>

<p>Text before screenreader-only text.</p>

<p class="screenreader-only">
  This text is hidden to sighted users, but is read by screen readers.</p>

<span class="screenreader-only">
  You can make any type of element a screenreader-only element.</span>

 <p>Text after screenreader-only text.</p>
```

CSS

```
.screenreader-only {
  position:absolute;
  left:-9999px;
  top:-9999px;
  width:1px;
  height:1px;
  overflow:hidden; }
```

Screenreader-only

Problem	You want text to be read by a screenreader program, and you don't want sighted users to see the text. This design pattern is useful when you want to provide instructions to nonsighted users that you don't want to give to sighted users.
Solution	Remove the element from the flow. Shrink the element to one pixel. Hide the text when it overflows its one-pixel size. Move the element offscreen. Use `position:absolute` to remove the element from the flow. Use `left:-9999px` to move the element off the left side of the viewport. Use `top:-9999px` to move the element above the top of the viewport. Use `width:1px` to shrink the element to one pixel wide. Use `height:1px` to shrink the element to one pixel tall. Use `overflow:hidden` to hide any text that overflows the one pixel height and width.
Pattern	`SELECTOR { position:absolute; left:-9999px; top:-9999px; width:1px; height:1px; overflow:hidden; }`
Location	This pattern applies to any element.
Tips	Occasionally, you may want to give instructions to nonsighted users that you don't want to give to sighted users. For example, when filling out a form, the layout, graphics, and colors may make something obvious to a sighted user that is unknowable to a nonsighted user. You can use this design pattern to create instructions for nonsighted users without cluttering the screen seen by sighted users. Such instructions should be brief like headings, captions, and tooltips. You may want to include a screenreader-only link at the beginning of the document that skips to the main content, such as "skip to main content." This keeps the visual interface uncluttered and makes the document easier for nonsighted users to navigate. On the other hand, visually impaired users, mobile users, and others benefit from seeing such a link, so you may not want to hide it.
Disadvantages	Screenreader-only text is visible in non-CSS browsers and browsers that don't support absolute positioning.
Related to	Text Replacement, Invisible Text; Absolute (Chapter 7); Left-aligned Sized Absolute Element (Chapter 9); Tabs, Flyout (Chapter 17)

CHAPTER 11

Spacing Content

This chapter discusses design patterns that put horizontal and vertical space around inline elements, which may contain text, images, objects, controls, and so on. This chapter contains the following design patterns:

- **Spacing** shows how to space text and content. It simply groups together the many properties built into CSS that put space around and between blocks, text, and content.

- **Blocked** shows how to render an inline element as a block element. This is a very important design pattern that is often combined with other patterns.

- **Nowrap** shows how to prevent the browser from wrapping text across lines.

- **Preserved** shows how to render whitespace in a document instead of collapsing it.

- **Code** shows how to mark up computer code, render it inline, display it as a block, preserve whitespace, and prevent it from being wrapped across lines.

- **Padded Content** shows how to put space around inline content to emphasize it.

- **Inline Spacer** shows how to insert a horizontal spacer into a line to put a precise amount of distance between content.

- **Inline Decoration** shows how to insert a decoration into a line. A decoration is style—not content. It lets you insert a colored background, a textured background, or a background image into the flow. You can put borders around it. You can use it to push content apart, to overlap prior content, and to underlap following content.

- **Line Break** shows how to insert *four different types of line breaks* into your document that can add extra space between lines or shrink the distance between lines.

- **Inline Horizontal Rule** shows how to insert a horizontal rule using an inline element. You can style the horizontal rule with images, borders, margins, and so on. This allows you to put extra space between lines, to overlap prior lines, and to underlap following lines. An *inline* horizontal rule is particularly useful because you can use an inline element anywhere. HTML's horizontal rule is a *block* element and has limited styling options.

Spacing

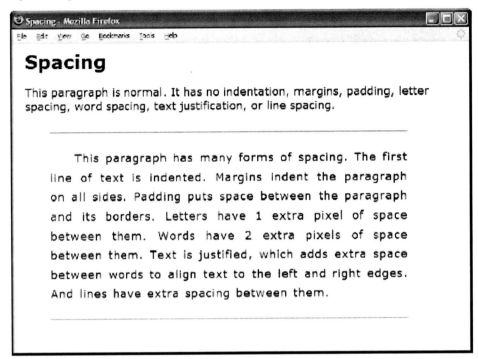

HTML

```
<h1>Spacing</h1>

<p>This paragraph is normal. It has no indentation, margins, padding,
  letter spacing, word spacing, text justification, or line spacing.</p>

<p class="elegant">This paragraph has many forms of spacing. The first line of text
  is indented. Margins indent the paragraph on all sides. Padding puts space
  between the paragraph and its borders. Letters have 1 extra pixel of space between
  them. Words have 2 extra pixels of space between them. Text is justified, which
  adds extra space between words to align text to the left and right edges. And
  lines have extra spacing between them.</p>
```

CSS

```
.elegant { margin-left:40px; margin-right:80px;
  margin-top:30px; margin-bottom:30px;
  padding-top:25px; padding-bottom:25px;
  letter-spacing:1px;
  word-spacing:2px;
  line-height:1.7em;
  text-indent:40px;
  text-align:justify;
  border-top:1px solid black; border-bottom:1px solid black; }
```

Spacing

Problem	You want to control the spacing around content.
Solution	
HTML	Tag a terminal block element with a class or ID of your choosing.
CSS	Apply styles to your chosen class or ID as follows:
	Use **margin-left** to indent the left side of any element.
	Use **margin-right** to indent the right side of any element.
	Use **margin-top** to indent the top of a block element.
	Use **margin-bottom** to indent the bottom of a block element.
	Use **padding-left** to pad the left side of any element.
	Use **padding-right** to pad the right side of any element.
	Use **padding-top** to pad the top of any element.
	Use **padding-bottom** to pad the bottom of any element.
	Use **letter-spacing** to add space between letters.
	Use **word-spacing** to add space between words.
	Use **line-height** to increase the spacing between lines.
	Use **text-indent** to indent the first line of a terminal block element.
	Use **text-align:justify** to justify text, which adds space between words.
Pattern	
HTML	`<TERMINAL-BLOCK class="elegant">text</TERMINAL-BLOCK>`

CSS	`.elegant {`
	`  margin-left:±VALUE; margin-right:±VALUE;`
	`  margin-top:±VALUE; margin-bottom:±VALUE;`
	`  padding-left:±VALUE; padding-right:±VALUE;`
	`  padding-top:±VALUE; padding-bottom:±VALUE;`
	`  letter-spacing:±VALUE;`
	`  word-spacing:±VALUE;`
	`  line-height:±VALUE;`
	`  text-indent:±VALUE;`
	`  text-align:justify; }`

Location	This pattern works on all elements, with the exception that **margin-top**, **margin-bottom**, **text-indent**, and **text-align** work only on block elements. It is most common to apply spacing to terminal block elements.
Limitations	**text-indent** works only on terminal block elements. It does not work on inline elements. You can assign **text-indent** to structural block elements, and it will be inherited by descendant terminal block elements.
Tips	You can use negative values in **margin**, **letter-spacing**, and **word-spacing** to shrink spacing. You can assign a value smaller than **1em** to **line-height** to shrink spacing between lines. You can assign an **em** measurement to **text-indent** to indent by an approximate number of letters. Since a letter is typically twice the height of its width, **2em** equals four letters.
Related to	Code, Inline Spacer; Invisible Text (Chapter 10); Text Indent, Hanging Indent (Chapter 12); First-Letter Dropcap, Hanging Dropcap (Chapter 18); Hanging Alert (Chapter 20)

Blocked

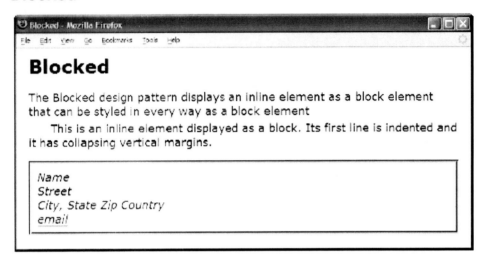

HTML

```
<h1>Blocked</h1>

<p>The Blocked design pattern displays an inline element as a block element
   that can be styled in every way as a block element.
   <span class="blocked">This is an inline element displayed as a block.
   Its first line is indented and it has collapsing vertical margins.</span></p>

<div class="vcard">
  <span class="fn org">Name</span>
  <p class="adr">
    <span class="street-address">Street</span>
    <span class="locality">City</span>,
    <span class="region">State</span>,
    <span class="postal-code">Zip Code</span>
    <span class="country-name">Country</span>
  </p>
  <a class="email" href="mailto:email@email.com">email@email.com</a>
</div>
```

CSS

```
.blocked { display:block; text-indent:2em; margin-top:5px; }


.vcard { border:4px solid green; padding:10px;  font-style:italic;}
.vcard .org { display:block; }
.vcard .street-address { display:block; }
.vcard .adr { display:block; }
.vcard .email { display:block; }
```

Blocked

Problem	You want to style text as a block. For example, you want to move an inline element to the next line, give it vertical margins, and indent its first line. Or, you want to use an element in your markup, such as **<code>**, **<samp>**, or **<address>**, that can contain only inline elements, and you want to display some or all of these inline elements as blocks.
Solution	You can display any inline element as a block. This moves the element to a new line and makes it possible for block properties to work properly. This means **text-indent**, **text-align**, **margin**, **border**, **padding**, **width**, and **height** work like they do on block elements. If an inline element were not displayed as a block, these properties would have no effect, or they would work differently. This design pattern is the converse of Inlined, which displays block elements as inline elements.
HTML	Wrap the text that you want to be indented in a span or other inline element and assign it to a class or ID of your choosing.
CSS	Apply styles to your chosen class or ID as follows: Use **display:block** to display the inline element as a block. Optionally apply **text-indent**, **text-align**, **margin**, **border**, **padding**, **width**, and **height** to format the inline element as if it were a block element.
Pattern	
HTML	`<INLINE class="indent"></INLINE>`

CSS	`.indent { display:block;`
	`    text-indent:±VALUE;`
	`    text-align: LEFT_CENTER_RIGHT;`
	`    margin: ±VALUE;`
	`    border: WIDTH STYLE COLOR;`
	`    padding: +VALUE;`
	`    width: +VALUE;`
	`    height: +VALUE; }`

Location	This pattern works anywhere you can use an inline element.
Tip	In spite of its simplicity, this is one of the most powerful design patterns. It allows you to combine the semantic meaning of inline elements with the styling features of block elements. In other words, you can feel free to tag elements based on their semantic meaning without sacrificing style.
Related to	Code, Padded Content, Line Break, Inline Horizontal Rule; Block Box, Display (Chapter 4); Inlined (Chapter 13); Image, Image Map, Content Over Image (Chapter 14); Tabled, Rowed, and Celled (Chapter 15); Outside-In Box, Opposing Floats, Tab Menu, Layout Links (Chapter 17); Center Callout, Block Quote, Inline Block Quote (Chapter 19)

Nowrap

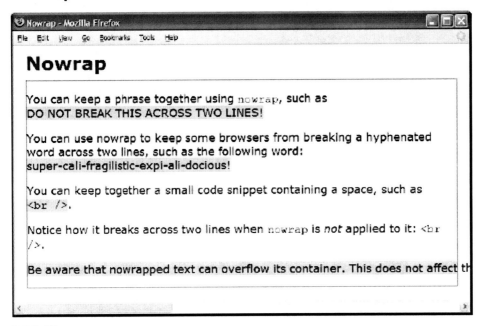

HTML

```
<h1>Nowrap</h1>
<div>
  <p>You can keep a phrase together using <code>nowrap</code>, such as
   <span class="nowrap">DO NOT BREAK THIS ACROSS TWO LINES!</span></p>

  <p>You can use nowrap to keep some browsers from breaking a hyphenated word
    across two lines, such as the following word:
    <span class="nowrap">super-cali-fragilistic-expi-ali-docious!</span></p>

  <p>You can keep together a small code snippet containing a space, such as
    <code class="nowrap">&lt;br /&gt;</code>.</p>
  <p>Notice how it breaks across two lines when <code>nowrap</code>
    is <em>not</em> applied to it: <code>&lt;br /&gt;</code>.</p>

  <p class="nowrap">Be aware that nowrapped text can overflow its container. This
    does not affect the width of other elements, but it may cause a browser to
    display a horizontal scrollbar requiring users to scroll to see the text.</p>
</div>
```

CSS

```
.nowrap { white-space:nowrap; background-color:gold; }
```

230

Nowrap

Problem	You want to prevent the browser from wrapping text to a new line. For example, you want to keep together a phrase, a hyphenated word, or a small code snippet containing a whitespace, such as ** **.
Solution	The rule **white-space:nowrap** prevents text from wrapping. You can apply **white-space:nowrap** to any inline element that you do not want wrapped.
Pattern	`SELECTOR { white-space:nowrap; }`
Location	This pattern applies to any inline element. If you assign **white-space:nowrap;** to a block element, it will be inherited by its child inline elements.
Disadvantages	When the browser viewport is smaller than the nonwrapped text, the browser viewport overflows, and the browser creates a horizontal scrollbar so the user can scroll to see all the unwrapped text. Even though it looks like the viewport has been resized, it has not. It is still the same width and height. All static, absolute, fixed, and floated elements are aligned and positioned as if the unwrapped text had never overflowed. Since users do not like to scroll horizontally, it is best to keep nowrapped text as short as possible.
Example	The example prevents the text in four elements from wrapping. The first unwrapped element contains a phrase that I wanted to stay in one line. The second unwrapped element contains a hyphenated word that I did not want broken across two lines. Most major browsers do not break at hyphens. The third unwrapped element is a code fragment that contains whitespace that I did not want to break across two lines. The fourth unwrapped element contains a large amount of unwrapped text that overflows the browser's viewport. This causes the browser to display horizontal scrollbars so the user can scroll to read the unwrapped text.
Related to	Preserved, Code; Overflow (Chapter 6); Flyout Menu, Layout Links (Chapter 17); Inline Alert (Chapter 20)

Preserved

HTML

```
<h1>Preserved</h1>

<pre>You   can   preserve   whitespace   using   <code>&lt;pre&gt;</code>.</pre>

<p>You can use <code>white-space:pre</code> to insert line breaks and spaces.
  <span class="preserved" >
    </span>Preserved moves this sentence to a new line and indents it five spaces.
  <br />     A better approach is to insert
  <code>&lt;br /&gt;</code> and <code> </code></p>

<p class="preserved">You can preserve
                whitespace in blocks.</p>

<p>You can preserve <span class="preserved" >
                whitespace </span>in inline elements.</p>

<p class="preserved">You can turn <code>white-space:pre</code>
                            <span class="not-preserved" >on and off
                                        at any time.</span></p>
```

CSS

```
.preserved { white-space:pre; }
.not-preserved { white-space:normal; }
```

Preserved

Problem	You want to selectively preserve whitespace around text and objects that you insert into the HTML document. For example, you want to preserve whitespace in code. You also may want to insert specific amounts of whitespace into your document without having to track the number of **
** elements and ** ** entities you need to insert to achieve the desired effect.
Solution	When whitespace is an intrinsic part of the content, you can mark up the content with **<pre>** to preserve the whitespace. This identifies whitespace as part of the content and preserves it. **<pre>** also works in non-CSS browsers.
	When whitespace is decorative or when you cannot use **<pre>**, you can use **white-space:pre** to prevent whitespace from being collapsed.
	You can assign **white-space:pre** to a span containing nothing but whitespace to direct the browser to render that whitespace—although this is probably not a good idea, as explained under "Disadvantages."
Pattern	
HTML	`<pre> CONTENT </pre>`
CSS	`SELECTOR { white-space:pre; }` `SELECTOR { white-space:normal; }`
Location	**white-space:pre** applies equally well to any type of element.
Advantages	**white-space:pre** has several advantages over **<pre>**. It can preserve whitespace in existing markup that you cannot modify to include **<pre>**. It allows preserved whitespace to intermingle with images, objects, and any other type of element. (The HTML specification prevents **<pre>** from containing **<img>**, **<object>**, **<sub>**, **<sup>**, **<big>**, and **<small>**.) It does not automatically style the content with a monospace font like **<pre>**. It can preserve whitespace in an inline element. (Since **<pre>** is a *block* element, **<pre>** cannot be embedded in paragraphs, headings, and other terminal block elements.) Lastly, it can turn whitespace on and off selectively.
Disadvantages	Since it is unusual for whitespace to be preserved in HTML markup, it is easy to accidentally change the layout of the document just by rearranging a little whitespace in a preserved element.
	Most HTML authoring software and utilities automatically rearrange whitespace to make code more readable or to remove whitespace to reduce document size. These programs break preserved whitespace in elements styled with **white-space:pre**, but most retain whitespace in **<pre>**.
Tip	You can use **white-space:normal** to override a rule that applies **white-space:pre** to an element. **white-space:normal** is the default.
Related to	Nowrap, Code; Inline Elements (Chapter 2)

233

Code

HTML

```
<h1>Code</h1>

<p>The following code is blocked and preserved:

<code class="blocked preserved">
  .blocked     { display:block; }
  .preserved   { white-space:pre; }
  .code        { font-family:monospace; }
</code>
</p>

<p>The following inline code uses the Nowrap design pattern:
<code class="nowrap preserved">a = x(y<sup>2</sup> + z<sup>3</sup>) + 1</code>.
 This prevents it from being wrapped across lines.</p>
```

CSS

```
.blocked { display:block; }
.preserved { white-space:pre; }
.nowrap { white-space:nowrap; }
```

Code

Problem	You want to identify an element as containing code, and you want to control when it preserves whitespace, when it breaks across lines, and when it is displayed as a block.
Solution	You can use **\<code\>** to identify text as computer code. The meaning of this element is well understood by search engines and document processors. By default, **\<code\>** is displayed inline, does not preserve whitespace, and can be wrapped across lines. When you want to display a block of code, add the Blocked design pattern. When you want to preserve whitespace in **\<code\>**, add the Preserved design pattern. When you do not want code to wrap across lines, add the Nowrap design pattern. Note that you cannot use Preserved and Nowrap at the same time.
HTML	Use the **\<code\>** element to tag text as code.
	Assign **blocked**, **preserved**, or **nowrap** classes to **\<code\>**, or assign classes or IDs with names of your choosing.
CSS	Apply styles to your chosen class or ID as follows:
	Use **white-space:preserve** to preserve whitespace in **\<code\>**.
	Use **white-space:nowrap** to prevent text in the **\<code\>** from wrapping.
	Use **display:block** to display **\<code\>** as a block.

Pattern	
HTML	```<code class="BLOCKED PRESERVED NOWRAP"> CODE </code>```

CSS	```.blocked { display:block; }```
	```.preserved { white-space:pre; }```
	```.nowrap { white-space:nowrap; }```

Location	This pattern works everywhere inline elements can be used.
Variations	HTML provides four additional inline elements that are similar to **\<code\>**. They are **\<var\>**, **\<samp\>**, **\<cite\>**, and **\<kbd\>**. **\<var\>** identifies its contents as a computer variable. **\<samp\>** identifies its contents as sample output from a computer program. **\<cite\>** identifies a title of work (e.g., a book, a song, a poem, a film, etc.). **\<kbd\>** identifies its contents as keypresses that a user should type on a keyboard to accomplish a specific task. This design pattern can easily be applied to these elements to fine-tune how they are rendered.
Related to	Blocked, Nowrap, Preserved; Inline Elements (Chapter 2)

Padded Content

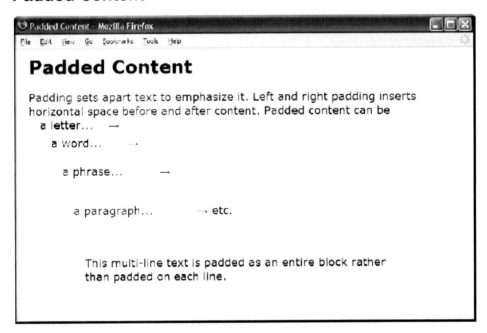

HTML

```
<h1>Padded Content</h1>

<p>Padding sets apart text to emphasize it.
  Left and right padding inserts horizontal space before and after content.
  Padded content can be
  <br /><span class="padded-mild">a letter...</span>&rarr;
  <br /><span class="padded-emphasized">a word...</span>&rarr;
  <br /><span class="padded-strong">a phrase...</span>&rarr;
  <br /><span class="padded-extreme">a paragraph...</span>&rarr; etc.
  <span class="padded-strong-BA">This multi-line text is padded as an
    entire block rather than padded on each line.
  </span>
</p>
```

CSS

```
.padded-mild { padding-left:1em; padding-right:1em; line-height:1em; }
.padded-emphasized { padding-left:2em; padding-right:2em; line-height:2em; }
.padded-strong { padding-left:3em; padding-right:3em; line-height:3em; }
.padded-extreme { padding-left:4em; padding-right:4em; line-height:4em; }

.padded-strong-BA { display:block; padding:2em 5em; }
```

Padded Content

Problem	You want to put extra space around content to emphasize it and set it apart.
Solutions	**Inline Padded Content** You can use **padding-left** and **padding-right** to pad the left and right of an inline element. This pads the beginning and end of the element—not each line spanned by the element. Padding the top and bottom does not affect the height of an inline element, but you can use **line-height** to change the height of each line spanned by the element. You cannot add space above just the first line and below just the last line spanned by the element. **Blocked Padded Content** You can use **display:block** to display an inline element as a block. This lets you use **padding-left** and **padding-right** to indent the left and right sides of all lines—not just the beginning of the first line and the end of the last. This lets you use **padding-top** and **padding-bottom** to add space above the top of the element and below the bottom of the element. You can also use **line-height** to change the height of each line in the element.

Patterns	**Inline Padded Content**
	
	`INLINE-SELECTOR { padding-left:+VALUE;`
	`  padding-right:+VALUE;`
	`  line-height:+VALUE; }`
	
	Blocked Padded Content
	
	`INLINE-SELECTOR { display:block;`
	`  padding-left:+VALUE;`
	`  padding-right:+VALUE;`
	`  padding-top:+VALUE;`
	`  padding-bottom:+VALUE;`
	`  line-height:+VALUE; }`

Location	This pattern applies to any inline element.
Limitations	**line-height** is used to pad the height of lines because **padding-top** and **padding-bottom** have no effect on the height of a line.
Tips	Padding is colored using the **background-color** or **background-image**. If you want transparent space around the element, use **margin** instead. If you want a different color or pattern than the background, use **border** instead.
Related to	Inline Spacer

Inline Spacer

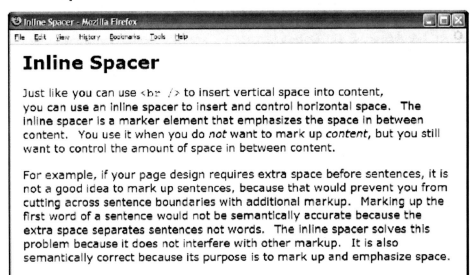

HTML

```
<h1>Inline Spacer</h1>

<p>Just like you can use <code>&lt;br /&gt;</code> to insert vertical space
   into content, <br /> you can use an inline spacer to insert and control
   horizontal space.
   <span class="space"> </span>The inline spacer is a marker element
   that emphasizes the space in between content.
   <span class="space"> </span>You use it when you do <em>not</em> want to
   mark up <em>content</em>, but you still want to control the amount of space
   in between content.</p>

<p>For example, if your page design requires extra space before sentences,
   it is not a good idea to mark up sentences, because that would prevent you from
   cutting across sentence boundaries with additional markup.
   <span class="space"> </span>Marking up the first word of a sentence would not
   be semantically accurate because the extra space separates sentences not words.
   <span class="space"> </span>The inline spacer solves this problem
   because it does not interfere with other markup.
   <span class="space"> </span>It is also semantically correct
   because its purpose is to mark up and emphasize space.</p>
```

CSS

```
.space { margin-left:0.5em; }
```

Inline Spacer

Problem	You want to insert a precise amount of horizontal space into inline content.
Solution	To create an inline spacer, you can insert a span with a class or ID of your choosing and set the amount of space using **margin-left**. A negative value in **margin-left** causes neighboring elements to overlap. Because you are styling space, it is a good idea to put whitespace in between the span's start and end tags, although this is not required for this design pattern to work.
Pattern	
HTML	`<span class="space" > </span>`
CSS	`.space { margin-left:±VALUE; }`
Location	This pattern works anywhere you can use an inline element.
Usage	In general, the best way to space content is to embed it within an element and style the element with **margin**. This begs the question, why would you ever need to use an inline spacer?
	Because the inline spacer is an empty element, it can be placed anywhere without interfering with the nesting of other elements. In those rare cases when the current markup does not align with where you need to control space, you can insert an inline spacer without compromising or complicating the nesting. This is why ** ** and **<hr />** are empty marker elements.
	The inline spacer has the same purpose as ** ** and **<hr />**. It inserts space without marking up content. In other words, it marks and emphasizes the presence of space. It has semantic meaning: it indicates that the following content is set apart from the previous content—because that is what space does. The larger the space, the stronger the meaning. ** ** and **<hr />** insert vertical space, and an inline spacer inserts horizontal space.
	If emphasizing or deemphasizing *space* is the point, it is semantically correct to mark up space, because marking up content would emphasize the content—not the space in between.
	In the past, spacer GIFs were improperly used for this purpose. Images are content—not spacing. Screenreaders announce the presence of these images, and the latency involved in downloading them slows the rendering of the document. The inline spacer has none of these problems.
Variations	You can use pixels or a fixed measurement to size the space. You can use a percentage to scale the size proportional to the width of the containing block.
Tips	This design pattern also works with an empty span, **<span></span>**, or an XML-style empty span, **<span />**. Like ** **, **<span />** works in all major browsers, and validates as valid XHTML, but not as valid HTML.
Related to	Inline Decoration, Line Break; Block Spacer (Chapter 13)

Inline Decoration

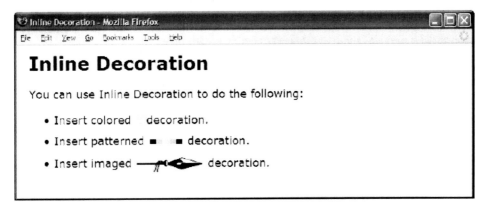

HTML

```
<h1>Inline Decoration</h1>

<div>You can use Inline Decoration to do the following:
  <ul>
    <li>Insert colored<span class="deco-solid"> </span> decoration.</li>
    <li>Insert patterned<span class="deco-groove"> </span> decoration.</li>
    <li>Insert imaged<span class="deco-spear"> </span> decoration.</li>
  </ul>
</div>
```

CSS

```
div { font-size:18px; }

.deco-solid { padding-left:40px;
  font-size:0.4em; vertical-align:middle; line-height:24px;
  margin-left:3px; margin-right:-15px;
  background-color:gold; }

.deco-groove { padding-left:10px;
  font-size:0.4em; vertical-align:middle; line-height:24px;
  border-left:20px groove black; border-right:20px ridge black;
  margin-left:3px; margin-right:3px;
  background-color:lightgray; }

.deco-spear { padding-left:100px;
  font-size:1em; vertical-align:-3px; line-height:24px;
  margin-left:3px; margin-right:3px;
  background-image:url("spear.jpg"); background-position:top right; }
```

Inline Decoration

Problem	You want to insert a decoration into the content, such as a block of color, a styled border, or a background image. You want to move the decoration closer or further away from previous and following content. You do not want to insert an image because you want pure decoration—not content.
Solution	
HTML	Insert a span containing nonbreaking space into the content. Assign to it a class or ID of your choosing.
CSS	Apply styles to your chosen class or ID as follows:
	Use **padding-left** to set the width of the decoration.
	Use **font-size** to set the height of the decoration.
	Use **vertical-align** to move the decoration up or down.
	Use **line-height** to size the height of the line to fit the decoration.
	Use a positive value in **margin-left** to move the decoration to the right.
	Use a negative value in **margin-left** to move the decoration to the left. A large enough value will cause the decoration to overlap previous content.
	Use a positive value in **margin-right** to move the following content to the right and farther away from the decoration.
	Use a negative value in **margin-right** to move the following content to the left and closer to the decoration. A large enough value will cause the content to overlap the decoration.
	Use **border** to insert a border on the left, right, top, or bottom.
	Use **background-color** to display a background color in the padding area.
	Use **background-image** to display an image in the padding area.
	Use **background-position** to position the background image.
Pattern	
HTML	`<span class="decoration"> </span>`

CSS	`.decoration { padding-left:+VALUE;`
	`    font-size:+VALUE;`
	`    vertical-align:±VALUE;`
	`    line-height:+VALUE;`
	`    margin-left:±VALUE; margin-right:±VALUE;`
	`    border-left:+W S C; border-right:+W S C;`
	`    background-color:COLOR;`
	`    background-image:url("FILE.EXT"); }`

Location	This pattern works anywhere you can use an inline element.
Trade-offs	Unlike the Inline Spacer, the Inline Decoration requires the span to contain a nonbreaking space and to have a closing tag. Without the closing tag, a browser renders the background color or image underneath the following text. Without a nonbreaking space, a browser ignores padding and borders.
Related to	Inline Spacer; Hanging Alert, Run-In Alert, Floating Alert, Left Marginal Alert, Right Marginal Alert (Chapter 20)

Line Break

```
Linebreak - Mozilla Firefox
File  Edit  View  Go  Bookmarks  Tools  Help

Linebreak

You can insert a linebreak anywhere.
↑ One-half linebreak.
↑ Normal linebreak.

↑ Linebreak plus 10 pixels.


↑ One-and-a-half linebreak.



↑ Double linebreak.




↑ Triple linebreak.





↑ Quadruple linebreak.
```

HTML

```html
<h1>Line Break</h1>

<p>You can insert a line break anywhere.
  <span class="lb-half"></span>&uarr; One-half line break.
  <span class="lb-single"></span>&uarr; Normal line break.
  <br /><br class="br10px" /> &uarr; Line break plus 10 pixels.
  <span class="lb-one-and-a-half"></span>&uarr; One-and-a-half line break.
  <span class="lb-double"></span>&uarr; Double line break.
  <br /><br class="br3" /> &uarr; Triple line break.
  <span class="lb-quad">&uarr; Quadruple line break.</span>
</p>
```

CSS

```css
.lb-half { display:block; margin-top:-0.5em; }
.lb-single { display:block; margin-top:0; }
.lb-one-and-a-half { display:block; margin-top:1.5em; }
.lb-double { display:block; margin-top:2em; }
.lb-quad { display:block; margin-top:4em; }

.br10px { line-height:10px; }
.br3 { line-height:3em; }
```

Line Break

Problem	You want to insert a line break. You also want to add or reduce the amount of vertical space between the lines.
Solutions	**Break** You can use HTML's break element, ** **, to move content to a new line. The height of the line following the break is determined by the line's content. **Double Break** You can move content to a new line and add extra space between the lines by inserting two ** ** elements in a row with *nothing* in between them. You can use **line-height** to style the second ** ** to control the amount of extra space inserted. **Line Break** You can move content to a new line and add extra space between lines or even shrink the space between the lines by inserting an empty **<span>** and using **display:block** to display it as a block. You can use **margin-top:+VALUE** to insert additional space between the lines. You can use **margin-top:-VALUE** to shrink the space between the lines. **Blocked** You can apply the Blocked design pattern to an *existing* inline element to move the element onto a new line.
Patterns	**Break** ` ` **Double Break** ` <br class="br" />` `.br { line-height:+VALUE; }` **Line Break** `<span class="lb"></span>` `.lb { display:block; margin-top:±VALUE; }` **Blocked** `<ELEMENT class="lb"></ELEMENT>` `.lb { display:block; margin-top:±VALUE; }`
Location	This pattern can be used in any inline context.
Trade-offs	Two ** ** elements can add extra space between lines, but they cannot reduce space between lines. A **<span>** displayed as a block can insert or reduce space between lines and requires only a single element.
Example	In the example, I named classes *descriptively* to make it easier to match the code to the screenshot. In a real document, I would name classes *functionally* because it makes it easier to restyle the document later.
Related to	Inline Horizontal Rule; Block Horizontal Rule, Block Spacer, Block Space Remover (Chapter 13)

Inline Horizontal Rule

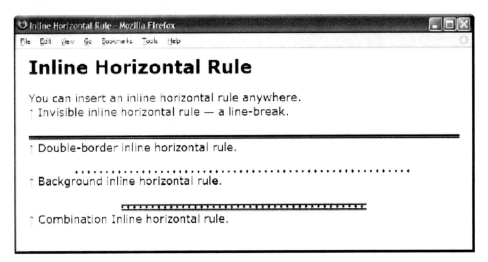

HTML

```
<h1>Inline Horizontal Rule</h1>

<p>You can insert an inline horizontal rule anywhere.
  <span class="hr"></span>&uarr; Invisible inline horizontal rule – a line-break.
  <span class="hr border"></span>&uarr; Double-border inline horizontal rule.
  <span class="hr background"></span>&uarr; Background inline horizontal rule.
  <span class="hr combo"></span>&uarr; Combination Inline horizontal rule.
</p>
```

CSS

```
.hr { display:block; margin:0; }

.border { padding-top:1px; margin-top:25px; margin-bottom:0;
  width:auto; margin-left:0; margin-right:0;
  border-top:4px ridge blue; border-bottom:4px groove blue;
  background:none; background-color:yellow; }

.background { padding-top:5px; margin-top:25px; margin-bottom:0;
  width:auto; margin-left:76px; margin-right:76px; border:none;
  background:repeat-x left center url("diamond-blue.gif");
  background-color:transparent; }

.combo { padding-top:5px; margin-top:25px; margin-bottom:0;
  width:400px; margin-left:auto; margin-right:auto;
  border-top:4px ridge blue; border-bottom:4px groove blue;
  background:repeat-x left center url("diamond-blue.gif");
  background-color:white; }
```

Inline Horizontal Rule

Problem	You want to insert a styled line break in between inline elements. You cannot use the horizontal rule because that works only between block elements.
Solution	Apply styles to your chosen class or ID as follows:

Use **display:block** to display the inline element as a block element. This puts the horizontal rule on its own line and stretches it across the width of its containing block.

Use **padding-top** to make space for the background color and image.

Use **margin-top:+VALUE** to insert space above the horizontal rule.

Use **margin-top:-VALUE** to overlap the rule with the previous line.

Use **margin-bottom:+VALUE** to insert space below the rule.

Use **margin-bottom:-VALUE** to overlap the rule with the next line.

Use **width:auto**, **margin-left:0**, and **margin-right:0** to stretch the rule to the left and right sides of the containing block.

Use **width:auto**, **margin-left:±VALUE**, and **margin-right:±VALUE** to stretch the rule to the left and right margins of the containing block.

Use **width:+VALUE**, **margin-left:auto**, and **margin-right:auto** to size and center the rule.

Use **border-top** to display a border above the rule.

Use **border-bottom** to display a border below the rule.

Use **background-image** to display a background image in the rule.

Use **background-repeat:repeat-x** to tile an image across the rule.

Use **background-position:left center** to position the background image in the vertical middle of the rule.

Use **background-color** to display a background color in the rule.

Pattern	HTML	CSS

	`<span class="hr"></span>`	`.hr { display:block;`
		`  padding-top:+VALUE; width:+VALUE;`
		`  margin-top:±VALUE; margin-bottom:±VALUE;`
		`  margin-left:±VALUE; margin-right:±VALUE;`
		`  border-top:WIDTH STYLE COLOR;`
		`  border-bottom:WIDTH STYLE COLOR;`
		`  background-image:url("FILE.EXT");`
		`  background-position:left center;`
		`  background-repeat:repeat-x;`
		`  background-color:COLOR; }`

Location	This pattern applies to inline elements.
Tip	**display:block;** is the only required rule. The rest are optional and can be used in any combination. This design pattern is much more versatile than the line break, which cannot be styled.
Related to	Line Break; Block Horizontal Rule, Block Spacer, Block Space Remover (Chapter 13)

Aligning Content

This chapter discusses design patterns that align text and content horizontally and vertically to their containing blocks. These alignment patterns work in the normal flow without using absolute or relative positioning.

The first three design patterns align content horizontally. The next three design patterns align content vertically. The last design pattern and the example at the end of the chapter are quite esoteric and have little practical application. I have included them to demonstrate the powerful capabilities built into the inline formatting context.

- **Text Indent** shows how to indent the first line of text.

- **Hanging Indent** shows how to create a hanging indent.

- **Horizontal-Aligned Content** shows how to align text and inline content to the left, right, or center. It also shows how to justify text and inline content.

- **Vertical-Aligned Content** shows how to vertically align an inline element to its parent's fontlines. These fontlines define an alignment context.

- **Vertical-Offset Content** shows how to vertically offset an inline element from its parent's baseline.

- **Subscript and Superscript** shows how to create subscript and superscript text, and how to make it look consistent across all browsers.

- **Nested Alignment** shows how to nest alignment contexts.

- **Advanced Alignment Example** is not a design pattern, but a fun example showing off how alignment and relative positioning can create sophisticated inline layouts.

Text Indent

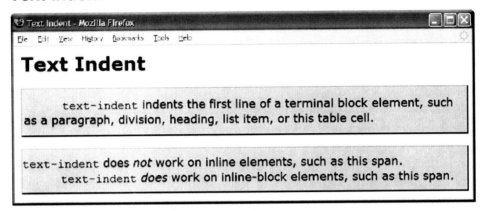

HTML

```
<h1>Text Indent</h1>

<table><tr><td class="text-indent"><code>text-indent</code>
   indents the first line of a terminal block element, such as a paragraph,
   division, heading, list item, or this table cell.
</td></tr></table>

<p><span class="text-indent"><code>text-indent</code> does
   <em>not</em> work on inline elements, such as this span.</span>
   <span class="text-indent inline-block"><code>text-indent</code>
     <em>does</em> work on inline-block elements, such as this span.</span></p>
```

CSS

```
.text-indent { text-indent:60px; }
.inline-block { display:inline-block; }

/*  Nonessential rules are not shown. */
```

Text Indent

Problem	You want to indent the first line of a terminal block element, such as a paragraph.
Solution	You can use a positive value in **text-indent** to indent the first line of text.
Pattern	
HTML	`<TERMINAL-BLOCK class="text-indent"> content </TERMINAL-BLOCK>`
CSS	`.text-indent { text-indent:+VALUE; }`
Location	**text-indent** works only on terminal block elements. It does not work on structural block elements or inline elements. By default, **text-indent** is inherited by child elements. This means you can assign **text-indent** to a structural block element, and all descendant terminal block elements will inherit the value you assigned to **text-indent**.
	Furthermore, this design pattern works only on content. If an element contains no content, there is nothing to indent, and this property will have no visual impact. Even though the name of the property is **text-indent**, it indents all content, regardless of whether it is text.
Tip	Normally you want indentation and margins to be consistent. All major browsers set the indents of their list items at 40 pixels.
Variation	You could create a first-line indent using **first-letter** to select the first letter of a terminal block element and then style it with a positive **margin-left**. This is more work and is less reliable than **text-indent**.
Related to	Hanging Indent; Invisible Text (Chapter 10); Blocked, Spacing (Chapter 11); First-Letter Dropcap, Hanging Dropcap (Chapter 18); Hanging Alert (Chapter 20)

Hanging Indent

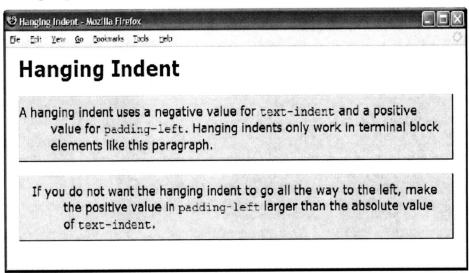

HTML

```
<h1>Hanging Indent</h1>

<p class="hanging-indent">A hanging indent uses a negative value for
   <code>text-indent</code> and a positive value for <code>padding-left</code>.
   Hanging indents work only in terminal block elements like this paragraph.</p>

<p class="hanging-indent2">If you do not want the hanging indent to
   go all the way to the left, make the positive value in <code>padding-left</code>
   larger than the absolute value of <code>text-indent</code>.</p>
```

CSS

```
.hanging-indent { text-indent:-50px; padding-left:50px; }
.hanging-indent2 { text-indent:-50px; padding-left:70px; }

/*  Nonessential rules are not shown. */
```

Hanging Indent

Problem	You want to insert a hanging indent on the first line in a terminal block element, such as a paragraph.
Solution	You can use a negative value in **text-indent** to extend the first line of text into the left padding area of a terminal block element so that it hangs over the left side of the element. You can use a positive value in **padding-left** to make room for the hanging indent.
Pattern	
HTML	`<TERMINAL-BLOCK class="hanging-indent">content</TERMINAL-BLOCK>`
CSS	`.hanging-indent { text-indent:-VALUE; padding-left:+VALUE; }`
Location	**text-indent** works only on terminal block elements that contain content. It does not work on structural block elements or inline elements. By default, **text-indent** is inherited by child elements. You will notice the hanging indent only if the element contains more than one line.
Advantages	Because this design pattern uses **padding-left** to indent the block, the border surrounds the entire block. If you use **margin-left** to indent the block, the negative indent will stick outside of the border.
Disadvantages	This design pattern does not apply to inline elements. You can use the Padded Content or Inline Spacer design patterns to achieve this same effect using inline elements.
Tips	A hanging indent is normally used to create list items. HTML provides the unordered list **<ul>** and the ordered list **<ol>** for this purpose. Normally, you want indentation and margins to be consistent. The default indentation for a list item is 40 pixels. You may also want to use –40 pixels for **text-indent** and 40 pixels for **padding-left**.
Variation	You could create a first-line indent using **first-letter** to select the first letter of a terminal block element and then style it with a negative **margin-left**. This is more work and is less reliable than **text-indent**.
Related to	Text Indent; Blocked, Spacing (Chapter 11); Hanging Dropcap (Chapter 18); Hanging Alert (Chapter 20)

Horizontal-Aligned Content

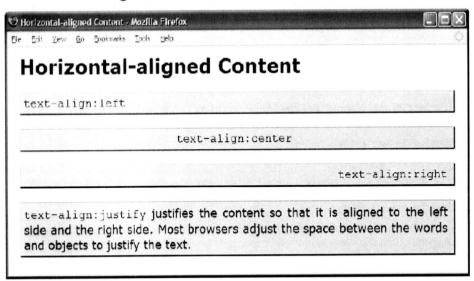

HTML

```
<h1>Horizontal-Aligned Content</h1>

<p class="align-left"><code>text-align:left</code></p>
<p class="align-center"><code>text-align:center</code></p>
<p class="align-right"><code>text-align:right</code></p>
<p class="align-justify"><code>text-align:justify</code> justifies the content so
    that it is aligned to the left side and the right side. Most browsers adjust
    the space between the words and objects to justify the text.</p>
```

CSS

```
.align-left { text-align:left; }
.align-center { text-align:center; }
.align-right { text-align:right; }
.align-justify { text-align:justify; }

/*  Nonessential rules are not shown. */
```

Horizontal-Aligned Content

Problem	You want to left-align, center-align, right-align, or justify the content in a terminal block element, such as a paragraph. For example, you may want to center-align text in a heading, right-align a label assigned to a control, or left-align data in one table column and right-align data in another.
Solution	You can use **text-align** to align the text within its terminal block.
	Use **text-align:left** to align the text to the left of the block.
	Use **text-align:center** to align the text to the center of the block.
	Use **text-align:right** to align the text to the right of the block.
	Use **text-align:justify** to justify the text to both sides of the block. Browsers typically justify text by increasing space between words to stretch the text to the sides of the block.
Patterns	
HTML	```<TERMINAL-BLOCK class="align-left">content</TERMINAL-BLOCK> <TERMINAL-BLOCK class="align-center">content</TERMINAL-BLOCK> <TERMINAL-BLOCK class="align-right">content</TERMINAL-BLOCK> <TERMINAL-BLOCK class="align-justify">content</TERMINAL-BLOCK>```
CSS	```.align-left { text-align:left; } .align-center { text-align:center; } .align-right { text-align:right; } .align-justify { text-align:justify; }```
Location	This design pattern works only on terminal block elements containing content. Without content, there is nothing to align. It does not work on inline elements. It does not work directly on structural block elements, but you can assign **text-align** to a structural block element, and it can be inherited by child elements.
Tips	When justifying text, it is important to size the block large enough to prevent a browser from putting unpleasant amounts of extra whitespace between words. The justification algorithm is not sophisticated. It only adds space between words. It does not automatically hyphenate words, and it does not put extra space between letters.
	In spite of the name, **text-align** aligns all types of content including text, images, objects, controls, and so on.
Related to	Aligned Static Inline (Chapter 8); Left Aligned, Left Offset, Right Aligned, Right Offset, Center Aligned, Center Offset (Chapter 9); Spacing (Chapter 11); Opposing Floats, Tab Menu, Tabs, Layout Links (Chapter 17); Center Callout (Chapter 19)

Vertical-Aligned Content

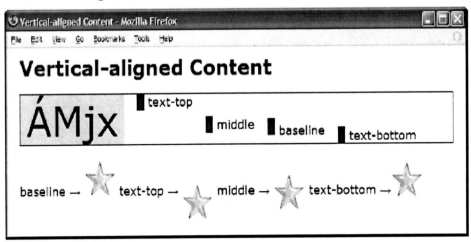

HTML

```
<h1>Vertical-Aligned Content</h1>

<div><span class="main">ÁMjx</span>
    <img  class="text-top" src="bar.gif" alt="bar"
   /><span class="text-top text"> text-top</span>
    <img  class="middle" src="bar.gif" alt="bar"
   /><span class="middle text"> middle</span>
    <img  class="baseline" src="bar.gif" alt="bar"
   /><span class="baseline text"> baseline</span>
    <img  class="text-bottom" src="bar.gif" alt="bar"
   /><span class="text-bottom text"> text-bottom</span></div>

<p class="text">
 baseline &rarr; <img class="baseline" src="star.gif" alt="star" />
 text-top &rarr; <img class="text-top" src="star.gif" alt="star" />
 middle &rarr; <img class="middle" src="star.gif" alt="star" />
 text-bottom &rarr; <img class="text-bottom" src="star.gif" alt="star" /></p>
```

CSS

```
div { font-size:60px; line-height:normal; border:1px solid black; }
.main { background-color:gold; padding:0 10px; }

.text { font-size:18px; }

.text-top { vertical-align:text-top; }
.middle { vertical-align:middle; }
.baseline { vertical-align:baseline; }
.text-bottom { vertical-align:text-bottom; }
```

Vertical-Aligned Content

Problem	You have different sizes of inline elements that you want to align to a common set of reference points. For example, when you have images and text on the same line, you want to align the images to the top, middle, baseline, or bottom of text.
Solution	You can use **vertical-align** to align an inline element to one of its parent's four fontlines: **text-top**, **middle**, **baseline**, and **text-bottom**. By default, inline content is aligned to the baseline.
	Fontlines provide four reference points to which you can align inline content. They define what I call an **alignment context**. Notice how the star image in the example is aligned to each of the four fontlines established by its paragraph, and its neighboring text is aligned to the paragraph's baseline. This is a key point. The star and text are not aligned to each other. They are aligned to the fontlines established by their parent, the paragraph.
	A terminal block establishes the initial alignment context for its inline children and text. The **font** and **font-size** of a block defines the location of the four font lines. The **text-top** is located at the top of characters with accents, like the letter "Á." The **baseline** is located at the bottom of characters that do not have descenders, like the letter "M." The **text-bottom** is located at the bottom of characters that have descenders, like the letter "j." The **middle** is located in the middle of the **ex** height, which is the middle of the letter "x."
	You can use **vertical-align:top** or **bottom** to align an inline element to the top or bottom of a *line*. **top** and **bottom** are typically the same as **text-top** and **text-bottom**—unless the height of a line is taller than its content. A line can be taller than its content when it contains images, objects, different font sizes, different vertical alignment, or a larger **line-height**.
	If a parent and child share the same **font** and **font-size**, their fontlines are located in the same vertical positions. Aligning to the same fontlines produces no change in alignment. To see changes, elements need to have different font sizes, or in the case of images and objects, their height needs to be larger or smaller than the **font-size** of the alignment context.
Pattern	
HTML	`<TERMINAL_BLOCK>  <INLINE> content </INLINE>  </TERMINAL_BLOCK>`
CSS	`TERMINAL_BLOCK_SELECTOR { font-size:+em; }` `INLINE_SELECTOR { vertical-align:FONTLINE; }`
Example	The division in the example defines an alignment context with a **font-size** of 60 pixels. The letters "ÁMjx" show the font size rendered at its full height from the accent on top of the "Á" to the bottom of the "j." The height of the letter "M" is the em height. The height of the letter "x" is the ex height. The images and spans inside the division are aligned to each of the division's fontlines.
	Notice how the closing **/>** of each **<img />** element is placed on the next line with no spaces between it and the following **<span>**. This prevents the whitespace from collapsing out of the span into the division. Since the division has a **font-size** of 60 pixels and the span has a **font-size** of 18 pixels, whitespace in the division is much wider than whitespace in the spans.
Related to	Vertical-Offset Content, Subscript and Superscript, Nested Alignment; HTML Whitespace (Chapter 2); Table, Vertical-Aligned Data (Chapter 15); Layout Links (Chapter 17)

Vertical-Offset Content

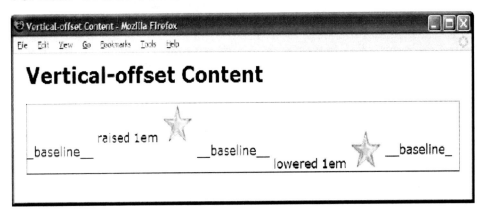

HTML

```
<h1>Vertical-Offset Content</h1>

<div>
  _baseline__

  <span class="raised">raised 1em </span>
  <img class="raised" src="star.gif" alt="star" />

  __baseline__

  <span class="lowered">lowered 1em </span>
  <img class="lowered" src="star.gif" alt="star" />

  __baseline_
</div>
```

CSS

```
div { border:1px solid black; }

.baseline { vertical-align:baseline; }
.raised { vertical-align:1em; }
.lowered { vertical-align:-1em; }
```

Vertical-Offset Content

Problem	You want to vertically offset two or more inline elements that are on the same line. For example, you want to vertically position an image in relation to neighboring text, or you want to position two or more images in relation to each other, or you want to position a drop cap in relation to the following text, or you want to offset text to create a subscript or superscript effect.
Solution	You can use **vertical-align** to offset a child inline element from the baseline of its parent. Positive values raise an element above the baseline, and negative values lower it below the baseline. A line automatically expands to accommodate the offset element.
	You can use ems in **vertical-align**. One em is equal to the element's **font-size**. For example, **1em** raises text above where its top is normally located, and **-1em** lowers text below where its bottom is normally located. Ems have the advantage of scaling along with the text. Thus, if a browser zooms in or out, ems scale proportionally.
	You can use pixels in **vertical-align**. Pixels do not change when a browser zooms in or out, and the offset does not change. This is usually not desirable when offsetting text, but it may be exactly what you want when you are offsetting images.
	vertical-align:0 is the same as aligning to the baseline.
Pattern	
HTML	`<INLINE> content </INLINE>`
CSS	`INLINE_SELECTOR { vertical-align:±VALUE; }`
Location	This pattern works on inline text elements.
Limitations	Vertical offsets are for contrasting the position of two or more inline elements that are on the same line. Since a browser always centers content in a line, if you vertically offset only one element on a line, you will not see the offset because it is centered away.
Tip	I do not recommend using percentages to vertically offset inline elements because the results are hard to predict. The percentage is a proportion of the element's **line-height**. This would be useful if percentages offset an element from the bottom of a line, but they offset it from the baseline. Since a browser centers content within a line, the location of the baseline within a line is not easy to predict.
Example	The division in the example defines an alignment context with a **font-size** of 60 pixels. The letters "ÁMjx" show the rendered font size. The images and spans inside the division are offset from the baseline of the division's alignment context.
Related to	Vertical-Aligned Content, Subscript and Superscript, Nested Alignment; Inline Decoration (Chapter 11); Button (Chapter 17); Aligned Dropcap, First-Letter Dropcap, Padded Dropcap (Chapter 18)

Subscript and Superscript

HTML

```
<h1>Subscript and Superscript</h1>
<p class="large">sub<sub>1</sub> super<sup>2</sup> M<sup>lle</sup></p>
```

CSS

```
sub { vertical-align:-0.5em; font-size:0.75em; }
sup { vertical-align:0.5em;  font-size:0.75em; }

.large { font-size:32px; }
```

CSS Internet Explorer

```
sub { font-size:0.9em; }
sup { font-size:0.9em; }
```

Subscript and Superscript

Problems	You want to use subscripts and superscripts.
	Since each browser uses different vertical offsets and font sizes for subscripts and superscripts, you may also want to standardize their styles to fit your tastes. For example, Firefox 2 lowers subscripts just a little, and Opera 9 uses a larger font size for subscripts and superscripts. The first three screenshots in the example show how subscripts and superscripts look in Firefox 2, Internet Explorer 7, and Opera 9. The fourth screenshot shows subscripts and superscripts styled to look the same in all browsers.
Solutions	You can mark up inline content with **\<sub\>** for subscripts and **\<sup\>** for superscripts. Subscripts and superscripts are semantic elements. In foreign languages, such as French, certain characters must be superscripts to be correct, such as the "lle" in the abbreviation for "mademoiselle." In math, subscripts and superscripts change the meaning of a number.
	If you want to ensure all browsers render subscripts and superscripts the same, you can assign **vertical-align** and **font-size** to **\<sub\>** and **\<sup\>**. You can use **em** values so the location and size of the subscript always remain proportional to the font size.
	You can assign a negative **em** to **vertical-align** to lower a subscript. For example, **-0.5em** lowers the text by half its **font-size**.
	You can assign a positive **em** to **vertical-align** to raise a superscript. For example, **0.5em** raises the text by half its **font-size**.
	You can assign a positive **em** to **font-size** to size the subscript or superscript to be proportional to the font size of its parent. For example, **0.75em** shrinks the subscript or superscript to 75% of its parent's size.
	Since Internet Explorer 7 and earlier versions have a "feature" that sizes subscripts and superscripts 75% smaller than the value you specify with **font-size**, you can compensate by assigning a positive value to **font-size** that is 120% larger than the **em** value you assign to other browsers. You can use the Conditional Style Sheet design pattern to load a style sheet specific to Internet Explorer to assign these values. For example, if you assign **0.75em** to all browsers, you can assign **0.9em** to Internet Explorer.
Patterns	
HTML	`<sub>text</sub>` `<sup>text</sup>`
CSS	`sub { vertical-align:-em; font-size:+em; }` `sup { vertical-align:+em; font-size:+em; }`
Location	This pattern works only on inline text elements.
Related to	Vertical-Offset Content; Inline Elements, Conditional Style Sheet (Chapter 2)

Nested Alignment

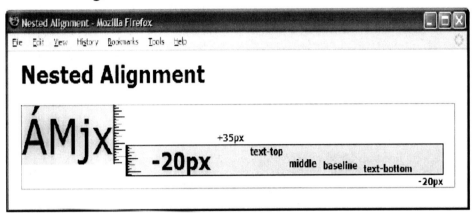

HTML

```
<h1>Nested Alignment</h1>

<div class="ac1">
  <span class="main">ÁMjx</span><span class="ruler"> </span>
  <span class="ac2 lower20px main ruler" >    -20px
    <span class="ac3 raise35px">+35px</span>
    <span class="ac3 text-top">text-top</span>
    <span class="ac3 middle">middle</span>
    <span class="ac3 baseline">baseline</span>
    <span class="ac3 text-bottom">text-bottom</span>
    <span class="ac3 lower20px">-20px</span>
  </span>
</div>
```

CSS

```
.ac1 { font-size:50px; }
.ac2 { font-size:30px; }
.ac3 { font-size:12px; }

.raise35px { vertical-align:35px; }
.lower20px { vertical-align:-20px; }
.text-top { vertical-align:text-top; }
.middle { vertical-align:middle; }
.baseline { vertical-align:baseline; }
.text-bottom { vertical-align:text-bottom; }

/*  Nonessential rules are not shown. */
```

Nested Alignment

Problem	You want to nest alignment contexts. *Nested alignment contexts* are a unique layout feature built into CSS. You will probably never need to use it. I have included this design pattern mainly for completeness.
Solution	You can nest alignment contexts by nesting inline elements and assigning them to different **font-size** values. Each nested inline element defines its own independent alignment context based on the size of the font assigned to the element.
	Fontlines define two alignment contexts for each element: the alignment context in which an element is rendered, and the alignment context an element supplies for its children.
Pattern	
| HTML | ```
<INLINE class="ac1"> content
    <INLINE class="ac2"> content </INLINE>
</INLINE>
``` |
| CSS | ```
.CLASS { font-size:±em;
    white-space:nowrap;
    vertical-align:±em;
    left:±em;
    position:relative; }
``` |
Location	This pattern works only on inline elements.
Limitations	Nested alignment contexts work well as long as they stay on the same line. When a nested alignment context is wrapped to another line, the results vary depending on the browser. In Opera 11, there is a rendering error when **vertical-align: text-bottom** is used with multiple different font sizes. The text can display outside the container.
Tip	You can nest inline elements indefinitely to create as many alignment contexts as you want.
Example	In the example, I have three alignment contexts: **<div class="ac1">**, **<span class="ac2">**, and **<span class="ac3">**. Each is set to three different font sizes: **60px**, **30px**, and **12px**, respectively. Each **font-size** defines a different set of fontlines to which child elements can align. There are six elements using the third alignment context, **<span class="ac3">**, and each one is aligned to a fontline or offset from the baseline of **<span class="ac2">**. **<span class="ac2">** is offset from the baseline of **<div class="ac1">**.
	Notice how **ac2**'s alignment context is preserved internally while it is aligned to **ac1**'s alignment context externally. Internally, each inline element defines its own alignment context to which its children can be aligned. Externally, each inline element is aligned to the alignment context of its parent.
Related to	Vertical-Aligned Content, Vertical-Offset Content, Advanced Alignment Example; Positioned, Relative (Chapter 7); Offset Relative (Chapter 8); Nowrap (Chapter 11)

Advanced Alignment Example

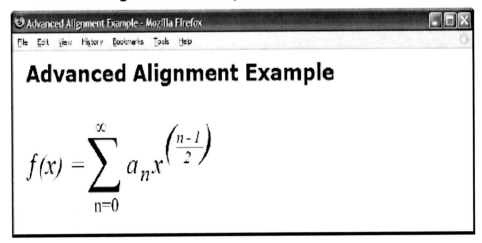

HTML

```
<h1>Advanced Alignment Example</h1>

<p class="large">
  <span class="ac1">
    <span class="ac1-func">&fnof;(x) = </span>
    <span class="ac1-sum">&sum;</span>
    <span class="ac1-min">n=0</span>
    <span class="ac1-max">&infin;</span>
    <span class="ac1-formula">a<sub>n</sub>x
    <span class="ac2">
      (<span class="ac2-num">n-1</span><span class="ac2-dnm">2</span>
        <span class="ac2-close" >)</span>
</span></span></span></p>
```

CSS

```
sub { vertical-align:-0.3em; font-size:0.75em; }

.ac1 {font-size:4em; font-family:"Times New Roman" serif; white-space:nowrap; }
.ac1-func{vertical-align:0.6em; font-size:0.3em; font-style:italic; }
.ac1-sum {vertical-align:0.2em; font-size:0.6em; position:relative; left:-0.1em; }
.ac1-max {vertical-align:3em;   font-size:0.2em; position:relative; left:-6em; }
.ac1-min {vertical-align:-1em;  font-size:0.2em; position:relative; left:-3.3em; }
.ac1-formula { vertical-align:0.6em; font-size:0.3em; font-style:italic;
  position:relative; left:-4em; letter-spacing:0.1em; }

.ac2 {vertical-align:0.4em; font-size:1.5em; position:relative; left:-0.3em; }
.ac2-num {vertical-align:0.7em;   font-size:0.4em; border-bottom:1px solid black; }
.ac2-dnm {vertical-align:-0.4em; font-size:0.4em; position:relative; left:-1.4em; }
.ac2-close { position:relative; left:-0.65em; }
```

Advanced Alignment Example

Example	I have included this example for fun. It uses advanced alignment techniques and relative offsets. This is not an actual design pattern. Something this complex is probably better rendered as an image or as MathML. This is simply an example of how powerful CSS can be.
	This example is sizable. You can use the zoom feature in your browser to enlarge or shrink it. Everything remains aligned properly as it changes size.
	This example works the same in all major browsers, which shows how consistently browsers have implemented alignment contexts.
	The example uses **font-size** to set the size of each alignment context. The two alignment contexts in the example are defined by the elements assigned to the classes **ac1** and **ac2**. I assigned a large enough **font-size** to **ac1** to make room for all its vertically aligned children. The second alignment context is the **(n-1)/2** part of the formula. Notice how all its children are aligned relative to the second alignment context.
	I used **white-space:nowrap** to prevent the example from wrapping to another line. I used **vertical-align** to align elements to various parts of the example. I used **position:relative** and **left** to move elements into horizontal position. I used **em** measurements for **vertical-align** and **left** so they would scale proportionally to the **font-size**. This allows them to grow or shrink as the **font-size** grows and shrinks. You can assign different font sizes to the paragraph in the example to see this in action.

Features

HTML	``` <INLINE class="ac1"> content <INLINE class="ac2"> content </INLINE> </INLINE> ```

CSS	```
	.CLASS { font-size:±em;
	    white-space:nowrap;
	    vertical-align:±em;
	    position:relative;
	    left:±em; }
	``

Location	These features work only on inline elements.
Related to	Vertical-Aligned Content, Vertical-Offset Content, Nested Alignment; Positioned, Relative (Chapter 7); Offset Relative (Chapter 8); Nowrap (Chapter 11)

CHAPTER 13

Blocks

The main purpose of this chapter is to show various ways you can emphasize document structure by styling blocks. Many design patterns in other chapters apply to blocks, but this chapter contains patterns specific to styling block elements to reveal document structure.

Chapter Outline

- **Structural Meaning** shows how blocks create hierarchical and sequential structure.

- **Visual Structure** shows how to style blocks to bring out the document structure.

- **Section** shows how to organize your document into sections for easy styling and for better structural meaning for search engines and document processors.

- **Lists** shows many ways to create lists and list markers.

- **Background Bulleted** shows how to add bullets to a list using background images.

- **Inlined** shows how to render a block element as if it were an inline element. This allows blocks to be rendered from left to right and to wrap across lines.

- **Collapsed Margins** shows how to collapse and uncollapse vertical margins between block elements.

- **Run-In** shows how to run a block into the following sibling block as if it were an inline element within the following block. Run-in headings save space and are very attractive.

- **Horizontal Rule** shows how to use and style a horizontal rule in spite of the problems caused by Internet Explorer 7, which refuses to remove its built-in styles from `<hr />`.

- **Block Spacer** shows how to insert a precise amount of vertical space between selective blocks without having to adjust margins individually.

- **Block Space Remover** shows how to remove a precise amount of vertical space between selective blocks without having to adjust margins individually.

- **Left Marginal** shows how to extract headings, notes, alerts, and images from the normal flow and move them into a wide left margin.

- **Right Marginal** works like Left Marginal except items are moved to the right.

Structural Meaning

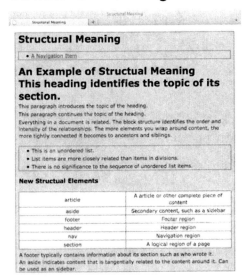

HTML

```
<body>
<div id="wrapper">
  <header><h1>Structural Meaning</h1></header>

  <nav><ul><li><a href="#">A Navigation Item</a></li></ul></nav>

  <article>
    <header><h1>An Example of Structural Meaning</h1></header>
    <section>
      <header><hgroup>
        <h1>This heading identifies the topic of its section.</h1>
        <p>This paragraph introduces the topic of the heading.</p>
        <p>This paragraph continues the topic of the heading.</p> </hgroup></header>

      <p>Everything in a document is related. The block structure identifies the
order and intensity of the relationships. The more elements you wrap around
content, the more tightly connected it becomes to ancestors and siblings.</p>

      <ul>
        <li>This is an unordered list.</li>
        <li>List items are more closely related than items in divisions.</li>
        <li>There is no significance to the sequence of unordered list items.</li> </ul>

      <h3>New Structural Elements</h3>
      <table><tbody>
        <tr><td>article</td><td>An article or other complete piece of content</td></tr>
        <tr><td>aside</td><td>Secondary content, such as a sidebar</td></tr>
        <tr><td>footer</td><td>Footer region</td></tr>
        <tr><td>header</td><td>Header region</td></tr>
        <tr><td>nav</td><td>Navigation region</td></tr>
        <tr><td>section</td><td>A logical region of a page</td></tr> </tbody></table>
```

```
    </section>
    <footer>
        <p>A footer typically contains information about its section such as who wrote it.</p>
    </footer>
    </article>

    <aside id="sidebar">
        <p>An aside indicates content that is tangentially related to the content around it. Can
be used as a sidebar.</p> </aside>
    </div></body>
```

Structural Meaning

Problem	You want to identify the structure of a document using blocks.
Solution	Blocks define the structure of a document, and the structure of a document helps readers and computers understand the meaning of a document. Everything in a document is related. The block structure identifies the order and intensity of the relationships. The more elements you wrap around content, the more closely it relates to ancestors and siblings.

HTML makes four assumptions about the *meaning* of document structure:

1) A parent element defines the topic of its children.

2) Siblings are ordered unless the parent element specifies otherwise.

3) As the hierarchy deepens, meaning becomes more focused and connected.

4) All content in the document body is related. Content in a division or a form is more closely related. Content in lists is even more closely related. Content in tables is the most closely related.

Two types of structures exist in HTML: **hierarchies** and **sets**. You create hierarchies by nesting elements. You create sets by placing multiple elements inside a parent. There are two types of sets: **ordered** and **unordered**.

Each structure in HTML starts out as a hierarchy and ends in a set.

For example, a table creates a hierarchy of nested rows and cells. Within that hierarchy, a table contains an ordered set of rows, and each row contains an ordered set of cells. Cells in the same column are related, and cells in the same row are related. Because a cell is the intersection of a row and a column, it ties together the meaning of both. As a result, content in tables is *most* strongly related (that is why it is called **relational data**).

Take another example: a list starts out as a hierarchy where a parent list element contains a set of list items. An ordered list contains an ordered set of related list items. An unordered list contains an unordered set of related list items. A dictionary list is an associative entity containing an unordered set of related terms and definitions. Lists can be nested within each other to create a hierarchy of lists. You can put content in lists when you want it to be *more* strongly related than content in the document body, a division, or a form.

As a final example, a division organizes headings and paragraphs into a series of related topics where each heading introduces an ordered series of related paragraphs. Divisions can be nested to create a hierarchy of subtopics.

Pattern HTML	```<PARENT_BLOCK>
<CHILD_BLOCK_1> related content </CHILD_BLOCK_1>
<CHILD_BLOCK_2> related content </CHILD_BLOCK_2>
...
<CHILD_BLOCK_N> related content </CHILD_BLOCK_N>
</PARENT_BLOCK>```
Location	This pattern applies to block elements.
Related to	Visual Structure; HTML Structure, Structural Block Elements, Terminal Block Elements, Multi-purpose Block Elements (Chapter 2)

Visual Structure

See the Structural Meaning design pattern for the example.

CSS (for the Structural Meaning Design Pattern)

```
h1 { margin:0; font-size:1.9em; }
h2 { margin:0; margin-top:3px; font-size:1.2em; }

header,nav,section,aside,footer,article{ display:block; }
ul,div,td,th { border:1px solid black; background-color:gold; margin-top:20px; }
div { padding:0 10px; }
table { border-collapse:collapse; margin:5px 0; }
td,th { background-color:white; width:20%; text-align:center; padding:2px; }
ul { margin-left:0; padding:0 40px; }
p,li { margin:0; padding:2px 0; }
```

STYLING EXCEPTIONS

A style sheet works well when you style classes of items, but it quickly becomes cumbersome when you style exceptions. To style one element, you typically add an ID to it and style the ID in the style sheet. This is a minor inconvenience in a single document, but this inconvenience turns into a maintenance problem over time as documents change, styles change, and hundreds of documents share common style sheets. For example, since an ID used for exceptional styling is part of an element, when the element moves, the exceptional styling moves with it. This will likely cause unexpected results when you modify a document and will send you on a wild goose chase looking for the cause of the problem.

The Horizontal Rule, Block Spacer, or Block Space Remover design patterns are good solutions for styling exceptional cases because they insert an element into the document. The element has structural meaning, is self-documenting, and is easy to reposition. You can style these spacer elements using standard classes so you are no longer styling exceptions. Spacer elements are only for exceptional cases.

POSITIONAL STYLING

At times you may want to style an element because it is in a certain position. For example, you may want to change the amount of margin before the first child and after the last child of a block because collapsed margins work differently for the first and last child elements. If you apply an exceptional margin directly to the first child element, and then you move the first child so that it becomes a middle child, its exceptional margin moves with it. This is not the result you want because you want to *style the position*—not the element.

One way to style a position is to use the Horizontal Rule, Block Spacer, or Block Space Remover design patterns. This works because it is easy to keep a spacer element in the right position—especially if you name its class intuitively, such as "first-child" and "last-child". CSS 3 positional selectors are powerful enough for positional styling and are almost completely supported by modern browsers.

Visual Structure

Problem	You want to reveal the structure of a document visually.
Solution	CSS provides a number of ways you can style blocks to reveal document structure. You can put vertical margins between blocks or use first-line indents to visually separate content into blocks. You can put bullets or numbers in a block's margin to enumerate blocks. You can use margins, borders, and padding to put boxes around blocks to reveal how they are nested inside each other. You can also assign font sizes to heading levels so that headings with a larger scope have a larger font size—this can reveal the nesting of blocks without having to put them inside boxes.
	You can help the user see the structural meaning of a document by visually styling the structure. To emphasize a close structural relationship, you can position elements closer together and give them a similar look. For example, elements inside lists and tables have a similar look to show they belong together. To set elements apart, you can position them further apart and style them differently. For example, lists, tables, and blocks have different default styles to emphasize the different meanings of their structures. Also, unordered lists use bullets to point out that their items are unordered.
	To create a consistent look and feel, it is a common practice to apply a standard set of styles to all blocks of the same type. For example, you may want all paragraphs and list items to have a 2-pixel vertical padding. In your style sheet, you can select all elements of a certain type or all elements of a certain class and style them as desired. This is demonstrated in the example.
	Occasionally, you may want to change the space between *two specific blocks*. You can bring them closer together to emphasize the closeness of their relationship or push them further apart to emphasize their differences. Structurally, you are styling the space between the blocks. Since the relationship is not part of either block, but is *between* the blocks, it is more structurally accurate and simpler to insert a spacer block than it is to style the margin of one of the two blocks as an *exception* to its normal styling.
	HTML provides the **<hr />** element for the purpose of inserting a structural break between blocks (and ** ** to insert a line break between inlines). The Horizontal Rule design pattern shows how to use and style **<hr />**.
	When you want to insert a structural break that is not as strong as a horizontal rule or you want to bring two blocks closer together, you can use the Block Spacer and Block Space Remover design patterns.
	Using a horizontal rule, a block spacer, or a block space remover should be the exception, not the norm. The structural meaning of breaks and links between elements is not as strong as nested structures.
	You may want to merge two blocks to emphasize a very close relationship between them. This is explored in the Inlined and Run-In design patterns.
Related to	Structural Meaning, Horizontal Rule, Block Spacer, Block Space Remover

Section

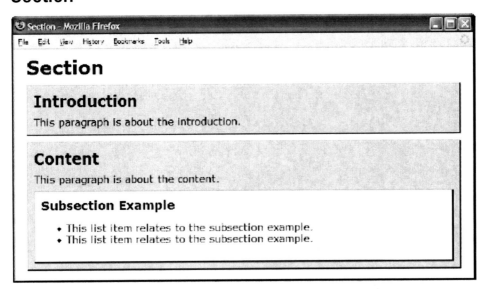

HTML

```
<h1>Section</h1>

<section class="introduction">
   <h2>Introduction</h2>
   <p>This paragraph is about the introduction.</p>
</section>

<section class="content">
  <h2>Content</h2>
  <p>This paragraph is about the content.</p>

  <section class="section example">
    <h3>Subsection Example</h3>
      <ul><li>This list item relates to the subsection example.</li>
        <li>This list item relates to the subsection example.</li></ul>
  </section>
</section>
```

CSS

```
section { padding:10px; margin:10px 0; background-color:gold;
  border-left:1px solid gray; border-right:2px solid black;
  border-top:1px solid gray; border-bottom:2px solid black; display:block; }
section p { margin:0; margin-top:5px; }
section h2 { margin:0; margin-bottom:10px; }
section h3 { margin:0; margin-bottom:10px; }
section.example { background-color:white; }
section section { margin-bottom:0; }
```

Section

Problem	You want to organize your document into sections, and you want to style various sections differently.
Solution	HTML provides the **section** element to identify sections of a document. A section is generic and has no meaning by itself. A section is a part of a document that contains content relating to a specific theme or purpose. A section normally contains a heading followed by blocks of supporting statements that are logically related to each other. Subsections are often nested within sections to identify subthemes relating to the theme of the parent section.
	Any heading element can be used, such as **‹h1›**, **‹h2›**, **‹h3›**, **‹h4›**, **‹h5›**, and **‹h6›**. The heading level identifies the relative importance of the section. **‹h1›** is the most important heading in a document. Following the heading are blocks of content and subsections.
	This design pattern imposes no constraints on the structure of sections and subsections, other than each section should contain a heading as its first content-containing child element. I use the phrase "content-containing child element" because a section may contain any number of decorative child elements, such as divisions and spans, prior to the heading. Such decorative child elements could be used to layer background images behind the section, for example.

Pattern	HTML

```
<section class="TYPE">
  <HEADING> content </HEADING>
  <BLOCK> content </BLOCK>
  ...
</section>
```

CSS

```
section { STYLES }
section.TYPE { STYLES }
section.TYPE HEADING { STYLES }
section.TYPE BLOCK { STYLES }
section section { STYLES }
```

Location	This pattern applies to block elements.
Tips	There are no limits to the names you can use to classify your sections. Here are a few examples: callout, caution, content, example, figure, introduction, listing, note, quote, summary, table, tip, and warning. For 200 more examples, see the file **Common Section Names.txt** in the example folder.
Related to	Structural Meaning, Run-In; Floating Section (Chapter 17)

Lists

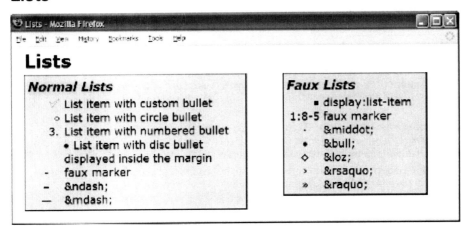

HTML

```
<h1>Lists</h1>
<section id="section1"><h2>Normal Lists</h2>
  <ul><li class="custom">List item with custom bullet</li>
    <li class="circle">List item with circle bullet</li>
    <li class="decimal">List item with numbered bullet</li>
    <li class="inside">List item with disc bullet displayed inside the margin</li>
    <li class="none"><span class="marker">-</span>faux marker</li>
    <li class="none"><span class="marker">&ndash;</span>&amp;ndash;</li>
    <li class="none"><span class="marker">&mdash;</span>&amp;mdash;</li></ul></section>
<section id="section2"><h2>Faux Lists</h2>
  <span class="listed">display:list-item</span>
    <p class="list"><span class="marker">1:8-5</span>faux marker</p>
    <p class="list"><span class="marker">&middot;</span>&amp;middot;</p>
    <p class="list"><span class="marker">&bull;</span>&amp;bull;</p>
    <p class="list"><span class="marker">&loz;</span>&amp;loz;</p>
    <p class="list"><span class="marker">&rsaquo;</span>&amp;rsaquo;</p>
    <p class="list"><span class="marker">&raquo;</span>&amp;raquo;</p></section>
```

CSS

```
ul { margin-left:0; padding-left:0; } /* Normalized list */
ul li { margin-left:60px; }

.listed { margin-left:60px; display:list-item; list-style:square; }

.list { margin-left:60px; }
.marker { float:left; margin-left:-60px; width:60px; text-align:center; }

.custom  { list-style-image:url("check.gif"); }
.circle  { list-style-type:circle; }
.decimal { list-style-type:decimal; }
.inside  { list-style-position:inside; }
.none    { list-style-type:none; }

/* Nonessential rules are not shown. */
```

Lists

Problem	You want to lay out a block as a bulleted or numbered list.
Solution	You can embed content in list items (**<li>**). You can embed list items in unordered (bulleted) lists (**<ul>**) or ordered (numbered) lists (**<ol>**).
	You can use the list-style-type property to assign the type of marker displayed to the left of a list item. The bullet markers include **disc** (the default), **circle**, and **square**. The numbered markers that work in all major browsers include **decimal** (the default), **lower-alpha**, **upper-alpha**, **lower-roman**, and **upper-roman**. Using **list-style-type**, you can even force numbered list items to display bullets and vice versa! You can hide the marker using **list-style-type:none**.
	You can use list-style-image to display an image in place of the marker. In the example, the **marker-custom** class uses the rule **list-style-image:url("check.gif")** to display a check-mark image as the marker.
	You can use list-style-position:inside to place the marker inside the list's margin, which allows subsequent lines to wrap under the marker.
	You can use display:list-item to render any block or inline element as a list item, and a browser will display a marker in its left margin. You can apply any **list-style** rule to the element to style the marker. This can be useful when you have inline elements in MicroFormats that you want to style as lists (see **http://microformats.org** for more information on using MicroFormats).
	All major browsers indent lists by 40 pixels, but they differ in how they do it. Some set margins to 40 pixels, and others set padding. For consistent results, you can assign **margin-left:0;** and **padding-left:0;** to **<ul>** and **<ol>**, and you can assign **margin-left:WIDTH** to list items (**<li>**). You can increase the left margin to make more room for markers, as I did in the example.
	You can create a faux marker by wrapping any content you want in a span. This allows you to use any text as a marker, and you can style it in any way! You can use **float:left** to float the span to the left. You can use **margin-left:-WIDTH** to move it into the left margin the same distance as its width and its parent's left margin. You can also align its content to center.

Patterns
 	
HTML
	```<ul><li> CONTENT </li></ul>```
	or ```<ol><li> CONTENT </li></ol>```
	or ```<ul><li> <span class="faux-marker"> MARKER </span> </li></ul>```
	or ```<ELEMENT class="listed"> CONTENT </ELEMENT>```
	or ```<PARENT class="list">```
	    ```<CHILD class="marker"> MARKER </CHILD> CONTENT </PARENT>```

CSS	```ul { margin-left:0; padding-left:0; }```
	```ul li { margin-left:WIDTH; }```
	```.listed { margin-left:WIDTH; display:list-item; list-style:disc; }```
	```.list { margin-left:WIDTH; }```
	```.marker { float:left; margin-left:-WIDTH; width:WIDTH; }```

Related to	Structural Meaning, Visual Structure, Background Bulleted, Inlined; Structural Block Elements, Multi-purpose Block Elements (Chapter 2); Display, Block Box (Chapter 4); Margin, Padding (Chapter 6); Float and Clear, Relative Float (Chapter 7); Offset Float (Chapter 8); Rollup, Tab Menu, Tabs, Flyout Menu, Layout Links (Chapter 17)

273

Background Bulleted

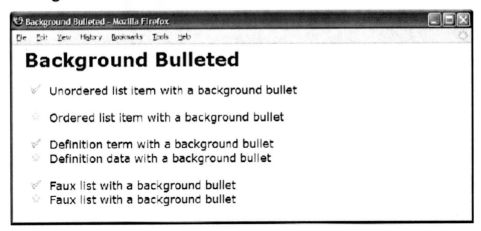

HTML

```
<h1>Background Bulleted</h1>

<ul class="bb-list">
  <li class="bb1">Unordered list item with a background bullet</li></ul>

<ol class="bb-list">
  <li class="bb2">Ordered list item with a background bullet</li></ol>

<dl class="bb-list">
  <dt class="bb1">Definition term with a background bullet</dt>
  <dd class="bb2">Definition data with a background bullet</dd></dl>

<div class="bb-list">
  <p class="bb1">Faux list with a background bullet</p>
  <p class="bb2">Faux list with a background bullet</p></div>
```

CSS

```
.bb-list { padding-left:40px; margin-left:0; margin-top:20px; }
.bb-list li,
.bb-list dt,
.bb-list dd,
.bb-list p { padding-left:40px; margin-left:-40px; list-style-type:none;
  margin-top:0; margin-bottom:0; }

.bb1 { background:url("check.gif") no-repeat 10px 1px; }
.bb2 { background:url("star.gif") no-repeat 10px 1px; }
```

Background Bulleted

Problem	You want to control the precise placement of a list item's bullet.
Solution	Since CSS does not provide properties for controlling the position of a bullet, you can use a background image as the bullet of each list item, and you can use **background-position** to position it precisely.

You can assign a positive left padding to a list element (**<ol>**, **<ul>**, or **<dl>**) to make room for bullets on its list items. You should also remove the default left margin that some browsers add to lists. In the example, I assigned **padding-left:40px** and **margin-left:0** to each list.

You can assign a negative left margin to each list item to move it into the padding area of its parent list. The negative left margin should be the exact inverse of the amount assigned to the left padding of its parent. In the example, I assigned **margin-left:-40px** to each list item.

You can assign the exact amount of left padding to each list item that you assigned to its parent list. This moves a list item's content away from the bullet. In the example, I assigned **padding-left:40px** to each list item. You should also hide each list item's built-in marker using **list-style-type:none**.

You can assign a nonrepeating background image to each list item and use **background-position** to offset its position. In the example, I used a left offset of 10 pixels and a top offset of 1 pixel. You can use different classes as needed to assign and position different background images to individual list items.

You can assign the **bb-list** class to each list. This distinguishes between normal lists and background-bulleted lists, which is important because they each have different values for margin and padding. You can combine ***.bb-list** with the descendant operator and a list-item element to select background-bulleted list items. Since there are three different types of list-item elements, you can use the grouping operator to assign multiple selectors to this pattern's rules.

Since a list item is a block element, this pattern applies to all block elements. Nonetheless, it is better to mark up items as a list when they function as a list. In the example, I applied this pattern to a division and its child paragraphs, but only to show how it can be done—not to recommend that you do it.

Pattern HTML	``` <LIST class="bb-list"> <LIST_ITEM class="BULLET_STYLE"> list content </LIST_ITEM> </LIST> ```
CSS	``` .bb-list { padding-left:+INDENT; margin-left:0; } .bb-list li, .bb-list dt, .bb-list dd,.bb-list p { padding-left:+INDENT; margin-left:-INDENT; list-style-type:none; } .BULLET_STYLE { background:url("FILE.EXT") LEFT_OFFSET TOP_OFFSET no-repeat; } ```
Related to	Lists; Block Box (Chapter 4); Margin, Padding, Background (Chapter 6)

Inlined

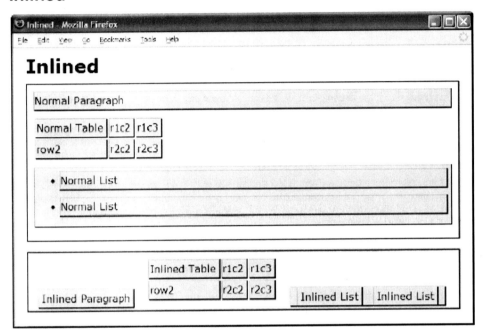

HTML

```
<h1>Inlined</h1>
<div>
  <p>Normal Paragraph</p>
  <table><tr><td>Normal Table</td><td>r1c2</td><td>r1c3</td></tr>
    <tr><td>row2</td><td>r2c2</td><td>r2c3</td></tr></table>
  <ul><li>Normal List</li><li>Normal List</li></ul></div>

<div>
  <p class="inlined">Inlined Paragraph</p>
  <table class="inlined">
    <tr><td>Inlined Table</td><td>r1c2</td><td>r1c3</td></tr>
    <tr><td>row2</td><td>r2c2</td><td>r2c3</td></tr></table>
  <ul class="inlined"><li class="inlined">Inlined List</li>
  <li class="inlined">Inlined List</li></ul></div>
```

CSS

```
div { padding:10px; margin-bottom:15px; border:2px solid black; }
table, p, td, ul, li { margin-top:0px; margin-bottom:10px; padding-right:5px; }
p, td, ul, li { background-color:gold; padding-top:5px; padding-bottom:5px;
  border-left:1px solid gray; border-right:2px solid black;
  border-top:1px solid gray; border-bottom:2px solid black; }

.inlined { display:inline; line-height:normal; padding:5px; margin:5px; vertical-align:bottom;
}
table.inlined{ display:inline-table; }
```

Inlined

Problem	You want the browser to render a block element as if it were an inline element. In other words, you want a block element to be displayed inline.
Solution	CSS provides **display:inline** for this purpose. You can assign this rule to any element to display it inline. Since **margin** and **padding** work differently inline, you often need to adjust the margin and padding to work inline. This is particularly true for lists displayed inline. Since **height** does not work inline, you can use **line-height** in its place.
Pattern	`SELECTOR { display:inline; line-height:+VALUE;` `    margin:±VALUE; padding:+VALUE; }`
Location	This pattern applies to any type of element.
Limitations	List items lose their bullets and numbers when inlined. Version 8+ of Google Chrome requires tables use inline-table to render a table inline.
Advantages	Inlining a block element allows it to be rendered from left to right (or right to left in some languages) and wrapped to additional lines as needed. This is the most compact way to display elements.
Tips	Rendering a table inline can be useful when you have a few rows of tabular data that you want to flow along with other inline content. The table retains its internal structure of rows and columns, but is located in the inline formatting context. A table rendered inline is very similar to an inline block: both are rendered as blocks within an inline formatting context. When a parent block is inlined, its child blocks must be inlined too, or they will break out of the inline formatting context and create new block formatting contexts. For example, list elements need to be inlined along with their list container. (This does *not* apply to rows and cells of inlined tables.)
Example	The first division in the example contains a paragraph, a table containing two rows of cells, and a list containing two list items. The second division contains the same elements, but each element is inlined.
Related to	Run-In; Display, Inline Box, Inline-Block Box (Chapter 4); Blocked (Chapter 11); Tabled, Rowed, and Celled (Chapter 15); Flyout Menu (Chapter 17); Hanging Alert, Run-In Alert (Chapter 20)

Collapsed Margins

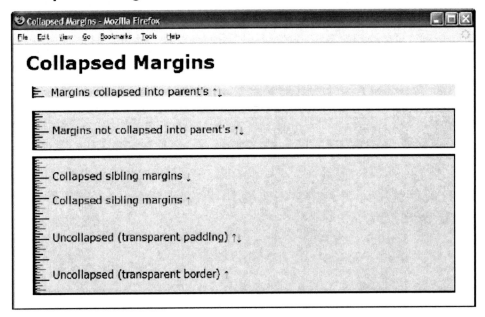

HTML

```
<h1>Collapsed Margins</h1>
<div><p class="collapsed">Margins collapsed into parent's &uarr;&darr;</p></div>
<div class="border">
  <p class="collapsed">Margins not collapsed into parent's &uarr;&darr;</p></div>

<div class="border">
  <p class="collapsed">Collapsed sibling margins &darr;</p>
  <p class="collapsed">Collapsed sibling margins &uarr;</p>
  <p class="uncollapsed1">Uncollapsed (transparent padding) &uarr;&darr;</p>
  <p class="uncollapsed2">Uncollapsed (transparent border) &uarr;</p></div>
```

CSS

```
div { margin:10px; padding-left:30px; background-color:gold;
  background-image: url("ruler.gif"); background-repeat:repeat-y; }
.border { border:2px solid black; }

.collapsed { margin-top:20px; margin-bottom:20px; }

.uncollapsed1 { margin-top:0; margin-bottom:0;
  padding-top:20px; padding-bottom:20px;
  background-color:transparent; }

.uncollapsed2 { margin-top:0; margin-bottom:0;
  border-top:20px solid transparent;
  border-bottom:20px solid transparent; }
```

Collapsed Margins

Problem	You want to collapse or uncollapse vertical margins between blocks.
Solution	Browsers collapse vertical margins into the larger of the bottom and top margins between *sibling* blocks. For example, if the bottom margin of one block is 15 pixels and the top margin of the next sibling block is 10 pixels, the collapsed margin is 15 pixels (the uncollapsed margin is 25 pixels).
	You can literally prevent the collapsing of the first child's top margin into its parent's top margin by assigning a top padding or a top border to the parent. Likewise, you can prevent the collapsing of the last child's bottom margin into its parent's bottom margin by assigning bottom padding or a bottom border to the parent. You can hide the padding or border by making it transparent and as small as one pixel. In the example, the vertical margins of the second paragraph do not collapse into its parent because its parent has top and bottom borders.
	You cannot prevent vertical margins from collapsing *between sibling blocks*. If you want to avoid the collapsing effect between siblings, you can set margins to zero and use transparent borders or transparent padding instead. Borders and padding do not collapse.
	When a parent block does not have a border, the top margin of its first child collapses into its top margin. Likewise, the bottom margin of the last child collapses into the parent's bottom margin.
| **Patterns** | **Uncollapsed Margins Between Parent and Child Blocks**<br><br>```
PARENT_SELECTOR { border-top: WIDTH STYLE COLOR;
    border-bottom: WIDTH STYLE COLOR;
    padding-top:+VALUE; padding-bottom:+VALUE; }
```<br>**Uncollapsed Margins Between Sibling Blocks**<br><br>```
SIBLING_SELECTOR { padding-top:+VALUE; margin-top:0;
    padding-bottom:+VALUE; margin-bottom:0;
    background-color:transparent; }
```<br>*or*<br>```
SIBLING_SELECTOR { margin-top:0; margin-bottom:0;
    border-top:+VALUE solid transparent;
    border-bottom:+VALUE solid transparent;
    background-color:transparent; }
``` |
Location	This pattern applies to block elements and elements displayed as blocks.
Disadvantage	Using padding or borders to prevent collapsing margins prevents you from using padding and borders for what they were intended.
Related to	Horizontal Rule, Block Spacer, Block Space Remover; Margin, Border, Padding (Chapter 6); Spacing, Blocked (Chapter 11), Collapsed Borders (Chapter 15)
```

Run-In

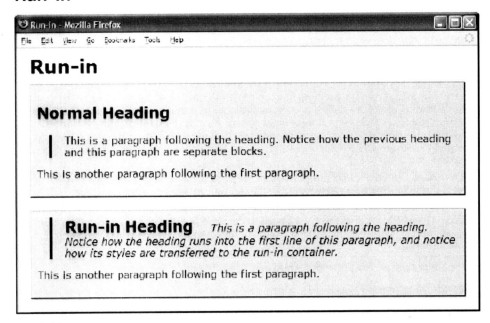

HTML

```
<h1>Run-In</h1>
<section>
  <h2>Normal Heading</h2>
  <p class="indent">This is a paragraph following the heading. Notice
    how the previous heading and this paragraph are separate blocks.</p>
  <p>This is another paragraph following the first paragraph.</p></section>

<section>
  <div  class="run-in-container indent">
    <h2 class="run-in">Run-In Heading</h2>
    <p  class="run-in">This is a paragraph following the heading. Notice how
      the heading runs into the first line of this paragraph, and notice how
      its styles are transferred to the run-in container.</p>
  </div>
  <p>This is another paragraph following the first paragraph.</p></section>
```

CSS

```
section { padding:10px; margin-bottom:20px; background-color:gold;
  border-left:1px solid gray; border-right:2px solid black;
  border-top:1px solid gray; border-bottom:2px solid black; display: block; }
.indent { margin-left:20px; border-left:4px solid black; padding-left:20px; }

.run-in { display:inline; }
.run-in-container h2 { padding-right:20px; }
.run-in-container p { font-style:italic; }
```

Run-In

Problem	You want to run a block into the following sibling block as if it were an inline element within the following block. For example, you may want to run a heading into the following paragraph for a more compact presentation. You may also want to run a series of blocks into another block.
Solution	CSS provides the rule **display:run-in** for this purpose, but only Opera, Safari, and Konquerer support it. You can implement a run-in by wrapping the run-in block and the destination block inside a container block. You can then assign **display:inline** to these two blocks to render them inline. Displaying them inline causes the run-in block to merge into the first line of the destination block. By wrapping both blocks in a container block, you can transfer any block styles to the container block that you would have applied to the destination block, such as margins, borders, padding, or a background.
	If you want to run multiple blocks into a final block, you can assign the entire series of blocks to **display:inline** and wrap them all in one block.
	Of course, it would be much better if Internet Explorer and Firefox simply implemented run-ins.

Pattern HTML	``` <RUN_IN_CONTAINER_BLOCK> <RUN_IN_BLOCK> content </RUN_IN_BLOCK> <DESTINATION_BLOCK> content </DESTINATION_BLOCK> </RUN_IN_CONTAINER_BLOCK> ```
CSS	``` RUN_IN_BLOCK_SELECTOR { display:inline; } DESTINATION_BLOCK_SELECTOR { display:inline; } ```

Location	This pattern applies to block elements.
Tips	Because the run-in container encloses the run-in and destination blocks, you can take advantage of descendant selectors to apply additional styles to the run-in block and the destination block.
	This design pattern works even if you do not wrap the run-in and destination blocks in a container block. Since the run-in and destination blocks are displayed inline, the browser creates an anonymous block box to hold them. The problem with the anonymous block box is that you cannot transfer any block styles from the destination block to the anonymous block box. This is a problem only if you have block styles you need to transfer, such as margins, borders, padding, or a background.
Example	In the example, I transferred the **indent** class from the destination paragraph to the run-in container. I also used a descendant selector to insert extra padding between the run-in heading and the destination paragraph. Using another descendant selector, I styled the destination paragraph as italic.
Related to	Section, Inlined; Run-In Alert (Chapter 20)

Horizontal Rule

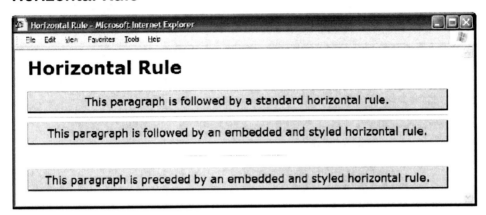

HTML

```
<h1>Horizontal Rule</h1>

<p>This paragraph is followed by a standard horizontal rule.</p>

<hr />

<p>This paragraph is followed by an embedded and styled horizontal rule.</p>

<div class="hr"><hr /></div>

<p>This paragraph is preceded by an embedded and styled horizontal rule.</p>
```

CSS

```
.hr { height:40px; width:200px;
  margin:0 auto 0 auto;
  border:0;
  background:url("hr.gif") repeat-x left center;
  line-height:1px; font-size:1px; }

.hr hr { display:none; }

/* Nonessential rules are not shown. */
```

Horizontal Rule

Problem	You want to insert a horizontal rule between block elements to indicate the beginning of a new section. You want the horizontal rule to insert styled vertical space between blocks in the normal flow. You want to style the horizontal rule with margins, borders, background colors, and tiled images.
Solution	HTML provides the **‹hr /›** element for this purpose. Browsers render it as a gray, 2-pixel tall, 3D stretched line. Each browser uses a different shade of gray and a slightly different amount for the vertical margins.
	You can style its margins, borders, padding, and background color just like you would style any block. If you give it a nonzero height, you can even assign it a background image. Unfortunately, Internet Explorer 7 and earlier versions do not properly apply box model rules to the horizontal rule, such as padding. And worse, Internet Explorer adds *extra* vertical margins and interior borders that you cannot remove. This makes styling the horizontal rule the same in all major browsers impossible.
	If you want to style a horizontal rule and have it work in Internet Explorer, it is best to embed the horizontal rule within a division, hide the rule, and style the division instead. You can use **display:none** to hide the embedded horizontal rule. Because the horizontal rule is still present, a browser that does not use CSS will still display a horizontal rule, and the semantic meaning of the horizontal rule is preserved.
	You can use **width** and horizontal margins to align, indent, and offset the parent division. You can use **height** to set its height. You can use **margin-top** and **margin-bottom** to insert transparent space above and below the division. You can render a styled line across the width of the division using **border-top** and **border-bottom**. You can also use the background properties to show or tile an image across the division.
Patterns	
HTML	**‹hr /›**
	or
	‹div class="hr"›‹hr /›‹/div›

CSS	**.hr { width:+VALUE;**
	   height:+VALUE;
	   margin:±VALUE; border: WIDTH STYLE COLOR;
	   background:COLOR IMAGE REPEAT H_POSITION V_POSITION; }
	.hr hr { display:none; }

Location	This pattern applies to horizontal rules.
Related to	Block Spacer; Linebreak, Inline Horizontal Rule (Chapter 11)

Block Spacer

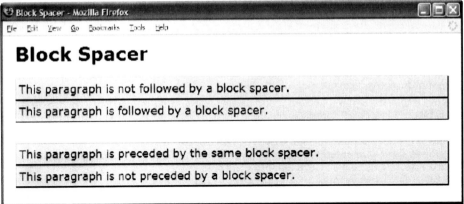

HTML

```
<h1>Block Spacer</h1>

<p>This paragraph is not followed by a block spacer.</p>
<p>This paragraph is followed by a block spacer.</p>

<div class="spacer-large"></div>

<p>This paragraph is preceded by the same block spacer.</p>
<p>This paragraph is not preceded by a block spacer.</p>
```

CSS

```
p { margin:0; padding:5px; background-color:gold;
   border-left:1px solid gray; border-right:2px solid black;
   border-top:1px solid gray; border-bottom:2px solid black; }

.spacer-large { padding-bottom:32px; }
```

Block Spacer

Problem	You want to put space between two blocks to show that they do not belong together. You want the separation to imply that a new series of thoughts follows, but unlike the horizontal rule, you do not want to imply that a whole new section follows. You want the structure of the markup to mirror the structure of the content, which has a slight separation of thought. You also want to control the amount of vertical space inserted—the more space, the stronger the structural separation of content.
Solution	You can insert an empty division between the blocks. You can assign a specific amount of bottom or top padding to the division to insert the desired amount of space.
	Since the purpose of this design pattern is to separate two blocks, the class name you assign to the block spacer element should reflect this purpose.
Pattern	HTML
	`<div class="CLASS"></div>`
	CSS
	`.CLASS { padding-bottom:+VALUE; }`
Location	This pattern applies to block elements.
Advantages	The block spacer is best used when you want the markup to communicate a separation between blocks because this reflects the meaning of the content. It is a simple, reliable, and semantic way to insert extra vertical space between any two blocks.
Disadvantages	This design pattern requires an extra element to be inserted into the markup. You may be tempted to use this for visual effects rather than for its structural purpose. In that case, you should assign a **margin** to one of the blocks.
Tips	Because a block spacer is inserted between two elements, it has the side effect of stopping the previous block's bottom margin from collapsing into the following block's top margin. Thus, you can insert a 1-pixel block spacer between blocks to uncollapse their margins (and add one extra pixel of space). Note that a zero-pixel block spacer does not uncollapse margins.
	You could insert the **padding-bottom** rule directly inside the **style** attribute of the spacer division. I recommend against this because you will likely need to change this value as margins in the style sheet change. I find it speeds software development to keep all style rules in style sheets. I also avoid using class names that imply specific measurements, such as **spacer32px**, because the amount of space removed is likely to change.
Related to	Visual Structure, Block Space Remover, Horizontal Rule; Padding (Chapter 6); Spacing, Inline Spacer, Linebreak, Inline Horizontal Rule (Chapter 11)

Block Space Remover

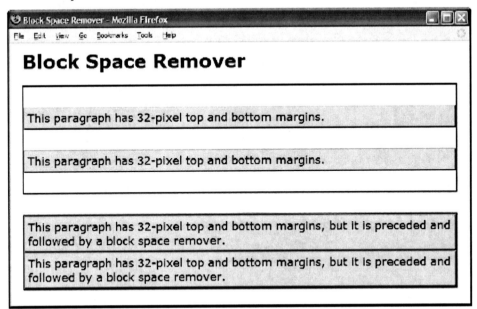

HTML

```
<h1>Block Space Remover</h1>
<div class="section">
  <p>This paragraph has 32-pixel top and bottom margins.</p>
  <p>This paragraph has 32-pixel top and bottom margins.</p>
</div>

<section>
  <div class="space-remover-large"></div>
  <p>This paragraph has 32-pixel top and bottom margins,
    but it is preceded and followed by a block space remover.</p>
  <div class="space-remover-large"></div>
  <p>This paragraph has 32-pixel top and bottom margins,
    but it is preceded and followed by a block space remover.</p>
  <div class="space-remover-large"></div>
</section>
```

CSS

```
section { border:2px solid black; margin-bottom:32px; display:block; }
p { margin-top:32px; margin-bottom:32px; padding:5px; background-color:gold;
  border-left:1px solid gray; border-right:2px solid black;
  border-top:1px solid gray; border-bottom:2px solid black; }

.space-remover-large { margin-top:-32px; }
```

286

Block Space Remover

Problem	You want to bring two blocks closer together because they are closely related. You also want to remove a precise amount of space between blocks based on their location in the markup. For example, you want to remove some or all of the top margin before the first child element in a block; or you want to remove some or all of the bottom margin after the last child element in a block; or you want to remove some or all of the margin between two specific blocks.
Solution	To remove vertical space between any two blocks, you can insert an empty division between the blocks. You can assign a negative top margin to the division to remove the desired amount of space. For example, if you want to remove 32 pixels of space, you can insert a division assigned to the rule **margin-top:-32px**.

Pattern	HTML	CSS
	`<div class="CLASS"></div>`	`.CLASS { margin-top:-VALUE; }`

Location	This pattern applies to block elements.
Explanation	This pattern is the opposite of the Block Spacer design pattern and has the exact opposite structural meaning. By drawing two blocks closer together, the markup indicates they are more closely related. The class name you assign to the block space remover element should reflect this purpose.
	Furthermore, the structural relationship created by a block space remover or block spacer element does not belong to either block. It belongs *in between* the blocks because it links or separates them. It is best to use structural markup to create structural meaning because it is easiest to maintain—you can see it and manipulate it directly in the HTML.
Advantages	Unlike the block spacer, the block space remover does not uncollapse margins. This makes using the block spacer remover simpler and more predictable.
Disadvantages	This design pattern requires an extra element to be inserted into the markup for each space you want to remove. If you remove too much space, you can cause blocks to overlap.
Example	In the example, each paragraph has been assigned to top and bottom margins of 32 pixels. The two paragraphs in the second section are preceded and followed by block space removers, which remove the space before, between, and after these paragraphs.
Related to	Visual Structure, Collapsed Margins, Block Spacer; Margin (Chapter 6)

Left Marginal

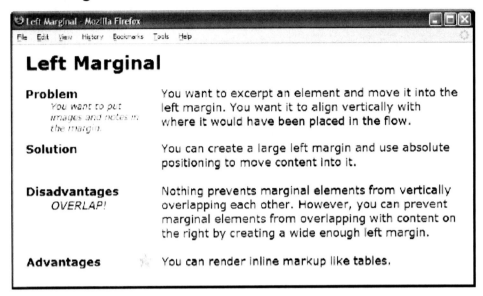

HTML

```
<h1>Left Marginal</h1>
<p class="left-marginal"><span class="marginal-header">Problem</span>You want to
  excerpt an element and move it into the left margin.<span class="marginal-note">
  You want to put images and notes in the margin.</span> You want it to align
  vertically with where it would have been placed in the flow.</p>
<p class="left-marginal"><span class="marginal-header">Solution</span>You can
  create a large left margin and use absolute positioning to move content
  into it.<br /><br /> <span class="marginal-header">Disadvantages</span>
  Nothing prevents marginal elements from vertically overlapping each other.
  <span class="marginal-alert">OVERLAP!</span>
  However, you can prevent marginal elements from overlapping with content on
  the right by creating a wide enough left margin. <br /><br />
  <span class="marginal-header">Advantages</span><img class="marginal-flag"
  src="star.gif" alt="star"/>You can render inline markup like tables.</p>
```

CSS

```
.left-marginal { position:relative; width:480px;
  margin-left:230px; margin-right:auto; }
.marginal-header { position:absolute; left:-220px; width:160px; font-weight:bold; }
.marginal-note { position:absolute; left:-180px; width:150px;
  font-style:italic; font-size:14px; font-weight:normal; }
.marginal-alert { position:absolute; left:-180px; font-style:italic; }
.marginal-flag { position:absolute; left:-40px; margin-top:-5px; }
```

Left Marginal

Problem	You want to excerpt elements out of the normal flow and move them into the left margin. These elements could contain headers, notes, tips, alerts, comments, images, and so on. You want elements in the margin to be positioned vertically where they would have been in the flow. You do not mind using fixed widths.
Solution	You can indent a block to create a margin on the left and then use absolute positioning to remove elements from the normal flow into the margin.
	You can mark up a block element with the **left-marginal** class to make it easy to select. You can indent it using **margin-left**. You can set it to **position:relative**, **position:absolute**, or **position:fixed** so its children can be positioned relative to its margin. You can use **margin-right:auto** and **width** to fix the width of the block so that content does not reflow when the viewport resizes. Reflow may change the vertical location of marginal elements, which could cause them to overlap.
	You can mark up a marginal element with a class that describes its purpose, such as **marginal-header**, **marginal-note**, and so forth. You can use **position:absolute** to remove the element from the flow, and you can use a negative value in **left** to move it into the left margin. You can use **margin-top** to move the element up or down. You can use **width** to size the element to fit into the width of the margin.
Pattern	
HTML	``` <TERMINAL-BLOCK class="left-marginal"> <INLINE-TEXT class="marginal-TYPE"> text </INLINE-TEXT> <img class="marginal-TYPE" src="FILE.EXT" alt="ALT_TEXT" /> </TERMINAL-BLOCK> ```

CSS	```
	.left-marginal { position:relative;
	  width:+VALUE;
	    margin-left:+VALUE; margin-right:auto; }
	.marginal-TYPE { position: absolute;
	    left: -VALUE;
	    width: +VALUE;
	    margin-top: ±VALUE; }
	``

Location	This pattern works on any element.
Caution	The layout created by this pattern does *not* protect elements from overlapping in the margin. It is easy to move an element into the margin and have it overlap other elements in the margin. Also, a browser that does not support absolute positioning renders marginal text inline where it occurs.
Tips	You can combine this pattern with Right Marginal.
	This pattern is visually similar to HTML tables, but the markup is more flexible. You can pull out any element and move it into the margin.
Related to	Right Marginal; Box Model (Chapter 4); Margin (Chapter 6); Positioning Models, Positioned, Closest Positioned Ancestor, Absolute, Relative (Chapter 7); Offset Absolute and Offset Fixed (Chapter 8); Marginal Dropcap, Marginal Graphic Dropcap (Chapter 18); Left Marginal Callout (Chapter 19); Left Marginal Alert (Chapter 20)

Right Marginal

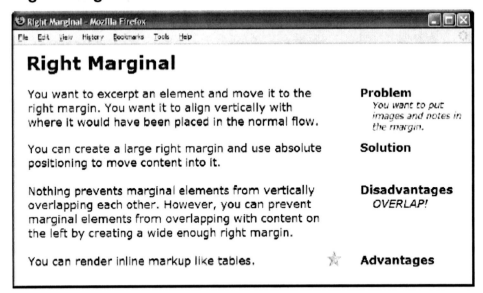

HTML

```
<h1>Right Marginal</h1>
<p class="right-marginal"><span class="marginal-header">Problem</span>You want to
  excerpt an element and move it to the right margin. <span class="marginal-note">
  You want to put images and notes in the margin.</span> You want it to align
  vertically with where it would have been placed in the normal flow.</p>
<p class="right-marginal"><span class="marginal-header">Solution</span>You can
  create a large right margin and use absolute positioning to move content
  into it.<br /><br /> <span class="marginal-header">Disadvantages</span>
  Nothing prevents marginal elements from vertically overlapping each other.
  <span class="marginal-alert">OVERLAP!</span>
  However, you can prevent marginal elements from overlapping with content on
  the left by creating a wide enough right margin. <br /><br />
  <span class="marginal-header">Advantages</span><img class="marginal-flag"
  src="star.gif" alt="star"/>You can render inline markup like tables.</p>
```

CSS

```
body { width:702px; }
.right-marginal { position:relative; width:480px;
  margin-right:210px; margin-left:auto; }

.marginal-header {position:absolute; right:-230px; width:170px; font-weight:bold; }
.marginal-note { position:absolute; right:-230px; width:150px;
  font-style:italic; font-size:14px; font-weight:normal; }
.marginal-alert {position:absolute; right:-230px; width:150px; font-style:italic; }
.marginal-flag { position:absolute; right:-30px;  margin-top:-5px; }
```

Right Marginal

Problem	You want to excerpt elements out of the normal flow and move them into the right margin. These elements could contain headers, notes, tips, alerts, comments, images, and so on. You want elements in the margin to be positioned vertically where they would have been in the flow. You do not mind using fixed widths.
Solution	You can indent a block to create a margin on the right and then use absolute positioning to remove elements from the normal flow into the margin.
	You can mark up a terminal block element with the **right-marginal** class to make it easy to select. You can indent it using **margin-right**. You can set it to **position:relative**, **position:absolute**, or **position:fixed** so its inline children can be positioned relative to its margin. You can use **margin-left:auto** and **width** to fix the width of the terminal block so that the content does not reflow when the viewport resizes. Reflow may change the vertical location of marginal elements, which could cause them to overlap. You can set the **width** of **<body>** or the width of one of the terminal block's ancestors to a fixed measurement to prevent the block from moving to the right as the viewport grows larger.
	You can mark up a marginal element with a class that describes its purpose, such as **marginal-header**, **marginal-note**, and so forth. You can use **position:absolute** to remove the inline element from the flow, and you can use a negative value in **right** to move it into the right margin. You can use **margin-top** to move the inline element up or down. You can use **width** to size the inline element to fit into the width of the margin.
| **Pattern** **HTML** | ```
<TERMINAL-BLOCK class="right-marginal">
    <INLINE-TEXT class="marginal-TYPE"> text </INLINE-TEXT>
    <img class="marginal-TYPE" src="FILE.EXT" alt="ALT_TEXT" />
</TERMINAL-BLOCK>
``` |
| **CSS** | ```
.right-marginal { position:relative; width:+VALUE;
    margin-right:+VALUE; margin-left:auto; }
.marginal-TYPE { position: absolute;
    right: -VALUE;
    width: +VALUE;
    margin-top: ±VALUE; }
``` |
Location	This pattern works on any element.
Caution	The layout created by this pattern does *not* protect elements from vertically overlapping in the margin. You need to plan carefully to avoid this problem.
Tips	You can combine this pattern with Left Marginal.
	This pattern is visually similar to HTML tables, but the markup is more flexible. You can pull out any element and move it into the margin.
Related to	Left Marginal; Box Model (Chapter 4); Margin (Chapter 6); Positioning Models, Positioned, Closest Positioned Ancestor, Absolute, Relative (Chapter 7); Offset Absolute and Offset Fixed (Chapter 8); Marginal Dropcap, Marginal Graphic Dropcap (Chapter 18); Right Marginal Callout (Chapter 19); Right Marginal Alert (Chapter 20)

CHAPTER 14

Images

This chapter shows how to use images to create beautiful and functional documents that remain accessible and download quickly.

Chapter Outline

- **Image** shows how to use the `<img>` element. It also contrasts the advantages and disadvantages of the GIF, JPG, and PNG image formats.
- **Image Map** shows how to overlay an image with clickable areas that link to other pages.
- **Fade-Out** shows how to use gradient images to add subtle shading behind content. It also shows how to create chameleon gradients that adapt to the current background.
- **Semi-transparent** shows how to put a partially transparent background behind an element so that it stands out from the background below it without obscuring it.
- **Replaced Text** shows how to replace text with an image while remaining accessible to nonsighted users. This technique also shows the text when the image is unavailable.
- **Content over Image** shows how to overlay text and other images on top of an image.
- **Content over Background Image** shows how to overlay text and other images on top of a background image.
- **CSS Sprite** shows how to embed multiple images into one file and display them independently as the background of different elements of a document.
- **Basic Shadowed Image** shows how to create and apply a simple shadow to an image without modifying the image itself.
- **Shadowed Image** shows a generic way of applying a shadow to an image of any size.
- **Rounded Corners** shows how to round the corners of an element's borders and how to create custom borders of any style imaginable.
- **Image Example** showcases these patterns in one document.

Image

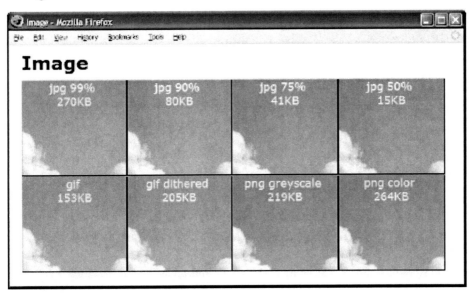

HTML

`<img width="742" height="556" src="cl1-99.jpg" alt="Crater Lake 1" />`

`<!-- Nonessential markup is not shown. -->`

CSS

`img { display:block; width:auto; height:auto; }`

`/* Nonessential rules are not shown. */`

Example

The example contains eight different versions of a picture that I took of Crater Lake on August 4, 2003. The source image is 742×556 pixels with a file size of 1,238,822 bytes. I processed the image to create eight separate files—each with a different image type and quality.

The first image is a JPG image at maximum quality, which reduces the file size to 275,798 bytes. This is a reduction of five times. At a JPG's highest quality, it is difficult to see any loss of quality. The second image is a JPG at 90% quality, which reduces the file size to 81,248 bytes. This is a reduction of 15 times. At 90% quality, you can barely see a difference with a magnifying glass. You can see a difference in the third and fourth images, which are JPGs at 75% and 50% quality and 41,290 and 14,841 bytes. This is a reduction of 30 and 84 times.

The fifth and sixth images are GIFs. These images have less quality and larger sizes than the JPG images. This is not a fair test of GIFs because they are not designed for real-world images containing thousands of colors. GIFs produce smaller files and have better quality when used for computer-generated images containing 256 or fewer colors.

The seventh and eighth images are PNGs. These images have the best quality with slightly smaller file sizes than the best-quality JPG, but there is no way to increase the compression to shrink the file size.

Image

Problem	You want to insert an image into the document because it is part of the content.
Solution	You can insert an image into your document using **<img>**. You can use the **src** attribute to specify the URL containing the image.
	You should put a brief description of the image in the **alt** attribute. This alternative description should be written specifically for screen readers to read and for displaying when the image fails to download. Decorative images are best displayed as background images, but if you must use a decorative **<img>** element, include the **alt** attribute, but leave it empty.
	Because a browser downloads each image separately, it needs to know the image's height and width so it can create a placeholder for the image while the image downloads. Otherwise, after *each* image is downloaded and its real size becomes known, a browser has to reflow the page. This slows the rendering and annoys the user. To set an image's size, you can use the **width** and **height** attributes of **<img>** or the **width** and **height** CSS properties. There is no need to use both. CSS properties override HTML attributes.
Pattern **HTML**	`<img src="FILE.EXT" width="IMAGE_WIDTH" height="IMAGE_HEIGHT"` `    alt="BRIEF_IMAGE_DESCRIPTION" />`
Location	This pattern applies to images.
Tips	An image is an inline element. It vertically aligns to the baseline of the line in which it occurs. You can use **vertical-align** to adjust the alignment.
	When you want to treat an image as a block, you should use **display:block** to display it as a block. This removes a small amount of extra space that a browser places below an image when it is inline, and it preserves the image's size when it fails to download.
	JPG, GIF, and PNG are the most common types of images on the Internet.
	JPG is the best image format for photographs. JPG supports up to 16 million colors and lossy compression. You control the amount of lossy compression from none to extreme. More compression produces smaller files and poorer quality. JPG does not support transparency.
	GIF is the best image format for line art and computer-generated images. GIF supports a transparent background, but it does not support an alpha channel. GIF supports up to 256 colors in the palette. To get more colors, a graphics program may use dithering to simulate them. GIF uses lossless compression. You cannot control the amount of compression. The main problem with GIF is its limit of 256 colors and its lack of an alpha channel.
	PNG is an improvement over GIF. It supports alpha channel transparency, 16 million colors, grayscale, and palette-based colors. PNG uses lossless compression, which you cannot control. Internet Explorer 7 and other major browsers support PNG transparency. Internet Explorer 6 does not.
Related to	Image Map; Inline-Block Box (Chapter 4); Width, Height, Sized, Shrinkwrapped, Stretched (Chapter 5); Margin, Border, Padding (Chapter 6); Vertical-Aligned Content, Vertical-Offset Content (Chapter 12); Left Marginal, Right Marginal (Chapter 13); Flyout Menu (Chapter 17); JavaScript Alert, Tooltip Alert, Pop-Up Alert (Chapter 20)

Image Map

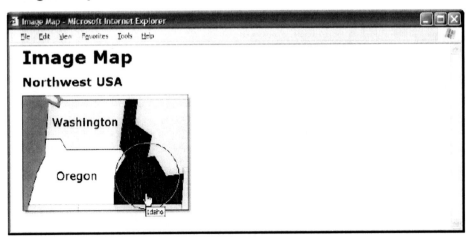

HTML

```
<h1>Image Map</h1>

<h2><a id="home" href="example.html">Northwest USA</a></h2>

<img src="nw.gif" usemap="#nw-map" alt="Northwest USA" width="290" height="200" />

<map id="nw-map" name="nw-map">

  <area href="washington.html" alt="Washington"
    shape="poly" coords="176,8, 164,89, 75,89, 40,72, 45,8" />

  <area href="oregon.html" alt="Oregon"
    shape="rect" coords="9,90, 155,180" />

  <area href="idaho.html" alt="Idaho"
    shape="circle" coords="212, 134,55" />
</map>
```

CSS

```
/* There are no CSS properties for styling image maps. */
```

Image Map

Problem	You want to overlay an image with clickable areas that link to other pages.
Solution	You can link an image to a **map** element that defines clickable areas and associates each area with a URL. When a user clicks an area, a browser jumps to its associated link. You can add a **usemap** attribute to an image to link the image to the **map** element with the same value in its **name** attribute. Multiple images can be linked to the same **map** element. For easy access to the element through JavaScript, it is a good practice for **map** elements to have an **id** attribute with the same value as its **name** attribute.
	A **map** element contains one or more **area** elements. Each **area** defines a region of an image that can be clicked. Areas should not overlap, but if they do, the document order of **area** elements determines the stacking order.
	Each **area** has four required attributes: **href**, **alt**, **shape**, and **coords**. **href** is the URL of the link that a browser jumps to when a user clicks the area. **alt** is read by screenreaders to describe the link—it is not visible. **shape** is the shape of the area, which is one of three shapes: **rect**, **circle**, and **poly**. **coords** define the location and extent of the shape.
	The number and meaning of coordinates in **coords** vary with each type of shape. Rectangles require four comma-delimited numbers. The first two are x, y coordinates of the upper-left corner of the rectangle, and the second two are x, y coordinates of the lower-right corner. Circles require three comma-delimited numbers. The first two are x, y coordinates of the circle's center, and the third is its radius. Polygons require a series of comma-delimited numbers in pairs of x, y coordinates that define the points of the polygon.
	This design pattern does not use any CSS styles.
| **Pattern**<br><br>HTML | ```html
<img usemap="MAP_NAME" src="FILE.EXT"
    width="WIDTH" height="HEIGHT" alt="DESCRIPTION" />


<map name="MAP_NAME" id="MAP_NAME">
    <area href="URL" shape="RECT_CIRCLE_POLY" coords="x,y..."
        alt="SCREENREADER_DESCRIPTION" />
</map>
``` |
Location	This pattern applies to images and image maps.
Tip	Image maps work well when you want a user to explore something visual, such as a real-world map. The problem is that image maps are invisible. Other than the mouse pointer changing shape when it is over a clickable area, a user cannot tell where areas are located, how many areas there are, and which areas have already been visited. For this reason, image maps are often paired with redundant links that are absolutely positioned over the image. These links make it clear what is clickable and what has already been visited. The example at the end of the chapter shows how this works.
Related to	Image, Content over Image, Content over Background Image
```

Fade-Out

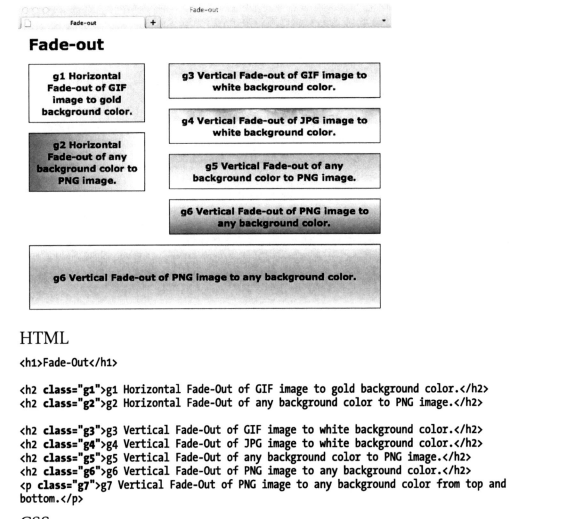

HTML

```
<h1>Fade-Out</h1>

<h2 class="g1">g1 Horizontal Fade-Out of GIF image to gold background color.</h2>
<h2 class="g2">g2 Horizontal Fade-Out of any background color to PNG image.</h2>

<h2 class="g3">g3 Vertical Fade-Out of GIF image to white background color.</h2>
<h2 class="g4">g4 Vertical Fade-Out of JPG image to white background color.</h2>
<h2 class="g5">g5 Vertical Fade-Out of any background color to PNG image.</h2>
<h2 class="g6">g6 Vertical Fade-Out of PNG image to any background color.</h2>
<p class="g7">g7 Vertical Fade-Out of PNG image to any background color from top and
bottom.</p>
```

CSS

```
.g1 { background:url("h-white2gold.gif") repeat-y left top gold; }
.g2 { background:url("h-trans2white.png") repeat-y right top royalblue; }

.g3 { background:url("v-gold2white.gif") repeat-x left top white; }
.g4 { background:url("v-lightning.jpg") repeat-x left top white; }
.g5 { background:url("v-trans2white.png") repeat-x left bottom red; }
.g6 { background:url("v-white2trans.png") repeat-x left top green; }
.g7 {background:url("v-white2trans.png") repeat-x left top, url("v-trans2white.png") repeat-x
left bottom green; }

/* Nonessential rules are not shown. */
```

Fade-Out

Problem	You want to create a gradient background behind an element. You want the gradient to work well regardless of how wide or tall the element grows.
Solution	There are two keys to creating a scalable background **gradient**: (1) fading the gradient into the background color, and (2) tiling it in the opposite direction of the gradient. For example, when the gradient is horizontal, you can tile the image vertically, and vice versa. This allows the element to grow in any direction while preserving the gradient effect. As an element grows, the background color fills in where the background image ends, and the image tiles to fill in the opposite direction.
	Using a graphics program, you can create a **gradient image**, such as a JPG, GIF, or PNG, that transitions from the forecolor and backcolor of your choosing. For example, if your document's background color is white and you want your forecolor to be gold, you could create a gradient image that transitions from white to gold or vice versa.
	Using a graphics program, you can use a **gradient mask** to fade any image, illustration, or graphical text into the background color. In the example, the fourth heading has a background image created from a texture that fades out to the white background color.
	You can also create a generic PNG image that fades from a predefined forecolor to whatever background color is currently assigned to the element. In the example, the second, fifth, and sixth headings use PNG images that fade from white to *transparent*. You can change the background color, and the image fades from white to that color. It just takes one of these **chameleon PNG gradients** to transition to *any* background color!
	Using multiple background images, you could also have a gradient that fades from a predefined foreground color to a background color and back to a predefined foreground color. In the example, the paragraph uses PNG images used in the fifth and sixth headers to accomplish this.
	The following design patterns show how to align and tile gradients in all four directions.
Patterns	**Horizontal Left-to-Right Fade-Out**
	`SELECT { background:url("FILE.EXT") repeat-y left top COLOR; }`
	Horizontal Right-to-Left Fade-Out
	`SELECT { background:url("FILE.EXT") repeat-y right top COLOR; }`
	Horizontal Top-to-Bottom Fade-Out
	`SELECT { background:url("FILE.EXT") repeat-x left top COLOR; }`
	Horizontal Bottom-to-Top Fade-Out
	`SELECT { background:url("FILE.EXT") repeat-x left bottom COLOR; }`
Location	This pattern applies to all elements.
Limitations	Internet Explorer 6 does not support PNG transparency, but Internet Explorer 7 and the other major browsers do. In the example, the PNG images show up in Internet Explorer 6 as gray gradients, which is not a bad effect in and of itself.
	Modern browsers support multiple backgrounds, but earlier browsers, such as Firefox 2 and versions of IE before 9, do not.
Related to	Semi-transparent; Background (Chapter 6)

Semi-transparent

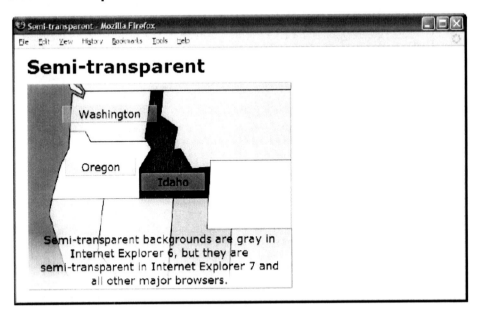

HTML

```
<h1>Semi-transparent</h1>

<div id="nw">
  <img src="nw.gif" alt="Northwest" width="437" height="328" />

  <span id="washington" class="overlay">Washington</span>
  <span id="oregon" class="overlay">Oregon</span>
  <span id="idaho" class="overlay">Idaho</span>

  <p id="note1">
    Semi-transparent backgrounds are gray in Internet Explorer 6, but they are
    semi-transparent in Internet Explorer 7 and all other major browsers.</p>
</div>
```

CSS

```
.overlay { background:url("semi-transparent.png") repeat; }

#note1 { background:url("trans2white.png") bottom left repeat-x; }

/* Nonessential rules are not shown. */
```

Semi-transparent

Alias	Translucent
Problem	You want an element to have a partially transparent background so that it stands out from the background below it without obscuring it.
Solution	You can use a graphics program to create a semi-transparent PNG image. You can set the transparency of its background to some value less than 100% to make it partially transparent. You can also use a gradient mask to fade into transparency. The color or colors you use in this image are important. Semi-transparent grayscale colors are color-neutral when they overlay a background. Nongrayscale semi-transparent colors colorize.
	If the image has the same transparency throughout, it needs to have a height and width of only about 10 pixels so a browser can efficiently tile it to fill the background of its container. For example, the **semi-trnsparent.png** image in the example is 10 pixels square, and I use **background:repeat** to tile it throughout the background. If the image contains a vertical transparent gradient, it needs to be about 10 pixels wide and as tall as the gradient. For example, the **trans2white.png** in the example is 10 pixels wide and 100 pixels tall to fit the gradient. I use **background:repeat-x** to tile it horizontally across the background. If the image contains a horizontal gradient, it needs to be about 10 pixels tall and as wide as the gradient, and you can tile it vertically down the background.
Pattern	
CSS	`SELECT { background:url("SEMI_TRANSPARENT_FILE.png") repeat; }`
Location	This pattern applies to all elements.
Limitations	Internet Explorer 6 does not support PNG transparency, but Internet Explorer 7 and the other major browsers do. In the example, the PNG images show up in Internet Explorer 6 as gray gradients, which is a nice way for the effect to degrade.
Advantages	Semi-transparency is practical and looks great as long as the color of the text contrasts well with the background. I expect to see more demand for this technique now that Windows Vista has joined the other major operating systems in building transparency effects into the desktop.
Example	In the example, the four spans positioned over the image have semi-transparent gray backgrounds. I created this effect by tiling **semi-transparent.png** across their background. Since this image is semi-transparent, you can partially see the image of the map behind them.
	In the example, paragraph **#note1** has a semi-transparent gradient that starts out transparent at the top and transitions to white at the bottom. This allows the background image to show through at the top of its background and gradually fade out to white at the bottom. This is the same **trans2white.png** image that I used in the Fade-Out design pattern.
Related to	Fade-Out; Background (Chapter 6)

Replaced Text

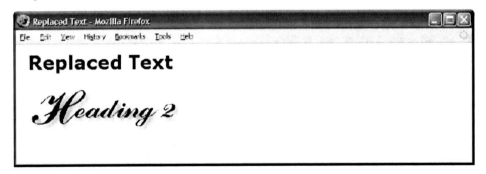

HTML

```
<h1>Replaced Text</h1>

<h2 id="h2">Heading 2<span></span></h2>
```

CSS

```
#h2 { position:relative; width:250px; height:76px;
  padding:0; overflow:hidden; }

#h2 span { position:absolute; width:250px; height:76px;
  left:0; top:0; margin:0;
  background:url("heading2.jpg") no-repeat; }
```

Replaced Text

Problem	You want to replace text with an image. You also want the text to be read by a screenreader. You also want the text to be visible if the image is unavailable.
Solution	You can insert an empty **<span>** into the block element that contains text that you want to replace with an image. You can assign the image to be the span's background image. You can relatively position the block element and absolutely position the span at the top left of the block. This displays the span in front of the block. You can size both the block and the span to fit the image exactly. Since the block and the span are the same size and the span is in front of the block, the background image of the span covers the text in the block. If the span's image is unavailable, the text behind it is visible because the span's background is transparent.
	You can assign a unique ID to the block containing the text you want to replace. Using a unique ID is important when text you are replacing with the image is unique in the document. If you repeatedly replace the same text with the same image, you may want to use a class instead.
	It is important that the block has no padding and the span has no margin. Otherwise, the hidden text might be visible. In addition, you can use **overflow:hidden** to ensure text does not overflow from behind the image. Also make sure the text fits within the area of the image so that if a user turns off images, the text does not overflow and get cut off.

Pattern

HTML

```
<BLOCK id="UNIQUE-ID"> TEXT <span></span></BLOCK>
```

CSS

```
#UNIQUE-ID { position:relative; padding:0; overflow:hidden;
    width:IMAGE_WIDTH;
    height:IMAGE_HEIGHT; }
#UNIQUE-ID span { position:absolute; margin:0;
    left:0; top:0;
    width:IMAGE_WIDTH;
    height:IMAGE_HEIGHT;
    background:url("FILE.EXT") no-repeat; }
```

Location	This pattern applies to any block element.
Limitations	When a user zooms in on a document in Firefox 2 and Internet Explorer 6, images do not enlarge along with the text. This does not apply to modern browsers such as versions of IE greater than 6 and Opera 8, which properly zoom images and text. Users typically zoom in because they need to see everything larger. When replaced images do not enlarge, the document is less accessible. This is usually not an issue because replaced text is typically a heading, and the text in the image is large to begin with.
Tips	Text replacement works well with links and buttons that use rollover effects.
Related to	Width, Height, Sized (Chapter 5); Background (Chapter 6); Positioning Models, Positioned, Closest Positioned Ancestor, Absolute (Chapter 7); Left Aligned, Top Aligned (Chapter 9)

Content over Image

HTML

```
<h1>Content over Image</h1>

<div class="figure">
  <h3 class="caption">Crater Lake North Rim</h3>
  <p id="crater-date"><img src="star.gif" alt="" /> August 4, 2003
    <img src="star.gif" alt="" /></p>
  <img class="framed" width="518" height="389"
    src="crater-lake.jpg" alt="Crater Lake North Rim August 4, 2003" /></div>
```

CSS

```
.figure { float:left; position:relative;
  color:white; background-color:black; }

.figure .caption { position:absolute; margin:15px; left:0; top:0;
  font-size:1.05em; }

.framed { display:block;
  border-left:1px solid gray; border-right:2px solid black;
  border-top:1px solid gray; border-bottom:2px solid black; }

#crater-date { position:absolute; left:0; bottom:10px; width:518px;
  text-align:center; color:white; font-size:0.8em; }
```

Content over Image

Problem	You want to place text on top of an image. You want to position the text relative to the image. You want the text to be visible if the image does not load. You want search engines to give the text a high priority and to index the *image* because it is part of the content.
Solution	You can embed a heading, an image, and any other type of object in a block element. You can shrinkwrap the block around the image by floating it or absolutely positioning it. This makes this design pattern work with any size of image. You can relatively position the block so it is the closest positioned ancestor of the image. This allows you to position text elements at any location over the image.
	You can absolutely position the heading and use the alignment design patterns in Chapter 9 to position it within the image. Aligning the heading to the block is the same as aligning to the image because the block is shrinkwrapped to the image and is the closest positioned ancestor.
Pattern	
HTML	``` <BLOCK class="figure"> <HEADING class="caption"> TEXT_OVER_TEXT </HEADING> <p id="UNIQUE_ID"> TEXT_OVER_TEXT </p> <img src="FILE.EXT" alt="IMAGE_DESCRIPTION" width="IMAGE_WIDTH" height="IMAGE_HEIGHT" /> </BLOCK> ```
CSS	``` .figure { float:LEFT_OR_RIGHT; position:relative; color:COLOR; background-color:COLOR; } .figure .caption { position:absolute; POSITIONING_STYLES; } .framed { display:block; border:WIDTH STYLE COLOR; } #UNIQUE_ID { position:absolute; POSITIONING_STYLES; } ```
Location	This pattern can be used anywhere a block element can be used.
Tips	You can use any type of element for text-over effects. I use a heading because search engines prioritize headings, and speech readers use headings to create an aural table of contents for the page.
	You can include any number and type of child elements in the figure. You can assign each to a unique ID so that you can position it within the image.
	In case a down-level browser does not shrinkwrap the block around the image, you should put borders around the image instead of the block.
Example	The example assigns text in the block to a white color over a black background. This ensures the text is visible if the image does not load. Also, the **alt** text is purposefully omitted from the two star images because they are meant to be decorative—the Inline Decoration design pattern is a better choice for displaying decorative images, but I wanted to keep the example simple.
Related to	Content over Background Image; Display, Block Box (Chapter 4); Border, Background (Chapter 6); Positioning Models, Positioned, Closest Positioned Ancestor, Absolute, Float and Clear, Relative Float (Chapter 7); Aligned and Offset Absolute (Chapter 8); Inline Decoration (Chapter 11)

Content over Background Image

HTML

```
<h1>Content over Background Image</h1>

<div id="crater-lake">
  <h3 class="caption">Crater Lake North Rim</h3>
  <p id="crater-date"><img src="star.gif" alt="" /> August 4, 2003
  <img src="star.gif" alt="" /></p></div>
```

CSS

```
#crater-lake { position:relative; padding:0; width:700px; height:500px;
  background:black url("crater-lake.jpg") no-repeat center center; }

#crater-lake .caption { position:absolute; margin:15px; left:0; top:0;
  font-size:1.05em; color:white; }

#crater-date { position:absolute; left:0; bottom:10px; width:700px;
  text-align:center; color:white; font-size:0.8em; }

/* Nonessential rules are not shown. */
```

Content over Background Image

Problem	Like the Content over Image design pattern, you want to place text and objects on top of an image, but you do not want the image to be part of the document's content, and you do *not* want search engines to index the image. You want to position the text relative to the image. You want the text to be visible when the image does not load. You want search engines to give the text priority.
Solution	You can assign a background image to a *sized* block element. Unique IDs work well for linking unique background images to these blocks. If you use the same image multiple times, you may want to use a class instead. You can use **background** to center a nontiled background image in the block. You can size the block to the exact size of the image or to an arbitrary size. If you size it larger than the image, the background color of the block becomes visible and creates a picture-frame effect around the image. The same thing happens if you apply padding to the block. If you size the block smaller than the image, it crops the image. You can relatively position the block so you can absolutely position its child elements relative to it. You can use the alignment design patterns in Chapter 9 to position child elements within the image.

Pattern

HTML

```
<BLOCK id="IMAGE-NAME">
  <HEADING class="caption"> TEXT_OVER_TEXT </HEADING>
  <p id="UNIQUE_ID"> TEXT_OVER_TEXT </p>
</BLOCK>
```

CSS

```
#IMAGE-NAME {
  position:relative;
  width:IMAGE-WIDTH; height:IMAGE-HEIGHT;
  padding:VALUE;
  background:url("FILE.EXT") COLOR center center no-repeat; }
#IMAGE-NAME .caption { position:absolute; POSITIONING_STYLES; }
#UNIQUE_ID { position:absolute; POSITIONING_STYLES; }
```

Location	This pattern can be used anywhere a block element can be used.
Advantages	There is less HTML markup than the Content over Image pattern because there is no image element. There is no need for **alt** text because a text-over caption serves the same purpose. This works better when the image fails to download because a browser does not try to display **alt** text in its place, which might get in the way of the content rendered on top of the image.
Tip	GIF and PNG images with transparent backgrounds overlay background images nicely. PNGs can even blend their edges into the background.
Example	In the example, I increase the height and width of the block to create a picture frame around the image.
Related to	Content over Image; Width, Height (Chapter 5); Padding, Background (Chapter 6); Positioning Models, Positioned, Closest Positioned Ancestor, Absolute (Chapter 7); Aligned and Offset Absolute (Chapter 8); Inline Decoration (Chapter 11)

CSS Sprite

HTML

```
<h1>CSS Sprite</h1>

<div id="nw">
  <img src="nw.gif" width="290" height="200" alt="Northwest USA" />

  <a id="olympia" class="bang-bg" href="olympia.html" title="Olympia">
    <span class="screenreader-only">Olympia</span></a>

  <a id="salem" class="flag-bg" href="salem.html" title="Salem">
    <span class="screenreader-only">Salem</span></a>

  <a id="boise" class="star-bg" href="boise.html" title="Boise">
    <span class="screenreader-only">Boise</span></a>
</div>
```

CSS

```
.bang-bg { background:url("bt.gif") -48px -16px; width:16px; height:16px; }
.flag-bg { background:url("bt.gif") -64px -16px; width:16px; height:16px; }
.star-bg { background:url("bt.gif") -64px -32px; width:16px; height:16px; }

.star-bg:hover { background-image:url("wt.gif"); background-color:black; }
.flag-bg:hover { background-image:url("wt.gif"); background-color:black; }
.bang-bg:hover { background-image:url("wt.gif"); background-color:black; }

.screenreader-only { position:absolute; left:-9999px; top:-9999px;
  width:1px; height:1px; overflow:hidden; }

/* Nonessential rules are not shown. */
```

CSS Sprite

Problem	You want to use many images on a page, but you do not want the performance penalty caused by downloading multiple image files. Even on a broadband connection, it is not unusual for latency alone to slow the rendering of a page by 100 milliseconds *per image*. In other words, the latency of downloading ten images will likely delay the rendering of a page by one second—no matter how small the image files. Of course, delays caused by latency vary depending on web server proximity and how busy it is.
Solution	You can combine multiple background images into one image file. This file is called a **CSS sprite**. For example, you could include most, if not all, of a page's background images in one file. You could also embed a library of list bullets, icons, and text decorations in a CSS sprite that is shared across your web site.
	The key to using a sprite is to display it as the background image of a sized element and to position the background image at the exact horizontal and vertical offset of the embedded image. The element must be the exact width and height of the desired embedded image; otherwise, parts of several embedded images may be visible in its background. The element must be set to the proper horizontal and vertical offset, or the background will show the wrong embedded image or will show parts of several embedded images. The measurements used in **width**, **height**, and **background-position** must all be in pixels because embedded images are measured in pixels. The values in **background-position** are *negative* because they move the composite background image up and to the left to position it.
	You can replace **<img>** elements with CSS sprites by displaying them as background images within sized spans or divisions, but unless content images cause performance problems, it is more natural to use **<img>** elements. When replacing an image with a CSS sprite, you can use the Screenreader-Only design pattern to embed hidden alternate text that will be read only by screenreaders. This makes the CSS sprite accessible.

Pattern

| HTML | ```
<ELEMENT>
  <span class="screenreader-only"> ALTERNATE_TEXT </span>
</ELEMENT>
``` |
| CSS | ```
SELECTOR { width:SPRITE_WIDTH; height:SPRITE_HEIGHT;
  background-image:url("SPRITE_FILE.EXT");
  background-position:-HORIZONTAL_OFFSETpx -VERTICAL_OFFSETpx; }
SELECTOR:hover { background-image:url("HOVER_SPRITE_FILE.EXT");
  background-color:COLOR; }
``` |
| **Location** | This pattern applies to any type of element. |
| **Limitations** | Background images using CSS sprites cannot be tiled because the entire composite image would be tiled rather than just the embedded image. |

CSS Sprite cont.

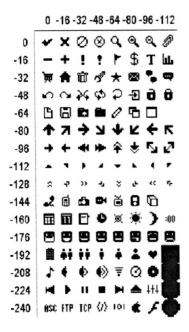

Offsets for 16×16 sprites as used in `bt.gif`

Example

I use two CSS sprite files in the example: `bt.gif` (see Figure 14-1) and `wt.gif`. These file names stand for a black image on a transparent background and a white image on a transparent background. When the user mouses over the image, the hover selector switches out the `bt.gif` and replaces it with `wt.gif`, which inverts the color from black to white. The background is also changed to black, which shows through the transparent parts of the image.

I include two other sprite files in the example directory that are not used in the example. They are named `tb.gif` and `tw.gif`. These file names stand for transparent images in black boxes and transparent images in white boxes. These embedded images are little black and white boxes with transparent images in the center, which change color to match the background.

I created these four CSS sprites from an icon set called bitcons. I made all the embedded images exactly 16×16 pixels, like the originals. These icons are freely licensed and are available at `http://somerandomdude.net/srd-projects/bitcons`. Likewise, you are free to use these four CSS sprite files in your projects.

When making your own CSS sprite images, you can embed any image of any size into the sprite. Embedded images do not need to be the same size. All you need to know is the offset and size of each embedded image.

CSS Sprite cont.

Advantages	By reducing the number of files that are downloaded, you can dramatically speed the loading of a page. Embedding multiple images in a single file typically results in a smaller overall file size than the combined file sizes of separate images.
Disadvantages	Combining images to create sprites and tracking their offsets can be time-consuming and error-prone. This makes managing images harder. It works best when you create a sprite containing a library of images that work together to skin a document. Whenever you want to change the look and feel of a document, you change the sprite.
Tip	Managing sprite offsets is easier if all embedded images are the same size.
Latency	Over a broadband connection to the Internet, downloading data in a small file is very quick, but the communication latency involved in requesting a small file can often take several times longer than actually downloading the file! HTTP and TCP/IP communications protocols require handshake messages to be sent back and forth before content can be downloaded, messages traveling across the Internet compete for bandwidth, and servers queue requests until they can get to them. My measurements show latency delays the rendering of a page by approximately 100 milliseconds plus the time it takes to download the data.
	Using Google Load Time Analyzer for Firefox, I tracked web page download times on my high-speed broadband connection. For example, the home page of MSN.com took 5 seconds to download 41 files: 1 HTML document, 3 CSS stylesheets, 4 JavaScript files, 15 GIFs, 10 JPGs, and 8 ad callbacks. The total download size was 136K, which took 1,742 ms to download. The time it took to send messages to the server and to wait for replies was 15,960 ms! In other words, for each millisecond that data was downloaded, 9 milliseconds were spent waiting: 3 milliseconds were lost waiting for messages to travel back and forth across the Internet, and 6 milliseconds were lost due to server latency. I have documented the results in an Excel spreadsheet included in this design pattern's example directory.
	If all 25 images in the MSN home page were merged into one composite file, latency would be reduced from 9,000 ms to 500 ms. This would save 8,500 ms! Since a browser downloads using three connections simultaneously, the actual savings are one-third of 8,500 ms, or 2,800 ms. This one change alone would reduce the download time of the MSN home page from 5.2 seconds to 2.4 seconds—more than doubling its download speed!
Sprite history	A sprite gets its name from a technique used in two-dimensional video games of compositing multiple images into one file where each image is a frame of animation. You can animate a sprite simply by rotating the display through offsets in the composite image. Animated GIFs use this technique, and you can use this technique to create rollover effects.
Related to	Image; Width, Height (Chapter 5); Background (Chapter 6)

Basic Shadowed Image

HTML

```
<h1>Basic Shadowed Image</h1>

<img class="shadowed"
  src="crater-lake.jpg"
  alt="Crater Lake"
  width="518"
  height="389" />
```

CSS

```
img.shadowed { padding-right:20px;
  padding-bottom:20px;
  background-image:url("shadow.jpg");
  background-position:right bottom;
  background-repeat:no-repeat; }
```

Basic Shadowed Image

Problem	You want to place a shadow behind an image without having to modify the original image. You also want to control the distance the shadow is offset from behind the image.
Solution	You can create a shadow image that is the same size as the image it is shadowing. You can assign the shadow as the nontiled background of the image. You can use **background-position** to move the background shadow to the bottom right of the padding area. You can use **padding-right:+VALUE** and **padding-bottom:+VALUE** to control how much the shadow extends below the bottom right of the image.
	Shadows are traditionally displayed in the bottom-right corner, but if you want to display them in a different corner, you can extend the padding into that corner and position the shadow there.

Pattern	

HTML	```
	<img class="shadowed"
	  src="FILE.EXT" alt="DESCRIPTION"
	  width="WIDTH" height="HEIGHT" />
	``

CSS	```
	.shadowed { padding-right:+VALUE;
	  padding-bottom:+VALUE;
	  background-image:url("FILE.EXT");
	  background-position:right bottom;
	  background-repeat:no-repeat; }
	``

Location	This pattern applies to images.
Advantages	Because the shadow is an image, there is no limit to what you can do with the shadow. You can use any color, blur, and texture to fit the style of your document.
	This pattern is simple and does not require you to process images to embed shadows in them. You can also change the look and feel of all shadows on a web site by simply changing the shadow image.
Disadvantages	This pattern requires you to create a shadow image for each size of image. If all your images are the same size or have a limited number of sizes, this pattern works well. If your images come in unpredictable sizes, you may want to use the more complicated, yet more versatile, Shadowed Image pattern.
	The *latency* caused by a browser checking to see whether the shadowed image has already been downloaded slows the rendering of a page—even on broadband connections.
Related to	Image, Shadowed Image; Padding, Background (Chapter 6)

Shadowed Image

shadow.jpg

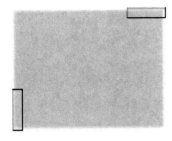

shadow-rt.jpg and *shadow-lb.jpg* are created by extracting them from *shadow.jpg*.

shadow-rt.jpg indents and closes off the top-right edge of the shadow.

shadow-lb.jpg indents and closes off the left-bottom edge of the shadow.

Shadowed Image

Problem

You want to place a shadow behind an image without having to modify the original image. You also want to control how much the shadow is offset from the image. You also want the shadow to work automatically with any size of image.

Solution

You can use three image files to create a shadow that will automatically fit any image. This can be a great timesaver because you do not need to embed shadows within images, and it makes it easy to change the style of the shadows on the fly.

Like the Basic Shadowed Image pattern, the first step is to create a shadowed image, as shown in Figure 14-2, or reuse one previously created like the one in the example. I name this file **shadow.jpg**. Unlike the Basic Shadowed Image pattern, **shadow.jpg** should be as large as the *largest* image it will shadow.

In addition, you need to create two additional images by extracting them from the shadowed image (see Figure 14-3). One indents and closes off the right-top edge of the shadow (see Figure 14-4), and one indents and closes off the left-bottom edge of the shadow (see Figure 14-5). These images are the key to creating an automatically sized shadow because they create the illusion that the shadow is indented on the right-top and the left-bottom, as shown in Figure 14-6. I call these the **indentor images**.

In the example, I created the two indentor images as follows. I extracted the right-top corner of the shadow image and saved it as **shadow-rt.jpg** (see Figure 14-4). I also extracted the left-bottom corner of the shadow image and saved it as **shadow-lb.jpg** (see Figure 14-5). I made **shadow-rt.jpg** 100 pixels *wide* and only as tall as needed to capture the shadow's blur. I made **shadow-lb.jpg** 100 pixels *tall* and only as wide as needed to capture the shadow's blur. I then expanded the canvas of each of these two images to make them 100 pixels square. I put the background color in the expanded part of these images. This allows the indentors to indent up to 100 pixels of the shadow by covering it with the background color (see Figure 14-6).

You need to stack the images in the following order from bottom to top: **shadow.jpg**, **shadow-rt.jpg**, and **shadow-lb.jpg**. The image receiving the shadow gets stacked on top of them all, as shown in Figure 14-6. You can stack these three background images by assigning them to three nested block elements. I typically use divisions. The order is important. You can assign **shadow.jpg** to the outermost block element. You can assign **shadow-rt.jpg** to the second nested element. You can assign **shadow-lb.jpg** to the third nested element. You can place the **<img>** element inside the third nested block.

To shrinkwrap these three elements to the size of the image, you need to float them or absolutely position them.

Shadowed Image cont.

Composite view of the shadowed image

Shadowed Image cont.

Solution cont.	Apply styles to your chosen class or ID as follows:

You can use **background-image** to load the shadow images into the backgrounds of their respective elements.

You can use **background-position:right bottom;** to position the shadow image in the right-bottom corner of the image.

You can use **background-position:right TOP_OFFSET;** to position **shadow-rt.jpg** at an offset from the right-top corner of the image. You can calculate the value of **TOP_OFFSET** by adding **BOTTOM_OFFSET** to the negative of the height of **shadow-rt.jpg**. For example, if the height of **shadow-rt.jpg** is 100 pixels and **BOTTOM_OFFSET** is 20 pixels, you would add 20 to -100 to get a **TOP_OFFSET** of **-80px**. By offsetting **shadow-rt.jpg** by the inverse of its height, you are aligning its bottom to the top of the background. By adding back in the **BOTTOM_OFFSET**, you move it down the same amount that you move down the shadow.

You can use **background-position:LEFT_OFFSET bottom;** to **position shadow-lb.jpg** at an offset from the left-bottom corner of the image. You can calculate the value of **LEFT_OFFSET** by adding **RIGHT_OFFSET** to the negative of the width of **shadow-lb.jpg**. For example, if the width of **shadow-lb.jpg** is 100 pixels and **RIGHT_OFFSET** is 20 pixels, you would add 20 to -100 to get a **LEFT_OFFSET** of **-80px**. By offsetting **shadow-lb.jpg** by the inverse of its width, you are aligning its right side to the left side of the background. By adding back in the **LEFT_OFFSET**, you move it to the right by the same amount that you move the shadow to the right.

You can use **background-repeat:no-repeat** to prevent each background image from being tiled.

You can use **padding-right:RIGHT_OFFSET** to move the shadow image past the right side of the image.

You can use **padding-bottom:BOTTOM_OFFSET** to move the shadow image below the bottom of the image.

Shadowed Image cont.

HTML

```
<h1>Shadowed Image</h1>

<div class="shrinkwrapped">
  <div class="shadowed">
    <div class="shadowed-rt">
      <div class="shadowed-lb">
        <img src="crater-lake.jpg" alt="Crater Lake" width="518" height="389" />
</div></div></div></div>
```

CSS

```
.shrinkwrapped { float:left; }

.shadowed { background-image:url("shadow.jpg");
  background-position:right bottom; background-repeat:no-repeat; }

.shadowed-rt { background-image:url("shadow-rt.jpg");
  background-position:right -80px; background-repeat:no-repeat; }

.shadowed-lb { padding-right:20px; padding-bottom:20px;
  background-image:url("shadow-lb.jpg");
  background-position:-80px bottom; background-repeat:no-repeat; }
```

Shadowed Image cont.

Pattern

HTML
```
<div class="shrinkwrapped">
  <div class="shadowed">
    <div class="shadowed-rt">
      <div class="shadowed-lb">
        <img src="FILE.EXT" alt="" width="WIDTH" height="HEIGHT" />
</div></div></div></div>
```

CSS
```
.shrinkwrapped { float:LEFT_OR_RIGHT; }
.shadowed { background-image:url("FILE.EXT");
  background-position:right bottom;
  background-repeat:no-repeat; }
.shadowed-rt { background-image:url("FILE-rt.EXT");
  background-position:right TOP_OFFSET;
  background-repeat:no-repeat; }
.shadowed-lb {
  padding-right:RIGHT_OFFSET;
  padding-bottom:BOTTOM_OFFSET;
  background-image:url("FILE-lb.EXT");
  background-position:LEFT_OFFSET bottom;
  background-repeat:no-repeat; }
```

Location	This pattern applies to images. Because this pattern wraps the image in block elements, it cannot be used inline.
Advantages	Because the shadow is an image, there is no limit to what you can do with the shadow. You can use any color, amount of blur, and texture to fit the style of your document. Because this pattern automatically fits the shadow to the size of the image, you need to create only three images to put a shadow behind any image of any size. The browser has to download only three image files to create an unlimited number of shadows.
Disadvantages	This pattern requires you to insert extra divisions into the markup to create this shadow effect.
	This pattern requires you to shrinkwrap the parent division to the image. Otherwise, it will be stretched to the width of its container, and the nested background images will extend beyond the image to fill the width of the container. This breaks the shadow effect. In the pattern, I floated the element to shrinkwrap it. You could also position it to shrinkwrap it. The only block element that shrinkwraps naturally is the table.
Related to	Image, Basic Shadowed Image, Rounded-Corners; Padding, Background (Chapter 6); Float and Clear (Chapter 7)

Rounded Corners

Rounded Corners

You can nest two divisions to create two opposite rounded corners.

You can nest two divisions to create two opposite rounded corners.

You can nest four divisions to create four rounded corners.

You can have a single division with multiple backgrounds.

HTML

```
<div class="bg"><div class="tl"><div class="br pad">
You can nest two divisions to create two opposite rounded corners.
</div></div></div>

<div class="bg"><div class="tr"><div class="bl pad">
You can nest two divisions to create two opposite rounded corners.
</div></div></div>

<div class="bg">
  <div class="tl"><div class="br"><div class="trc"><div class="blc pad">
You can nest four divisions to create four rounded corners.
</div></div></div></div></div>
<div class="mbg pad">You can have a single division with multiple backgrounds</div>
```

CSS

```
.bg { background:url("bg.gif") bottom left repeat-x white; margin-top:20px; }

.tl { background:url("rc.gif") top left no-repeat; }
.br { background:url("rc.gif") bottom right no-repeat; }
.tr { background:url("rc.gif") top right no-repeat; }
.bl { background:url("rc.gif") bottom left no-repeat; }

.trc { background:url("rc-trc.gif") top right no-repeat; }
.blc { background:url("rc-blc.gif") bottom left no-repeat; }

.pad { padding:10px; }
.mbg{ background: url("rc-trc.gif") top right no-repeat, url("rc-blc.gif") bottom left no-
repeat, url("rc.gif") top left no-repeat, url("rc.gif") bottom right no-repeat, url("bg.gif")
bottom left repeat-x white; margin-top:20px; }
```

Rounded Corners

Problem	You want to round the corners of an element's box. You want the corners to expand and shrink with the box so it will work with any amount of content.
Solution	You can create rounded corners by embedding background images of rounded corners inside an element. These images also include the borders that connect the rounded corners to each other. Because these are images, you can create any style of corner and border you can imagine. In Chapter 6, you learned that with CSS3 you can implement rounded corners with only CSS. The solution for implementing rounded corners with images is still applicable where support for rounded corners in CSS is not available, such as older browsers, mobile browsers, and modern browsers that don't fully support CSS rounded corners.
	Since versions of CSS before 3 allowed for only one background image per element, you can insert extra divisions inside the element you want to have rounded corners—one division for each rounded corner. Embedded divisions with no margins and padding are located in exactly the same position as their parent. This allows you to layer background images on top of each other. Note that when a parent element has a fixed height, its child divisions must also have the same fixed height.
	The first two boxes in the example have two rounded corners and two nested divisions. The third box has four rounded corners and four nested divisions. A detailed explanation follows.
	Support for CSS3 multiple backgrounds has been widely adopted by modern browsers and has been implemented for Firefox 3.6+, Chrome/Safari 1.3+/1.0, Opera 10.5+, and Internet Explorer 9.0+.

Patterns

HTML

```
<div class="bg"><div class="tl"><div class="br">
    CONTENT
</div></div></div>
```

or

```
<div class="bg"><div class="tr"><div class="bl">
    CONTENT
</div></div></div>
```

or

```
<div class="bg"><div class="tl"><div class="br">
  <div class="trc"><div class="blc">
      CONTENT
  </div></div></div></div></div>
```

or

```
<div class="mbg">CONTENT</div>
```

CSS

```
.bg { background:BACKGROUND_STYLES; margin-top:20px; }
.tl { background:url("RC_FILE.EXT") top left no-repeat; }
.tr { background:url("RC_FILE.EXT") top right no-repeat; }
.br { background:url("RC_FILE.EXT") bottom right no-repeat; }
.bl { background:url("RC_FILE.EXT") bottom left no-repeat; }
.trc { background:url("TRC_FILE.EXT") top right no-repeat; }
.blc { background:url("BLC_FILE.EXT") bottom left no-repeat; }
.mbg { background:url("TRC_FILE.EXT") top right no-repeat, url("TLC_FILE.EXT") top
left no-repeat, url("BRC_FILE.EXT") bottom right no-repeat, url("BLC_FILE.EXT")
bottom left no-repeat; }
```

Location	This pattern applies to block elements and inline elements that are positioned, floated, or displayed as blocks.

Rounded Corners cont.

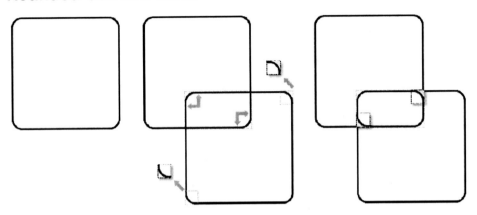

Creating rounded corners from rounded rectangle images

Creating the Three Rounded Rectangle Images

In the example, I started with a 1600×1600 transparent canvas. I added a rounded rectangle that hugged the edges of the canvas. The rounded rectangle had a transparent interior. I filled in the *exterior* pixels of each rounded corner with the external background color, which is white in my example. This makes them opaque so the outside of each corner overlays the interior background with the background color. Notice in Figure 14-7 how the outside of the top-left corner of the first rounded rectangle and the outside of the bottom-right corner of the second rounded rectangle would display the internal background if they were not opaque. Lastly, I saved the image as `rc.gif`.

To create the cutout images, I cut out the bottom-left corner and the top-right corner of the rounded rectangle image and saved them as separate GIF images named `tr.gif` and `bl.gif`. I made sure the exterior part of the corner remained opaque and the interior remained transparent. Otherwise, they would not do their job of hiding the external square borders on the outside and letting the background show through on the inside. I sized each cutout just large enough to cover the square corner with a rounded corner.

Creating the three rounded rectangle images is simple: create a transparent rounded rectangle; fill in the exterior of its rounded corners; and save the bottom-left and top-right corners as separate images.

Rounded Corners cont.

Detailed Solution	You can assign a background image to each nested division. I use six classes for that purpose: **tl**, **br**, **tr**, **trc**, **bl**, and **blc**, which stand for top left, bottom right, top right, top-right corner, bottom left, and bottom-left corner.
	To create two opposite rounded corners, you can apply the same background image to two child divisions. The image should be a large rounded rectangle with a transparent *interior* so the background image or color will show through. The *exterior* of its rounded corners should be opaque and should be the same color as the exterior background color.
	The key is to position the same rounded rectangle image in the top-left corner and in the bottom-right corner (see Figure 14-7). This creates two overlapping rounded rectangles. As the element expands or contracts, so do the rounded rectangles. The content of the element can grow as large as the size of the rounded rectangle before the illusion breaks. This is not a problem because you can make this rectangle as large as you want. In the example, I made the rounded rectangle image 1600×1600 pixels, and yet it has a file size of only 8,278 bytes because most of it is transparent.
	To create four rounded corners, you can position the same rounded rectangle image in the top-left corner and in the bottom-right corner. You then assign two additional background images to two additional nested divisions: one is positioned in the top-right corner, and the other in the bottom-left. These new images are tiny rounded corners that cover up the square intersections of the two overlapping rounded rectangles, as shown in Figure 14-7. It is important that these two corner divisions are placed *after* the first two rounded rectangle divisions. This allows the corner divisions to be stacked on top of the others.
	You can set the interior **background** by assigning a background color or image to the parent of the rounded corner box. In the example and the pattern, I use the **bg** class to assign this background. Likewise, the best place to set the **margin** is the parent. The best place to set the **padding** is the last embedded division. In the example, I assign the **pad** class to the last embedded division to set the padding for the interior of the rounded corner box. You should not apply a **border** to any of these elements because it would conflict with the rounded corners.
Limitations	The exterior of the cutout corner images must not be transparent. When they are transparent, they show the intersection of the rounded rectangle borders. This breaks the illusion. Since the exterior of the cutout corner images must be opaque, the opaque exterior needs to match the background color that surrounds the *outside* of the rounded rectangle. This requires that you create a different set of cutout corner images for each different external background color you intend to use.
	There is a bug in Internet Explorer 6 that sometimes causes the background to leak out from behind the element. You can assign **zoom:1** to the parent element to give it "layout," which prevents the background from leaking out. See the Atomic pattern in Chapter 7 for more details on "layout."
Related to	Image, Basic Shadowed Image, Shadowed Image; Margin, Background (Chapter 6)

Image Example

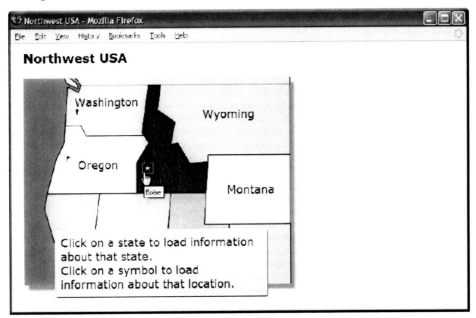

Representative Excerpts from the HTML

```
<h1>Northwest USA</h1>

<div id="states">
  <img src="nw.gif" width="437" height="328"
    alt="Northwest" usemap="#nw-map" class="shadowed" />

  <a id="washington" href="washington.html" class="overlay">Washington</a>
  <a id="oregon" href="oregon.html" class="overlay">Oregon</a>
  <a id="idaho" href="idaho.html" class="overlay">Idaho</a>

  <a id="olympia" class="bang-bg" href="olympia.html" title="Olympia">
    <span class="screenreader-only">Olympia</span></a>
  <a id="salem" class="flag-bg" href="salem.html" title="Salem">
    <span class="screenreader-only">Salem</span></a>

  <div id="info" class="bg">
    <div class="tl"><div class="br"><div class="trc"><div class="blc pad">
      <p>Click a state to load information about that state.</p>
      <p>Click a symbol to load information about that location.</p>
      </div></div></div></div></div>
</div>
```

Image Example

Example	This is not a design pattern but an example that illustrates how the design patterns in the chapter can work together.
Explanation	The main image in the example is a map of the Pacific Northwest. I used the Basic Shadowed Image design pattern to put a shadow behind it. The image is linked to the **nw-map** element to make areas on the map clickable. I used the Content over Image design pattern to put links on top of the map. When the user hovers over these links, the background displays a semi-transparent PNG image, which partially hides the content under the image. I also use the CSS Sprite design pattern to put clickable rollover images on top of the map. I also use the Rounded Corners and Fade-Out design patterns to style the message below the map.

Representative Excerpts from the CSS

```
.shadowed { padding-right:12px; padding-bottom:12px;
  background:url("shadow.jpg") right bottom no-repeat; }

.screenreader-only { position:absolute; left:-9999px; top:-9999px;
  width:1px; height:1px; overflow:hidden; }

a { text-decoration:none; color:black; }
a:hover { border-left:1px solid silver; border-right:1px solid gray; color:white;
  border-top:1px solid silver; border-bottom:1px solid gray;
  background-image:url("semi-transparent.png"); background-repeat:repeat-x; }
.overlay { padding:2px 4px; }

.bg { background:url("white2trans.png") top left repeat-x yellow;
  margin-top:20px; }
.tl { background:url("rc.gif") top left no-repeat; }
.br { background:url("rc.gif") bottom right no-repeat; }
.trc { background:url("rc-trc.gif") top right no-repeat; }
.blc { background:url("rc-blc.gif") bottom left no-repeat; }
.pad { padding:10px; }

.bang-bg { background:url("bt.gif") -48px -16px; width:16px; height:16px; }
.flag-bg { background:url("bt.gif") -64px -16px; width:16px; height:16px;
  }
.star-bg { background:url("bt.gif") -64px -32px; width:16px; height:16px; }

.bang-bg:hover { background-image:url("wt.gif"); background-color:black; }
.star-bg:hover { background-image:url("wt.gif"); background-color:black; }
.flag-bg:hover { background-image:url("wt.gif"); background-color:black; }

#states { position:relative; float:left; }
  #washington { position:absolute; top:35px; left:80px; }
  #oregon { position:absolute; top:135px; left:85px; }
  #idaho { position:absolute; top:150px; left:210px; }
```

CHAPTER 15

Tables

Tables are one of the most useful and complex structures in HTML. This is the first of two chapters on tables. This chapter explores the HTML structure of tables and how you can style them. The next chapter explores the many ways you can automatically lay out columns in tables. The purpose of tables is to identify and style tabular data.

Chapter Outline

- **Table** shows how to create and style the fundamental structure of a table.
- **Row and Column Groups** shows how to create and style row headers, row footers, row groups, column groups, and columns.
- **Table Selectors** shows how to select cells from columns, rows, and row groups.
- **Separated Borders** shows how to separate table borders from cell borders.
- **Collapsed Borders** shows how to combine table and cell borders.
- **Styled Collapsed Borders** shows how to style collapsed borders.
- **Hidden and Removed Cells** shows how to hide or remove cells.
- **Removed and Hidden Rows and Columns** shows how to remove or hide rows, row groups, and columns of cells.
- **Vertical-Aligned Data** shows how to vertically align data to the top, middle, bottom, or baseline of a cell.
- **Striped Tables** shows how to assign alternating backgrounds to rows.
- **Accessible Tables** shows how to create a table that is friendly to nonsighted users.
- **Tabled, Rowed, and Celled** shows how to turn any element into a table, row, or cell.
- **Table Layout** shows how to create the four types of tables: **shrinkwrapped**, **sized**, **stretched**, and **fixed**.

Table

Table

Simple Table

1	2	3	4	5	6
7	8	9	10	11	12

Table with Spanned Rows and Cells

1	2-6				
	8	9			12

HTML

```
<h1>Table</h1>

<h2>Simple Table</h2>
<table>
  <tr> <th>1</th> <th>2</th> <th>3</th> <th>4 </th> <th>5 </th> <th>6 </th> </tr>
  <tr> <th>7</th> <td>8</td> <td>9</td> <td>10</td> <td>11</td> <td>12</td> </tr>
</table>

<h2>Table with Spanned Rows and Cells</h2>
<table>
  <tr> <td rowspan="2">1</td> <td colspan="5">2-6</td>              </tr>
  <tr> <td>8</td> <td>9</td>  <td> </td> <td> </td> <td>12</td> </tr>
</table>
```

CSS

```
table { width:auto; height:1px; table-layout:auto; border-collapse:collapse;
  margin-left:20px; border:1px solid black; }

td, th { width:50px; height:1px; overflow:hidden; visibility:visible;
  border:1px solid black; padding:5px; background:gold;
  text-align:center; vertical-align:middle; text-indent:5px; }
```

Table

Problem	You want to create a table to present data in rows and columns.
Solution	At its simplest, a table consists of a **\<table\>** element containing one or more row **\<tr\>** elements, which contain one or more cells. Cells can be **header cells**, **\<th\>**, or **data cells**, **\<td\>**.

Header cells contain text describing the purpose of the columns and rows that they head. You may have zero or more rows of header cells to describe each column. You may have zero or more columns of header cells in each row to describe each row. Header cells and data cells may contain any content including nested tables, blocks, text, and objects. It is a common practice to restrict data cells to tabular data and header cells to text.

You can add the **colspan** and **rowspan** attributes to a cell to have it span one or more columns and/or one or more rows. To prevent missing cells, you need to use the same number of cells in each row or to use **colspan** to span cells across multiple columns. In the second table of the example, the first cell spans two rows, the second cell spans two columns, and the first row is missing three cells.

The major browsers apply box model properties in limited ways to tables, cells, rows, row groups, columns, and column groups. **background** is the only property that applies to all these elements. **margin** applies only to tables. **border** applies only to tables and cells. **padding**, **overflow**, and **vertical-align** apply to cells. **text-indent**, **text-align**, and other text-styling properties apply only to cells but can be inherited from row, row group, and table elements. **width** applies to tables, cells, and columns. **width** is important enough for the next chapter to be devoted to showing how it creates column layouts.

height applies to tables, rows, and cells, and specifies the *minimum* height of a table, row, or cell. It is a minimum height because content can always expand the height of a cell, row, or table. Contrast this with block elements where content overflows a fixed-height block instead of expanding it. A percentage-height block assigned to a table is a percentage of the height of the table's container. A percentage-height block is ignored when assigned to rows and cells. In the example, **height:1px** is applied to cells, but is overridden by the height of cell content and padding.

There are several unique table properties including **border-collapse** and **table-layout**. **border-collapse** is discussed in this chapter. **table-layout** is discussed in the next chapter. Additional unique table properties exist, but are implemented inconsistently by the major browsers: **table-layout**, **border-collapse**, **border-spacing**, **caption-side**, and **empty-cells**.

Pattern	
| HTML | ```
<table>
  <tr>
    <td colspan="NUMBER" rowspan="NUMBER"> CONTENT </td>
  </tr>
</table>
``` |
| **Location** | Tables can be used anywhere blocks can be used. |
| **Related to** | Structural Block Elements, Terminal Block Elements (Chapter 2); Display, Table Box (Chapter 4); Width, Height, Sized, Shrinkwrapped, Stretched (Chapter 5); Margin, Border, Padding (Chapter 6); Atomic (Chapter 7); Offset or Indented Static Table, Aligned and Offset Static Table (Chapter 8); Structural Meaning, Visual Structure, Inlined (Chapter 13); all design patterns in Chapters 15 and 16 |
```

Row and Column Groups

Row and Column Groups

Row Groups

thead	2	3	4
tbody	6	7	8
tfoot	10	11	12

Columns

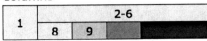

HTML

```
<h1>Row and Column Groups</h1>

<h2>Row Groups</h2>
<table class="example1">
  <thead> <tr> <th>thead</th> <th>2 </th> <th>3 </th> <th>4 </th> </tr> </thead>
  <tfoot> <tr> <th>tfoot</th> <td>10</td> <td>11</td> <td>12</td> </tr> </tfoot>
  <tbody> <tr> <th>tbody</th> <td>6 </td> <td>7 </td> <td>8 </td> </tr> </tbody>
</table>

<h2>Columns</h2>
<table class="example2">
  <colgroup><col class="col1" /><col class="col2" /><col class="col3" />
          <col class="col4" /><col class="col5" /><col class="col6" /></colgroup>

  <tr> <td rowspan="2">1</td> <td colspan="5">2-6</td>                </tr>
  <tr> <td>8</td> <td>9</td>  <td> </td> <td> </td> <td>12</td> </tr>
</table>
```

CSS

```
table.example1 thead { background:orange; color:black; }
table.example1 tbody { background:gold; color:black; }
table.example1 tfoot { background:firebrick; color:white; }
.col1 { background:wheat; }
.col2 { background:gold; }
.col3 { background:orange; }
.col4 { background:tomato; }
.col5 { background:firebrick; }
.col6 { background:black; color:white; }

/* Nonessential styles are not shown */
```

Row and Column Groups

Problem	You want to group together rows and columns to make it easy to style groups of rows and columns.
Solution	You can optionally use the following elements to group together rows and columns: **<thead>** (table header row group), **<tfoot>** (table footer row group), **<tbody>** (table body row group), **<colgroup>** (column group), and **<col>** (column).

Row groups are useful for styling groups of rows and cells with **background**, **visibility**, **display:none**, and text properties. You can also use descendant selectors to select rows and cells in row groups. On the other hand, column groups and columns are limited to styling with **background** and **width**.

Row groups may surround any number of rows. You can use data cells or header cells in any row of any row group. You may include any number of **<tbody>** elements in a table, but you should include at most only one **<thead>** and one **<tfoot>**. This is because a browser renders table header and footer groups once per table. Table header groups are placed at the beginning of the table, and the footer groups are placed at the end (even though footer rows are placed before body rows in *HTML code*). When a document is printed, table headers and footers are supposed to be repeated at the top and bottom of each page, but only Firefox 2 does this. Because of this, **<tfoot>** is unsuitable for containing summary data.

Because of inheritance, cells inherit text styles assigned to tables, row groups, and rows. Cells cannot inherit from column groups and columns. **visibility:hidden** and **display:none** apply to tables, rows, row groups, and cells, but not to column groups and columns. **background** applies to all.

Table backgrounds are layered from back to front as follows: table, column groups, columns, row groups, rows, and cells. Since there is no padding between these elements, you can see the background of an element only when its children have a transparent background. For example, to see a row group's background, its rows and cells must have a transparent background.

A table may contain one or more column groups (**<colgroup>**), which may contain one or more columns (**<col>**). Browsers can reliably style column groups and columns with only two properties: **background** and **width**. This is a problem and a severe limitation. In the second table of the example, I select column elements to apply different background colors to each column. Notice how you cannot see the text in cell 12, for it is black on black because browsers apply **background:black** to column elements but not **color:white**.

Pattern	
HTML	```<table>
<colgroup> <col /> </colgroup>
<thead> <tr> <th> CONTENT </th> </tr> </thead>
<tfoot> <tr> <th> CONTENT </th> </tr> </tfoot>
<tbody> <tr> <td> CONTENT </td> </tr> </tbody>
</table>```
Location	This pattern applies to tables.
Related to	Table

Table Selectors

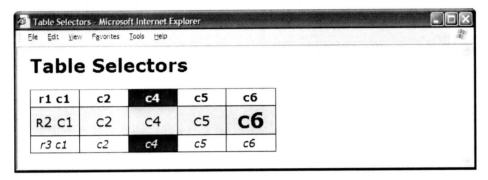

HTML

```
<h1>Table Selectors</h1>
<table id="t1">
  <thead>
    <tr class="r1"> <td class="c1">r1 c1</td> <td class="c2">c2</td>
                    <td class="c3">c3</td>    <td class="c4">c4</td>
                    <td class="c5">c5</td>    <td class="c6">c6</td> </tr></thead>
  <tfoot>
    <tr class="r3"> <td class="c1">r3 c1</td> <td class="c2">c2</td>
                    <td class="c3">c3</td>    <td class="c4">c4</td>
                    <td class="c5">c5</td>    <td class="c6">c6</td> </tr></tfoot>
  <tbody class="b1">
    <tr class="r2"> <td class="c1">r2 c1</td> <td class="c2">c2</td>
                    <td class="c3">c3</td>    <td class="c4">c4</td>
                    <td class="c5">c5</td>    <td class="c6">c6</td> </tr></tbody>
</table>
```

CSS

```
table,td,th { border:1px solid black; }        /* Selecting all tables and cells */
td,th { background-color:white; }              /* Selecting all cells */

#t1 { border-collapse:collapse; }              /* Selecting table */
#t1 thead td { font-weight:bold; }             /* Selecting cells in head */
#t1 tfoot td { font-style:italic; }            /* Selecting cells in foot */
#t1 tbody td { font-variant:small-caps; }      /* Selecting cells in body */
#t1 .b1  td { font-size:1.2em; }               /* Selecting cells in body */
#t1 .c3 { display:none; }                       /* Selecting cells in column */
#t1 .c4 { background-color:firebrick; color:white; }
#t1 .r1 { background-color:gold; color:black; }       /* Selecting row-no effect*/
#t1 .r2 td { background-color:gold; color:black; }  /* Selecting cells in row */
#t1 .r2 .c6 { font-size:1.8em; font-weight:bold; } /* Selecting cell */

/* Nonessential styles are not shown */
```

Table Selectors

Problem	You want a simple, flexible, and generic way to select a column, a row, or a cell for styling.
Solution	You can assign a unique ID to each table, such as **t1**. This allows you to select each table individually. You can label each row with a class that is unique within the table, such as **r1**, **r2**, and so on. You can label each cell with a class that is unique within each row, such as **c1**, **c2**, and so on. Because each table has a unique ID, you can reuse the same class names for rows and columns. By using the table ID with descendant selectors, you can select the table, any row in the table, any cell in any row, and any cell in any column.
	You can also enclose rows within **<thead>**, **<tfoot>**, and **<tbody>** elements. If you have multiple **<tbody>** elements, you can also label each one with a unique class, such as **b1**, **b2**, and so on. You can use descendant selectors following the table's ID to select and style the cells in a table header, footer, or one of the row groups defined by **<tbody>**. This makes it easy to style cells in groups of rows.
	Selecting a row, table header, table footer, or table body is of little use because you can style only its background, and even then you cannot see the background unless cell backgrounds are transparent. In the example, I style all cells with a white background. I also style the first *row* element with a gold background, but you cannot see its gold background because it is covered by the white cell backgrounds. On the other hand, I style *cells* in the second row with a gold background, which you can see because the selector styles cells, not the row. Thus, selecting cells within a row or row group is very useful. All of the following selector design patterns select cells.

Patterns	**All Table and Cells Selector**
	`table,td,th { STYLES }`
	
	All Cells Selector
	`td,th { STYLES }`
	
	Table Selector
	`#tx { STYLES }`
	
	Column Cells Selector
	`#tx .cx { STYLES }`
	
	Row Cells Selector
	`#tx .rx td { STYLES }` *or* `#tx .rx th { STYLES }`
	
	Cell Selector
	`#tx .rx .cx { STYLES }`
	
	Row Group Selector
	`#tx thead td { STYLES }` *or* `#tx thead th { STYLES }`

Location	This pattern applies to cells, rows, row groups, and tables.
Related to	Table

Separated Borders

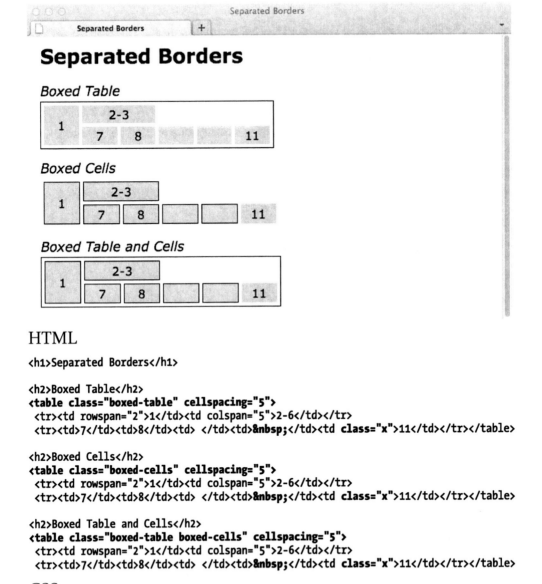

HTML

```
<h1>Separated Borders</h1>

<h2>Boxed Table</h2>
<table class="boxed-table" cellspacing="5">
 <tr><td rowspan="2">1</td><td colspan="5">2-6</td></tr>
 <tr><td>7</td><td>8</td><td> </td><td> </td><td class="x">11</td></tr></table>

<h2>Boxed Cells</h2>
<table class="boxed-cells" cellspacing="5">
 <tr><td rowspan="2">1</td><td colspan="5">2-6</td></tr>
 <tr><td>7</td><td>8</td><td> </td><td> </td><td class="x">11</td></tr></table>

<h2>Boxed Table and Cells</h2>
<table class="boxed-table boxed-cells" cellspacing="5">
 <tr><td rowspan="2">1</td><td colspan="5">2-6</td></tr>
 <tr><td>7</td><td>8</td><td> </td><td> </td><td class="x">11</td></tr></table>
```

CSS

```
table { border-collapse:separate; }
.boxed-table { border:1px solid black; }
.boxed-cells td { border:1px solid black; }
.boxed-cells td.x { border:none; }

/* Nonessential styles are not shown */
```

Separated Borders

Problem	You want to put independent borders around tables and cells.
Solution	You can apply the **border-collapse:separate** property to a table to separate table borders from cell borders. You can use the **border** property to put a border around a table or around a cell. When borders are separate, borders around tables are distinct from borders around cells. You can use the **cellspacing** attribute to control the amount of spacing around cell borders.
Pattern	

HTML	`<table cellspacing="WIDTH">`
	`    <tr> <td> CONTENT </td> </tr>`
	`</table>`

CSS	`TABLE_SELECTOR { border-collapse:separate;`
	`    border:WIDTH STYLE COLOR; }`
	
	`CELL_SELECTOR { border:WIDTH STYLE COLOR; }`

Location	This pattern applies to tables and cells.
Limitations	Internet Explorer 7 does not render a border around empty cells. An empty cell does not contain content. Whitespace is not content. In IE7 the example will display differently; cell 9 will have no border because it is empty. In contrast, cell 10 will have a border because it contains a nonbreaking space—even though it looks empty. You can prevent this problem by always putting a nonbreaking space in empty cells.
	No major browser renders borders or backgrounds for missing cells. Missing cells occur when a row has fewer cells than the table has columns and existing cells do not span enough columns to compensate. In the example, cells 4, 5, and 6 are missing.
	Browsers ignore borders applied to rows, columns, column groups, and row groups. This means the only way to put borders around columns or rows is to put them around each cell in the column or row.
Advantages	Unlike collapsed borders, separated borders do not have border conflicts between adjacent cells and between the table and its cells.
Disadvantages	Separated borders require an HTML attribute, **cellspacing**, to control the distance between cells because Internet Explorer 7 and earlier versions do not implement the **border-spacing** property.
Tips	You can use **border:none** to remove a border applied by another rule. Notice in the example how **border:none** removes the border from cell 11.
	You can use **border-left**, **border-right**, **border-top**, and **border-bottom** to apply borders independently to each side of a cell or table. In other words, any side of a table or cell can have a different border width, style, and color.
Related to	Collapsed Borders; Border (Chapter 6)

Collapsed Borders

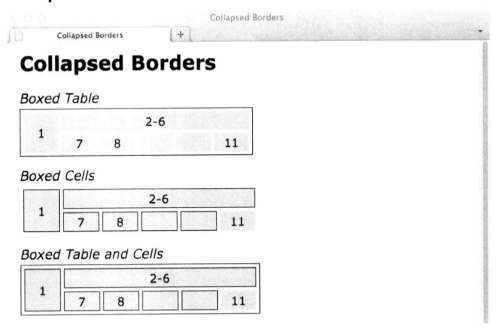

HTML

```
<h1>Collapsed Borders</h1>

<h2>Boxed Table</h2>
<table class="boxed-table" cellspacing="0">
 <tr><td rowspan="2">1</td><td colspan="5">2-6</td> </tr>
 <tr><td>7</td><td>8</td><td> </td><td> </td><td class="x">11</td></tr></table>

<h2>Boxed Cells</h2>
<table class="boxed-cells" cellspacing="0">
 <tr><td rowspan="2">1</td><td colspan="5">2-6</td> </tr>
 <tr><td>7</td><td>8</td><td> </td><td> </td><td class="x">11</td></tr></table>

<h2>Boxed Table and Cells</h2>
<table class="boxed-table boxed-cells" cellspacing="0">
 <tr><td rowspan="2">1</td><td colspan="5">2-6</td> </tr>
 <tr><td>7</td><td>8</td><td> </td><td> </td><td class="x">11</td></tr></table>
```

CSS

```
table { border-collapse:collapse; }
.boxed-table { border:1px solid black; }
.boxed-cells td { border:1px solid black; }
.boxed-cells td.x { border:none; }

/* Nonessential styles are not shown */
```

Collapsed Borders

Problem	You want to merge table and cell borders.
Solution	You can apply the **border-collapse:collapse** property to a table to merge its borders with its cell borders. You can use the **border** property to put borders around a table and its cells. When borders are collapsed, you must omit the **cellspacing** attribute from the table element or set it to **0** to avoid problems in Internet Explorer 7 and earlier versions.
Pattern	
| HTML | ```
<table cellspacing="0">
  <tr> <td> CONTENT </td> </tr>
</table>
``` |
| CSS | ```
TABLE_SELECTOR { border-collapse:collapse;
  border:WIDTH STYLE COLOR; }
CELL_SELECTOR { border:WIDTH STYLE COLOR; }
``` |
Location	This pattern applies to tables and cells.
Advantages	In contrast to separated borders, all major browsers render collapsed borders around empty cells. Notice in the example how cell 9 is empty and has a border; in the Separated Borders design pattern, it does not have a border.
Disadvantages	Unlike separated borders, collapsed borders have border conflicts between adjacent cells and between the table and its cells.
Tips	If adjacent borders have different styles, width, or color, the most visible border wins. Wider borders override narrower ones. Border styles override each other in the following order from most prominent to least: **double**, **solid**, **dashed**, **dotted**, **ridge**, **outset**, **groove**, and **inset**. When colors conflict, cell border color overrides table border color. Also, left border color overrides right, and top overrides bottom.
Related to	Separated Borders; Border (Chapter 6)

Styled Collapsed Borders

HTML

```
<h1>Styled Collapsed Borders</h1>

<table id="t1">
  <tr class="r1"> <td class="c1">1</td> <td class="c2">2</td> </tr>
  <tr class="r2"> <td class="c1">1</td> <td class="c2">2</td> </tr> </table>
```

CSS

```
table { border-collapse:collapse; }              /* Table and cells borders */
table,td,th { border:5px solid red; }

#t1 { border-left:1px solid black; }             /* Left table border */
#t1 .c1 { border-left:1px solid black; }

#t1 { border-right:2px solid black; }            /* Right table border */
#t1 .c2 { border-right:2px solid black; }

#t1 .c1 { border-right:1px dotted black; }       /* Interior column border */
#t1 .c2 { border-left:1px dotted black; }

#t1 { border-top:1px solid black; }              /* Top table border */
#t1 .r1 td { border-top:1px solid black; }

#t1 { border-bottom:2px solid black; }           /* Bottom table border */
#t1 .r2 td { border-bottom:2px solid black; }

#t1 .r1 td { border-bottom:1px dotted black; }   /* Interior row border */
#t1 .r2 td { border-top:1px dotted black; }

/* Nonessential styles are not shown */
```

Styled Collapsed Borders

Problem	You want to assign borders to rows and columns in a table with collapsed borders. The problem is that the table shares borders with its cells, and cells share borders with each other. Thus, each visible border is actually two borders that have been merged, such as the left table border and the left border of each cell in the first column. If you do not style merged borders the same, a browser decides which of the merged borders to display, which may not be the border you want.
Solution	You can use the Table Selectors design pattern to mark up the table to make it easy to select columns and rows of cells. A table with collapsed borders has six types of borders: left table border, interior column border, right table border, top border, interior row border, and bottom border. The design patterns that follow show how to style these six types of merged borders.

Patterns	**Left Table Border**
	
	`#t1 { border-left: WIDTH_1 STYLE_1 COLOR_1; }`
	`#t1 .cx_FIRST { border-left: WIDTH_1 STYLE_1 COLOR_1; }`
	
	Right Table Border
	
	`#t1 { border-right: WIDTH_2 STYLE_2 COLOR_2; }`
	`#t1 .cx_LAST { border-right: WIDTH_2 STYLE_2 COLOR_2; }`
	
	Interior Column Border
	
	`#t1 .cx { border-right: WIDTH_3 STYLE_3 COLOR_3; }`
	`#t1 .cx+1 { border-left: WIDTH_3 STYLE_3 COLOR_3; }`
	
	Top Table Border
	
	`#t1 { border-top: WIDTH_4 STYLE_4 COLOR_4; }`
	`#t1 .rx_FIRST td { border-top: WIDTH_4 STYLE_4 COLOR_4; }`
	
	Bottom Table Border
	
	`#t1 { border-bottom: WIDTH_5 STYLE_5 COLOR_5; }`
	`#t1 .rx_LAST td { border-bottom: WIDTH_5 STYLE_5 COLOR_5; }`
	
	Interior Row Border
	
	`#t1 .rx td { border-bottom: WIDTH_6 STYLE_6 COLOR_6; }`
	`#t1 .rx+1 td { border-top: WIDTH_6 STYLE_6 COLOR_6; }`

Location	This pattern applies to cells and tables. `<colgroup>` and `<col />` cannot be used to style borders.
Tip	When a table uses separated borders, you do not need this design pattern because separated borders are not shared.
Example	In the example, I use the **table,td,td {}** selector to set all table and cell borders to be 5 pixels wide and solid red. If you want all borders to be the same, this selector is all you need. The example overrides these red borders with a variety of smaller black borders assigned to each row and column.
Related to	Table Selectors, Collapsed Borders; Border (Chapter 6)

Hidden and Removed Cells

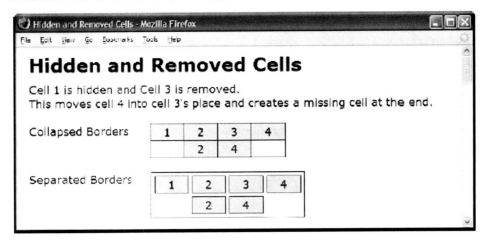

HTML

```
<h1>Hidden and Removed Cells</h1>

<h3>Cell 1 is hidden and Cell 3 is removed. <br /> This moves cell 4
   into cell 3's place and creates a missing cell at the end.</h3>

<br /><div>Collapsed Borders</div>
<table class="collapsed" cellspacing="0">
 <tr><td>1</td><td>2</td><td>3</td><td>4</td></tr>
 <tr><td class="h">1</td><td>2</td><td class="x">3</td><td>4</td></tr></table>

<br /><div>Separated Borders</div>
<table class="separated" cellspacing="5">
 <tr><td>1</td><td>2</td><td>3</td><td>4</td></tr>
 <tr><td class="h">1</td><td>2</td><td class="x">3</td><td>4</td></tr></table>

<!-- Many additional examples are not shown -->
```

CSS

```
table, td, th { border:1px solid black; }

.separated { border-collapse:separate; }
.collapsed { border-collapse:collapse; }

.x { display:none; }
.h { visibility:hidden; }

/* Nonessential styles are not shown */
```

Hidden and Removed Cells

Problem	You want to hide or remove one or more cells.
Solution	You can use **visibility:hidden** to hide cells. Hidden cells are not rendered, but their location and the space they would have occupied is preserved. This is the most common way to hide a cell because it keeps cells in their proper locations. Notice in the example how the first cell in the second row is hidden without changing the location of the following cells.
	When a table has collapsed borders, the borders around hidden cells are still rendered. Thus, when you hide a cell in a table with collapsed borders, its contents are hidden, but its borders are not. Notice in the first table of the example how borders surround the hidden cell in the first column of the second row. On the other hand, borders are not rendered around hidden cells in a table with separate borders. In the second table in the example, there are no borders around the hidden cell in the first column of the second row.
	You can use **display:none** to remove cells. Removed cells are not rendered. It is as if they never existed. This means that cells to the right of removed cells slide over to take the place of removed cells! In the example, cell 3 is removed. Notice how cell 4 slides into its place. Because cell 3 is removed, there are fewer cells in the second row than in the first row, which creates a missing cell at the end. Thus, if you do not want cells to be shuffled around, you should hide cells instead of removing them. On the other hand, it is common to remove columns, rows, row groups, and tables because you typically do not want these items to leave behind empty space. This is explored further in the Removed and Hidden Rows and Columns design pattern.
Pattern	**Hidden Tables, Rows, and Cells**
	`SELECTOR { visibility:hidden; }`
	Removed Tables, Rows, and Cells
	`SELECTOR { display:none; }`
Location	This pattern applies to cells.
Limitations	In Opera and Internet Explorer, when you use **visibility:hidden** or **display:none** to hide cells, it will also hide the borders that don't touch other cells. There are a few solutions for this problem. Hide the content by using **text-indent: -9999px** to shift the content off the page or wrap the content in a **div** and set **visibility:hidden** on the **div** instead.
	This should be fixed when **empty-cell:show** is properly implemented, which tells the browser to render the background and border of an empty table cell as if it were there. However, at this time, it is extremely buggy and considered not supported.
Tip	When you hide a table with collapsed borders, the table's outer borders are hidden and its contents are hidden, but its internal borders remain visible. To completely hide the table, you can assign **visibility:hidden** to the table and **border:none** to its cells. This is not necessary for tables with separate borders.
Example	The code and the screenshot shown here are a small part of the full example, which includes many more examples of hidden columns, hidden rows, hidden row groups, and hidden tables.
Related to	Removed and Hidden Rows and Columns; Display (Chapter 4); Border, Visibility (Chapter 6)

Removed and Hidden Rows and Columns

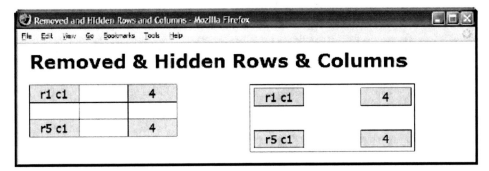

HTML

```
<h1>Removed &amp; Hidden Rows &amp; Columns</h1>

<table id="t1">
  <tbody class="b1">
    <tr  class="r1"> <td class="c1">r1 c1</td>  <td class="c2">2</td>
                     <td class="c3">r1 c3</td>  <td class="c4">4</td> </tr>

    <tr  class="r2"> <td class="c1">r2 c1</td>  <td class="c2">2</td>
                     <td class="c3">r2 c3</td>  <td class="c4">4</td> </tr></tbody>

  <tbody class="b2">
    <tr  class="r3"> <td class="c1">r3 c1</td>  <td class="c2">2</td>
                     <td class="c3">r3 c3</td>  <td class="c4">4</td> </tr>

    <tr  class="r4"> <td class="c1">r4 c1</td>  <td class="c2">2</td>
                     <td class="c3">r4 c3</td>  <td class="c4">4</td> </tr></tbody>

  <tbody class="b3">
    <tr  class="r5"> <td class="c1">r5 c1</td>  <td class="c2">2</td>
                     <td class="c3">r5 c3</td>  <td class="c4">4</td> </tr></tbody>
</table>

<!-- Second identical table with separated borders is not shown -->
```

CSS

```
#t1 .c2 { display:none; }        /* Removing column */
#t1 .c3 { visibility:hidden; }   /* Hiding column */
#t1 .r2 { visibility:hidden; }   /* Hiding row */
#t1 .b2 { display:none; }        /* Removing row group */

/* Nonessential styles are not shown */
```

Removed and Hidden Rows and Columns

Problem	You want to remove a column, a row, or a group of rows so that following columns slide over and following rows slide up to take the place of the removed row or column. You want to hide a row or column when you want to leave behind empty space where the row, row group, or column would have been rendered.
Solution	You can use the Table Selectors design pattern to mark up a table to make it easy to select any row or column. You can use **display:none** to remove rows, row groups, and columns. To remove a column, you can assign **display:none** to each cell in the column. To remove a row or a row group, you can assign **display:none** to **<tr>**, **<thead>**, **<tfoot>**, or **<tbody>** elements. Removed elements are not rendered. It is as if they never existed. Columns on the right slide over into the place of removed columns. This causes a shrinkwrapped table to shrink because there is one less column. Rows slide up into the place of removed rows. This causes the height of a shrinkwrapped table to shrink. In the example, the cells in the second column are removed, which causes the third and fourth columns to slide over. Also, the third and fourth rows in the third row group are removed, which causes the fifth row to slide up into their place.
	You can use **visibility:hidden** instead of **display:none** to hide rows and columns instead of removing them. This is less common than removing rows and columns because it leaves blank space behind. In the example, I hide the third column and the second row. The space where the rows and columns would have been rendered remains behind.
	When columns and rows are *removed*, a browser does not render their borders. On the other hand, when columns and rows are *hidden*, a browser renders borders when borders are collapsed, but not when separated. In the first table of the example, borders are collapsed, and you can see the borders around hidden rows and columns. In the second table, borders are separated, and you cannot see the borders around the hidden rows and columns.
Patterns	**Hidden Rows, Row Groups, and Cells**
	`SELECTOR { visibility:hidden; }`
	Removed Rows, Row Groups, and Cells
	`SELECTOR { display:none; }`
Location	This pattern applies to cells, rows, and row groups.
Limitations	You may be tempted to remove or hide columns using the two column elements: **<colgroup>** and **<col />**. Internet Explorer has a proprietary feature that allows this, but other major browsers do not. You may also want to apply **visibility: collapse** to these elements, but this does not work in Internet Explorer 7 or Opera 9. This design pattern is the best way to hide or remove columns.
	The limitations mentioned in Hidden and Removed Cells apply here as well.
Related to	Hidden and Removed Cells; Display (Chapter 4); Border, Visibility (Chapter 6)

Vertical-Aligned Data

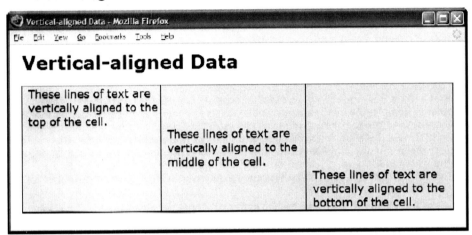

HTML

```
<h1>Vertical-Aligned Data</h1>

<table>
  <tr>
    <td class="align-top" >These lines of text are vertically aligned
      to the top of the cell.</td>

    <td class="align-middle">These lines of text are vertically aligned
      to the middle of the cell.</td>

    <td class="align-bottom">These lines of text are vertically aligned
      to the bottom of the cell.</td></tr></table>
```

CSS

```
.align-top    { height:200px; vertical-align:top; }
.align-middle { height:200px; vertical-align:middle; }
.align-bottom { height:200px; vertical-align:bottom; }

/* Nonessential styles are not shown */
```

Vertical-Aligned Data

Problem	You want to align multiple lines of data as a group to the top, middle, or bottom of a cell.
Solution	You can place multiple lines of data in a cell and use **vertical-align** to automatically align it to the top, middle, or bottom of the cell. For this to work, the cell needs to have a height greater than the height of the data; otherwise, there is no space for the data to move up or down within the cell.

vertical-align applies to cells and to inline elements. Just as you can use **vertical-align** to offset inline elements from the baseline, you can do the same to the contents of a cell.

There are three **vertical-align** settings that apply in unique ways to cells. These are **top**, **middle**, and **bottom**. **top** is the top of the cell, **middle** is the middle of the cell, and **bottom** is the bottom of the cell. When **top**, **middle**, and **bottom** are applied to inline elements, **top** is the top of the line, **bottom** is the bottom of the line, and **middle** is roughly the middle of the line.

What is unique and useful about **top**, **middle**, and **bottom** when applied to a cell is that they align *the entire contents of a cell **including multiple lines of content*** to the top, middle, or bottom of the cell. In contrast, when you apply **vertical-align** to an inline element, it aligns an inline element to another inline element *within a line*. In other words, **vertical-align** positions inline elements in relation to each other within a *single line*, whereas **vertical-align** applied to a cell vertically positions its content within the cell—including *multiple lines* of content.

There is no other mechanism in CSS and HTML that can vertically align multiple lines of *content*. The closest approximations are the absolute design patterns that vertically align an element (not its content) to the top, middle, or bottom of its closest positioned ancestor. These design patterns include Align Top, Align Middle, and Align Bottom. The main problem with absolute design patterns is that they remove elements from the flow. A cell can align its contents without leaving the normal flow.

Patterns	
HTML	`<table><tr><td class="ALIGNMENT"> CONTENT </td></tr></table>`

CSS	`.align-top     { height:+VALUE; vertical-align:top; }`
	`.align-middle { height:+VALUE; vertical-align:middle; }`
	`.align-bottom { height:+VALUE; vertical-align:bottom; }`

Location	This design pattern works on any cell.
Related to	Vertical-Aligned Content, Vertical-Offset Content (Chapter 12)

Striped Tables

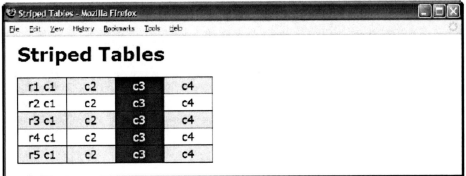

HTML

```
<h1>Striped Tables</h1>

<table id="t1">

  <tr class="r1 odd"> <td class="c1">r1 c1</td> <td class="c2">c2</td>
                      <td class="c3">  c3</td> <td class="c4">c4</td> </tr>

  <tr class="r2">     <td class="c1">r2 c1</td> <td class="c2">c2</td>
                      <td class="c3">  c3</td> <td class="c4">c4</td> </tr>

  <tr class="r3 odd"> <td class="c1">r3 c1</td> <td class="c2">c2</td>
                      <td class="c3">  c3</td> <td class="c4">c4</td> </tr>

  <tr class="r4">     <td class="c1">r4 c1</td> <td class="c2">c2</td>
                      <td class="c3">  c3</td> <td class="c4">c4</td> </tr>

  <tr class="r5 odd"> <td class="c1">r5 c1</td> <td class="c2">c2</td>
                      <td class="c3">  c3</td> <td class="c4">c4</td> </tr>

</table>
```

CSS

```
#ts td { background:white; }                    /* Background of all cells */
#t1 .odd td { background:palegreen; }           /* Alternating Row Background */
#t1 td.c3 { background:darkgreen; color:white; } /* Column Background */

/* Nonessential styles are not shown */
```

Striped Tables

Aliases	Greenbar, Zebra Stripes
Problem	You want to style alternating rows with different background colors—much like reports printed on greenbar paper.
Solution	You can optionally assign a standard background color to all cells or leave them all transparent. You can add a class to odd rows, even rows (or any arbitrary row for that matter), and you can use this class to select and style the **background** of cells in these rows. You can optionally style the backgrounds of cells in columns as well.
Pattern	
HTML	`<table><tr><td class="ALIGNMENT"> CONTENT </td></tr></table>`

CSS	`#TABLE_ID .odd  td { background:COLOR; }`
	or
	`#TABLE_ID .odd  th { background:COLOR; }`

Location	This pattern applies to cells in a row.
Advantages	Styling alternate rows in alternating background colors makes it easier to read extra wide tables. It also enables the user to read data in rows.
Disadvantages	When styling the backgrounds of columns, it takes careful planning and color coordination to make the background of columns blend well with the alternating backgrounds of rows. Furthermore, if you want a column background to override an alternating row background, you need to make sure the column selector has a higher priority in the cascade order than the row selector. In the example, I made the column selector equal priority to the alternating selector by using **#t1 td.c3** instead of **#t1 .c3**, and I made it a higher priority by placing it after the alternating row selector in the style sheet.
Tips	The most important point of this simple design pattern is selecting and styling cells within rows. If you style the background of a row element, you will not see the background unless the background of each cell in the row is transparent. This is because the background of each cell overlays the background of its row. Even when you use separated borders, the spacing between cells does not reveal a row's background—it reveals the table's background. Thus, this design pattern uses the descendant operator to select and style the cells in a row rather than the row itself.
	In addition to **background**, you may also want to style **border** and **padding** differently for alternating cells. You may also want to style text properties differently, such as **font-size**, **font-style**, **font-variant**, **font-weight**, **text-decoration**, **text-transform**, **line-height**, **letter-spacing**, and **word-spacing**.
Related to	Border, Padding, Background (Chapter 6); Font (Chapter 10); Spacing (Chapter 11)

Tabled, Rowed, and Celled

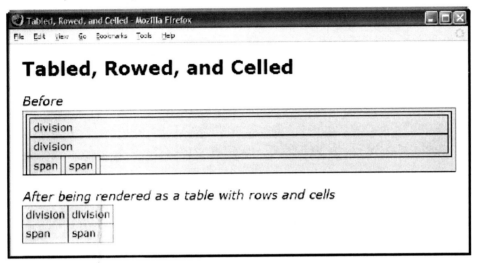

HTML

```
<h1>Tabled, Rowed, and Celled</h1>

<h2>Before</h2>
<div>
  <div>
    <div>division</div>
    <div>division</div></div>
  <span>
    <span>span</span>
    <span>span</span></span></div>

<h2>After being rendered as a table with rows and cells</h2>
<div class="tabled">
  <div class="rowed">
    <div class="celled">division</div>
    <div class="celled">division</div></div>
      <span class="rowed">
      <span class="celled">span</span>
        <span class="celled">span</span></span></div>
```

CSS

```
div,span { border:1px solid black; background-color:gold; padding:5px; }

.tabled { display:table; border-collapse:collapse; }
.rowed { display:table-row; }
.celled { display:table-cell; }
```

Tabled, Rowed, and Celled

Problem	You want to render ordinary inline and block elements as tables, rows, and cells.
Solution	You can use the **display:table**, **display:table-row**, and **display:table-cell** rules to transform elements into tables, rows, and cells.
	Typically you nest an element rendered as a cell within an element rendered as a row. In turn, you nest an element rendered as a row within an element that is rendered as a table. It does not matter what type of element is used as long as it is valid XHTML. A table can be created completely out of inline elements, block elements, or a mixture of both.
	You can also render an element as a stand-alone cell, and a browser will automatically create a row box and table box. Since tables shrinkwrap by default and since blocks stretch by default, rendering a block as a cell is a good way to shrinkwrap it without having to leave the normal flow.
Patterns	
HTML	``` <ELEMENT class="tabled"> <ELEMENT class="rowed"> <ELEMENT class="celled"> CONTENT </ELEMENT> <ELEMENT class="rowed"> </ELEMENT> ```
CSS	``` .tabled { display:table; border-collapse:collapse; } .rowed { display:table-row; } .celled { display:table-cell; } ```
Location	This pattern applies to block and inline elements.
Limitations	This pattern does not work in Internet Explorer 7 or earlier versions. This is unfortunate because this is a very useful design pattern. If Internet Explorer supported this part of the CSS standard, you could take advantage of all the unique features offered only by tables. For example, an element displayed as a table automatically shrinkwraps instead of stretches—without leaving the normal flow. This is very useful when you want to create shrinkwrapped buttons, menus, boxes around images, and so on. Displaying an element as a table also allows you to lay out its child elements using the many powerful and automatic layouts presented in Chapter 16. In short, you can take nontabular elements and lay them out in rows and columns for pure presentational pleasure without guilt.
Example	In the example, I transform four divisions and three spans into a table with two rows and two columns. Notice how block elements and inline elements can be combined to create a table.
Related to	Table; Display, Table Box (Chapter 4); Blocked (Chapter 11); Inlined (Chapter 13)

Table Layout

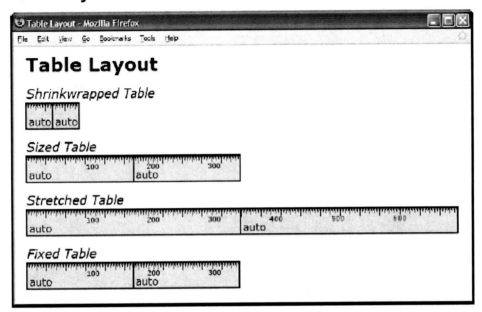

HTML

```
<h1>Table Layout</h1>

<h2>Shrinkwrapped Table</h2>
<table class="auto-layout shrinkwrapped">
 <tr><td>auto</td><td>auto</td></tr></table>

<h2>Sized Table</h2>
<table class="auto-layout sized"> <tr><td>auto</td><td>auto</td></tr></table>

<h2>Stretched Table</h2>
<table class="auto-layout stretched"> <tr><td>auto</td><td>auto</td></tr></table>

<h2>Fixed Table</h2>
<table class="fixed-layout sized"> <tr><td>auto</td><td>auto</td></tr></table>
```

CSS

```
.auto-layout { table-layout:auto; }
.fixed-layout { table-layout:fixed; }
.shrinkwrapped { width:auto; }
.sized { width:350px; }
.stretched { width:100%; }

/* Nonessential styles are not shown */
```

Table Layout

Problem	You want to create shrinkwrapped, sized, stretched, or fixed tables.
Solution	There are four types of tables: **shrinkwrapped**, **sized**, **stretched**, and **fixed**. Each has unique capabilities for laying out columns. These layouts are explored in detail in the next chapter.
	A **shrinkwrapped table** shrinks to the width of its columns and will not expand beyond the width of its container. A **sized** or **stretched table** can lay out its columns in proportion to the table's width, and can expand beyond the width of its container. A **fixed table** is a variation of a sized or stretched table, except it ignores the width of its content when laying out columns. This greatly speeds the rendering and prevents content from expanding a column's width.
	The following two properties assigned to a table determine the type of table: **table-layout** and **width**.
	There are two values for **table-layout**: **auto** and **fixed**. The default value is **auto**. An **auto-layout table** lays out columns based on the minimum and maximum widths of cell contents and on the **width** assigned to its cells. A **fixed-layout table** ignores content and lays out columns based only on the **width** assigned to the cells in its first row.
	The type of width assigned to the table determines whether a table is shrinkwrapped, sized, or stretched. There are three types of width: auto, fixed, and percentage. An auto width is created using **width:auto**. A fixed width is created using **width:VALUE**, such as **width:100px**. A percentage width is created using **width:PERCENT%**, such as **width:100%**.
	A shrinkwrapped table is auto layout and auto width. A stretched table is auto layout and has a percentage width of 100%. A sized table is auto layout and fixed width, or has a percentage width other than 100%. A fixed table is fixed layout and has a fixed width or percentage width.
Patterns	**Shrinkwrapped Table**
	`TABLE_SELECTOR { table-layout:auto; width:auto; }`
	Sized Table
	`TABLE_SELECTOR { table-layout:auto; width:VALUE_OR_PERCENT; }`
	Stretched Table
	`TABLE_SELECTOR { table-layout:auto; width:100%; }`
	Fixed Table
	`TABLE_SELECTOR { table-layout:fixed; width:VALUE_OR_PERCENT; }`
Location	This pattern applies to table elements.
Tip	A good way to set the width of columns is to assign **width** to each cell in the first row of the table. This works in fixed-layout and auto-layout tables, and it does not require **<colgroup>** and **<col>** elements.
Related to	Table; Sized, Shrinkwrapped, Stretched (Chapter 5); Offset or Indented Static Table, Aligned and Offset Static Table (Chapter 8); all design patterns in Chapter 16

CHAPTER 16

Table Column Layout

Browsers have many built-in capabilities for *automatically* sizing columns in tables. This chapter shows how to harness these automatic features to shrinkwrap columns, size them to specific widths, size them proportionally to each other, size them proportionally to their content, size them equally, size them flexibly, and undersize or oversize them.

Table Layout Models

There are four types of tables: shrinkwrapped, sized, stretched, and fixed. Each type of table has unique column layouts that only it can create.

The main purpose of a shrinkwrapped table is shrinking columns to fit their content. The main purpose of a sized or stretched table is proportionally dividing its width among its columns. The main purpose of a fixed table is setting its columns to fixed widths and speeding the rendering of the table.

Shrinkwrapped tables shrink to fit their content. This gives them the unique capability to shrink columns to fit the width of their content. A shrinkwrapped table can be narrower than its container and will not expand beyond the width of its container. Shrinkwrapped tables are the best choice when you want flexible layouts that adapt to different devices, screen resolutions, and viewport sizes. The following unique layouts apply to shrinkwrapped tables: Shrinkwrapped Columns, Sized Columns, Equal Content-Sized Columns, and Inverse-Proportioned Columns.

Sized and stretched tables divide their width proportionally among their columns while ensuring no column is narrower than its content. Sized and stretched tables work exactly the same when laying out columns. The only difference is that a sized table can be narrower or wider than its container, and a stretched table stretches to the width of its container. The following layouts apply to stretched tables: Content-Proportioned Columns, Size-Proportioned Columns, Percentage-Proportioned Columns, Equal-Sized Columns, and Flex Columns.

Fixed tables are a variation of sized or stretched tables. They can be sized or stretched, but not shrinkwrapped. They are different from sized and stretched tables in that they ignore the width of their content when laying out columns. This prevents a cell's content from having any influence over a column's width. Because fixed tables ignore content, they render much faster than the other types of tables. For shrinkwrapped, sized, and stretched tables, a browser must wait for the entire table to download so it can calculate the minimum and maximum width of the content in *each cell* before it can even begin rendering the table. Fixed tables can be rendered progressively as soon as the first row downloads. Fixed tables can size columns smaller than their content and wider than the table width. Fixed tables have unique support for Sized Columns and Undersized Columns. Fixed tables support all the layouts of sized and stretched tables except for Content-Proportioned Columns. These layouts include Size-Proportioned Columns, Percentage-Proportioned Columns, Equal-Sized Columns, and Flex Columns.

The type of layout algorithm chosen by the browser depends on the type of table and on the *type of width* assigned to its cells. In other words, it makes a big difference whether you assign a value of auto, 100px, or 20% to a cell. Not only are these different widths, but they are also different *types* of width: auto, fixed, or percentage. These different types of width combined with the type of table cause the browser to use different algorithms for sizing columns.

A value of auto assigned to width creates an **auto width**. A measurement assigned to width, such as pixels or ems, creates a **fixed width**. A percentage assigned to width, such as 50%, creates a **percentage width**.

Finally, a browser examines the width assigned to all cells in the same column in all rows to determine the column width and the type of column width. How a browser reconciles different cell widths in the *same* column is explained in the Column Width design pattern. Also, assigning different types of width to *different* columns causes the browser to use multiple layout algorithms in the same table. How a browser combines column layouts is explained in the Mixed Column Layouts design pattern.

Even though a browser examines the width of all cells in nonfixed tables to determine the column width, you only need to assign a width to the cells in the first row.

The following design patterns are created by combining the four types of tables with the three types of widths.

Using Column Layouts

For many years, designers and developers have used the many automatic and powerful layout features of columns to lay out nontabular content. In fact, this extensive use has promoted browser vendors to enhance these capabilities more than any other feature. It has also caused the major browser vendors to ensure column layouts work consistently and are bug-free.

Even though you can use column layouts to lay out *nontabular* data, I do not recommend it because it leads to less-accessible content.

The purpose of this chapter is to show you how to lay out *tabular* data. Tabular data needs to be styled and laid out. Each example in this chapter shows how you can automatically lay out columns using the many powerful and automatic algorithms built into browsers.

Chapter Outline

- **Column Width** shows how a browser calculates the column width when cells in the same column in different rows have different widths, different types of widths, different minimum content widths, and different maximum content widths. This pattern applies to shrinkwrapped, sized, and stretched tables.

- **Shrinkwrapped Columns** shows how to shrinkwrap columns to fit the width of their content. This pattern applies to shrinkwrapped tables.

- **Sized Columns** shows how to assign fixed widths to columns while keeping the table's width within a minimum or maximum value. This pattern applies to shrinkwrapped or fixed tables.

- **Content-Proportioned Columns** shows how to automatically distribute a table's width among its columns *proportionally* to the width of the content in each column. Columns with wider content are assigned to a wider width than columns with narrower content. This pattern applies to sized and stretched tables. It also applies to shrinkwrapped tables when their content stretches them to the width of their containers.

- **Size-Proportioned Columns** shows how to automatically distribute a table's width among its columns *proportionally* to the width assigned to each column. In this design pattern, a browser does not necessarily render a column at its assigned width. Instead, it renders a column proportionally to the widths assigned to other columns. This pattern applies to sized, stretched, and fixed tables. It also applies to shrinkwrapped tables when assigned cell widths stretch them to the width of their containers.

- **Percentage-Proportioned Columns** shows how to distribute a table's width among its columns *proportionally* to the percentage assigned to the width of each column. In this design pattern, a browser does not necessarily render a column at its assigned percentage of the table's width. Instead, it renders a column proportionally to the percentages assigned to other columns. This pattern applies to sized, stretched, and fixed tables.

- **Inverse-Proportioned Columns** shows how to size columns in proportion to their content. For example, a cell can be sized to be double the width of its content. This pattern applies to shrinkwrapped tables.

- **Equal Content-Sized Columns** shows how to automatically shrink a table to its smallest possible width while sizing all columns equally. In other words, it sets all columns to the same width while using the smallest possible width that will display each cell's content. It creates compact tables with uniform columns. It works best with tables containing numbers and short text. This pattern applies to shrinkwrapped tables.

- **Equal-Sized Columns** shows how to automatically divide a table's width into equal proportions for each cell. This pattern applies to sized, stretched, and fixed tables.

- **Undersized Columns** shows how to create columns that are narrower than their content. This pattern applies to fixed tables.

- **Flex Columns** shows how to create dynamically sized columns alongside fixed-width or percentage-width columns. These columns fill in the space not taken by sized or percentage cells. As a table's container grows or shrinks, so do flex columns. This pattern is most useful when applied to stretched and fixed tables, but also applies to sized tables.

- **Mixed Column Layouts** shows how to combine fixed-width, percentage-width, and auto-width columns to create additional layouts. It shows how browsers assign different priorities to fixed-width, percentage-width, and auto-width columns depending on whether a table is shrinkwrapped, sized, stretched, or fixed.

Column Width

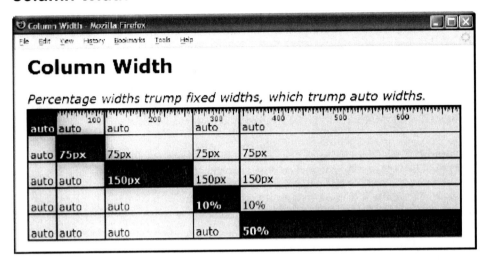

HTML

```
<h1>Column Width</h1>
<h2>Percentage widths trump fixed widths, which trump auto widths.</h2>

<table class="auto-layout sized">
 <tr> <td class="a i">auto</td><td class="a">auto</td>    <td class="a">auto</td>
      <td class="a">auto</td>  <td class="a">auto</td></tr>
 <tr> <td class="a">auto</td>  <td class="b i">75px</td> <td class="b">75px</td>
      <td class="b">75px</td>  <td class="b">75px</td></tr>
 <tr> <td class="a">auto</td>  <td class="a">auto</td>    <td class="c i">150px</td>
      <td class="c">150px</td> <td class="c">150px</td></tr>
 <tr> <td class="a">auto</td>  <td class="a">auto</td>    <td class="a">auto</td>
      <td class="d i">10%</td> <td class="d">10%</td></tr>
 <tr> <td class="a">auto</td>  <td class="a">auto</td>    <td class="a">auto</td>
      <td class="a">auto</td>  <td class="e i">50%</td></tr>
</table>
```

CSS

```
.i { background-color:black; color:white; font-weight:bold; }
.auto-layout { table-layout:auto; }
.sized { width:700px; }

.a { width:auto; }
.b { width:75px; }
.c { width:150px; }
.d { width:10%; }
.e { width:50%; }

/* Nonessential styles are not shown */
```

Column Width

Problem	You want to know how a browser chooses the width of a column when you assign different widths to cells in the same column in different rows.
Solution	This design pattern is the algorithm built into each browser that determines the width of a column. You do not have to do anything to use this pattern.

It is simplest to assign widths only to cells in the first row. However, you may want to assign different styles with different widths to arbitrary cells in a table, and let a browser figure out the width of a column.

This design pattern does not apply to *fixed* tables, because a browser determines column widths using only the widths of cells in the first row. Content in subsequent rows is truncated when it exceeds the column width. The following discussion applies only to nonfixed tables.

A browser assigns a *minimum content width* to each cell. This is the minimum width needed to display cell content. On nonfixed tables, a browser will not shrink a column smaller than this width. For text, the minimum content width is the width of the widest word in the cell. For a replaced element, such as an image, it is the width of the replaced element.

A browser assigns a *maximum content width* to each cell. This is the width of a cell's content up to the width of the table's container. Some design patterns use this width to size or proportion columns.

A browser downloads the entire table and scans all its rows to determine the following for each column: width *type*, maximum width *value*, minimum content width, and maximum content width.

A browser uses the following rules to reconcile different types and values:

1. A column defaults to auto width.
2. A fixed width changes the column's type to fixed width.
3. A percentage width changes the column's type to percentage width.
4. A larger fixed width replaces a smaller one.
5. A larger percentage width replaces a smaller one.
6. A larger *minimum* content width replaces a smaller one.
7. A larger *maximum* content width replaces a smaller one.

A browser chooses a layout design pattern based on the type of table and the type of each column (auto, fixed, or percentage width). The column is sized using the largest width value in the column that matches its type.

Location	This pattern applies to shrinkwrapped, sized, and stretched tables.
Example	The table is 700 pixels wide. The second column in the example is 75 pixels wide, showing how a fixed-width cell overrides an auto cell in the same column. The third column is 150 pixels wide, showing how a larger fixed-width value (**150px**) overrides a smaller one (**75px**). The fourth column is 70 pixels wide, showing how a percentage-width cell (**10%**) overrides a fixed-width cell (**150px**) in the same column. The fifth column is 350 pixels wide, showing how a larger percentage width (**50%**) overrides a smaller one (**10%**).
Related to	All the design patterns in this chapter

Shrinkwrapped Columns

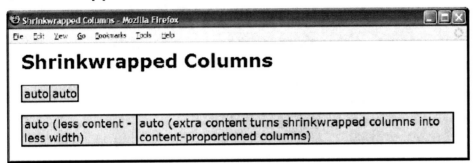

HTML

```
<h1>Shrinkwrapped Columns</h1>

<table class="auto-layout shrinkwrap">
  <tr>
    <td class="shrinkwrap">auto</td>
    <td class="shrinkwrap">auto</td>
  </tr>
</table>

<br />

<table class="auto-layout shrinkwrap">
  <tr> <td class="shrinkwrap">auto (less content - less width)</td>
      <td class="shrinkwrap">auto (extra content turns shrinkwrapped columns
        into content-proportioned columns)</td></tr></table>
```

CSS

```
table { border-collapse:collapse; }
td { overflow:hidden; }

.auto-layout { table-layout:auto; }
.shrinkwrap { width:auto; }

/* Nonessential styles are not shown */
```

Shrinkwrapped Columns

Problem	You want to shrinkwrap columns to fit the width of their content.
Solution	You can shrinkwrap columns by applying `table-layout:auto` and `width:auto` to the table and `width:auto` to its cells. Since these rules are the default, this happens by default. The width of each cell expands to its *maximum* content width, which is the width of a cell's content up to the width of the table's container. The content can expand a table up to the width of the table's container. If this happens, the cells are laid out using the Content-Proportioned Columns design pattern.
Pattern	
HTML	``` <table> <tr> <td> CONTENT </td> </tr> </table> ```
CSS	``` TABLE_SELECTOR { width:auto; table-layout:auto; } CELL_SELECTOR { width:auto; } ```
Location	This pattern applies to shrinkwrapped tables.
Advantages	Browsers use this design pattern by default because it is the most adaptable and natural. It automatically sizes columns and tables to fit their content. It adapts automatically to any device and display size. This is a very powerful feature that requires a lot of code to implement in other graphical user interfaces.
Disadvantages	A browser determines the layout of columns. Other design patterns allow you to control column width, to size columns equally, or to size them proportionally.
Tips	The only time shrinkwrapped columns can expand a table *beyond* the width of its container is when the combined *minimum content width* of each column is greater than the width of the container. For example, replaced elements, such as images, tables nested in cells, or text set to `white-space:nowrap` can easily expand a shrinkwrapped table beyond the width of its container. This causes the table to overflow its container.
Example	The first table in the example shows how cells can shrinkwrap to fit their content. The second table shows how wider content expands a table up to the width of its container and automatically uses the Content-Proportioned Columns design pattern to lay out columns.
Related to	Content-Proportioned Columns

359

Sized Columns

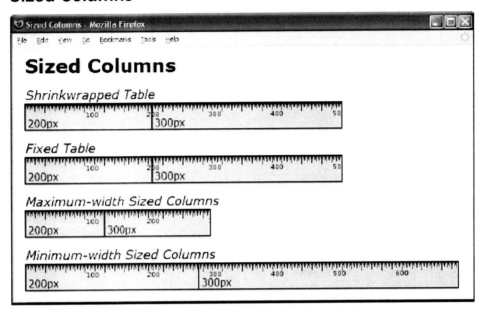

HTML

```
<h1>Sized Columns</h1>
<h2>Shrinkwrapped Table</h2>
<table class="auto-layout shrinkwrapped">
  <tr> <td class="sized1">200px</td> <td class="sized2">300px</td></tr></table>

<h2>Fixed Table</h2>
<table class="fixed-layout min-width1">
  <tr> <td class="sized1">200px</td> <td class="sized2">300px</td></tr></table>

<h2>Maximum-width Sized Columns</h2>
<div class="sized2">
 <table class="auto-layout shrinkwrapped">
  <tr> <td class="sized1">200px</td><td class="sized2">300px</td></tr></table></div>

<h2>Minimum-width Sized Columns</h2>
<table class="fixed-layout min-width2">
  <tr> <td class="sized1">200px</td> <td class="sized2">300px</td></tr></table>
```

CSS

```
.auto-layout { table-layout:auto; }
.fixed-layout { table-layout:fixed; }
.shrinkwrapped { width:auto; }
.min-width1 { width:1px; } .min-width2 { width:700px; }
.sized1 { width:200px; } .sized2 { width:300px; }

/* Nonessential styles are not shown */
```

Sized Columns

Problem	You want to assign fixed widths to columns while keeping the table's width within a minimum or maximum value.
Solution	You can size columns by applying **table-layout:auto** and **width:auto** to the table and **width:VALUE** to its cells. If the total width of the columns is greater than the width of the container, the layout changes to the Sized-Proportioned Columns design pattern. I call this the **Maximum-Width Sized Columns** design pattern because columns are rendered at the width you assigned only as long as their total width is *less than or equal to* the width of the *table's container.* In other words, the container's width sets the maximum width of the table. Finally, regardless of the assigned width, columns cannot be smaller than their minimum content width.
	You can also size columns by applying **table-layout:fixed** and **width:MIN_WIDTH** to the table and **width:VALUE** to cells in the first row. If you assign a 1-pixel width to the table, a browser will expand the table as necessary to fit the fixed width of its cells. There is no maximum width—the table overflows its container as needed to ensure its columns are sized to their assigned width. If you assign a larger width to the table than the total width of the columns, the layout changes to the Sized-Proportioned Columns design pattern. I call this the **Minimum-Width Sized Columns** design pattern because columns are rendered at the width you assigned only as long as their total width is *greater than or equal to* the width assigned to the *table.* Finally, minimum content width has no effect on column width.
Limitations	In select versions of webkit browsers (Chrome, Safari), there is a documented bug associated with table-layout:fixed where the browser will not render padding assigned to the width of a table cell.
Patterns	**Maximum-Width Sized Columns**
HTML	`<table> <tr> <td> CONTENT </td> </tr> </table>`
CSS	`TABLE_SELECTOR { width:auto; table-layout:auto; }` `CELL_SELECTOR { width:VALUE; }`
	Minimum-Width Sized Columns
HTML	`<table> <tr> <td> CONTENT </td> </tr> </table>`
CSS	`TABLE_SELECTOR { width:MIN_WIDTH; table-layout:fixed; }` `CELL_SELECTOR { width:VALUE; }`
Location	This pattern applies to shrinkwrapped or fixed tables.
Example	The columns in all four tables are sized the same. The first column is 200 pixels, and the second is 300 pixels. The difference is the type of table (fixed or shrinkwrapped) and the table's width or its container's width.
Related to	Sized-Proportioned Columns

Content-Proportioned Columns

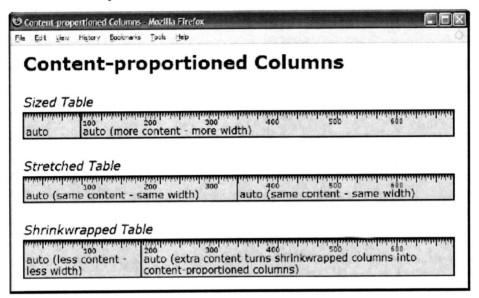

HTML

```
<h1>Content-Proportioned Columns</h1>

<h2>Sized Table</h2>
<table class="auto-layout sized">
  <tr> <td class="auto-width">auto</td>
       <td class="auto-width">auto (more content - more width)</td></tr></table>

<h2>Stretched Table</h2>
<table class="auto-layout stretched">
  <tr> <td class="auto-width">auto (same content - same width)</td>
       <td class="auto-width">auto (same content - same width)</td></tr></table>

<h2>Shrinkwrapped Table</h2>
<table class="auto-layout shrinkwrapped">
  <tr> <td class="auto-width">auto (less content - less width)</td>
       <td class="auto-width">auto (extra content turns shrinkwrapped columns
       into content-proportioned columns)</td></tr></table>
```

CSS

```
.auto-layout { table-layout:auto; }
.fixed-layout { table-layout:fixed; }
.sized { width:700px; }
.stretched { width:100%; }
.shrinkwrapped { width:auto; }
.auto-width { width:auto; }

/* Nonessential styles are not shown */
```

Content-Proportioned Columns

Problem	You want columns to fill the specified width of a table, and you want columns with wider content to have a wider width than columns with narrower content. In other words, you want to distribute a table's width automatically among its columns while keeping the table stretched or sized, and you want columns to be sized *proportionally* to the width of their *content*.
Solution	You can size columns proportionally to the width of their content by applying **table-layout:auto** and **width:VALUE_OR_PERCENT** to the table and **width:auto** to its cells. In other words, you size or stretch the table and make cells auto width. A browser automatically calculates the maximum content width of each column and totals the maximum content widths of all columns. It then sizes each column based on the percentage of its maximum content width divided by the total maximum content width of all columns. Thus, it gives columns with a larger maximum content width a proportionally larger width compared to cells with a smaller maximum content width.
	A shrinkwrapped table cannot expand beyond the width of its container. When content expands a shrinkwrapped table to the full width of its container, the table behaves as if it were stretched and turns shrinkwrapped columns into content-proportioned columns.
Pattern	
HTML	`<table> <tr> <td> CONTENT </td> </tr> </table>`
CSS	`TABLE_SELECTOR { width:VALUE_OR_PERCENT; table-layout:auto; }` `CELL_SELECTOR { width:auto; }`
Location	This pattern applies to sized and stretched tables. It also applies to shrinkwrapped tables when their content stretches them to the width of their containers. It does not apply to fixed tables.
Advantages	Sized and stretched tables are particularly useful when you have multiple tables that you want to be the same size. This gives a document a consistent look and feel. Stretched tables have an advantage over sized tables in that they automatically resize to fit smaller displays.
Disadvantages	Sized tables do not adapt to small displays, such as mobile devices.
Example	In the example, the first table is sized, and its first column is smaller than its second column because it has less content. Notice that both columns are wider than they would have been if they were shrinkwrapped. In the second table, both columns have identical content, and the browser makes them the same size. The third table is shrinkwrapped, but its content stretches the table to the width of its container. This makes its columns content-proportioned. Notice how the second column is twice as wide as the first column because its content is twice as wide.
Related to	Shrinkwrapped Columns

Size-Proportioned Columns

Size-Proportioned Columns

Sized or Stretched Table

Shrinkwrapped Table

Fixed Table

HTML

```
<h1>Size-Proportioned Columns</h1>
<h2>Sized or Stretched Table</h2>
<table class="auto-layout stretched">
  <tr> <td class="size3">100px</td>
       <td class="size4">300px</td></tr></table>

<h2>Shrinkwrapped Table</h2>
<table class="auto-layout shrinkwrapped">
  <tr> <td class="size1">1000px</td>
       <td class="size2">3000px</td></tr></table>

<h2>Fixed Table</h2>
<table class="fixed-layout sized">
  <tr> <td class="size3">100px</td>
       <td class="size4">300px</td></tr></table>
```

CSS

```
.auto-layout { table-layout:auto; }
.fixed-layout { table-layout:fixed; }
.sized { width:700px; }
.stretched { width:100%; }
.shrinkwrapped { width:auto; }
.size1 { width:1000px; } .size2 { width:3000px; }
.size3 { width:100px; } .size4 { width:300px; }

/* Nonessential styles are not shown */
```

Size-Proportioned Columns

Problem	You want columns to fill the specified width of a table, and you want columns with larger width to be proportionally wider than columns with smaller width. In other words, you want to distribute a table's width among its columns *proportionally* to each column's assigned width.
Solution	You can size columns proportionally to their width by applying **table-layout:auto** and **width:VALUE_OR_PERCENT** to the table and **width:VALUE** to its cells. In other words, you size or stretch the table and assign fixed widths to cells.
	When all column widths, padding, borders, and cell spacing add up to the width you assign to the table, a browser renders each column at the exact width you assigned. Since this is tedious to calculate and error-prone, it is easy for column widths to add up to more or less than the table's width. When this happens, a browser renders a column *proportionally* to the widths you assigned to other columns.
Pattern	
HTML	`<table> <tr> <td> CONTENT </td> </tr> </table>`
CSS	`TABLE_SELECTOR { width:VALUE_OR_PERCENT; table-layout:auto; }` `CELL_SELECTOR { width:VALUE; }`
Location	This pattern applies to sized and stretched tables.
	This pattern applies to a **shrinkwrapped table** when the total width of all its columns is *greater than* the width of its container. This stretches it to the sides of its container, causing it to behave like a stretched table.
	This pattern applies to a **fixed table** when the total width of all its columns is *less than* the width assigned to the table. In contrast, if the total width of the columns is greater than the width of a fixed table, the width of the table expands, and the columns are not size-proportioned.
Advantages	Size-proportioned columns give you the ability to specify the relative size of each column in relation to the other columns while preserving the width you assigned to the table. Size-proportioned columns are most common in stretched and sized tables where you want multiple tables to have a uniform width and you want to tweak the width of individual columns.
Tips	Since the widths you assign to columns are proportional, you can make widths huge or tiny because only the ratio between widths matters.
Example	Notice how the columns in the shrinkwrapped table had to be set to a width large enough to stretch the table to the width of its container. This allows the columns to be size-proportioned. Notice how the total width of the columns in the fixed table is much smaller than the width of the table. This allows the fixed table to be size-proportioned.
Related to	Sized Columns

Percentage-Proportioned Columns

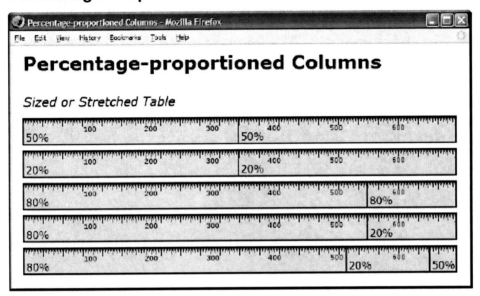

HTML

```
<h1>Percentage-Proportioned Columns</h1>
<h2>Sized or Stretched Table</h2>
<table class="auto-layout sized">
  <tr> <td class="p3">50%</td> <td class="p3">50%</td></tr></table>

<table class="auto-layout sized">
  <tr> <td class="p1">20%</td> <td class="p1">20%</td></tr></table>

<table class="auto-layout sized">
  <tr> <td class="p2">80%</td> <td class="p2">80%</td></tr></table>

<table class="auto-layout sized">
  <tr> <td class="p2">80%</td> <td class="p1">20%</td></tr></table>

<table class="auto-layout sized">
  <tr> <td class="p2">80%</td> <td class="p1">20%</td>
       <td class="p3">50%</td></tr></table>
```

CSS

```
.auto-layout { table-layout:auto; }
.fixed-layout { table-layout:fixed; }
.sized { width:700px; }
.stretched { width:100%; }
.p1 { width:20%; } .p2 { width:80%; } .p3 { width:50%; }

/* Nonessential styles are not shown */
```

Percentage-Proportioned Columns

Problem	You want to size columns as a percentage of a table's width. In other words, you want columns to fill the specified width of a table, and you want to distribute a table's width among its columns using percentages. When the total column percentage falls short of 100%, you want a browser to scale the percentages to equal 100%.
Solution	You can size columns as a percentage of a table's width by applying `width:VALUE_OR_PERCENT` to the table and `width:PERCENT` to its cells. In other words, you size or stretch the table and assign percentages to cells. The table can be fixed layout or auto layout.
	When the total percentage of all columns is less than 100%, a browser scales percents to equal 100%. In the example, the two columns in the second table are both assigned to 20%, which totals 40%. These percents are scaled to 100%, laying out the table as if each column were assigned to 50%.
	A browser works from left to right when sizing percentage-width columns. When a browser encounters a percentage that increases the total beyond 100%, it truncates the percentage assigned to that column so the total equals 100% and it treats any remaining columns as `width:auto`. In the example, the two columns of the third table are both set to 80%, which totals 160%. The percentage assigned to the second table is reduced to 20% so that the columns total 100%. In the last table of the example, the third column occurs after the percentage totals 100%. This causes a browser to shrinkwrap the third column and to scale the previous columns to fit in the remaining space.
	In fixed tables, when percentages total 100% or less, percentages work the same as they work in sized and shrinkwrapped tables. When they exceed 100%, the results vary from browser to browser.
Pattern	
HTML	`<table> <tr> <td> CONTENT </td> </tr> </table>`
CSS	`TABLE_SELECTOR { width:VALUE_OR_PERCENT; }` `CELL_SELECTOR { width:PERCENT; }`
Location	This pattern applies to sized, stretched, and fixed tables.
Advantages	Percentages are an intuitive, self-documenting way to proportion columns.
Disadvantages	Size-proportioned columns are more forgiving because they do not have to add up to 100%.
Tip	It is best *not* to allow column percentages to exceed 100% for any type of table. If you want some cells to be shrinkwrapped and others to be percentage proportioned, your intention is clearer and the result more reliable when you assign `width:auto` to shrinkwrapped cells and `width:PERCENT` to percentage-proportioned cells.
Related to	Size-Proportioned Columns

Inverse-Proportioned Columns

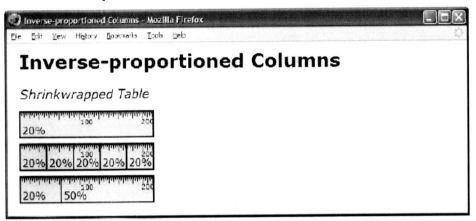

HTML

```
<h1>Inverse-proportioned Columns</h1>
<h2>Shrinkwrapped Table</h2>
<table class="auto-layout shrinkwrapped">
  <tr> <td class="p1">20%</td></tr></table>

<table class="auto-layout shrinkwrapped">
  <tr> <td class="p1">20%</td>
       <td class="p1">20%</td>
       <td class="p1">20%</td>
       <td class="p1">20%</td>
       <td class="p1">20%</td></tr></table>

 <table class="auto-layout shrinkwrapped">
  <tr> <td class="p1">20%</td>
       <td class="p2">50%</td></tr></table>
```

CSS

```
.auto-layout { table-layout:auto; }
.shrinkwrapped { width:auto; }

.p1 { width:20%; }
.p2 { width:50%; }

/* Nonessential styles are not shown */
```

Inverse-Proportioned Columns

Problem	You want to size a table in proportion to its column with the widest content, and you want its columns to be percentage-proportioned within this width. For example, you want a table to be automatically sized at twice the width of the column containing the widest content.
Solution	You can size a table in proportion to the column with the widest content by assigning **table-layout:auto** and **width:auto** to the table and **width:PERCENT** to its cells. In other words, you shrinkwrap the table and assign percentages to cells.
	A browser calculates the table width by multiplying the maximum content width by the inverse of the percentage assigned to each column. The largest resulting width becomes the width of the table. Once the table width is calculated, a browser percentage-proportions each column to fit into the table's width.
	This design pattern provided by browsers is too unintuitive to be useful as it stands. But it can be used to create equal-sized columns based on the content width, which is the basis of the next design pattern, Equal Content-Sized Columns. And this is a very useful design pattern.
Pattern	
HTML	`<table> <tr> <td> CONTENT </td> </tr> </table>`
CSS	`TABLE_SELECTOR { width:auto; table-layout:auto; }` `CELL_SELECTOR { width:PERCENT; }`
Location	This pattern applies to shrinkwrapped tables.
Limitations	This pattern works only when the total of all columns is less than or equal to 100%.
Example	In the example, the first table has one column assigned to **width:20%**. A browser multiplies the content's width, which is 40 pixels, by the inverse of 20%, which is 5. This sizes the table at 200 pixels plus cell spacing, padding, and borders around each cell. The second table shows that the table width is wide enough to hold five equal-sized columns shrinkwrapped to their content. The third table shows that columns with different percentages are percentage-proportioned within the calculated width of the table.
	Also notice in the example how *smaller percentages* and wider content make wider tables. For example, given a content width of 40 pixels, the first column of the third table with a width of 20% suggests a table width of 200 pixels (5×40). The second column with a width of 50% suggests a table width of 80 pixels (2×40). The first column wins because it suggests a larger table width. If the content width of the second column were wider, say 150 pixels, it would win and size the table at 300 pixels (2×150).
Related to	Equal Content-Sized Columns

Equal Content-Sized Columns

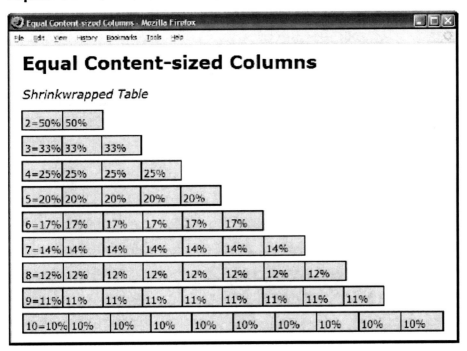

HTML

```
<h1>Equal Content-Sized Columns</h1>

<h2>Shrinkwrapped Table</h2>
<table class="auto-layout shrinkwrapped">
 <tr> <td class="p2">2=50%</td> <td class="p2">50%</td></tr></table>

<!-- Additional tables are not shown -->
```

CSS

```
.auto-layout { table-layout:auto; }
.shrinkwrapped { width:auto; }

.p2 { width:50%; }   /* 2 columns */
.p3 { width:33.5%; } /* 3 columns */
.p4 { width:25%; }   /* 4 columns */
.p5 { width:20%; }   /* 5 columns */
.p6 { width:16.5%; } /* 6 columns */
.p7 { width:14.1%; } /* 7 columns */
.p8 { width:12.3%; } /* 8 columns */
.p9 { width:11%; }   /* 9 columns */
.p10 { width:10%; }  /* 10 columns */

/* Nonessential styles are not shown */
```

Equal Content-Sized Columns

Problem	You want to create a compact table with uniformly sized columns. In other words, you want to automatically shrink a table to its smallest possible width while sizing all columns equally.
Solution	You can use a variation of the Inverse-Proportioned Columns design pattern to set all columns to the same width while ensuring the width is no larger than necessary to display the table's content.

You can do this by assigning **table-layout:auto** and **width:auto** to the table and **width:PERCENT** to its cells. In other words, you shrinkwrap the table and assign percentages to cells. The key is to apply the same percentage to all cells and to use a percentage that is the inverse of the number of columns in the table.

A two-column table requires each column to be sized at 50%.

A three-column table requires each column to be sized at 33.5%.

A four-column table requires each column to be sized at 25%.

A five-column table requires each column to be sized at 20%.

A six-column table requires each column to be sized at 16.5%.

A seven-column table requires each column to be sized at 14.1%.

An eight-column table requires each column to be sized at 12.3%.

A nine-column table requires each column to be sized at 11%.

A ten-column table requires each column to be sized at 10%.

Note that some percentages are not exact inverses of the number of columns because the inexact value works better in some browsers.

Pattern	
HTML	`<table> <tr> <td> CONTENT </td> </tr> </table>`
CSS	`TABLE_SELECTOR { width:auto; table-layout:auto; }` `CELL_SELECTOR { width:PERCENT; }`
Location	This pattern applies to shrinkwrapped tables.
Advantages	You can automatically shrinkwrap a table and its columns, and at the same time have all columns be equal width. This scales nicely on all devices, and when a small display shrinks a table's container to the width of the table or smaller, a browser automatically switches the table to the Equal-Sized Columns design pattern.
Disadvantages	This design pattern works best only when you have columns containing numbers and short text. When content is wide enough to stretch a table to the width of its container, a browser automatically switches to the Equal-Sized Columns design pattern.
Related to	Inverse-Proportioned Columns, Equal-Sized Columns

Equal-Sized Columns

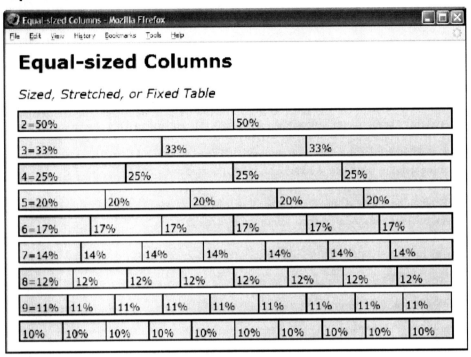

HTML

```
<h2>Sized, Stretched, or Fixed Table</h2>
<table class="auto-layout sized">
 <tr> <td class="p2">2=50%</td> <td class="p2">50%</td></tr></table>

<!-- Additional tables are not shown -->
```

CSS

```
.auto-layout { table-layout:auto; } .fixed-layout { table-layout:fixed; }
.sized { width:700px; } .stretched { width:100%; }

.p2 { width:50%; }    /* 2 columns */
.p3 { width:33.5%; } /* 3 columns */
.p4 { width:25%; }    /* 4 columns */
.p5 { width:20%; }    /* 5 columns */
.p6 { width:16.5%; } /* 6 columns */
.p7 { width:14.1%; } /* 7 columns */
.p8 { width:12.3%; } /* 8 columns */
.p9 { width:11%; }    /* 9 columns */
.p10 { width:10%; }  /* 10 columns */

/* Nonessential styles are not shown */
```

Equal-Sized Columns

Problem	You want to automatically divide a table's width into equal proportions for each cell. In other words, you want to size all columns equally as a percentage of a table's width.
Solution	You can size columns equally as a percentage of a table's width by applying `width:VALUE_OR_PERCENT` to the table and `width:PERCENT` to its cells. In other words, you size or stretch the table and assign percentages to cells. The table can be fixed layout or auto layout. The key is to apply the same percentage to all cells.

The same percentages that work for the Equal Content-Sized Columns design pattern work for this design pattern:

A two-column table requires each column to be sized at 50%.

A three-column table requires each column to be sized at 33.5%.

A four-column table requires each column to be sized at 25%.

A five-column table requires each column to be sized at 20%.

A six-column table requires each column to be sized at 16.5%.

A seven-column table requires each column to be sized at 14.1%.

An eight-column table requires each column to be sized at 12.3%.

A nine-column table requires each column to be sized at 11%.

A ten-column table requires each column to be sized at 10%.

Note that some percentages are not exact inverses of the number of columns because the inexact value works better in some browsers. It does not matter if the total percentage exceeds 100%, because a browser compensates by proportionately shrinking the width of all columns to fit into its width.

The difference between this design pattern and the Equal Content-Sized Columns design pattern is that this pattern divides columns equally into the table's width, and the Equal Content-Sized Columns pattern shrinkwraps columns to create the narrowest possible table with equal-width columns.

Pattern	
HTML	`<table> <tr> <td> CONTENT </td> </tr> </table>`
CSS	`TABLE_SELECTOR { width:VALUE_OR_PERCENT; }` `CELL_SELECTOR { width:PERCENT; }`
Location	This pattern applies to sized, stretched, and fixed tables.
Advantages	Equal-sized columns are most common in stretched and sized tables where you want multiple tables to have a uniform width and you want their columns to have a uniform width.
Disadvantages	Sized tables do not adapt to small displays, such as mobile devices.
Tips	Fixed tables automatically create equal-sized columns by default because assigning `width:auto` to cells triggers this unique behavior of fixed tables.
Related to	Equal Content-Sized Columns, Percentage-Proportioned Columns

Undersized Columns

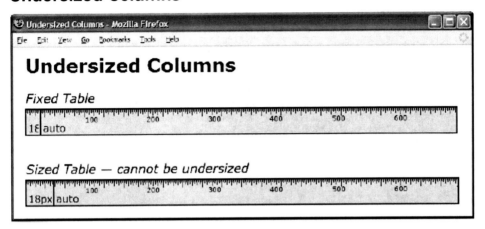

HTML

```
<h1>Undersized Columns</h1>

<h2>Fixed Table</h2>
<table class="fixed-layout sized">
 <tr> <td class="undersized">18px</td> <td class="flex">auto</td></tr></table>

<h2>Sized Table – cannot be undersized</h2>
<table class="auto-layout sized">
 <tr> <td class="undersized">18px</td> <td class="flex">auto</td></tr></table>
```

CSS

```
td { overflow:hidden; }

.fixed-layout { table-layout:fixed; }
.auto-layout { table-layout:auto; }

.sized { width:700px; }
.stretched { width:100%; }

.undersized { width:18px; }
.flex { width:auto; }

/* Nonessential styles are not shown */
```

Undersized Columns

Problem	You want to create columns that will be the exact width assigned to them. They may even be undersized, which means a column may be narrower than its content, and its content may be truncated.
Solution	You can fix the size of columns by applying **table-layout:fixed** and **width:VALUE_OR_PERCENT** to the table and **width:VALUE_OR_PERCENT** to its cells. In other words, you can size or stretch a fixed table, and assign fixed widths to cells.
	A fixed-layout table truncates content in a cell if the content cannot fit within the column's assigned width. Contrast this with auto-layout tables, where a browser always increases the width of a cell to fit its minimum content width. To ensure consistent behavior in browsers, you can assign **overflow:hidden** to all table cells. **overflow:hidden** is the only overflow setting that is consistently applied by major browsers to tables.
Pattern	
HTML	`<table> <tr> <td> CONTENT </td> </tr> </table>`
CSS	`TABLE_SELECTOR { width:VALUE_OR_PERCENT; table-layout:fixed; }` `CELL_SELECTOR { width:VALUE_OR_PERCENT; overflow:hidden; }`
Location	This pattern applies only to fixed tables.
Advantages	This design pattern works best when you need to ensure pixel-perfect precision that cannot be broken by content. For example, you need to align tabular data with a background image.
	Fixed tables render much faster than auto-layout tables because a browser reads only the widths assigned to the first row of cells, and it completely ignores the width of content. This means a browser does not have to wait for the entire table to download, and it does not have to calculate minimum and maximum content widths.
Disadvantages	Fixed tables do not adapt to small displays, such as mobile devices.
Example	The example contains two tables. The first is a fixed table showing how it can create undersized columns. The second is an auto-layout table showing how it cannot create undersized columns.
Related to	Column Width

Flex Columns

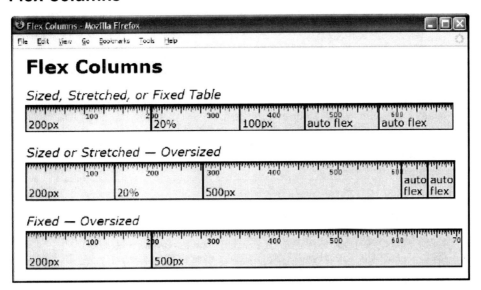

HTML

```
<h1>Flex Columns</h1>
<h2>Sized, Stretched, or Fixed Table</h2>
<table class="fixed-layout sized"><tr><td class="sized1">200px</td>
  <td class="p1">20%</td> <td class="sized2">100px</td>
  <td class="flex">auto flex</td> <td class="flex">auto flex</td></tr></table>

<h2>Sized or Stretched — Oversized</h2>
<table class="auto-layout sized"><tr><td class="sized1">200px</td>
  <td class="p1">20%</td> <td class="sized3">500px</td>
  <td class="flex">auto flex</td> <td class="flex">auto flex</td></tr></table>

<h2>Fixed — Oversized</h2>
<table class="fixed-layout sized"><tr><td class="sized1">200px</td>
  <td class="p1">20%</td> <td class="sized3">500px</td>
  <td class="flex">auto flex</td> <td class="flex">auto flex</td></tr></table>
```

CSS

```
.fixed-layout { table-layout:fixed; }
.auto-layout { table-layout:auto; }
.sized { width:700px; }
.stretched { width:100%; }
.flex { width:auto; }
.sized1 { width:200px; }
.sized2 { width:100px; }
.sized3 { width:500px; }
.p1 { width:20%; }
.fixed-layout .p1{ padding:0; }

/* Nonessential styles are not shown */
```

376

Flex Columns

Problem	You want to create dynamically sized columns alongside fixed-width or percentage-width columns. You want these columns to fill in space that is not used by sized or percentage cells. As a table's container grows or shrinks, you want flex columns to grow or shrink (i.e., to flex with the table).
Solution	You can flex the size of one or more columns by applying **width:VALUE_OR_PERCENT** to the table and **width:auto** to its cells. In other words, you can size or stretch a table, assign fixed widths and percentage width to most cells, and apply auto width to those cells you want to flex.
	When there are multiple flex columns in fixed tables, each one is sized equally. In auto-layout tables, flex columns are content-proportioned.
	Flex columns stretch to fill any space left over after fixed-width and percentage-width columns are calculated. If there is no remaining width, flex columns collapse or shrinkwrap. In auto-layout tables, flex columns shrinkwrap to their minimum content width. In fixed tables, flex columns completely disappear—with the exception of Firefox 6, which will render the padding of a flex column if allowed to.
Pattern	
HTML	`<table> <tr> <td> CONTENT </td> </tr> </table>`

CSS	`TABLE_SELECTOR { width:VALUE_OR_PERCENT; }`
	`FLEX_CELL_SELECTOR { width:auto; }`
	`FIXED_CELL_SELECTOR { width:VALUE; }`
	`PERCENTAGE_CELL_SELECTOR { width:PERCENT; }`

Location	This pattern applies to stretched and fixed tables. It does not apply to shrinkwrapped tables because their auto-width columns shrinkwrap rather than flex. It applies to sized tables, but this serves no purpose since a sized table does not flex.
Example	The first table in the example is 700 pixels wide and has two flex columns, two fixed-width columns, and one percentage-width column. The fixed-width columns take up 300 pixels, and the percentage-width column takes up 140 pixels. This leaves 260 pixels for the flex columns. Since this is a fixed table, both flex columns are sized equally to fit in the remaining 260 pixels.
	The second table shows how flex columns shrink to their minimum content width in auto-layout tables when the total width of nonflex columns (840 pixels in the example) is larger than or equal to the table's width.
	The third table shows how flex columns disappear in fixed tables when the total width of nonflex columns (700 pixels in the example) is larger than or equal to the table's width.
Related to	Mixed Column Layouts

Mixed Column Layouts

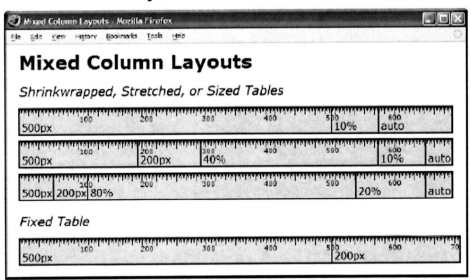

HTML

```
<h1>Mixed Column Layouts</h1>

<h2>Shrinkwrapped, Stretched, or Sized Tables</h2>
<table class="auto-layout stretched"> <tr> <td class="sized1">500px</td>
  <td class="p1">10%</td> <td class="flex">auto</td></tr></table>

<table class="auto-layout stretched"> <tr> <td class="sized1">500px</td>
  <td class="sized2">200px</td> <td class="p3">40%</td>
  <td class="p1">10%</td> <td class="flex">auto</td></tr></table>

<table class="auto-layout stretched"> <tr> <td class="sized1">500px</td>
  <td class="sized2">200px</td> <td class="p4">80%</td>
  <td class="p2">20%</td> <td class="flex">auto</td></tr></table>

<h2>Fixed Table</h2>
<table class="fixed-layout stretched"> <tr> <td class="sized1">500px</td>
  <td class="sized2">200px</td> <td class="p4">80%</td>
  <td class="p2">20%</td> <td class="flex">auto</td></tr></table>
```

CSS

```
.fixed-layout { table-layout:fixed; } .auto-layout { table-layout:auto; }
.shrinkwrapped { width:auto; }
.stretched { width:100%; }
.flex { width:auto; }
.sized1 { width:500px; } .sized2 { width:200px; }
.p1 { width:10%; } .p2 { width:20%; }
.p3 { width:40%; } .p4 { width:80%; }
.fixed-layout .p2 { padding:0; }

/* Nonessential styles are not shown */
```

Mixed Column Layouts

Problem	You want to use a mixture of columns in a table. For example, you want some columns to have a fixed width, some to be a percentage of the table's width, and some to fill in the remaining space.
Solution	This design pattern is the algorithm built into each browser that prioritizes how much width to give different types of columns when the table is not wide enough for all its columns to fit.
	In a shrinkwrapped, sized, or stretched table, *percentage-width columns have highest priority* followed by fixed-width and auto-width columns. In other words, auto-width columns are shrunk to the minimum width of their content to make room for other columns. If there is still not enough room, fixed-width columns are shrunk to the minimum width of their content. Percentage-width columns are percentage-proportioned in the remaining space. If there is space left over for fixed-width columns, they are size-proportioned to fill the remaining space.
	In a fixed table, *fixed-width columns have highest priority* followed by percentage-width and auto-width columns. In other words, auto-width columns are collapsed as needed to make room for other columns—they completely disappear. If there is still not enough room for all the columns, percentage-width columns are collapsed to make room—they completely disappear. Fixed-width cells are displayed at their assigned width—even if it increases the width of the table beyond its specified width. If there is space left over for percentage-width columns, they are percentage-proportioned to fill the remaining space.
Location	This pattern applies to shrinkwrapped, stretched, and fixed tables that are stretched. This is because a browser resizes them automatically to fit their content and to fit large or small displays. In this situation, you may want some columns to be a fixed width, some to be a percentage of the table's width, some to shrinkwrap, or some to flex to fill in the remaining width.
	There is no need to mix columns in sized tables, because you already know their width, and you can simply use fixed-width columns.
	Firefox 6 will render the padding of flex columns on fixed tables.
Example	The first table in the example is a stretched table with mixed columns that do not exceed the width of the table. Notice how the auto-width column flexes to take up the extra space. The remaining tables have columns with a combined width that exceeds the width of the table. Notice in the second table how the percentage-width columns are fully sized to their assigned percentages, the auto-width column is forced down to the minimum width of its content, and the fixed-width columns are size-proportioned to fit the remaining space. The third table shows how large percentage-width columns can force fixed-width and auto-width columns to shrink to their minimum content width. The fourth table is identical to the third table, except it is fixed. Notice how the fixed-width columns in this fixed table have completely removed the percentage-width and auto-width columns!
Related to	Flex Columns

CHAPTER 17

Layouts

This chapter shows how to create fluid layouts, which automatically adapt to different devices, fonts, widths, and zoom factors. These design patterns are accessible, modular, and easily customized. The dynamic patterns use open source JavaScript libraries to attach event handlers to elements. This allows you to create dynamic effects without putting a single line of JavaScript in your document! The libraries use *CSS selectors* to determine which elements to process in response to events, and they can modify the class attribute of elements so your stylesheet has complete control over how events dynamically style an element.

Chapter Outline

- **Fluid Layout Overview** explores problems and solutions in creating fluid layouts.
- **Outside-in Box** shows how to size the *outer width* of a box instead of the *inner width*.
- **Floating Section** shows how to render sections in columns using a fluid layout.
- **Float Divider** shows how to separate and integrate floats and content predictably.
- **Fluid Layout** shows how to create layouts that automatically adapt to any display.
- **Opposing Floats** shows how to move content to opposite sides of its container.
- **Event Styling** shows how to assign events to elements without putting code in your document. It shows how events can modify classes to change how elements are styled.
- **Rollup** shows how to collapse and open sections with a mouse click.
- **Tab Menu** shows how to create a tabbed interface that loads new pages when clicked.
- **Tabs** shows how to create a tabbed interface that dynamically switches content in and out of the display when the user clicks a tab—without loading a new page.
- **Flyout Menu** shows how to create a menu that opens when clicked or hovered over.
- **Button** shows how to create buttons and process their events using JavaScript.
- **Layout Links** shows how to use links as part of the layout, such as breadcrumbs.
- **Multi-column** shows how to distribute content over multiple columns.

- **Template** shows how to define positions using an alphabetical character and the position property.
- **Layout Example** shows how these design patterns can be combined and extended.

Fluid Layout Overview

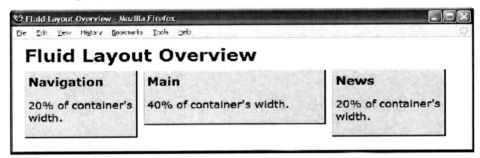

HTML

```
<body>

  <h1>Fluid Layout Overview</h1>

  <div id="nav">
    <h2>Navigation</h2>
    <p>20% of container's width.</p></div>

  <div id="main">
    <h2>Main</h2>
    <p>40% of container's width.</p></div>

  <div id="news">
    <h2>News</h2>
    <p>20% of container's width.</p></div>

</body>
```

CSS

```
body { max-width:1000px; margin-left:auto; margin-right:auto; }

div { background-color:gold; margin-right:10px; padding:5px;
  border-left:1px solid gray; border-right:2px solid black;
  border-top:1px solid gray; border-bottom:2px solid black; }

#nav  { float:left; width:20%; min-width:170px; }
#main { float:left; width:40%; min-width:170px; }
#news { float:left; width:20%; min-width:170px; }

/*  Nonessential rules are not shown. */
```

Fluid Layout Overview

Problems	You want to create fluid layouts that automatically adapt to different devices, fonts, widths, and zoom factors.
	You want to lay out content in columns and rows that dynamically expand and contract to fit the width of the viewport. You want to use columns even for nontabular data, but you can't use tables for nontabular content because this is less accessible. (Content is tabular only when the content of each cell is related to *all* cells in its row and *all* cells in its column.)
	You want *columns* automatically to reflow *into rows* when the width of the viewport is narrow, such as on a handheld device. You can't use tables because they can't render columns as rows.
	You want the width of columns to expand automatically to take advantage of a wide viewport, but only to a certain point because extremely wide columns aren't very readable.
	You want the width of columns to shrink automatically when the width of the viewport is narrow, but not so much that content becomes unreadable.
	You want to lay out columns proportionally so that some columns have a greater percentage of their parent's width and some have less.
	You want some columns to be aligned to the left side and others to the right—see the Opposing Floats design pattern.
Solutions	Each of these problems is solved by the design patterns in this chapter. The Fluid Layout design pattern shows how to lay out content in rows and columns without using tables. In turn, it relies on the Outside-in Box, Float Divider, and Floating Section design patterns.
Example	The example shows only the minimum markup and styles needed to create fluid layouts. As the chapter progresses, additional markup and styles are added to implement additional capabilities and better reliability when combined with other markup.
	The example illustrates several key capabilities of the Fluid Layout design pattern. A maximum width is assigned to the body element so that the width doesn't get too wide to be usable. (For fun, I have also centered the body in the viewport.) In addition, I floated the divisions to the left to display them as columns, but when the viewport is too narrow for all of them to be displayed side by side, a browser automatically wraps one or more of them to the next row. I assigned a minimum width to each division so that it doesn't shrink too small to be readable. Finally, I assigned a percentage to the width of each division so that it scales proportionately to the width of the viewport.
	You may want to resize the example in a browser to see how it responds to different widths.
Related to	Outside-in Box, Floating Section, Float Divider, Fluid Layout

Outside-in Box

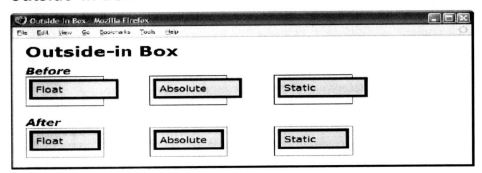

HTML

```
<h1>Outside-in Box</h1>

<h2>Before</h2>
<div class="container"><div class="before float"> Float </div></div>
<div class="container"><span class="before absolute"> Absolute </span></div>
<div class="container"><div class="before static"> Static </div></div>

<div class="float-divider"></div><h2>After</h2>

<div class="container">
   <div class="after float"><div class="oi"> Float </div></div></div>

<div class="container">
   <span class="after absolute"><span class="oi"> Absolute </span></span></div>

<div class="container">
   <div class="after static"><div class="oi"> Static </div></div></div>
```

CSS

```
.before { width:100%; margin:5px; padding:5px; border:5px solid black; }

.after { width:100%; }
.after .oi { margin:5px; padding:5px; border:5px solid black; display:block; }

.float { float:left; }
.absolute { position:absolute; }
.static { position:static; }

/*  Nonessential rules are not shown. */
```

Outside-in Box

Alias	Outer Width
Problem	You want to set the *outer width* of a float, an absolute, or a static element to a specific measurement or percentage. You don't want margins, borders, and padding to increase the outer width. This is a problem because CSS doesn't provide an outer-width property. The **width** property is the inner width of an element; and margins, borders, and padding expand the outer width.
Solution	Instead of assigning margins, borders, and padding to an element, you can assign them to an embedded element. Because the outer element doesn't have margins, borders, and padding, its outer width is its inner width. This lets you set its outer width using **width**.

I call the embedded element the *outside-in box* because it moves the margins, borders, and padding from the outside of the box to the inside. In the example, I identify outside-in boxes using a class named **oi**.

The outside-in box must be stretched to fill the width and height of its parent so its margins, borders, and padding are indented inside its container. (You could also use negative margins to outdent the outside-in box.) A block element or an inline element displayed as a block makes a great outside-in box because a browser automatically stretches it. |
| **Application** | When creating layouts, you often need to set the outer width of child elements to a percentage of the width of their parent. For example, you may want each of two floats in a container to be set to 50% of the container's width. If you apply margins, borders, or padding directly to these floats, their *outer width* expands to more than 50%. This causes the second float to move *below* the first float instead of beside it. You can solve this problem by applying margins, borders, and padding to embedded outside-in boxes.

This pattern is essential when using percentages to lay out elements in *fluid layouts* because it's impossible to anticipate in advance what *percentage* assigned to **width** will compensate for *fixed* margins, borders, and padding. |
Pattern	

HTML	`<BLOCK><div class="oi"> CONTENT </div></BLOCK>`
	or
	`<INLINE><span class="oi"> CONTENT </span></INLINE>`

CSS	`SELECTOR { width:PERCENT; min-width:+VALUE; }`
	`SELECTOR .oi { margin:+VALUE; border:WIDTH STYLE COLOR;`
	`    padding:+VALUE; background:STYLES; display:block; }`

Location	This pattern works anywhere.
Limitations	This pattern doesn't apply to tables. It also doesn't apply to *outer height* because a static block box's height shrinkwraps instead of stretches.
Related to	Fluid Layout; Display, Box Model, Block Box (Chapter 4); Width, Stretched (Chapter 5); Margin, Border, Padding, Background (Chapter 6); Blocked (Chapter 11)

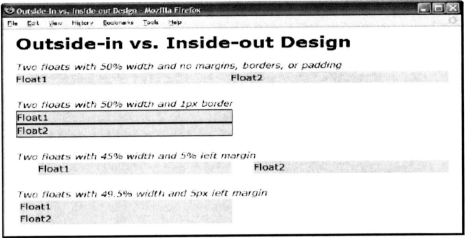

HTML

```
<h1>Outside-in vs. Inside-out Design</h1>

<h2>Two floats with 50% width and no margins, borders, or padding</h2>
<div class="ex1"> Float1 </div> <div class="ex1"> Float2 </div><hr />

<h2>Two floats with 50% width and 1px border</h2>
<div class="ex2"> Float1 </div> <div class="ex2"> Float2 </div><hr />

<h2>Two floats with 45% width and 5% left margin</h2>
<div class="ex3"> Float1 </div> <div class="ex3"> Float2 </div><hr />

<h2>Two floats with 49.5% width and 5px left margin</h2>
<div class="ex4"> Float1 </div> <div class="ex4"> Float2 </div>
```

CSS

```
body { max-width:1200px; }
div { min-width:100px; }

.ex1 { float:left; width:50%; }
.ex2 { float:left; width:50%; border:1px solid; }
.ex3 { float:left; width:45%; margin-left:5%; }
.ex4 { float:left; width:49.5%; margin-left:5px; }

/*  Nonessential rules are not shown. */
```

OUTSIDE-IN VS. INSIDE-OUT DESIGN

Fluid layouts are designed from the *outside to the inside*. This is because you start with the width of the viewport and divide its width among elements using percentages, minimum widths, and maximum widths.

The problem is that the `width` property sets the *inner width* of an element. Padding, borders, and margins surround the inner width of an element and thus increase its *outer width*. Because CSS doesn't have an outer-width property, CSS requires you to design from the *inside to the outside*. The result is that margins, borders, and padding can break fluid layout designs.

For example, you may want to float two elements to the left and assign each to `width:50%` so they're positioned side by side and evenly divide the width of the viewport. The first two divisions in the example show how this works. No matter how you resize the viewport, these elements stay positioned side by side (until their minimum width no longer allows them to fit within the width of the viewport).

If you assign *any* margins, borders, and padding to these two side-by-side floats, the floats no longer fit within the width of the viewport. For example, if you assign a 1-pixel border around each of them, their total outer width exceeds the width of the viewport by 4 pixels (1 pixel for the left and right sides of each element). When floats don't fit side by side within their container, they wrap to the next line. This isn't what you want! The second set of divisions in the example shows how a tiny 1-pixel border can break the fluid layout. No matter how you resize the viewport, the floats will *not* fit side by side.

To fit two elements with margins, borders, and padding within their container, you have to reduce the percentage width of each element, but by how much? If you assign percentages to margins and padding, you can simply subtract each of their percentages from the percentage you assign to the width. For example, if you assign a 5% left margin to each of two elements, you can assign a width of 45% to each element. This is demonstrated by the third set of divisions in the example. No matter how you resize the viewport, these elements stay positioned side by side (until their minimum width prevents them from fitting in the viewport).

Per the CSS specification, browsers ignore percentages assigned to borders, which means you must use a fixed measurement to create borders. It's also unusual to assign percentages to margins and padding because margins and padding typically look better when they don't resize with the viewport. You can resize the example to contrast the behavior of percentage margins and fixed margins.

In *fluid layouts*, assigning *fixed* margins, borders, and padding to an element isn't compatible with a *percentage* assigned to its `width`. As the viewport shrinks, percentages shrink the width of an element, but its fixed margins, borders, and padding don't shrink. For example, given a viewport width of 1000 pixels containing two side-by-side child elements where each has 5-pixel left margins, the available width is 990 pixels, or 99%—that is, (1000px – 5px – 5px) / 1000px. If you were to divide this equally among the two elements, you would assign `width:49.5%` to each. Given a viewport width of 100 pixels, the available width is 90 pixels, or 90%—that is, (100px – 5px – 5px) / 100px. To divide that equally among the two elements, you would assign `width:45%` to each. Thus, mixing fixed margins, borders, and padding with percentage widths doesn't work in fluid layouts. In the example, the fourth set of divisions is set to 49.5%, with left margins set to 5 pixels. The screenshot is taken at 750 pixels wide, which isn't wide enough for them to fit side by side; but if you enlarge the browser window to 1000 pixels or more, they fit.

Note that Internet Explorer 7 and earlier versions don't quite play by the rules. When floating two elements set to `width:50%`, Internet Explorer guesses you want them to be side by side, so it breaks the rules and puts them side by side. All other major browsers behave properly. Furthermore, Internet Explorer 6 has bugs that sometimes cause floats *not* to be placed side by side when they should be. For example, in the third set of divisions, Internet Explorer 6 moves the second float below the first. Internet Explorer 7 fixes these bugs.

The Outside-in design pattern solves all these problems (including the ones with Internet Explorer). Thus, it's an essential design pattern for creating fluid layouts. The alternative is to hack away at percentages until you find something that works in most browsers and looks close to what you want most of the time.

Floating Section

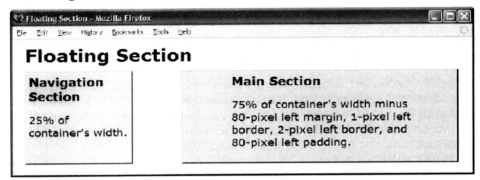

HTML

```
<h1>Floating Section</h1>
<div id="nav" class="section">
  <div class="oi">
      <h2>Navigation Section</h2>
      <p>25% of container's width.</p>
  </div>
</div>
<div id="main" class="section">
  <div class="oi">
      <h2>Main Section</h2>
      <p>75% of container's width minus 80-pixel left margin, 1-pixel left border,
          2-pixel left border, and 80-pixel left padding.</p>
  </div>
</div>
```

CSS

```
.oi { background-color:gold;
  border-left:1px solid gray; border-right:2px solid black;
  border-top:1px solid gray; border-bottom:2px solid black; }

#nav { float:left; width:25%; min-width:170px; }
#nav .oi { min-height:150px; margin:0; padding:5px; }

#main { float:left; width:75%; min-width:170px; }
#main .oi { min-height:150px; margin-left:80px; padding:5px; padding-left:80px; }

/* Nonessential rules are not shown. */
```

Floating Section

Problem	You want sections to be rendered in columns instead of rows. You want a browser to reflow sections automatically into rows to fit small displays. You also want sections to be sized proportionally to the width of their parent while controlling spacing between sections. And you want to set minimum and maximum heights and widths to ensure that a browser doesn't automatically size sections too small or too large.
Solution	You can use the Section design pattern to create a section, and you can float it to the left to render it as a column instead of a row. You can assign a unique ID to it so you can select it, style it, and target it with hyperlinks.
	You can embed an outside-in box within each float and style its margins, borders, padding, and background instead of the float's. This makes it easy and reliable to size floats proportional to their container.
	You can assign **min-width** to a section to prevent it from shrinking too small. You can assign **max-width** to a section to prevent it from growing too wide. You can also assign **min-height** to the outside-in box to ensure that floats with less content have the same minimum height as those with more content.
Pattern	
HTML	<pre><code><div id="SECTION_ID" class="section">
<div class="oi">
<h2> HEADING </h2>
<p> CONTENT </p>   </div></div></code></pre>
CSS	<pre><code>#SECTION_ID { float:left; width:PERCENT;
min-width:VALUE; max-width:VALUE; }
#SECTION_ID .oi { min-height:+VALUE;
margin:+VALUE; border:WIDTH STYLE COLOR;
padding:+VALUE; background:STYLES; }</code></pre>
Location	This pattern works anywhere sections can be used.
Limitations	Internet Explorer 6 doesn't implement **min-width** and **max-width**, but Internet Explorer 7 and higher versions do. These properties aren't essential to this design.
Example	In the example, the first float's width is 25% of its container's width, and the second float's is 75%. Notice how the percentages add up to 100%. Without the outside-in box, you would have to play around with percentages to find values that compensate for margins, borders, and padding around floats.
	Notice how the floats in the example have no margin, border, padding, or background. What you see is the border and background of the outside-in box inside each float. For example, the outside-in box in the second float has an 80-pixel left margin, which creates the illusion of space between the floats when it's actually *inside* the second float. It also has an 80-pixel left padding, which indents the content without changing the float's outer width.
Related to	Outside-in Box, Fluid Layout; Floated Box (Chapter 4); Width (Chapter 5); Margin, Border, Padding, Background (Chapter 6); Float and Clear (Chapter 7); Section (Chapter 13)

Float Divider

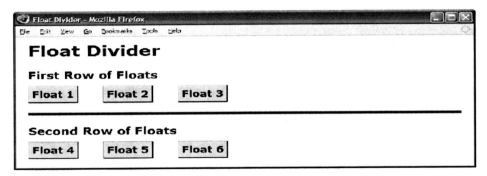

HTML

```
<h1>Float Divider</h1>
<h2>First Row of Floats</h2>

<div class="float box"><h3>Float 1</h3></div>
<div class="float box"><h3>Float 2</h3></div>
<div class="float box"><h3>Float 3</h3></div>

<div class="float-divider"></div>

<h2>Second Row of Floats</h2>
<div class="float box"><h3>Float 4</h3></div>
<div class="float box"><h3>Float 5</h3></div>
<div class="float box"><h3>Float 6</h3></div>
```

CSS

```
.float { float:left; }

.float-divider { clear:both;
  height:20px;
  margin-bottom:20px;
  border-bottom:5px solid black;
  font-size:1px; line-height:1px; }

/* Nonessential rules are not shown. */
```

Float Divider

Problem	You want to put a divider between two sets of floats or between floats and content—much like how you would put a line break or a horizontal rule in the normal flow. You want to control how much space the divider inserts, and you want to style it with borders and background.
Solution	You can add **clear:both** to the Horizontal Rule design pattern, which is an empty division styled with **width**, **height**, and **margin** to control how much space it inserts. You can use **font-size:1px** and **line-height:1px** to ensure that Internet Explorer 6 doesn't expand its height beyond the height you specify. You can also use **border** and/or **background** to style the divider's line.
	Instead of inserting a float divider, you may want to add a unique ID to an existing element and style it with **clear:both**.
Pattern	
HTML	`<div class="float-divider"></div>`

CSS	`.float-divider { clear:both; font-size:1px; line-height:1px;`
	`    height:+VALUE; width:+VALUE;`
	`    margin-left:±VALUE; margin-right:±VALUE;`
	`    margin-top:+VALUE; margin-bottom:+VALUE;`
	`    border-top:WIDTH STYLE COLOR;`
	`    border-bottom:WIDTH STYLE COLOR;`
	`    background-color:COLOR;`
	`    background-image:url("FILE.EXT");`
	`    background-repeat:REPEAT_OPTIONS; }`

Location	This pattern works anywhere a division can be located.
Advantages	A float divider is modular and self-documenting. Its borders, background, and margins are self-contained, which simplifies the stylesheet and avoids styles being overridden by the cascade order. You can quickly and easily reposition a float divider between any two elements to change the layout.
	When a block is collapsed because all its children are floated, you can use a float divider to expand the block to encompass its floated children. This is an essential technique explored in the Fluid Layout design pattern.
Tip	A float divider can be an *inline* element as long as you display it as a block (**display:block**).
Related to	Fluid Layout; Floated Box (Chapter 4); Margin, Border, Padding, Background (Chapter 6); Float and Clear (Chapter 7); Spacing, Inline Spacer, Linebreak, Inline Horizontal Rule (Chapter 11); Horizontal Rule, Block Spacer (Chapter 13)

Fluid Layout

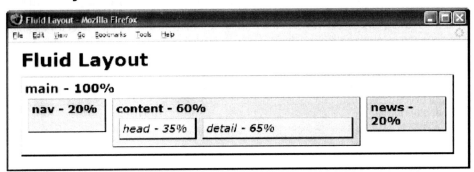

HTML

```
<h1>Fluid Layout</h1>

<div id="main"><div class="oi1"> <h2>main - 100%</h2>
  <div id="nav"><div class="oi2"> <h3>nav - 20%</h3> </div></div>

  <div id="content"><div class="oi2"> <h3>content - 60%</h3>
   <span id="head"><span class="oi3"> <em>head - 35%</em> </span></span>
   <span id="detail"><span class="oi3"> <em>detail - 65%</em> </span></span>
   <span class="float-divider"></span></div></div>

   <div id="news"><div class="oi2"> <h3>news - 20%</h3> </div></div>

   <div class="float-divider"></div></div></div>
```

CSS

```
.float-divider { clear:both; display:block;
  height:1px; font-size:1px; line-height:1px; }
.oi1 { background-color:white; margin:0; padding:5px; }
.oi2 { background-color:gold; margin:5px; padding:5px; }
.oi3 { background-color:yellow; margin:5px; padding:5px; }

#main { max-width:700px; }
#nav { float:left; width:20%; min-width:75px; }
#content { float:left; width:60%; min-width:150px; }
#news { float:left; width:20%; min-width:115px; }
#nav .oi2 { min-height:43px; }
#content .oi3 { display:block; }
#head { float:left; width:35%; min-width:75px; }
#detail { float:left; width:65%; min-width:75px; }

/* Nonessential rules are not shown. */
```

Fluid Layout

Problem	You want to lay out sections in rows and columns that dynamically and fluidly adapt to the width of the viewport, available fonts, and zoom level. You want the layout to grow and shrink with the width of the viewport, but you also want to limit how much it can grow and shrink. You want columns to revert automatically to rows when the viewport isn't wide enough for side-by-side display. You want to nest layouts within layouts, and you want to predictably intermingle them with content in the normal flow.
Solution	You can nest sections within sections to create multilevel layouts in rows and columns. A parent section can be floated or nonfloated! The initial section is the **\<body\>** element, which by default stretches to the width of the viewport. You can set the widths of all other sections to **width:PERCENT** or **width:auto** to scale the entire layout to the width of the viewport.
	You can lay out sections in columns by floating them left. Their parent becomes a row, and you can divide the row's width among its columns by assigning a percentage to each column's width. Column widths in a row normally total 100%. When a row grows or shrinks, so do its columns.
	You can embed an outside-in box within each section so you can size it without interference from margins, borders, and padding. To reliably select outside-in boxes at different levels of nested floats, you can assign a class to them that is unique to each level. In the example, I use three classes, **oi1**, **oi2**, and **oi3**, to identify outside-in boxes at specific nesting levels. This lets me select level 2 boxes without also selecting descendant level 3 boxes.
	You can ensure that a section always expands vertically to encompass all its content by inserting a float divider after the last float in the section. A float divider also starts the following section in a new row.

Pattern

HTML

```
<div id="SECTION_ID">
  <div class="oiLEVEL">
    NESTED_SECTIONS_AND_OR_SECTION_CONTENT
<div class="float-divider"></div></div></div>
```

CSS

```
#SECTION_ID { float:left; width:PERCENT;
  max-width:VALUE; min-width:VALUE; }
#SECTION_ID .oiLEVEL { min-height:+VALUE; margin:+VALUE;
  border:WIDTH STYLE COLOR;
  padding:+VALUE; background:STYLES;
  display:block; }
.float-divider { clear:both; display:block;
  height:1px; font-size:1px; line-height:1px; }
```

Location	This pattern works anywhere.
Related to	Outside-in Box, Floating Section, Float Divider; Floated Box (Chapter 4); Margin, Border, Padding, Background (Chapter 6); Float and Clear (Chapter 7); Offset Float (Chapter 8); Blocked (Chapter 11)

Opposing Floats

HTML

```
<div id="header">
  <h1  id="title">Opposing Floats</h1>
  <div id="search"> <h3>Search:</h3>
    <form method="post" action="http://www.tipjar.com/cgi-bin/test">
      <input type="text" value="" name="searchtext" id="searchtext" size="32" />
      <input type="submit" value="Search" name="find" id="find" /></form>
    <p class="message">This right float shrinks no smaller than its minimum width
      and grows no larger than its maximum width.</p>
  </div>
  <div class="float-divider"></div>
</div>

<div id="postheader">
  <p class="breadcrumbs"><a href="#">Home</a> » Floating Layout</p>
  <p class="post-msg">Postheader message 1</p>
  <div class="float-divider"></div>

  <p class="breadcrumbs"><a href="#">Home</a> » Floating Layout</p>
  <p class="post-msg">Postheader message 2</p>
  <div class="float-divider"></div>
</div>
```

CSS

```
.float-divider { clear:both; display:block;
  height:1px; font-size:1px; line-height:1px; }

.breadcrumbs { float:left;  max-width:350px; margin-left:10px; }
.post-msg { float:right; max-width:350px; margin-right:10px; }

#title  { float:left;  min-width:280px; max-width:350px; margin-left:0; }
#search { float:right; min-width:280px; max-width:350px; margin-right:0; }

/* Nonessential rules are not shown. */
```

Opposing Floats

Problem	You want two elements to be positioned at opposite sides of a container. You want a browser to shrinkwrap each one to fit its content. You want to put minimum and maximum limits on the width of each one.
Solution	You can assign **float:left** to one sibling element and **float:right** to the next. This moves both elements to opposite sides of their parent. It doesn't matter which element comes first in document order. This pattern applies only to pairs of adjacent sibling elements.
	The parent of the opposing floats can be floated or nonfloated. You can follow the floats with a float divider to ensure that no subsequent content comes in between the floats and to ensure that the parent expands vertically to encompass the opposing floats. If you want to float multiple pairs of opposing floats within the same parent, you can insert a float divider between each pair to prevent them from stacking next to each other.
	You can assign **min-width** and **max-width** to each float to set its minimum width and maximum width. You can assign **margin-left** to the left float and **margin-right** to the right float to adjust their positions.

Pattern

HTML

```
<div id="SECTION_ID">
    <ELEMENT id="ID1"> ANY_CONTENT </ELEMENT>
    <ELEMENT id="ID2"> ANY_CONTENT </ELEMENT>
    <div class="float-divider"></div>
</div>
```

CSS

```
#ID1 { float:left; min-width:VALUE; max-width:VALUE;
    margin-left:±VALUE; }
#ID2 { float:right; min-width:VALUE; max-width:VALUE;
    margin-right:±VALUE; }
.float-divider { clear:both; display:block;
    height:1px; font-size:1px; line-height:1px; }
```

Location	This pattern works anywhere because you can float inline or block elements.
Limitations	Internet Explorer 6 doesn't implement **min-width** and **max-width**, but Internet Explorer 7 and higher versions do. These properties aren't essential to this design.
Tips	When floating text to the right, it's often better to omit **min-width**. This allows a browser to shrinkwrap the float to the minimum width of the text, which keeps the text aligned to the right side of the parent. If you want multiple lines of text to be aligned to the right, you can assign **text-align:right** to the float.
Related to	Fluid Layout, Float Divider; Floated Box (Chapter 4); Margin (Chapter 6); Float and Clear (Chapter 7); Offset Float (Chapter 8); Blocked (Chapter 11)

Event Styling

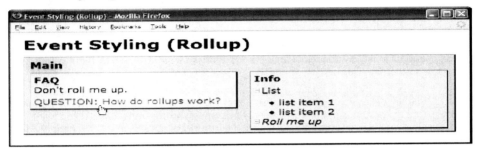

HTML

```
<head>
  <!-- only script elements are shown -->

  <script type="text/javascript"
    src="https://ajax.googleapis.com/ajax/libs/jquery/1.6.3/jquery.min.js"></script>
</head>
```

page.js

```
$(document).ready(function(e){
    $('.rollup-trigger').click(function(e){
        $(this).closest('.rollup').children().not('.rollup-trigger').toggleClass('hidden');
        $(this).parent().removeClass('hidden');
    });
});
```

Event Styling

Problem	You want to attach events to HTML elements without putting JavaScript in the body of the document. You want to attach events to elements using CSS selectors so there is a direct connection between how elements are styled and how they respond to events. You want events to modify element classes so you can use stylesheets to control how dynamic HTML styles a document. In other words, you want to completely separate content, style, and JavaScript. You don't want to put JavaScript or styles in the content, and you don't want to put styles or content in the JavaScript code.
Solution	You can use JavaScript libraries to attach events to elements *at runtime*. All you need are a few **<script>** tags in the document head to load the JavaScript libraries. This technique completely removes the need to put code in event attributes, such as **<div onclick="someFunction();">**. **To attach events to elements at runtime,** you can use one of many different JavaScript libraries. jQuery is used for this example; you can find documentation at **http://docs.jquery.com/**. You can use this library by attaching its JavaScript files to your document. A browser downloads and executes each JavaScript file in the order it occurs in the document. The last JavaScript file is typically unique to the current page. It initializes the libraries, and it assigns event handlers to elements. In the example, I name this file **page.js**. The code doesn't slow down the rendering of the document, and it ensures that events are added to elements after they exist.

Event Styling cont.

Solution cont.	The first **$('document').ready()** function in **page.js** executes a generic function when the document's DOM is ready and assigns events to elements.
Overall pattern	JavaScript in page.js **$('document').ready()** The purpose of the **$()** function is to select DOM elements using CSS selectors. This allows you to use the same CSS selectors to style elements and to attach events to elements! This conceptually ties the stylesheet into the dynamic HTML.

Detailed pattern	JavaScript in page.js
	
	``
	$('CSS_SELECTOR').click(function(e){
	$(this).closest('PARENT_CSS_SELECTOR').children().not('CSS_SELECTOR').toggleClass(
	'TOGGLE_CSS_SELCTOR');
	    $(this).parent().removeClass('TOGGLE_CSS_SELECTOR');
	});
	``
	
	Using click(), you can assign an event listener that waits for a click event. By chaining together generic event handlers, you can create powerful event handlers while writing very little code.
	
	The name of the event is the function name **click()**. The name doesn't include the "on" prefix. In the example, I used **click** instead of **onclick**.
	
	A CSS selector is used in the function **$()**. It's a string that determines which elements get assigned to the event. You can use *any* CSS selector, including child and attribute selectors.
	
	$(this) refers to the element that has been clicked.
	
	closest() selects the next first parent DOM element of the element that has been clicked that has the parent CSS selector.
	
	children() selects all the children of the node that is returned by **closest()**.
	
	not() filters out any results that match the CSS selector.
	
	toggleClass() adds a CSS selector to or removes it from elements.
	
	$(this).parent().removeClass('TOGGLE_CSS_SELECTOR'); removes the hidden CSS class from the parent of the clicked element. This is done so that the clicked element can't be hidden.

Explanation	By using event handlers to modify the classes assigned to elements, you can control how your document responds to events by using a stylesheet. This keeps content, code, and styles separate, which improves productivity and reduces maintenance. By simply toggling classes, swapping them in and out, and adding, removing, or replacing them, you can create just about any effect.
Tips	This design pattern is extensible. You can create your own event handler and helper functions. To make it easy to extend, jQuery contains additional utility functions to manipulate strings and elements, and to aid in debugging. The most commonly used events are **onclick**, **onmouseover**, and **onmouseout**. Forms often use **onsubmit** and **onreset**. Any event handler can affect accessibility, but the following events require much more effort and testing to keep a document accessible. Form elements can use **onchange**, **onfocus**, **onblur**, and **onselect**. Advanced techniques can use **onkeydown**, **onkeypress**, **onkeyup**, **onmousedown**, **onmousemove**, and **onmouseup**. With the availability of touch devices such as smart phones and tablets, you should also listen for **touchstart**, **touchmove**, and **touchend** events.
Example	In the example, when the user clicks a **rollup-trigger** element, the **hidden** class is applied to all children of the rollup element except for the child containing the rollup trigger. When the user clicks the rollup trigger again, the hidden class is removed. You can create a rollup effect by styling the **hidden** class to hide elements, or you could create some other effect.
Related to	Rollup, Tabs, Flyout Menu; Popup Alert (Chapter 20)

Rollup

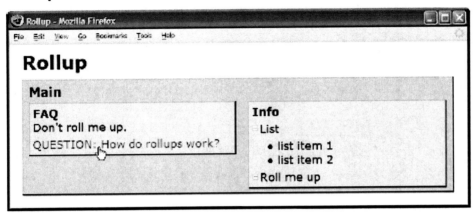

HTML

```
<h1>Rollup</h1>

<div id="main" class="rollup">
  <h2 class="rollup-trigger">Main</h2>

  <div id="faq"><div class="oi rollup">
    <h3 class="rollup-trigger">FAQ</h3> Don't roll me up.
    <dl class="rollup">
      <dt class="rollup-trigger">QUESTION: How do rollups work?</dt>
      <dd class="hidden">ANSWER: When the user clicks on a heading or button,
                         the content rolls up or down. </dd></dl></div></div>

  <div id="info"><div class="oi rollup">
    <h3 class="rollup-trigger">Info</h3>
    <div class="rollup">
      <p><span class="rollup-trigger"> </span>List</p>
      <ul> <li>list item 1</li> <li>list item 2</li></ul></div>
    <em><span class="rollup-trigger"> </span>Roll me up</em></div></div>
    <div class="float-divider"></div></div>
```

CSS

```
.rollup-trigger { cursor:pointer; }
.rollup-trigger:hover { color:firebrick; }

span.rollup-trigger { font-size:0.65em; padding-left:8px;
  background:url("hide.gif") no-repeat left top; }

span.rolledup { background:url("show.gif") no-repeat left top; }

.hidden { position:absolute; top:-99999px; left:-99999px;
  width:1px; height:1px; overflow:hidden; }

/* Nonessential rules are not shown. */
```

Rollup

Problem	You want the user to dynamically interact with sections, FAQs, lists, and so forth by rolling them up to hide information and rolling them down to show information. You want to do this without adding code to the HTML document. You want to use styles to control the dynamic behavior.
Solution	You can add the **rollup** class to any parent element. This identifies it as a container that can roll up its content. You can add the **rollup-trigger** class to *any* child in the rollup container. When the user clicks the **rollup-trigger** element, all content in the rollup element rolls up except for the **rollup-trigger** element. When the user clicks the **rollup-trigger** element again, the content rolls down.
	The **rollup** class is typically assigned to a section's container, and the **rollup-trigger** class is typically assigned to a section's heading. In the example, I assigned the **rollup** class to each section and the **rollup-trigger** class to each section heading. You can click a heading to roll up or roll down each section.
	The **rollup-trigger** class can be assigned to *any* descendant of the rollup container. In the example, I assign it to the dictionary term, **<dt>**. Its parent, **<dl>**, is its rollup container. You can click the dictionary term to roll up and roll down the dictionary definition, **<dd>**.
	When you want a child of a rollup container to start out rolled up, you can set it to the **hidden** class. In the example, the dictionary definition element is set to **hidden** so it starts out rolled up when the page loads.
	This design pattern rolls up elements by setting them to **hidden**. It rolls them down by removing **hidden** from their class. The **hidden** class is styled using the Screenreader-only design pattern (Chapter 10), which hides elements on the screen without hiding them from screen readers.

Pattern	
HTML	

```
<ELEMENT class="rollup">
  <ELEMENT class="rollup-trigger">CONTENT</ELEMENT>
  <ELEMENT class="hidden"></ELEMENT>
</ELEMENT>
```

CSS	

```
.rollup-trigger { cursor:pointer; }
.rollup-trigger:hover { STYLES }
span.rollup-trigger { font-size:VALUE; padding-left:VALUE;
  background:url("FILE.EXT") no-repeat; }
span.rolledup { background:url("FILE.EXT") no-repeat; }
.hidden { position:absolute;
  top:-99999px; left:-99999px;
  width:1px; height:1px; overflow:hidden; }
```

Location	This pattern works anywhere.

HTML Header

```
<head>
  <!-- only script elements are shown -->

  <script language="javascript" type="text/javascript"
    src=" https://ajax.googleapis.com/ajax/libs/jquery/1.6.3/jquery.min.js"></script>
</head>
```

page.js

```
$(document).ready(function(e){
    $('.rollup-trigger').click(function(e){
        $(this).closest('.rollup').children().not('.rollup-trigger').toggleClass('hidden');
        $(this).parent().removeClass('hidden');
    });
});
```

Rollup cont.

Limitations	Text placed directly inside the rollup container isn't rolled up. In the example, the text "Don't roll me up." doesn't get rolled up with the rest of the FAQ. If you want text to be rolled up, place it inside any element. It doesn't matter whether the element is block or inline. Also, this design pattern fails to roll up text when JavaScript isn't available.
Tips	You can insert an element specifically to be the rollup trigger, and you can place it anywhere inside the rollup parent. In the example, I insert two spans and assign them to the **rollup-trigger** class. Because these are inline elements, I use **font-size** and **padding** to size their height and width large enough to allow a background image to show through. This turns the span into a rollup button. Using this technique, you can put a rollup button in front of any element. (You can also float it to the right if you want.) When the user clicks a rollup button, everything in the rollup container rolls up except for the button and its ancestors.
	When the user clicks a rollup trigger, the JavaScript code dynamically adds or removes the **rolledup** class to the element. In the example, I use the **span.rolledup** selector to change the background image when the parent is rolled up. This creates a dynamic button effect.
Pattern	JavaScript ```$('.rollup-trigger').click(function(e){` ` $(this).closest('.rollup')children().not('.rollup-` `trigger').toggleClass('hidden');` ` $(this).parent().removeClass('hidden');` `});```
Related to	Event Styling; Margin, Padding, Background (Chapter 6); Positioned, Absolute (Chapter 7); Offset Absolute and Offset Fixed (Chapter 8); Font, Screenreader only (Chapter 10)

Tab Menu

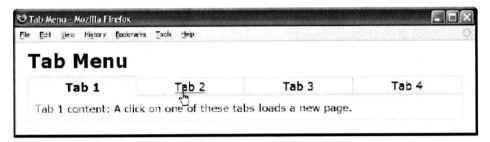

HTML

```
<h1>Tab Menu</h1>

<div id="main">
  <ul class="tabs">
    <li class="selected">
      <h3 class="tab-label"><a href="example.html">Tab 1</a></h3></li>
    <li><h3 class="tab-label"><a href="example2.html">Tab 2</a></h3></li>
    <li><h3 class="tab-label"><a href="example3.html">Tab 3</a></h3></li>
    <li><h3 class="tab-label"><a href="example4.html">Tab 4</a></h3></li>
  </ul>
  <p>Tab 1 content: A click on one of these tabs loads a new page.</p>
</div>
```

CSS

```
ul.tabs a:link, ul.tabs a:visited, ul.tabs a:active
    { text-decoration:none; color:maroon; }
    ul.tabs a:hover { text-decoration:underline; color:black; }
    ul.tabs a { display:block; }


    ul.tabs { float:left; width:100%; padding:0; margin:0;
      border-bottom:1px solid gold; margin-bottom:10px; }

    ul.tabs li { float:left; width:25%; list-style-type:none; }

    ul.tabs .tab-label { border:1px solid gold; margin:0; cursor:pointer;
      padding-bottom:2px; padding-top:2px;
      background:white url("g1.jpg") repeat-x left bottom;
      font-weight:normal; text-align:center; font-size:1.1em; }

    ul.tabs li.selected .tab-label { position:relative; border-bottom:none;
      top:1px; padding-bottom:4px;
      padding-top:5px; border-top:2px solid gold; margin-top:-5px;
      background:white url("g2.jpg") repeat-x left top; font-weight:bold; }

#main { border:1px solid gold; border-top:none; }
```

Tab Menu

Problem You want to create a menu of links that works like a tabbed user interface. You want it to adapt reliably and fluidly to different environments.

Solution You can place the list of links in an unordered list (`<ul>`) and assign the list to the **tabs** class. You can place a hyperlink inside each list item (`<li>`). Because each link functions as a tab heading, you can embed the link within a heading element. This gives the link a higher importance to search engines and makes it easier for nonsighted users to navigate with screen readers. The heading is also an outside-in box. This allows you to style the box of each tab without affecting the outer width of the tab.

When the user clicks a link, you want a browser to replace the current page with the page referenced by the link. If the new page also contains the same tabbed menu with the new tab selected, you can create the illusion of switching tabs. To change the look of selected tabs, you can assign the **selected** class to the list item containing the link of the currently displayed page. In the example, the first tab is selected. Moving the selected class to another list item makes it appear selected.

Pattern

HTML
```
<ul class="tabs">
    <li class="selected">
        <h3 class="tab-label">
            <a href="URL">Tab 1</a></h3></li></ul>
```

CSS
```
ul.tabs a:link, ul.tabs a:visited, ul.tabs a:active { STYLES }
ul.tabs a:hover, ul.tabs a:focus { STYLES }
ul.tabs a { display:block; }

ul.tabs { float:left; width:100%; padding:0; margin:0;
    margin-bottom:+VALUE; border-bottom:TAB_BOTTOM STYLE COLOR; }

ul.tabs li { float:left; width:PERCENT; list-style-type:none; }

ul.tabs .tab-label { border:BORDER_WIDTH STYLE COLOR;
    padding-bottom:PADDING_BOTTOM;
    padding-top:PADDING_TOP;
    margin:0; cursor:pointer;
    background:COLOR IMAGE REPEAT_OPTIONS POSITION;
    font-weight:normal; text-align:center; }

ul.tabs li.selected .tab-label
{ position:relative;  border-bottom:none; font-weight:bold;
    top:TAB_BOTTOM; cursor:auto;
    padding-bottom:TAB_BOTTOM+PADDING_BOTTOM+BORDER_WIDTH;
    border-top:BORDER_WIDTH+EXTRA_BORDER STYLE COLOR;
    padding-top:PADDING_TOP+EXTRA_PADDING;
    margin-top:-(TAB_BOTTOM+EXTRA_BORDER+EXTRA_PADDING);
    background:COLOR IMAGE REPEAT_OPTIONS POSITION; }

#SECTION { border:WIDTH STYLE COLOR; border-top:none; }
```

HTML (Same Code Shown Again for Convenience)

```
<h1>Tab Menu</h1>

<div id="main">
  <ul class="tabs">
    <li class="selected">
      <h3 class="tab-label">Tab 1</h3></li>
    <li><h3 class="tab-label"><a href="example2.html">Tab 2</a></h3></li>
    <li><h3 class="tab-label"><a href="example3.html">Tab 3</a></h3></li>
    <li><h3 class="tab-label"><a href="example4.html">Tab 4</a></h3></li>
  </ul>
  <p>Tab 1 content: A click on one of these tabs loads a new page.</p>
</div>
```

CSS (Same Code Shown Again for Convenience)

```
ul.tabs a:link, ul.tabs a:visited, ul.tabs a:active
    { text-decoration:none; color:maroon; }
    ul.tabs a:hover, ul.tabs a:focus
    { text-decoration:underline; color:black; }
    ul.tabs a { display:block; }

    ul.tabs { float:left; width:100%; padding:0; margin:0;
      border-bottom:1px solid gold; margin-bottom:10px; }

    ul.tabs li { float:left; width:25%; list-style-type:none; }

    ul.tabs .tab-label { border: 1px solid gold; margin:0; cursor:pointer;
      padding-bottom:2px; padding-top:2px;
      background:white url("g1.jpg") repeat-x left bottom;
      font-weight:normal; text-align:center; font-size:1.1em; }

    ul.tabs li.selected .tab-label { position:relative; border-bottom:none;
      top:1px; padding-bottom:4px; cursor:auto;
      padding-top:5px; border-top:2px solid gold; margin-top:-5px;
      background:white url("g2.jpg") repeat-x left top; font-weight:bold; }

#main { border:1px solid gold; border-top:none; }
```

Tab Menu cont.

Location	This pattern works anywhere a list can be used.
Styles	You can style tab links to interact dynamically with the user. The selectors are **ul.tabs a:link**, **ul.tabs a:visited**, **ul.tabs a:active**, **ul.tabs a:hover**, and **ul.tabs a:focus**. In the example, I hide a tab link's underline until the user mouses over it. This keeps the user interface uncluttered. You can render links as blocks so they will stretch to the width of their tab. This allows the user to click anywhere inside a tab to activate the link.
	You can float the tab menu container so it encompasses its floated tabs. The selector is **ul.tabs**. You can make the layout more flexible by setting its width to 100% so it stretches to the width of its container. When using an unordered list, you need to remove its default margins and padding so they don't interfere with the position of the tabs. You can use **margin-bottom** to put distance between the tab menu and subsequent content. You can also set the bottom border. In the example, I use a 1-pixel, solid, gold bottom border.
	To make list items look like tabs, you can float them to the left. The selector is **ul.tabs li**. You can assign a percentage to their width that is the inverse of the number of tabs, such as 16.66% for six tabs, 14.28% for seven, 12.5% for eight, 11.11% for nine, 10% for ten, and so forth. For percentages to work, the list item must have no left or right margins, borders, or padding. You can assign list items to **list-style-type:none** to hide their bullets.
	To style the tab's box, you can select the element that has the **tab-label** class. You can put a border around it, pad its content, and add a background image. In the example, I use a gradient image that transitions from white to gold going from top to bottom. Moving from a lighter color at the top to a darker color at the bottom supports the illusion that the tab isn't selected. The reverse makes the tab look selected. You should set its margins to zero; otherwise, they will break the tab effect. You can set the cursor to the hand pointer to signal that the tab can be clicked. You can set **font-weight** to normal when not selected and bold when selected. You can align text in the tab label to the center.
	To make a tab look selected, you can assign the **selected** class to it and style that class. The selector is **ul.tabs li.selected .tab-label**. You can use **border-bottom:none** to remove its bottom border, and you can increase its bottom padding to compensate. The selected tab also needs to cover the bottom border of the tab container **ul.tabs**. To do so, you can increase its bottom padding to cover the tab container's bottom border, and you can position it relatively to move it over the border. You can add extra thickness to the selected tab's top border to make it stand out. You can add extra top padding to raise it above nonselected tabs. You can use a negative value in **margin-top** to compensate for the extra padding and border.
	You can put a border around the left, right, and bottom of the section containing the tab menu to connect the tab menu with the section's content.
Related to	Floated Box (Chapter 4); Width, Sized, Stretched (Chapter 5); Margin, Border, Padding, Background, Overflow (Chapter 6); Positioned, Relative, Float and Clear, Relative Float (Chapter 7); Offset Float, Aligned Static Inline (Chapter 8); Font (Chapter 10); Blocked (Chapter 11); Lists (Chapter 13)

Tabs

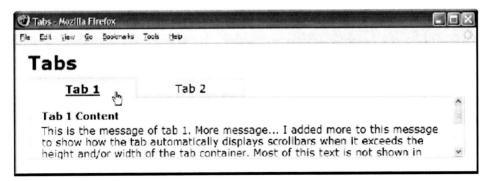

HTML

```
<h1>Tabs</h1>

<ul class="tabs">
 <li class="selected"><h3 class="tab-label"><a href="example.html">Tab 1</a></h3>
   <div id="section1" class="tab-content"><div class="oi2">
   <h4>Tab 1 Content</h4><p>This is the message of tab 1. More message...
   </p></div></div></li>

 <li><h3 class="tab-label"><a href="example2.html">Tab 2</a></h3>
   <div id="section2" class="tab-content"><div class="oi2">
   <h4>Tab 2 Content</h4><p>This is the message of tab 2.
   </p></div></div></li></ul>
```

CSS

```
/* All rules from the Tab Menu design pattern apply to Tabs.
   Only additional rules that apply to this design pattern are shown here. */

ul.tabs { position:relative; }

ul.tabs .tab-content { position:absolute; width:100%; height:6em;
  border:1px solid gold; border-top:none;
  left:-99999px; overflow:auto; }

ul.tabs li.selected .tab-content { left:0; }

ul.tabs li .oi2 { margin:10px; padding:10px; }

ul.tabs .tab-label a { display:block; text-decoration:none; color:black; }

ul.tabs .hover,
ul.tabs .tab-label:hover { text-decoration:underline; }

/*  Nonessential rules are not shown. */
```

Tabs

Problem	You want to create a tabbed user interface that displays the contents of tabs without loading new pages. You want it to adapt reliably and fluidly to different environments.
Solution	You can use the Tab Menu design pattern to turn a list into tabs. Inside each list item, you can insert a **tab-label** heading and a **tab-content** section. You can use a variation of the Screenreader-only design pattern to remove the section from the normal flow and hide it offscreen to the left.

The key to this design pattern is relatively positioning the tabs list in place and absolutely positioning each **tab-content** element in relation to it. This makes the tabs list the closest positioned ancestor of each **tab-content** element. Because of this, you can use **width:100%** to stretch the tab content to the width of the tabs list. Otherwise, the **tab-content** element would expand to the width of its *parent list item*, which has been floated left.

You should leave the **tab-content** element's **top** property set to its default value of **auto** so the **tab-content** element is automatically positioned at the same location it would have been if it weren't absolutely positioned. This keeps tabs and their content positioned properly—even if tabs become wrapped.

If you want the height to remain the same for all tabs, you can assign a height to the **tab-content** element, or you can leave it at its default value of **auto** and let a browser shrinkwrap the height of each tab to its content. If you size it, you can use **overflow:auto** to display scrollbars when content overflows.

You can assign the **selected** class to the list item you want to be displayed when the page loads.

You can insert a link around each **tab-label** element to load a fallback page when the user clicks a tab and JavaScript isn't available to switch tabs.

Pattern

HTML

```
<ul class="tabs">
  <li class="selected">
    <h3 class="tab-label">
     <a href="FALLBACK_PAGE.html"> TAB_LABEL </a></h3>
     <div id="SECTION_ID" class="tab-content"><div class="oi2">
       TAB CONTENT </div></div>
  </li>
</ul>
```

CSS

```
ul.tabs { position:relative; }
ul.tabs .tab-content { position:absolute;
  width:100%; height:VALUE;
  border:WIDTH STYLE COLOR; border-top:none;
  left:-99999px; overflow:auto; }
ul.tabs li.selected .tab-content { left:0; }
ul.tabs li .oi2 { margin:VALUE; padding:VALUE; }
ul.tabs .tab-label a { display:block; text-decoration:none; }
ul.tabs .hover,
ul.tabs .tab-label:hover { text-decoration:underline; }
```

407

HTML Header

```
<head>
 <!-- only script elements are shown -->

 <script language="javascript" type="text/javascript"
    src="https://ajax.googleapis.com/ajax/libs/jquery/1.6.3/jquery.min.js"></script>
</head>
```

page.js

```
$(document).ready(function(e){
        $('ul.tabs li').click(function(e){
                $('ul.tabs li.selected').removeClass('selected');
                $(this).addClass('selected');
        });
        $('ul.tabs li .tab-label').mouseover(function(e){
                $(this).addClass('hover');
        });
        $('ul.tabs li .tab-label').mouseout(function(e){
                $(this).removeClass('hover');
        });
        $('ul.tabs .tab-label a').click(function(e){
                e.preventDefault();
                $(this).blur();
        });
});
```

Tabs cont.

JavaScript	The first line in the first **click()** function applies the **onclick** event to all list items in the **tabs** list. When **onclick** fires, the generic function applies **removeClass()** to each child of the ancestor element that has the **tabs** class, except the child that contains the element that fired the event. In this case, the **removeClass()** function removes the **selected** class from the element. By removing this class, the **left** rule in the **ul.tabs .tab-content** selector applies to the element (instead of the **left** rule in **ul.tabs li.selected .tab-content**) and moves it far off the left side of the screen where it can't be seen but can still be read by screen readers.

The second line in the first **click()** function adds the **selected** class to the element. In the example, I styled the **selected** class to override the **left** rule in the **ul.tabs *.tab-content** so that it moves the **tab-content** element into the display area so the user can see it.

The **mouseover()** function applies the **onmouseover** event to all **tab-label** elements inside **tab** list items. When **onmouseover** fires, the **addClass()** function adds the **hover** class to the element that fired the event. In the example, I styled the **hover** class and the hover pseudo class to underline the element's text.

The **mouseout()** function works like the mouseover, except it applies **removeClass()** to the element that fired the event to remove the **hover** class from the element so it's no longer styled as being hovered over.

The second **click()** function captures clicks on links inside **tab-label** elements, hides the focus rectangle around the link, and cancels the jump. When JavaScript is available, clicks display tab content without loading new pages; and when JavaScript isn't available, clicks load pages just like the Tab Menu design pattern.

Pattern	JavaScript

```javascript
$('ul.tabs li').click(function(e){
    $('ul.tabs li.selected').removeClass('selected');
    $(this).addClass('selected');
});
$('ul.tabs li .tab-label').mouseover(function(e){
    $(this).addClass('hover');
});
$('ul.tabs li .tab-label').mouseout(function(e){
    $(this).removeClass('hover');
});
$('ul.tabs .tab-label a').click(function(e){
    e.preventDefault();
    $(this).blur();
});
```

Tip	The **tab-content** element can contain *any* content: blocks, inlines, tables, images, objects, and so on. This makes the Tabs design pattern a very powerful technique to make large amounts of information in a document easy and fast to navigate without compromising accessibility for nonsighted users.
Related to	Tab Menu, Event Styling; Absolute Box (Chapter 4); Width, Height, Stretched (Chapter 5); Margin, Border, Padding, Background, Overflow (Chapter 6); Positioned, Absolute, Relative (Chapter 7); Offset Absolute and Offset Fixed (Chapter 8); Left Aligned (Chapter 9); Screenreader-only (Chapter 10); Blocked, Inline Decoration (Chapter 11); Section (Chapter 13)

409

Flyout Menu

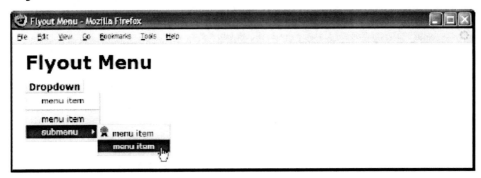

HTML

```
<div class="menu"><h3>Dropdown</h3>
  <ul class="dropdown hidden">
    <li><a href="#">menu item</a></li>
      <li class="separator"><a href="#">menu item</a></li>
    <li class="flyout-trigger"><h4>submenu</h4>
      <ul class="submenu hidden">
        <li><img src="award.gif" alt="award" /><a href="#">menu item</a></li>
        <li><a href="#">menu item</a></li></ul></li></ul></div>
```

CSS

```
.menu { float:left; position:relative; z-index:1; cursor:pointer;
    font-size:0.8em; white-space:nowrap; }
  .menu a { text-decoration:none; color:black; }

  .menu h3 { float:left; margin:0; padding:1px 5px;
    background:url("g1.jpg") repeat-x left bottom white; }
  .menu h4 { display:inline; margin:0; }
  .menu ul { position:absolute; margin:0; padding:0; padding-bottom:5px;
    background:url("g3.jpg") repeat-x left bottom white; }

  .menu li { margin:0; padding:2px 25px; list-style-type:none; color:black; }
  .menu li img { margin-left:-22px; padding-right:5px; }
  .menu li.separator { margin-top:5px; border-top:1px solid gray; padding-top:5px; }
  .menu li.flyout-trigger { background:url("flyout1.gif") no-repeat right center; }
  .menu li.flyout-trigger.hover
    { background:url("flyout2.gif") no-repeat right center firebrick; }
  .menu h3.hover { background:url("g2.jpg") repeat-x left top white; }
  .menu li.hover { background-color:firebrick; color:white; }
  .menu li.hover > a  { color:white; }
.menu ul.dropdown { top:100%;  clear:left; }
.menu ul.submenu { left:100%; margin-top:-1.5em; margin-left:-0.3em; }
.menu .hidden { left:-99999px; top:-99999px; }
  .menu h3,.menu ul { border-left:1px solid yellow; border-right:1px solid orange;
    border-top:1px solid yellow; border-bottom:1px solid orange; }

/* Nonessential rules are not shown. */
```

Flyout Menu

Problem   You want to create a flyout menu that can contain nested menus.

Solution   You can use a division assigned to the **menu** class as the overall container for the menu. You can insert a heading, such as **<h3>**, as the first child of the division to be the menu title. You can insert an unordered list assigned to the **dropdown** class to be the container for the drop-down menu. You can insert list items to create menu items. For the content of a menu item, you can insert an image followed by a link containing the menu item's text.

To create a nested flyout menu, you can embed another unordered list assigned to the **submenu** class inside a menu item assigned to the **flyout-trigger** class. When the user mouses over the **flyout-trigger** menu item, it triggers the display of the flyout menu. You can use a heading instead of a link to mark up the text of the **flyout-trigger** menu item.

To hide menus until the user activates them, you can assign unordered lists to the **hidden** class. To put a separator between list items, assign the **separator** class to them.

Pattern

HTML
```
<div class="menu">
    <h3> MENU_TTTLE_CONTENT </h3>
    <ul class="dropdown hidden">
    <li>
        <img src="FILE.EXT" alt="ALT_TEXT" />
        <a href="URL"> MENU_ITEM_CONTENT </a> </li></ul></div>
```

CSS
```
.menu { float:left; position:relative; z-index:VALUE;
  cursor:pointer; white-space:nowrap; }
.menu a { LINK_STYLES; }
.menu h3 { MENU_TITLE_BOX_STYLES; float:left; margin:0; }
.menu h3.hover { MENU_TITLE_HOVER_BOX_STYLES; }
.menu ul { MENU_CONTAINER_BOX_STYLES; position:absolute;
  margin:0; padding:0; padding-bottom:BUFFER; }

.menu li { MENU_ITEM_BOX_STYLES; margin:0;
 list-style-type:none; padding-left:LEFT_MENU_ITEM_PADDING; }
.menu li.hover { MENU_ITEM_HOVER_BOX_STYLES; }
.menu li.hover > a { MENU_ITEM_HOVER_LINK_STYLES; }
.menu li img { margin-left:-LEFT_MENU_ITEM_PADDING; }
.menu li.separator { margin-top:+VALUE; padding-top:+VALUE;
  border-top:WIDTH STYLE COLOR; }
.menu li.flyout-trigger { background:FLYOUT_ARROW; }
.menu li.flyout-trigger.hover { background:HOVER_FLYOUT_ARROW; }

.menu ul.dropdown { top:100%; clear:left; }
.menu ul.submenu { left:100%;
  margin-top:-1.5em; margin-left:-0.3em; }
.menu .hidden { left:-99999px; top:-99999px; }
```

HTML Header

```
<head>
  <!-- only script elements are shown -->

  <script type="text/javascript"
    src="https://ajax.googleapis.com/ajax/libs/jquery/1.6.3/jquery.min.js"></script>
</head>
```

page.js

```
$(document).ready(function(e){
    $('.menu').click(function(e){
        $('.dropdown', $(this)).toggleClass('hidden');
    });
    $('.menu').mouseover(function(e){
        $('.dropdown', $(this)).removeClass('hidden');
    });
    $('.menu').mouseout(function(e){
        $('.dropdown', $(this)).addClass('hidden');
    });
    $('.menu li, .menu h3').mouseover(function(e){
        $(this).addClass('hover');
    });
    $('.menu li, .menu h3').mouseout(function(e){
        $(this).removeClass('hover');
    });
    $('.menu li.flyout-trigger').mouseover(function(e){
        $('> .submenu', $(this)).removeClass('hidden');
    });
    $('.menu li.flyout-trigger').mouseout(function(e){
        $('> .submenu', $(this)).addClass('hidden');
    });
});
```

Flyout Menu cont.

Location	This pattern works anywhere a list can be used.
Styles	You can **float** the drop-down menu and its title to the left to shrinkwrap the menu and to stack multiple drop-down menus next to each other. You can assign **position:relative** to the drop-down menu so the unordered list can be absolutely positioned in relation to it. If you have other relatively positioned content, you can set **z-index** to a high-enough value to move the menu to the front. You can use **white-space:nowrap** to ensure that list items aren't wrapped across multiple lines.
	You can remove all the default margins and padding on headings, lists, and list items. You can use **list-style-type:none** to remove all bullets from list items. You can create extra left padding inside each list item so you can move images into this area with a negative left margin. This keeps images and text aligned in two columns when there is no image in a menu item.
	You can position a drop-down menu below its title by setting **top** to 100%. You can position a flyout menu to the right of its **flyout-trigger** element by setting **left** to 100%. You can compensate for a flyout menu being positioned lower than its **flyout-trigger** by using **margin-top:1.5em** to raise it. You can use **margin-left:-0.3em** to overlap the flyout menu over its parent menu; use em measurements because they scale with the text when the user zooms in. You can hide menus by moving them off screen.
	You can apply box styles to the following menu elements: **h3**, **ul**, and **li**.
JavaScript	The first three functions add, remove, or toggle the presence of the **hidden** class, which determines whether the drop-down menu is visible or not. Because the **hidden** class simply moves the menu off the screen, it's completely accessible to screen readers.
	The next two functions add or remove the **hover** class from menu items and the menu title. The **hover** class can be used to create hover effects. This is more reliable than the hover pseudo class, which isn't fully implemented in Internet Explorer 6.
	The last two functions add or remove the **hidden** class of submenus when the user hovers over a menu item assigned to the **flyout-trigger** class. Notice that the **applyToDescendants** selector, **'> *.submenu'**, contains a child selector to limit the scope to just the child submenu rather than all descendant submenus. Even though Internet Explorer 6 doesn't support the child selector, it works in this code because the jQuery library supports all CSS selectors.
Limitations	Single-level menus work fine, but nested menus have limitations. Nested menus don't work well on touchscreen devices because they require a mouseover to work, and touchscreens don't have a hover state. Because nested menus are absolutely positioned, they don't adapt to narrow displays. Finally, menus don't fly out when JavaScript isn't available.
Related to	Event Styling; Absolute Box, Floated Box (Chapter 4); Width, Height, Shrinkwrapped, Stretched (Chapter 5); Margin, Border, Padding, Background, Overflow (Chapter 6); Positioned, Atomic, Absolute, Relative, Float and Clear, Relative Float (Chapter 7); Offset Absolute and Offset Fixed, Aligned Outside (Chapter 8); Left Aligned (Chapter 9); Screenreader-only (Chapter 10); Blocked, Nowrap, Inline Decoration (Chapter 11); Section, Lists (Chapter 13)

Button

HTML

```
<h1>Button</h1>

<form id="form1" method="post" action="http://www.tipjar.com/cgi-bin/test">
  <input type="text" id="search" name="search"  class="search" value="Search" />
  <input type="submit" id="submit1" name="submit1" value="Submit" />
  <input type="submit" id="submit2" name="submit3" value="" />
  <input type="submit" id="submit3" name="submit2" class="button" value="Submit" />
  <input type="reset"  id="reset1"  name="reset1"  class="button" value="Reset" />
</form>
<input type="button" id="message" name="message" class="button" value="Message" />
<input type="button" id="submit4" name="submit4" class="button" value="J-Submit"/>
<input type="button" id="reset2"  name="reset2"  class="button" value="J-Reset" />

<button id="change" name="change" class="button">Change Me!</button>
<a id="link" class="button" href="http://cssdesignpatterns.com">Link</a>
```

CSS

```
form { margin:20px 0; }
    .button { margin:0; padding:3px 10px; font-size:1em; color:black;
      cursor:pointer; background:url("g1.jpg") repeat-x left bottom;
      border-left:1px solid yellow; border-right:1px solid orange;
      border-top:1px solid yellow; border-bottom:1px solid orange; }

    .button:hover, .button.hover
      { background:url("g2.jpg") repeat-x left top;
        border-left:1px solid orange; border-right:1px solid yellow;
        border-top:1px solid orange; border-bottom:1px solid yellow; }

    a.button { padding:5px 10px; line-height:2em; text-decoration:none; }

    #submit2 { width:32px; height:32px; border:none; cursor:pointer;
      background:url("go.jpg") no-repeat left top; }
#submit2:hover, #submit2.hover { background-position:1px 1px; }
```

Button

Problem	You want to use buttons to submit forms and run JavaScript. You want to style the buttons to fit the look and feel of the document. You want all actions to be accessible.
Solution	You can use the `<input type="submit">`, `<input type="reset">`, `<input type="button">`, `<button>`, and `<a>` elements to create buttons.
	To submit form values to a server or to reset form elements to their initial values, you can use one or more `<input type="submit">` and `<input type="reset">` buttons inside a `<form>` element. These buttons are designed to be used inside forms. The text displayed in them comes from their **value** attribute. When a submit button is clicked, the text in its value attribute is submitted along with the rest of the form data.
	To trigger JavaScript events, you can use `<input type="button">` and `<button>` elements outside a form. The `<button>` element allows you to put *any* content (including images, inline elements, and block elements) inside the button. Whatever content you put in the button is displayed inside the button. In the example, you can click the Change Me! button and literally enter any valid HTML to change the content it displays.
	To trigger JavaScript events, you can use a link, `<a>`. For example, when a user clicks an external link, you may want to ask the user whether they want to submit the form before leaving the page. In the example, I styled the link to look like a button to make the point that links can look and function like buttons. From an accessibility point of view, it's better to use button elements for buttons rather than links, because a screen reader says "button" when it encounters a button and says "link" for a link.
Pattern HTML	``` <form id="ID" method="post" action="URL"> <input type="submit" id="NAME" name="NAME" value="TEXT" /> <input type="reset" id="NAME" name="NAME" value="TEXT" /> </form> <input type="button" id="NAME" name="NAME" value="TEXT" /> <button id="NAME" name="NAME"> TEXT </button> <a id="NAME" href="URL"> TEXT </a> ```
Location	This pattern works anywhere inline elements work.
Styling	You can apply styles to the various types of button elements to replace proprietary styles supplied by the browser, but your results may vary in different browsers and operating systems. The example embeds three submit buttons and one reset button in a form. The first submit button is left unstyled, which renders it as a button, but the exact look varies in different browsers and operating systems. The second submit button, **#submit2**, displays a background image. I removed all text in the **value** attribute to prevent it from being displayed over the image. When this button is clicked, the form data is submitted, but there is no button value to submit. This is only a problem when you have multiple submit buttons in a form and want to take different actions depending on which one is clicked.

HTML Header

```
<head>
  <!-- only script elements are shown -->

  <script type="text/javascript"
    src="https://ajax.googleapis.com/ajax/libs/jquery/1.6.3/jquery.min.js"></script>
</head>
```

page.js

```
$(document).ready(function(e){
    $('#form1').submit(function(e){
        if(!confirm('Are you sure?')){e.preventDefault();}
    });
    $('#message').click(function(e){
        alert('Hi There');
    });
    $('#button').click(function(e){
        alert('Hi There');
    });
    $('#link').click(function(e){
        if(!confirm('Jump here?')){e.preventDefault();}
    });
    $('#change').click(function(e){
        try{
            var result = prompt('Enter content:',  $(this).text() );
            if ( result ) $(this).text( result );
        }catch(ex){ e.preventDefault(); }
    });
    $('#submit4').click(function(e){
        $('#form1').submit();
    });
    $('#reset2').click(function(e){
        $('#form1').reset();
    });
});
});
Button (Continued)
```

Styling cont.	I further styled the second submit button by removing its border and setting it to the exact height and width of its background image. When the button is hovered over, the **#submit2:hover** rule moves the background image down and right by 1 pixel to make it look like it's being depressed. The remaining buttons in the example are styled by the **button** class.
	I use the **button** class to normalize the display of all buttons by setting **margin**, **padding**, and **font-size**. This is important because browsers use different default values. I set the mouse pointer to **cursor:pointer** to further signal that the button is clickable.
	You can use any box styles to style a button. In the example, I set the background to a horizontally tiled gradient image that is lighter at the top and darker at the bottom to create a raised button effect. When the mouse hovers over the button, I change the background to a gradient image that is darker at the top and lighter at the bottom to create a depressed button effect. Likewise, I use lighter top-left borders and darker bottom-right borders when not hovered over and the reverse when hovered over.
Limitations	**<input type="image">** submits the coordinates of where its image is clicked. I don't recommend using it to process coordinates because nonsighted users can't see to click different areas of its image. A client-side image map is an accessible solution (see Image Map in Chapter 14).
	Because Internet Explorer 6 only responds to **a:hover**, I also use the **.hover** class and JavaScript to simulate **:hover**. Internet Explorer 7 and the other major browsers don't need this JavaScript workaround.
	If you omit the **name** attribute of a submit button, its value isn't submitted along with the rest of the form. For consistency, you can set a button's **id** attribute to the same value as its **name** attribute.
	The **name** and **id** attribute must not be the same name as a DOM element method, because this prevents you from executing the method. For example, if you give a submit button a **name** or **id** of "submit", you can't execute **document.getElementById("submit").submit()**, which prevents you from submitting the form using JavaScript. The same applies to "reset".
JavaScript	In the example, I use each button's unique ID to assign event handlers.
	This example shows how easy it is to extend the Event Styling framework with your own custom functions.
Related to	Event Styling; Inline Elements (Chapter 2)

Layout Links

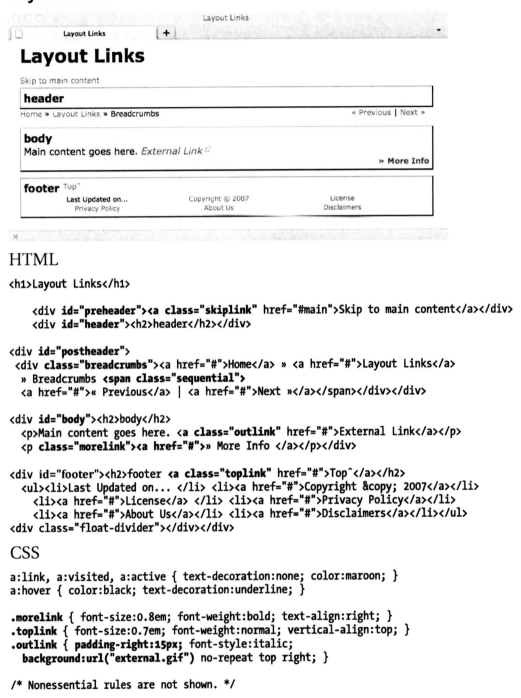

HTML

```
<h1>Layout Links</h1>

    <div id="preheader"><a class="skiplink" href="#main">Skip to main content</a></div>
    <div id="header"><h2>header</h2></div>

<div id="postheader">
 <div class="breadcrumbs"><a href="#">Home</a> » <a href="#">Layout Links</a>
  » Breadcrumbs <span class="sequential">
  <a href="#">« Previous</a> | <a href="#">Next »</a></span></div></div>

<div id="body"><h2>body</h2>
  <p>Main content goes here. <a class="outlink" href="#">External Link</a></p>
  <p class="morelink"><a href="#">» More Info </a></p></div>

<div id="footer"><h2>footer <a class="toplink" href="#">Top^</a></h2>
  <ul><li>Last Updated on... </li> <li><a href="#">Copyright &copy; 2007</a></li>
    <li><a href="#">License</a> </li> <li><a href="#">Privacy Policy</a></li>
    <li><a href="#">About Us</a></li> <li><a href="#">Disclaimers</a></li></ul>
<div class="float-divider"></div></div>
```

CSS

```
a:link, a:visited, a:active { text-decoration:none; color:maroon; }
a:hover { color:black; text-decoration:underline; }

.morelink { font-size:0.8em; font-weight:bold; text-align:right; }
.toplink { font-size:0.7em; font-weight:normal; vertical-align:top; }
.outlink { padding-right:15px; font-style:italic;
  background:url("external.gif") no-repeat top right; }

/* Nonessential rules are not shown. */
```

Layout Links

Problem	You want to enhance navigation within a document and to other documents using specially styled links including skip-to-main-content, breadcrumb, sequential, more-info, top, external, and footer links.
Solutions	**Section links** allow you to link to any section in a document. You can assign each section to a unique ID. The ID is an anchor that can be linked to by internal and external links. Using the section ID as a selector, you can uniquely style the section and its elements. There are five common sections: preheader, header, postheader, body, and footer. (The terms *preheader* and *postheader* are my own.) Different types of links occur in each of these sections.
	Skip-to-main-content links allow users to jump directly to the main content of a document. This link is useful for nonsighted users and users reading the document on small devices. It occurs in the preheader and should be the first item in the document other than perhaps the document heading.
	Breadcrumb links are a series of links that lead back to the home page. They typically occur in the postheader or header. To identify them as breadcrumbs, you can separate them with a right-pointing arrow symbol.
	Sequential links link to previous and next documents in a series. They typically have names like Previous and Next, the former often preceded by a left-pointing arrow and the latter followed by a right-pointing arrow.
	More-info links allow content in a section to be abbreviated to make it easier to read online. If users want more information, they can click a link to read more about it. The link is often labeled some variation of More Info. You can visually set apart more-info links by making them the last item in a section, embedding them in their own paragraph, aligning them to the right, and preceding them with a right-pointing arrow symbol.
	Top links allow users to jump to the top of a section or document. They typically occur in the header of a section when they link back to the top of the document. They also occur as the last item in a section when they link back to the top of the section. They're often raised above the baseline and are followed by an up-pointing arrow symbol.
	External links are styled to show that they lead to an external web site. This helps users decide whether they want to go to another web site. You can create a rule that adds right padding to a link and displays a background image of an up-right-pointing arrow in this padding.
	Footer links occur in the footer section and link to information about the copyright, licensing, privacy, company, disclaimers, affiliates, and so forth.
Pattern	
HTML	`<a class="LINK_TYPE" href="URL#SECTION_ID"> LINK_CONTENT </a>`
CSS	`.LINK_TYPE { STYLES }`
Related to	Inline Elements (Chapter 2); Lists (Chapter 13)
Location	This pattern works anywhere.

Multi-column Layout

HTML

```
<h1>Multi-column Layout</h1>

<div class="multi">
<p>Lorem ipsum dolor sit amet, consectetur adipiscing elit.
  Morbi sollicitudin posuere mauris sed in ...
<!-- Additional code can be found in sample -->
</div>
```

CSS

```
.multi { column-count:3; -moz-column-count:3;
  -webkit-column-count:3; -ms-column-count:3; }

/* Nonessential rules are not shown. */
```

Multi-column Layout

Problem	You want to distribute your content across multiple columns similar to a newspaper layout to save vertical screen space.
Solutions	The Multi-column module allows content to flow into multiple columns inside an element. It offers CSS properties that let you define the number of columns, column width, column gaps, and rules governing overflow.
	There is no specific markup for this solution. You use CSS to modify a given element and turn it into a multicol element, which occurs automatically when certain column styles are applied to an element.
	This also means that if a browser such as IE9 doesn't support the Multi-column layout module, the content remains in normal flow without any extra unused markup.
Pattern	
HTML	`<div>CONTENT </div>`
CSS	`div { column-count: 4; }` `div { column-width: 100px; }`
Limitations	A table element can't be made into a multicol element.
	IE9 and earlier versions don't support Multi-column Layouts.
	A vendor prefix, **-webkit**, **-ms**, and **-moz** for all browsers, is required.
Location	This pattern works anywhere.

421

Template Layout

HTML

```
<h1>Template Layout</h1>

<div id="template">
    <div id="a">Apple</div>
    <div id="b">Bear</div>
    <div id="c">Castle</div>
    <div id="d">Deer</div>
</div>
```

CSS

```
#template { display: "ab" "cd" 20% * 20%; }
    #d { position: a; }
    #c { position: b; }
    #b {   position: c; }
#a { position: d; }

/* Nonessential rules are not shown. */
```

Template Layout

Problem	You want to position elements based on templates with easy source arrangement for different media types (print, mobile, Web, and so on).
Solutions	The Template Layout module works like a grid. Each element is assigned a position using an alphabetical character and the position property. Once positions have been assigned, you can make layouts using a string of characters; each string equals a row, and each character in that string equals a column. This provides a method of implementing a table-like template without tables.
Limitations	At the time of writing, the Template Layout module hasn't been implemented in any browsers. A jQuery plugin called jQuery polyfill exists that implements it in modern browsers. Because jQuery is JavaScript based, any browser that doesn't support JavaScript isn't positioned correctly. It's important to lay out your content with this in mind.
Pattern	
| HTML | ```
<container>
  <element> HEADER_CONTENT </element>
  <element> NAV_CONTENT </element>
</container>
``` |
| CSS | `container { STYLES }` |
| **Location** | This pattern works anywhere. |
```

Layout Example

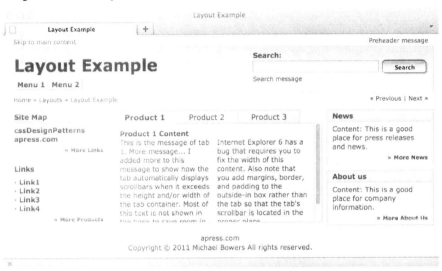

HTML Structural Elements

```
<div id="preheader"></div>
    <div id="header">
      <div id="title"><h1>Layout Example</h1></div>
      <div id="search"><h3>Search:</h3></div></div>
    <div id="postheader"></div>
    <div id="body">
      <div id="nav">
      <div id="site-map"><h3>Site Map</h3></div>
      <div id="links"><h3>Links</h3></div></div>
  <div id="main"></div>
  <div id="extras">
      <div id="news"><h3>News</h3></div>
      <div id="about-us"><h3>About us</h3></div></div></div>
<div id="footer"></div>
```

CSS Structural Styles

```
#preheader .part1 { float:left;  margin-left:10px; }
#preheader .part2 { float:right; margin-right:10px; }
#header { float:left; width:100%; }
#title { float:left; width:50%; margin-top:7px; }
#search { float:right; margin-top:2px; }
#postheader .breadcrumbs { float:left; margin-left:10px; }
#postheader .sequential { float:right; margin-right:10px; }
#body { float:left; width:100%; }
#nav { float:left; width:25%; min-width:160px; }
#main { float:left; width:50%; min-width:300px; }
#extras { float:left; width:25%; min-width:160px; }
#footer { clear:both; padding-top:40px; }
```

Layout Example

Example

This example combines the design patterns in this chapter. It shows how these design patterns can be nested and combined to create an unlimited variety of layouts.

There are five layout rows in the example corresponding to five typical sections: preheader, header, postheader, body, and footer. I created these sections using the Fluid Layout design pattern. This makes each section modular so its layout can be easily reorganized with confidence when floated or positioned.

The preheader section uses the Opposing Floats design pattern to move the skip-to-main-content link and the preheader message to opposite sides of the document. Placing information on opposite sides puts put more information in half the vertical space without overwhelming the reader. A user automatically separates content aligned to the left from content aligned to the right. Being floated allows the position of the breadcrumbs and preheader message to be adjusted automatically and dynamically to different viewport widths and zoom factors.

The header section contains two subsections, title and search, which are also floated to opposite sides using the Opposing Floats design pattern. This keeps the search section aligned to the right. The search button is styled with a custom background image using the Button design pattern.

The title section contains a heading and two flyout menus. A float divider moves the menus below the heading. You can create each menu using the Flyout Menu design pattern. You can stack together and nest as many menus as you like by adding more unordered lists and list items to the document. A float divider occurs before the end of the header to expand the section around its floated children—as specified in the Fluid Layout design pattern.

The postheader section (like the preheader and header) floats breadcrumbs and sequential links to opposite sides. This organizes the entire heading area into three rows and two columns aligned to opposite sides.

The body section contains three subsections: nav, main, and extras. Each is floated left using the Fluid Layout design pattern. This divides the body section into three columns.

The main section contains three tabs created using the Tabs design pattern. By using tabs, you can put more information in a smaller space. This is called *information hiding*. It hides information in the page and displays it as needed. Because the information is downloaded with the page, it can be displayed without having to fetch another page from the server.

The nav and extra sections each contain two subsections, which are rendered in normal flow. I applied the Rollup design pattern to them so that they roll up and down when you click their headings. Each of these sections also contains a more-info link. These are all additional information-hiding techniques.

The footer section contains standard footer links.

This example demonstrates how layout design patterns are modular, reusable, customizable, fluid, interactive, and accessible.

These layouts are modular and reusable. This example is created entirely using layout design patterns. I copied each design pattern's HTML *structure* into **example.html** and changed its *content* as desired. For each instance of the design pattern, I repeated this process. I then copied and pasted the CSS rules for each design pattern into **page.css**, and copied and pasted the JavaScript for each design pattern into **page.js**. The CSS styles and JavaScript code of a design pattern need to be copied only once into a page's stylesheet and script. For maximum reusability, you can place all layout design patterns in a site's stylesheet and script file to make them available to all pages. This works because HTML, CSS, and JavaScript are located in separate files, which makes them more reusable and interchangeable. On the other hand, for maximum performance, you may want to include only those styles and JavaScript that apply to the current page.

425

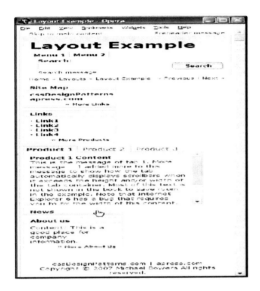 

Layout example displayed in a narrow viewport and displayed without a stylesheet

Layout Example cont.

These layouts are customizable. If you want to tweak the styles of a design pattern for all instances of the pattern, you can directly change the pattern's rules. If you want to tweak the styles of a design pattern for a specific section, you can copy the rule and prefix the copied selector with a section selector. For example, to change what a selected tab looks like in the **nav** section, you can copy the selector, `ul.tabs li.selected .tab-label`, and create a new one prefixed with `#nav`, as in `#nav ul.tabs li.selected .tab-label`. Because selectors containing an ID override those that don't, this selector overrides the standard selector. To change just one instance of a design pattern, you can wrap it in a division set to a unique ID, copy the desired rule, and prefix its selector with the unique ID.

These layouts are fluid. They adapt nicely to devices with different widths and zoom factors. Figure 17-1 shows the same page rendered in a narrow viewport. Notice how side-by-side columns automatically reflow into a single column to fit the viewport. This allows the page to work well on handheld devices. Furthermore, if a browser doesn't support stylesheets, each section renders as nicely structured HTML.

These layouts are interactive, allowing a user to collapse and expand sections, drop-down menus, and select tabs. Notice in Figure 17-1 how the News section is rolled up, which makes room to show other sections.

These layouts are accessible. Interactive elements such as rollups and drop-down menus play nicely with screen readers because content is never set to `visibility:hidden` or `display:none`; instead, hidden content is positioned offscreen and moved onscreen when it's made visible. Because all content is present in the document, search engines can index it. For browsers that don't support JavaScript or have disabled JavaScript, you should include an alternative version that doesn't rely on JavaScript.

Related to | All design patterns in this chapter and the majority of design patterns in the book

---

Drop Caps

This chapter discusses design patterns that create drop caps. A drop cap dramatically styles the first letter of a document to signal that it is the beginning of a document. Sometimes it is used at the beginning of a major section of a longer document. Sometimes it styles a word instead of just the first letter.

Typically, the drop cap enlarges the first letter and lowers it so that the top of the letter is aligned to the top of the following text, but there is no limit to how the drop cap can be styled.

The design patterns in this chapter are organized from simplest to most complex.

Chapter Outline

- **Aligned Drop Cap** shows how to create a simple drop cap by enlarging it and vertically aligning it.

- **First-letter Drop Cap** shows how to create a drop cap without inserting extra markup.

- **Hanging Drop Cap** shows how to use a hanging indent to create a drop cap.

- **Padded Graphical Drop Cap** shows how to add left padding to the drop cap to make room for a background image showing a banner, a grabber, or a decoration.

- **Floating Drop Cap** shows how to float the drop cap to the left so that text below the drop cap wraps back under the drop cap.

- **Floating Graphical Drop Cap** shows how to display a graphic on top of the dropcap text. It works great for screen readers, and it shows a styled text version of the drop cap when the image is unavailable. This is the best Graphical Drop Cap design pattern for allowing text below the drop cap to wrap back under the drop cap.

- **Marginal Drop Cap** shows how to use absolute positioning to move the drop cap into the left margin of a block. All lines of the block are indented.

- **Marginal Graphical Drop Cap** shows how to display a graphic on top of the dropcap text. It works great for screen readers, and it shows a styled text version of the drop cap when the image is unavailable. This is the best Graphical Drop Cap design pattern for preventing text below the drop cap from wrapping back under the drop cap.

Aligned Drop Cap

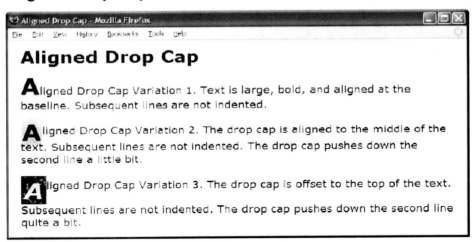

HTML

```
<p><span class="aligned-dropcap1">A</span>ligned Drop Cap Variation 1. Text is
  large, bold, and aligned at the baseline. Subsequent lines are not indented.</p>

<p><span class="aligned-dropcap2">A</span>ligned Drop Cap Variation 2. The
  drop cap is aligned to the middle of the text. Subsequent lines are not indented.
  The drop cap pushes down the second line a little bit.</p>

<p><span class="aligned-dropcap3">A</span>ligned Drop Cap Variation 3. The
  drop cap is offset to the top of the text. Subsequent lines are not indented.
  The drop cap pushes down the second line quite a bit.</p>
```

CSS

```
.aligned-dropcap1 { font-size:40px; line-height:normal; font-weight:bold;
  vertical-align:baseline; }

.aligned-dropcap2 { font-size:40px; line-height:0.8em; font-weight:bold;
  vertical-align:middle; background-color:gold; padding:0 2px; }

.aligned-dropcap3 { font-size:40px; line-height:normal; font-weight:bold;
  font-style:italic; vertical-align:-0.45em; color:white;
  background-color:black; background-image:url("marble.jpg");
  padding:0 4px; border:1px solid black; }
```

Aligned Drop Cap

Problem	You want to display the first letter of a block as a drop cap. An *aligned drop cap* is a letter that has a larger font size than the following text. Its baseline is typically dropped lower than the baseline of the following text. It may also be styled with a different font, weight, case, and so on.
	In general terms, you want to style a section of text and align it to other text.
Solution	You can mark up the first letter or letters of a terminal block element using an inline element. Assigning this element to a class, such as **"aligned-dropcap"**, makes it easy to style. You can use **font-size** to increase the height of the text. You can use a negative value in **vertical-align** to lower the text below the baseline. You can use a positive value in **vertical-align** to raise the text above the baseline. You can use **line-height** to fine-tune how all this affects the height of the line. You can use **line-height:normal** to ensure the drop cap does not overlap neighboring lines. You can use a value slightly smaller than **1em** in **line-height** to tighten up the space between the lines.
Pattern	
HTML	`<INLINE class="aligned-dropcap"> CONTENT </INLINE>`

CSS	`.aligned-dropcap { vertical-align:±VALUE;`
	`    font-size:+VALUE;`
	`    line-height:VALUE; }`

Location	This pattern works anywhere you can use an inline element.
Limitations	Using text with different fonts and font sizes increases the height of a line. Furthermore, offset text increases the height of a line. Thus, an aligned drop cap puts extra space between the first and second lines. The lower you place the drop cap, the more space you put between the lines.
Related to	Hanging Drop Cap, Floating Drop Cap; Vertical-Aligned Content, Vertical-Offset Content (Chapter 12); Font (Chapter 10); Spacing (Chapter 11)

First-Letter Drop Cap

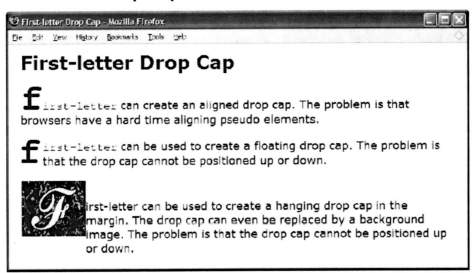

HTML

```
<p class="dropcap1"><code>first-letter</code> can create an aligned drop cap.
  The problem is that browsers have a hard time aligning pseudo elements.</p>

<p class="dropcap2"><code>first-letter</code> can be used to create a floating
  drop cap. The problem is that the drop cap cannot be positioned up or down.</p>

<p class="dropcap3">first-letter can be used to create a hanging drop cap in the
  margin. The drop cap can even be replaced by a background image.
  The problem is that the drop cap cannot be positioned up or down.</p>
```

CSS

```
.dropcap1:first-letter { font-size:60px; vertical-align:0px; font-weight:bold; }

.dropcap2:first-letter { float:left; margin-left:-3px; margin-right:3px;
  position:relative; top:-2000px; /* DOES NOT WORK */
  font-size:60px; line-height:normal; font-weight:bold; }

.dropcap3  { padding-left:105px; text-indent:-104px; margin-top:50px; }

.dropcap3:first-letter { padding:40px 50px; font-size:1px; line-height:1px;
  color:white; background-image:url("f.jpg");
  background-position:center center; }
```

First-Letter Drop Cap

Problem	You want to display the first letter of a block as a drop cap without adding elements to the HTML document. In general terms, you want to style the first letter of a terminal block element, such as a paragraph.
Solution	**first-letter** is a design pattern built into the CSS language. **first-letter** is called a pseudo-element selector because it selects a subset of content in an element rather than all the content in an element. You can tag a terminal block element with a class or ID of your choosing. You can combine the **first-line** pseudo-selector with classes, IDs, and types of your choosing. Make sure the **first-line** selector is the last item in the selector.
Pattern	

CSS	`.CLASS:first-letter { STYLES }`
	or
	`#ID:first-letter     { STYLES }`
	or
	`ELEMENT:first-letter { STYLES }`

Location	**first-letter** works just like **first-line**. It works only on terminal block elements. It does not work on structural block elements or inline elements. **first-letter** is not inherited by child elements.
Limitations	The **first-letter** selector works best with font and text properties. Browsers cannot position pseudo-elements and have trouble aligning them. This means you may not be able to control the vertical placement of the drop cap. Notice that the second drop cap in the example has been relatively positioned and offset 2000 pixels. This should move the drop cap off the screen, but as the example demonstrates, the text selected by **first-letter** does not respond to positioning. This solution displays correctly in all modern browsers. Be aware of the following for older browsers. Opera 9 does not select the first letter of table cells, and in a list item Internet Explorer 7 selects the list marker along with the first letter. Internet Explorer 6 positions a first-letter background image differently from Internet Explorer 7, and both position it differently from the other major browsers. As shown in the source code for the example, you can solve this problem by loading different style sheets for Internet Explorer versions 6 and 7 and using **background-position** to adjust the position of the background.
Related to	Pseudo-element Selectors (Chapter 3)

Hanging Drop Cap

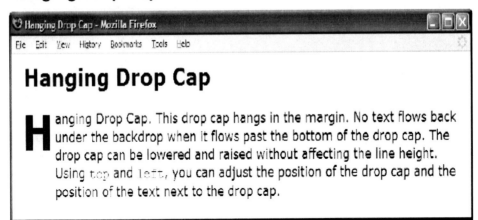

HTML

```
<p class="hanging-indent"><span class="hanging-dropcap">H</span>anging
Drop Cap. This drop cap hangs in the margin. No text flows back under
the backdrop when it flows past the bottom of the drop cap.
The drop cap can be lowered and raised without affecting the line height.
Using <code>top</code> and <code>left</code>,
you can adjust the position of the drop cap and the position of the text
next to the drop cap.</p>
```

CSS

```
.hanging-indent { padding-left:50px;
    text-indent:-50px;
    margin-top:-25px; }

.hanging-dropcap { position:relative;
    top:0.55em;
    left:-3px;
    font-size:60px;
    line-height:60px;
    font-weight:bold; }
```

Hanging Drop Cap

Problem	You want to display the first letter of a block as a drop cap without increasing the height of the first line. You also want to position the drop cap higher or lower and control its distance from neighboring text. You also want all text in all lines in a block element to stay to the right of the drop cap.
	In general terms, you want to move text or an image to the left and to move text to the right while controlling the position of both.
Solution	Mark up the first letter or letters of a terminal block element using an inline element assigned to the **"hanging-dropcap"** class. Also tag the terminal block element with the **"hanging-indent"** class.
	Style the **"hanging-dropcap"** class as follows:
	Use **position:relative** to prepare the drop cap for positioning.
	Use **top** to move the drop cap up or down.
	Assign a negative value to **left** to put space between drop cap and text.
	Assign **line-height** to the same value as **font-size** to prevent the large **font-size** of the drop cap from expanding the height of the first line.
	Style the **"hanging-indent"** class as follows:
	Assign a positive value to **padding-left** to move text to the right of the drop cap. The value should be larger than the width of the drop cap.
	Assign a negative value to **text-indent** to move the drop cap to the left of the text. The value should be equal to or less than the width of the drop cap.
	Assign a positive value to **margin-top** to make room for a drop cap that extends above the line, or a negative value when a drop cap is lowered.

Pattern	
| HTML | ```
<BLOCK class="hanging-indent">
  <INLINE class="hanging-dropcap"> TEXT </INLINE>
</BLOCK>
``` |
| CSS | ```
.hanging-indent { padding-left:+VALUE;
  text-indent:-VALUE;
  margin-top:±VALUE; }
.hanging-dropcap { position:relative;
  top:±VALUE; left:-VALUE;
  font-size:+SIZE; line-height:+SIZE; }
``` |
Location	The drop cap must be the first item in a terminal block element.
Limitations	Modern browsers all render this solution correctly.
	Internet Explorer 6 and Opera 9 position background images differently behind text that has been moved using **text-indent**. For this reason, if you must support older browsers, a graphical hanging drop cap is unfeasible.
Variations	You can style the **"hanging-dropcap"** class using properties such as **font**, **color**, **background-color**, **background-image**, **padding**, **border**, and so forth.
Related to	Aligned Drop Cap, Floating Drop Cap; Margin, Padding (Chapter 6); Relative (Chapter 7); Offset Relative (Chapter 8); Font (Chapter 10); Spacing (Chapter 11)

Padded Graphical Drop Cap

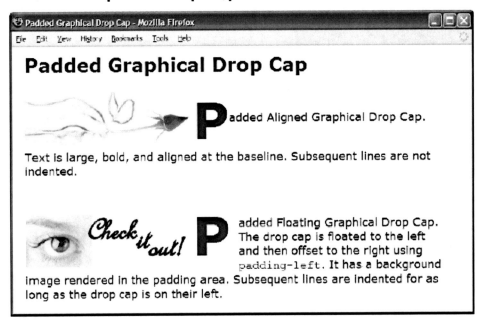

HTML

```
<h1>Padded Drop Cap</h1>

<p><span class="padded-dropcap1">P</span>added Aligned Drop Cap. Text is
   large, bold, and aligned at the baseline. Subsequent lines are not indented.</p>

<p><span class="padded-dropcap2">P</span>added Floating Drop Cap. The
   drop cap is floated to the left and then offset to the right using
   <code>padding-left</code>. It has a background image rendered in the
   padding area. Subsequent lines are indented for as long as the drop cap is on
   their left.</p>
```

CSS

```
.padded-dropcap1 { padding-left:39%; font-size:80px; line-height:normal;
   font-weight:bold; vertical-align:middle;
   background:url("rose.jpg") no-repeat -65px 0 white; }


.padded-dropcap2 { padding-left:275px; padding-right:10px; float:left;
   position:relative; top:-0.25em; margin-bottom:-0.2em;
   margin-left:-3px; margin-right:3px; color:black;
   background:url("grabber.jpg") no-repeat 5px 20px white;
   font-size:84px; line-height:normal; font-weight:bold; }
```

Padded Graphical Drop Cap

Problem	You want to indent or center a drop cap and style its background from the beginning of the line through the drop cap. Behind the padding, you want to put a background image, such as a banner, an ad, or a grabber, to draw the reader into the text.
	In general terms, you want to pad the starting position of an inline element.
Solution	A padded drop cap is indented using padding. You can use padding to center a drop cap or to indent it by a fixed amount. The background color or background image shows through the padding.
	To create a padded drop cap, you can mark up the first letter or letters of a terminal block element using an inline element. Assigning this element to a class, such as **"padded-dropcap"**, makes it easy to style. You can use **padding-left** to move the drop cap to the right. You can center the drop cap by using a value for **padding-left** that is slightly less than **50%**. Lower the percentage as needed to compensate for the width of the content in the drop cap. You can use **margin-left** to put transparent space on the left of the drop cap. You can use **padding-right** to put padding between the drop cap and the following text. You can also use **margin-right** to put transparent space between the drop cap and the following text.
Limitations	In Internet Explorer 8 and 9, the background of padded-dropcap1 is raised by 25px. This is addressed by a CSS rule for IE 8 and 9 that lowers the background image by 25px.
Pattern	
HTML	`<INLINE class="padded-dropcap"> CONTENT </INLINE>`

CSS	`.padded-dropcap { padding-left:+VALUE;`
	`    padding-right:+VALUE;`
	`    margin-left:+VALUE;`
	`    margin-right:+VALUE;`
	`    background:url("FILE.EXT") REPEAT HORIZONTAL VERTICAL COLOR; }`

Location	This pattern works anywhere you can use an inline element.
Limitations	If you are centering the drop cap and the width of the drop cap's parent is variable, the position of the drop cap will be close to center, but may not always remain perfectly centered as the parent's width changes. If you need it to be precisely centered, you need to set the width of the drop cap's parent to a fixed value.
	As you extend the padding on the left, you extend the background on the left. This is part of the design of this type of drop cap. If you have a background behind the drop cap, but you do not want to show the background on the left, you can use **margin-left** instead of **padding-left** to indent the drop cap.
Tip	You can combine this pattern with other Drop Cap design patterns.
Related to	Aligned Drop Cap, First-Letter Drop Cap, Hanging Drop Cap, Floating Graphical Drop Cap; Margin, Padding, Background (Chapter 6)

Floating Drop Cap

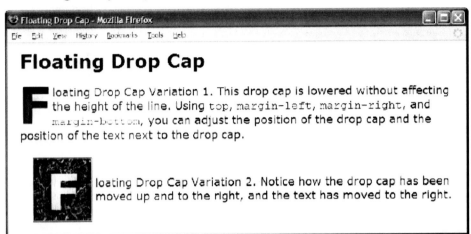

HTML

```
<h1>Floating Drop Cap</h1>
<p><span class="floating-dropcap1">F</span>loated Drop Cap Variation 1. This
    drop cap is lowered without affecting the height of the line.
    Using <code>top</code>, <code>margin-left</code>, <code>margin-right</code>,
    and <code>margin-bottom</code>, you can adjust the position of the drop cap
    and the position of the text next to the drop cap.</p>
<br />
<p><span class="floating-dropcap2">F</span>loated Drop Cap Variation 2.
    Notice how the drop cap has been moved up and to the right, and the text
    has moved to the right.</p>
```

CSS

```
.floating-dropcap1 { float:left; position:relative; top:-0.25em;
    margin-left:-3px; margin-right:3px; margin-bottom:-0.6em;
    font-size:80px; line-height:normal; font-weight:bold; }

.floating-dropcap2 { float:left; position:relative; top:-0.35em;
    margin-left:20px; margin-right:5px; margin-bottom:-0.7em;
    font-size:80px; line-height:normal; font-weight:bold;
    color:white; background-color:black; padding:0 20px;
    background-image:url("marble.jpg");
    border-left:2px groove black; border-right:2px ridge black;
    border-top:2px groove black; border-bottom:2px ridge black; }
```

Floating Drop Cap

Problem	You want to display the first letter of a block as a drop cap without increasing the height of the first line. You also need to position the drop cap higher or lower and control its distance from neighboring text.
Solution	In general, you can float a drop cap to the left and use margins and relative positioning to fine-tune its position. Specifically, you can mark up the first letter or letters of a terminal block element using an inline element. Assigning this element to a class, such as **"floating-dropcap"**, makes it easy to style. You can use **float:left** to float the drop cap to the left. You can use **position:relative** to prepare the drop cap for positioning. You can use **top** to move the drop cap up or down—negative values move it up, and positive values move it down. You can use **margin-left** to move the drop cap left or right—negative values move it to the left, and positive values move it to the right. You can use **margin-right** to change the space between the drop cap and text—positive values increase the space, and negative values shrink it. You can use **margin-bottom** to extend or shrink the transparent area below the drop cap. By using positive values in **margin-bottom**, you can extend down the influence of the float so that text continues to indent on its right.
Pattern	
HTML	`<INLINE class="floating-dropcap"> TEXT </INLINE>`
| CSS | ```
.floating-dropcap { float:left;
    position:relative;
    top:±VALUE;
    margin-left:±VALUE;
    margin-right:±VALUE;
    margin-bottom:±VALUE; }
``` |
Location	This pattern works anywhere you can use an inline element.
Limitations	If other elements in the same line are also floated left, they will be stacked between the drop cap and the text. This breaks the dropcap effect. Floats sometimes trigger bugs in browsers.
Advantages	The floating drop cap is simple to position, and is one of the most flexible to position and style. It allows text to wrap around the bottom of the float, which is the most common dropcap style.
Tips	To compensate for the extra empty space that occurs on the left of large fonts, you can shift the drop cap to the left by assigning a negative value to **margin-left**.

To compensate for the extra empty space below a drop cap that is created by a negative value in **top**, you can assign a negative value to **margin-bottom**. |
| **Related to** | Floating Graphical Drop Cap; Margin (Chapter 6); Relative, Float and Clear (Chapter 7); Offset Float, Offset Relative (Chapter 8) |
```

Floating Graphical Drop Cap

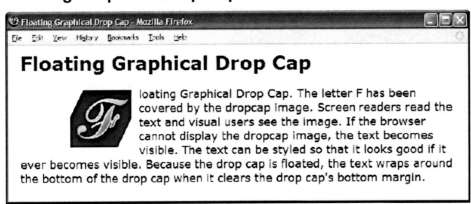

HTML

```
<h1>Floating Graphical Drop Cap</h1>

<p><span class="floating-dropcap">F<span></span></span>loating
  Graphical Drop Cap. The letter F has been covered by the dropcap image.
  Screen readers read the text and visual users see the image.
  If the browser cannot display the dropcap image, the text becomes visible.
  The text can be styled so that it looks good if it ever becomes visible.
  Because the drop cap is floated, the text wraps around the bottom of the drop cap
  when it clears the drop cap's bottom margin.</p>
```

CSS

```
.floating-dropcap { float:left; position:relative; top:5px;
  margin-left:80px; margin-right:12px; margin-bottom:0px;
  width:100px; height:90px;
  line-height:80px; text-align:right;
  font-size:100px; font-weight:bold;
  color:black; background-color:white; }

.floating-dropcap span { position:absolute;
  width:100px; height:90px; left:0; top:0; margin:0;
  background-image:url("f.jpg");
  background-repeat:no-repeat; }
```

Floating Graphical Drop Cap

Problem	You want to create a floating drop cap where the dropcap text is replaced by a graphic.
Solution	Combine the Floating Drop Cap pattern with the Text Replacement pattern.
	To use the Floating Drop Cap design pattern, tag the dropcap text in a terminal block element with an inline element assigned to the **"floating-dropcap"** class. Position the drop cap using **float:left**, **position:relative**, **top**, **margin-left**, **margin-right**, and **margin-bottom**. See Floating Drop Cap for details.
	To add in the Text Replacement design pattern, you can use **width** and **height** to size the float to the exact size of the dropcap image. You can also embed an empty span inside the float and use **background-image** to display the dropcap image as its background. You can style the embedded span to cover the text in the dropcap span using **position:absolute**, **left:0**, **top:0**, and **margin:0**. See Text Replacement in Chapter 10 for details.

Pattern

HTML
```
<INLINE class="floating-dropcap"> TEXT </INLINE>
```

CSS
```
.floating-dropcap { float:left;
    position:relative; top:-VALUE;
    margin-left:±VALUE; margin-right:±VALUE;
    margin-bottom:±VALUE;
    width:IMAGE_WIDTH; height:IMAGE_HEIGHT; }

.floating-dropcap span { position:absolute;
    width:IMAGE_WIDTH; height:IMAGE_HEIGHT;
    left:0; top:0; margin:0;
    background-image:url("FILE.EXT");
    background-repeat:no-repeat; }
```

Location	This pattern works anywhere you can use an inline element.
Advantages	The graphical floating drop cap is simple to position. It degrades gracefully when the graphic cannot be displayed because the dropcap text is displayed in its place. You can style the dropcap text so that it looks good whenever the browser cannot display the background image. Lastly, screen readers can read the dropcap text without any problem, while sighted users see the image in its place. A border around the terminal block containing the drop cap includes the drop cap.
Disadvantages	It has the disadvantages of a float, such as triggering browser bugs and interacting with other floats.
Related to	Padded Graphical Drop Cap, Floating Drop Cap, Marginal Graphical Drop Cap; Width, Height, Sized (Chapter 5); Margin, Background (Chapter 6); Positioned, Closest Positioned Ancestor, Absolute, Relative, Float and Clear (Chapter 7); Offset Float, Offset Relative, Aligned and Offset Absolute (Chapter 8); Text Replacement (Chapter 10)

Marginal Drop Cap

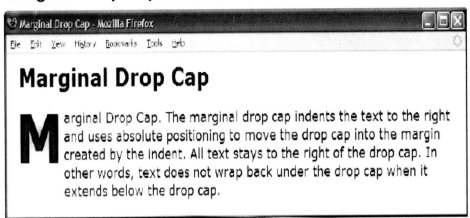

HTML

```
<h1>Marginal Drop Cap</h1>

<p class="indent"><span class="marginal-dropcap">M</span>arginal Drop Cap.
    The marginal drop cap indents the text to the right and uses absolute
    positioning to move the drop cap into the margin created by the indent. All
    text stays to the right of the drop cap. In other words, text does not wrap
    back under the drop cap when it extends below the drop cap.</p>
```

CSS

```
.indent { position:relative; margin-left:72px; margin-top:20px; }

.marginal-dropcap { position:absolute; left:-77px; top:-16px;
    font-size:80px; font-weight:bold;
    color:black; background-color:white; }
```

Marginal Drop Cap

Problem	You want to display the first letter of a block as a drop cap in the block's margin. You do not want the text to wrap back under the drop cap when it flows below the drop cap.
Solution	Use the Indented design pattern (Chapter 8) to create a left margin in the block and use absolute positioning to move the drop cap into the left margin. Use **margin-left** to indent the block element to make room for the drop cap in the left margin. Optionally, use **margin-top:+VALUE** to insert additional space above the block to make room for the drop cap. Assign **position: relative**, **position:absolute**, or **position:fixed** to the block so that the drop cap can be absolutely positioned relative to it. Tag the dropcap text with a span assigned to the **marginal-dropcap** class (or another class of your choosing). Use **position:absolute** and **left:-INDENT** to move the drop cap into the block's margin. The negative indent assigned to the drop cap is typically the negative of the indent assigned to the block. Occasionally, you may want to make it a few pixels larger than the block's indent because larger fonts have extra whitespace on their left. Use **top:±VALUE** to move the drop cap up or down.

Pattern	

HTML	`<BLOCK class="indent">`
	  `<INLINE class="marginal-dropcap"> TEXT </INLINE>`
	`</BLOCK>`

CSS	`.indent { position:relative;`
	  `margin-left:+INDENT;`
	  `margin-top:±VALUE; }`
	
	`.marginal-dropcap { position:absolute;`
	  `left:-INDENT;`
	  `top:±VALUE; }`

Location	This pattern works anywhere you can have a terminal block element.
Advantages	The marginal drop cap is simple to position, but it requires manually playing with the size of the margin and the size of the indent to accommodate the size of the drop cap's font.
Disadvantages	A border around the block containing the drop cap will not include the drop cap. This happens because the pattern uses **margin-left** instead of **padding-left** to create the indent. This avoids a positioning bug in Internet Explorer 6, but excludes the drop cap from being within the border around the block.
Related to	Margin (Chapter 6); Indented (Chapter 8); Positioned, Closest Positioned Ancestor, Absolute, Relative (Chapter 7); Indented, Offset Absolute, Aligned and Offset Absolute (Chapter 8); Left Marginal (Chapter 13)

Marginal Graphical Drop Cap

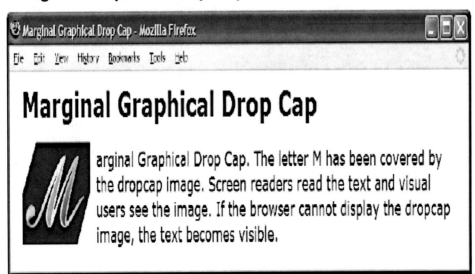

HTML

```
<h1>Marginal Graphical Drop Cap</h1>
<p class="indent"><span class="graphic-dropcap">M<span>arginal
  Graphical Drop Cap. The letter M has been covered by the dropcap image.
  Screen readers read the text and visual users see the image.
  If the browser cannot display the dropcap image,
  the text becomes visible.</p>
```

CSS

```
.indent { position:relative; margin-left:120px; margin-top:20px; }

.graphic-dropcap { position:absolute; left:-120px; top:6px;
  width:100px; height:90px;
  line-height:70px; padding-left:16px; text-align:right;
  font-size:80px; font-weight:bold;
  color:black; background-color:white; }

.graphic-dropcap span { position:absolute;
  width:100px; height:90px; left:0; top:0; margin:0;
  background-image:url("g.jpg");
  background-repeat:no-repeat; }
```

Marginal Graphical Drop Cap

Problem	You want to display the first letter of a paragraph as an image in a marginal drop cap. If the browser cannot display the image, you want the dropcap text to be visible. You want screenreader software to read the drop cap properly.
Solution	Combine the Marginal Drop Cap design pattern, the Text Replacement design pattern (Chapter 10), and the Top-Offset Sized Absolute Element design pattern.
	Indent a terminal block element to make room for the drop cap. Make the block positioned so the drop cap can be absolutely positioned relative to it. Tag the dropcap text with a span, and use absolute positioning to move it into the block's indent. Embed a span into the drop cap to display the dropcap graphic as its background image. Absolutely position the embedded span to cover the dropcap text so that it is hidden behind it.

Pattern

HTML

```
<BLOCK class="indent">
  <INLINE class="graphic-dropcap"> TEXT <span></span></INLINE>
</BLOCK>
```

CSS

```
.indent { position:relative;
  margin-left:+INDENT;
  margin-top:±VALUE; }

.graphic-dropcap { position:absolute;
  left:-INDENT;
  top:±VALUE;
  width:IMAGE_WIDTH;
  height:IMAGE_HEIGHT;
  line-height:+VALUE;
  padding-left:+VALUE;
  text-align:right; }

.graphic-dropcap span { position:absolute;
  width:IMAGE_WIDTH;
  height:IMAGE_HEIGHT;
  margin:0;
  left:0;
  top:0;
  background-image:url("FILE.EXT");
  background-repeat:no-repeat; }
```

Solution details	To make room for the drop cap, you can indent the terminal block element containing the drop cap using **margin-left:+VALUE**. The indent should be as large as or larger than the width of the dropcap image. The larger the indent, the more space you can put between the drop cap and the text. To move the drop cap above the block, you can use **margin-top: +VALUE** to make room for it. Because the drop cap is positioned relative to the block, you need to position the block using **position:relative**. You could also use **position:absolute** or **position:fixed** to make the block positioned.

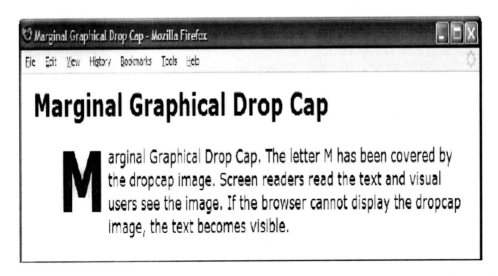

What the Marginal Graphical Drop Cap example looks like when the browser cannot load or display the image

Marginal Graphical Drop Cap cont.

Solution details cont.	You can tag the dropcap text with a span and assign it to the **graphic-dropcap** class. To move the drop cap into the space created by the indent, you can use **position:absolute**, and you can set **left** to the negative of the indent you assigned to **margin-left**. You can use **top** to move the drop cap up or down in relation to the block. You need to use **width** and **height** to size the drop cap to the exact size of the image. This ensures the dropcap text will be completely covered by the dropcap image.
	In case the image cannot be displayed (see Figure 18-1), you can use font properties to style the dropcap text. You can use **line-height** to move the dropcap text up or down. You can use **text-align:right** to move the dropcap text next to the block and **padding-left:+VALUE** to move it even closer to the block.
	To display the dropcap image over the top of the dropcap text, you can embed a span in the graphical dropcap span and use **background-image** to display the dropcap image in it. To hide the dropcap text behind the image, the image should not have a transparent background. To position the dropcap image over the dropcap text, you can use **position:absolute**, **left:0**, **top:0**, and **margin:0**. You need to use **width** and **height** to size the span to the image.
Location	This pattern works anywhere you can have a terminal block element.
Advantages	The graphical drop cap is simple to position. It degrades gracefully when the graphic cannot be displayed because the dropcap text is displayed in its place. You can style the dropcap text so that it looks good whenever the browser cannot display the background image. Lastly, screen readers can read the dropcap text without any problem, while sighted users see the image in its place.

Marginal Graphical Drop Cap cont.

Disadvantages	Like all marginal design patterns, a border around the terminal block containing the drop cap will not include the drop cap.
Related to	Floating Graphical Drop Cap, Padded Graphical Drop Cap; Margin (Chapter 6); Positioned, Closest Positioned Ancestor, Absolute, Relative (Chapter 7); Indented, Offset Absolute, Aligned and Offset Absolute (Chapter 8); Top-Offset Sized Absolute Element (Chapter 9); Text Replacement (Chapter 10), Horizontal-Aligned Content (Chapter 12); Left Marginal (Chapter 13)

CHAPTER 19

Callouts and Quotes

This chapter discusses design patterns that create **callouts** and **quotes**.

A callout is a key point pulled out of the document to grab a reader's attention so he or she will read the document and remember the point after having read it. A callout is repeated twice in a document: once as part of the body of the document and once again for display as a callout. A callout is displayed prominently so the reader cannot miss it. Because a callout is extracted from a document's text, it is often an inline element, although it could be a block element.

I have grouped callouts and quotes together because they are closely related. Callouts are also known as **pull quotes** because they are quotes pulled from the document. There are differences between pull quotes and quotes. A pull quote (or callout) requires the same text to be repeated twice within a document, whereas a quote occurs only once. Also, a quote typically includes a citation, whereas a pull quote does not. Lastly, quotes belong visually and semantically as part of the content, whereas callouts are visually and semantically set apart from the content and are often moved to the left or right sides or margins of a document. In the rest of this chapter, I will refer to pull quotes as callouts to avoid confusing them with regular quotes.

Chapter Outline

- **Left Floating Callout** shows how to create a callout and float it to the left.

- **Right Floating Callout** shows how to create a callout and float it to the right.

- **Center Callout** shows how to create a callout and center it.

- **Left Marginal Callout** shows how to create a callout in the left margin using the left marginal design pattern.

- **Right Marginal Callout** shows how to create a callout in the right margin using the right marginal design pattern.

- **Block Quote** shows how to create a block quote with a citation that is automatically centered and styled with graphical background quotes.

- **Inline Block Quote** shows how to render an inline quote as a block quote.

- **Inline Quote** shows how to create an inline quote with a citation.

Left Floating Callout

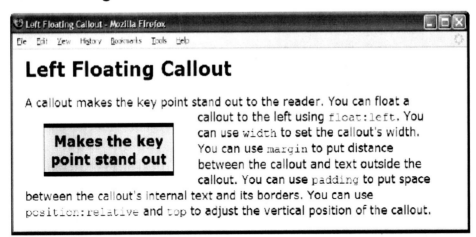

HTML

```
<h1>Left Floating Callout</h1>

<p>A callout makes the key point stand out to the reader.

    <span class="callout">Makes the key point stand out</span>

You can float a callout to the left using <code>float:left</code>.
You can use <code>width</code> to set the callout's width.
You can use <code>margin</code> to put distance between the callout and
text outside the callout. You can use <code>padding</code> to put space
between the callout's internal text and its borders. You can use
<code>position:relative</code> and <code>top</code> to adjust the vertical
position of the callout.</p>
```

CSS

```
.callout-left { float:left; width:200px; padding:6px;
  margin:10px 40px 10px 30px;
  position:relative; top:10px;
  font-size:22px; line-height:normal; font-weight:bold;
  text-align:center; color:black; background-color:gold;
  border-left:1px solid black; border-right:1px solid black;
  border-top:6px solid black; border-bottom:6px solid black; }
```

Left Floating Callout

Problem	You want to remove content from the flow and display it prominently to the reader on the left side. In general terms, you want to pull content out of the flow to emphasize it.
Solution	A callout is removed from the normal flow and styled to make its content stand out to the user. It usually has a larger font, margins, borders, and background around the outside to set it apart from surrounding content. Callouts can include all kinds of content, such as quotes, key phrases, attention getters, and so on. You can assign an inline element to the **callout** class. You can use **float:left** to float the callout to the left. You can use **padding** to put distance between the callout's content and its border. You can use **position:relative** to position the callout so you can move it. You can use **top** to move the callout up or down. You can use **margin-left** to move the callout to the right. You can use **margin-right** to put distance between the callout's right border and external text. You can use **margin-top** and **margin-bottom** to put distance between the callout's top and bottom borders and external text.
Pattern	
HTML	`<INLINE class="callout"> CONTENT </INLINE>`

CSS	`.callout { float:left; position:relative;`
	`    width:+VALUE;`
	`    padding:+VALUE;`
	`    margin-top:+VALUE; margin-bottom:+VALUE;`
	`    margin-left:±VALUE; margin-right:+VALUE;`
	`    top:±VALUE; }`

Location	This pattern works on any element.
Limitations	If you left-float any other elements close to where the callout is floated, they may stack next to each other. This would likely detract from the callout effect. Floats tend to bring out bugs in browsers.
Tips	A callout should be positioned in the text where it makes sense if it were read as part of the text. A screen reader will read it where it occurs, and a browser that does not support absolute positioning will display it inline where it occurs. I recommend placing the callout's markup immediately after the text it is quoting. Screen readers will read it twice, which emphasizes the callout aurally through repetition just like it is emphasized visually.
Related to	Right Floating Callout, Center Callout; Floated Box (Chapter 4); Width (Chapter 5); Margin, Padding (Chapter 6); Float and Clear, Relative Float (Chapter 7); Offset Float (Chapter 8)

Right Floating Callout

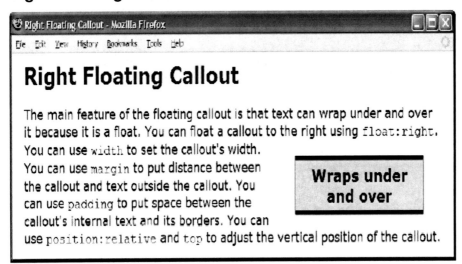

HTML

```
<h1>Right Floating Callout</h1>

<p>The main feature of the floating callout is that text can wrap
   under and over it because it is a float.

   <span class="callout">Wraps under and over</span>

   You can float a callout to the right using <code>float:right</code>.
   You can use <code>width</code> to set the callout's width.
   You can use <code>margin</code> to put distance between the callout and
   text outside the callout. You can use <code>padding</code> to put space
   between the callout's internal text and its borders. You can use
   <code>position:relative</code> and <code>top</code> to adjust the vertical
   position of the callout.</p>
```

CSS

```
.callout { float:right; width:200px; padding:6px;
   margin:10px 30px 10px 40px;
   position:relative; top:10px;
   font-size:22px; line-height:normal; font-weight:bold;
   text-align:center; color:black; background-color:gold;
   border-left:1px solid black; border-right:1px solid black;
   border-top:6px solid black; border-bottom:6px solid black; }
```

Right Floating Callout

Problem	You want to remove content from the flow and display it prominently to the reader on the right side.
	In general terms, you want to pull content out of the flow to emphasize it.
Solution	A callout is removed from the normal flow and styled to make its content stand out to the user. It usually has a larger font, margins, borders, and background around the outside to set it apart from surrounding content. Callouts can include all kinds of content, such as quotes, key phrases, attention getters, and so on.
	You can assign an inline element to the **callout** class. You can use **float:right** to float the inline element to the right content edge of its parent terminal block element. You can use **padding** to put distance between the callout's content and its border. You can use **position:relative** to position the callout so you can move it. You can use **top** to move the callout up or down. You can use **margin-left** to put distance between the callout's left border and external text. You can use **margin-right** to move the callout to the left. You can use **margin-top** and **margin-bottom** to put distance between the callout's top and bottom borders and external text.
Pattern	
HTML	`<INLINE class="callout"> CONTENT </INLINE>`
| CSS | ```
.callout { float:right; position:relative;
    width:+VALUE;
    padding:+VALUE;
    margin-top:+VALUE; margin-bottom:+VALUE;
    margin-left:+VALUE; margin-right:±VALUE;
    top:±VALUE;  }
``` |
Location	This pattern works on any element.
Limitations	If you right-float any other elements close to where the callout is floated, they may stack next to each other. This would likely detract from the callout effect. Floats tend to bring out bugs in browsers.
Tip	A callout should be positioned in the text where it makes sense if it were read as part of the text.
Related to	Left Floating Callout, Center Callout; Floated Box (Chapter 4); Width (Chapter 5); Margin, Padding (Chapter 6); Float and Clear, Relative Float (Chapter 7); Offset Float (Chapter 8)
```

Center Callout

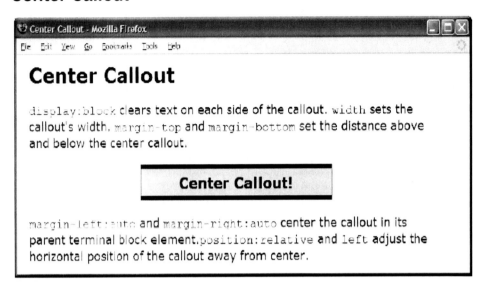

HTML

```
<h1>Center Callout</h1>

<p><code>display:block</code> clears text on each side of the callout. <code>
    width</code> sets the callout's width. <code>margin-top</code> and <code>
    margin-bottom</code> set the distance above and below the center callout.

    <span class="callout">Centered Callout!</span>

    <code>margin-left:auto</code> and <code>margin-right:auto</code> center the
    callout in its parent terminal block element.<code>position:relative</code>
    and <code>left</code> adjust the horizontal position of the callout
    away from center.</p>
```

CSS

```
.callout { display:block; width:300px; margin:20px auto; padding:6px;
    position:relative; left:0%;
    font-size:22px; line-height:normal; font-weight:bold;
    text-align:center; color:black; background-color:gold;
    border-left:1px solid black; border-right:1px solid black;
    border-top:6px solid black; border-bottom:6px solid black; }
```

Center Callout

Problem	You want to remove content from the flow and display it prominently to the reader in the center of the text with no content flowing to its left or right.
	In general terms, you want an inline element to be rendered like a block element.
Solution	A callout is removed from the normal flow and styled to make its content stand out to the user. It usually has a larger font, margins, borders, and background to set it apart from surrounding content. Callouts can include all kinds of content, such as quotes, key phrases, attention getters, and so forth.
	You can assign an inline element to the **callout** class. You can use **display:block** to display the inline element as a block element. You can use **width** to set the callout's width. If content is wider than the width, a browser wraps the content and extends the height of the callout. You can use **margin-left:auto** and **margin-right:auto** to center the callout. You can use **margin-top** and **margin-bottom** to put space above the callout's top border and below its bottom border. You can use **padding** to put distance between the callout's content and its border. You can use **position:relative** and **left** to move it to the left or right of center. Using a percentage in **left** is convenient because it is a percentage of the callout container's width.
Pattern	
HTML	`<INLINE class="callout"> CONTENT </INLINE>`

CSS	`.callout { display:block; position:relative;`
	`    width:+VALUE;`
	`    margin-top:+VALUE; margin-bottom:+VALUE;`
	`    left:±VALUE%; padding:+VALUE;`
	`    margin-left:auto; margin-right:auto; }`

Location	This pattern works on any element.
Limitations	CSS 3 provides no automatic way to flow content on the left or right of a centered callout. Thus, a centered callout extends across the entire width of its parent.
Tips	A callout should be positioned in the text where it makes sense if it were read as part of the text.
Related to	Left Floating Callout, Right Floating Callout; Display, Block Box (Chapter 4); Width (Chapter 5); Margin, Padding (Chapter 6); Relative (Chapter 7); Offset Relative (Chapter 8); Center Aligned (Chapter 9); Blocked (Chapter 11)

453

Left Marginal Callout

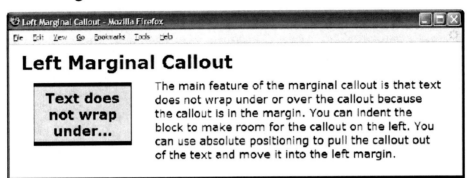

HTML

```
<h1>Left Marginal Callout</h1>

<p class="left-marginal">
  <span class="callout">Text does not wrap under...</span>
  The main feature of the marginal callout is that text does not wrap
  under or over the callout because the callout is in the margin.
  You can indent the block to make room for the callout on the left.
  You can use absolute positioning to pull the callout out of the text
  and move it into the left margin.</p>
```

CSS

```
.left-marginal { position:relative; width:470px; margin-left:230px; }

.callout { position:absolute; left:-220px; width:160px; margin-top:5px;
  line-height:normal; text-align:center; padding:5px 0;
  font-size:22px; font-weight:bold;
  color:black; background-color:gold;
  border-left:1px solid black; border-right:1px solid black;
  border-top:6px solid black; border-bottom:6px solid black; }
```

Left Marginal Callout

Problem	You want to excerpt text out of the normal flow and move it into the left margin as a callout. You want items in the margin to be positioned vertically where they would have been in the flow. You do not mind using fixed widths. You do not use many callouts, so the risk of overlap is minimal.
Solution	You can indent text to create a margin on the left and then use absolute positioning to remove content from the normal flow into the margin.
	You can use **margin-left** to indent the terminal block. You can use **position:relative** to position the block so its inline children can be positioned relative to its margin. You can use **margin-right:auto** and **width** to fix the width of the terminal block so that the content does not reflow. Without a fixed width, content reflows when the viewport resizes, and reflow may change the vertical location of callouts, causing them to overlap.
	You can assign an inline element to the **callout** class. You can use **position:absolute** to remove the inline element from the flow. You can use **width** to size the inline element to fit into the margin. You can assign a negative value to **left** to move the inline element into the left margin. You can use **margin-top** to move the inline element up or down.
Pattern	

HTML	<pre><code><TERMINAL_BLOCK class="left-marginal">
	  TEXT
	  <INLINE_TEXT class="callout"> CALLOUT TEXT </INLINE_TEXT>
	  TEXT
	</TERMINAL_BLOCK></code></pre>

CSS	<pre><code>.left-marginal { position:relative; width:+VALUE;
	  margin-left:+VALUE; margin-right:auto; }
	.callout { position:absolute;
	  left:-VALUE;
	  width:+VALUE;
	  margin-top:±VALUE; }</code></pre>

Location	This pattern works only on inline elements inside terminal block elements.
Caution	The layout created by this pattern does *not* protect content from overlapping. It is very easy to move callouts into the margin and to have them overlap each other and other content moved into the margin.
Tips	A callout should be positioned in the text where it makes sense if it were read as part of the text.
	You can combine this pattern with Right Marginal Callout.
	This pattern is visually similar to HTML tables, but the markup is more flexible. You can pull out any inline content and move it into the margin.
Related to	Right Marginal Callout; Left Marginal (Chapter 13)

Right Marginal Callout

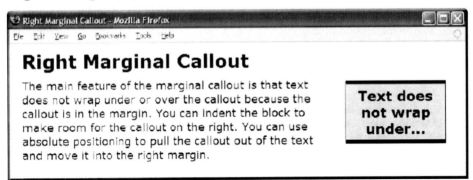

HTML

```
<h1>Right Marginal Callout</h1>

<p class="right-marginal">
    <span class="callout">Text does not wrap under...</span>

The main feature of the marginal callout is that text does not wrap
under or over the callout because the callout is in the margin.
You can indent the block to make room for the callout on the right.
You can use absolute positioning to pull the callout out of the text
and move it into the right margin.</p>
```

CSS

```
.right-marginal { position:relative; width:490px; margin-right:230px;  }

.callout { position:absolute; right:-200px; width:160px; margin-top:5px;
    line-height:normal; text-align:center; padding:5px 0;
    font-size:22px; font-weight:bold;
    color:black; background-color:gold;
    border-left:1px solid black; border-right:1px solid black;
    border-top:6px solid black; border-bottom:6px solid black; }
```

Right Marginal Callout

Problem	You want to excerpt text out of the normal flow and move it into the right margin as a callout. You want items in the margin to be positioned vertically where they would have been in the flow. You do not mind using fixed widths. You do not use many callouts, so the risk of overlap is minimal.
Solution	You can indent text to create a margin on the right and then use absolute positioning to remove content from the normal flow into the margin.
	You can use **margin-right** to indent the terminal block. You can use **position: relative** to position the block so its inline children can be positioned relative to its margin. You can use **margin-left:auto** and **width** to fix the width of the terminal block so that the content does not reflow. Without a fixed width, content reflows when the viewport resizes, and reflow may change the vertical location of callouts, causing them to overlap.
	You can assign an inline element to the **callout** class. You can use **position: absolute** to remove the inline element from the flow. You can use **width** to size the inline element to fit into the margin. You can assign a negative value to **left** to move the inline element into the left margin. You can use **margin-top** to move the inline element up or down.

Pattern

HTML	<pre><code><TERMINAL_BLOCK class="right-marginal">
TEXT
<INLINE_TEXT class="callout"> CALLOUT TEXT </INLINE_TEXT>
TEXT
</TERMINAL_BLOCK></code></pre>
CSS	<pre><code>.right-marginal { position:relative; width:+VALUE;
margin-right:+VALUE; margin-left:auto; }
.callout { position:absolute;
right:-VALUE;
width:+VALUE;
margin-top:±VALUE; }</code></pre>

Location	This pattern works only on inline elements inside terminal block elements.
Caution	The layout created by this pattern does *not* protect content from overlapping. It is very easy to move callouts into the margin and to have them overlap each other and other content moved into the margin.
Tips	A callout should be positioned in the text where it makes sense if it were read as part of the text.
	You can combine this pattern with Left Marginal Callout.
	This pattern is visually similar to HTML tables, but the markup is more flexible. You can pull out any inline content and move it into the margin.
Related to	Left Marginal Callout; Right Marginal (Chapter 13)

Block Quote

○ ○ ○   Mozilla Firefox

Block Quote

A block quote contains one or more paragraphs, and a citation. A block quote is not repeated twice in the document like a callout.

This example includes an embedded, decorative division so it can display a graphical closing quote.

Pro HTML5 and CSS3 Design Patterns

HTML

```
<h1>Block Quote</h1>

<blockquote><div>
  <p>A block quote contains one or more paragraphs, and a citation.
    A block quote is not repeated twice in the document like a callout.</p>

  <p>This example includes an embedded, decorative division so it can display
    a graphical closing quote.</p>
  <cite>Pro HTML5 and CSS3 Design Patterns<cite>
  </div></blockquote>
```

CSS

```
blockquote { width:500px; margin:10px auto;
  position:relative; left:0%; text-align:justify;
  line-height:1.3em; color:black;
  padding-top:40px; padding-left:40px;
  background:url("dq1.jpg") no-repeat top left; }

blockquote div { padding-bottom:10px; padding-right:40px;
  background:url("dq2.jpg") no-repeat bottom right; }

blockquote p { margin:0; margin-bottom:10px; }

blockquote cite { display:block; text-align:right; font-size:0.9em; }
```

Block Quote

Problem	You want to create a block quote. You want to set a quote apart from the rest of the content and make it easily recognizable as a block quote. You want the block quote to include one or more paragraphs and a citation. You want it to be styled with graphical opening and closing quotes.
Solution	Like a center callout, a block quote usually has a different font, margins, borders, and background to set it apart from surrounding content.
	You can embed the block quote in the **<blockquote>** element. You can use **width** to set its width. You can use **margin-left:auto** and **margin-right:auto** to center it. You can use **margin-top** and **margin-bottom** to put space above and below it. You can use **position:relative** and **left** to move it to the left or right of center.
	You can use **background** to apply a background image to the block quote. You can use **padding-top** and **padding-left** to put space between the image and the block quote's text. You can also embed a division immediately inside the block quote to display a second background image. You can use **padding-bottom** and **padding-right** to put space between its image and the block quote's text.
	You can use the **<cite>** element to place a citation following the block quote. You can place any inline content in **<cite>**. A citation represents the title of a work, e.g., a song, a paper, an essay, a script, etc.

Pattern

HTML
```
<blockquote><div>
  <p> QUOTE </p> <p> MORE QUOTE </p>
  <cite> <a href="URL"> CITATION </a> </cite>
</div></blockquote>
```

CSS
```
blockquote { width:+VALUE; margin:+VALUE;
  position:relative; left:±VALUE%;
  padding-top:+VALUE; padding-left:+VALUE;
  background:url("FILE.EXT") no-repeat top left; }

blockquote div { padding-bottom:+VALUE; padding-right:+VALUE;
  background:url("FILE.EXT") no-repeat bottom right; }

blockquote p { STYLING_PARAGRAPHS_IN_A_BLOCKQUOTE }

blockquote cite { STYLING_CITATIONS_IN_A_BLOCKQUOTE }
```

Location	This pattern works only inside block containers because **<blockquote>** is a block. See Inline Block Quote when you need the block quote to be inline.
Tip	A block quote can contain any inline content, including images and objects.
Related to	Center Callout, Inline Block Quote, Inline Quote; Display, Block Box (Chapter 4); Width (Chapter 5); Margin, Padding, Background (Chapter 6); Relative (Chapter 7); Offset Relative (Chapter 8)

Inline Block Quote

◉ ○ ○   Mozilla Firefox

Inline Block Quote

This quote is embedded in a paragraph, but looks like a block quote.

An inline block quote is marked up with inline elements, but looks like a block quote because its elements are rendered using display:block.

I embedded a decorative span in this example to display a graphical closing quote.

Pro HTML5 and CSS3 Design Patterns

HTML

```
<h1>Inline Block Quote</h1>

<p>This quote is embedded in a paragraph, but looks like a block quote.

<span class="blockquote"><span>
  An inline block quote is marked up with inline elements, but looks like a
  block quote because its elements are rendered using <code>display:block</code>.
  <br /> <br />I embedded a decorative span in this example to display
  a graphical closing quote.

  <cite>Pro HTML5 and CSS3 Design Patterns</cite></span></span> </p>
```

CSS

```
.blockquote { display:block; width:500px; margin:10px auto;
  position:relative; left:0%; text-align:justify;
  line-height:1.3em; color:black;
  padding-top:40px; padding-left:40px;
  background:url("dq1.jpg") no-repeat top left white; }

.blockquote span { display:block;
  padding-bottom:20px; padding-right:40px;
  background:url("dq2.jpg") no-repeat bottom right; }

.blockquote cite { display:block; text-align:right; font-size:0.9em; }
```

Inline Block Quote

Problem	You want to create a block quote inside a paragraph.
	You cannot use **<blockquote>** because it cannot be embedded in a paragraph since it is a block element. You should not use the **<q>** element, for the reasons cited in the discussion of the Inline Quote design pattern.
Solution	You can embed the block quote in **<span class="blockquote">** instead of **<blockquote>** or **<q>**. You can use **display:block** on the span and all child elements to display them as blocks. This is the key ingredient of this design pattern. Once all the elements are displayed as blocks, the rest of the rules work like the Block Quote design pattern.
Pattern	
| HTML | ```
<span class="blockquote"><span>
  QUOTE <br /><br /> MORE QUOTE
  <cite> <a href="URL"> CITATION </a> </cite>
</span></span>
``` |
| CSS | ```
.blockquote { display:block;
  width:+VALUE; margin:+VALUE;
  position:relative; left:±VALUE%;
  padding-top:+VALUE; padding-left:+VALUE;
  background:url("FILE.EXT") no-repeat top left; }

.blockquote span { display:block;
  padding-bottom:+VALUE; padding-right:+VALUE;
  background:url("FILE.EXT") no-repeat bottom right; }

.blockquote cite { display:block; }
``` |
Location	This pattern works in any inline context.
Tips	You can insert line breaks to simulate separate paragraphs within the quote.
	It is better to use **<blockquote>** for block quotes because search engines and document processors understand the meaning of **<blockquote>**. Search engines give greater importance to content in **<blockquote>** and **<cite>**.
Related to	Center Callout, Block Quote, Inline Quote; Display, Block Box (Chapter 4); Width (Chapter 5); Margin, Padding, Background (Chapter 6); Relative (Chapter 7); Offset Relative (Chapter 8); Blocked (Chapter 11)

Inline Quote

Mozilla Firefox

Inline Quote

"A quote should be followed by a citation." (*Pro HTML5 and CSS3 Design Patterns*)

" "If you embed a quote inside <q> most browsers will automatically insert double quotes — whether or not you want them!" (*Pro HTML5 and CSS3 Design Patterns*)"

HTML

```
<h1>Inline Quote</h1>

<p><span class="quote">
  "A quote should be followed by a citation."
  (<cite>Pro HTML5 and CSS3 Design Patterns</cite>)</span></p>

<p><q>  <!-- Do not use <q>. -->
  "If you embed a quote inside <code>&lt;q&gt;</code> most browsers
  will automatically insert double quotes — whether or not you want them!"
  (<cite> Pro HTML5 and CSS3 Design Patterns</cite>)</q></p>
```

CSS

```
.quote { letter-spacing:0.07em; }
.quote cite { font-size:0.9em; }
```

Inline Quote

Problem	You want to create an inline quote.
	You cannot use **\<blockquote\>** because it is a block element.
	You should not use the **\<q\>** element, even though it was designed for inline quotes, because most browsers automatically insert English-style double quotes around the contents of **\<q\>**. This is a problem because there are over 23 different types of international quotation marks and many ways these can be combined to indicate quotes in different languages, dialects, and writing styles. Because of this complexity, only an author can make the choice of quotation marks. It is unfortunate that the HTML specification requires browsers to automatically insert quotes around the contents of **\<q\>**. Internet Explorer does not insert quotes, and other browsers should follow its lead.
Solution	You can enclose an inline quote in **\<span class="quote"\>** to identify it as a quote. You can include a citation following the text of the quote and before the end tag of the **\</span\>**. A citation is typically placed within parentheses and is enclosed in the **\<cite\>** element. You can place any inline content in **\<cite\>**. A citation commonly contains a description of the source of the quote, which is commonly embedded in a hyperlink to the actual source.
	The double quote marks shown in the following pattern can be replaced by any type of quote marks.
Pattern	
| HTML | ```
<span class="quote">
    "QUOTE" (<cite><a href="URL"> SOURCE </a></cite>)</span>
``` |
| CSS | ```
.quote { STYLES }
.quote cite { STYLES }
``` |
Location	This pattern works on any element.
Tips	Because it is natural to put line breaks between elements like **\<cite\>** and **\<a\>**, it is easy to introduce undesirable whitespace between the parentheses and the contents of the citation. The obvious solution is not to put whitespace between these elements. If that is not an option, you can put a line break inside a tag instead of between tags. In my example, I put a line break inside the **\<a\>** tags just before the closing greater-than sign.
Example	Notice how Firefox added quotation marks around the second example because it was embedded in **\<q\>** instead of **\<span class="quote"\>**.
Related to	Inline Block Quote; Inline Elements (Chapter 2)

Alerts

This chapter discusses design patterns that create an **alert**. An alert points out important information to the reader by separating it from the content. There are two basic types of alerts: **dynamic** and **static**. The first three design patterns in this chapter are dynamic alerts, which dynamically display information as a user interacts with the document. The remaining alerts in this chapter are static alerts, which are always displayed in a document. The Alert design pattern is an HTML pattern, which is basically a heading followed by the alert's message. The design patterns following Alert combine it with other design patterns, demonstrating how you can combine existing design patterns to create new design patterns.

Chapter Outline

- **JavaScript Alert** shows how to dynamically pop up an alert based on an event.

- **Tooltip Alert** shows how to create a tooltip to show the user extra information.

- **Pop-Up Alert** shows how to pop up an alert to show the user extra information.

- **Alert** shows the basic HTML structure of an alert.

- **Inline Alert** shows how to make an alert using an inline element.

- **Hanging Alert** shows how to move the alert's heading to the left side and the content to the right side by using a hanging indent that does not require extra markup.

- **Graphical Alert** shows how to move the alert's heading to the left side and the content to the right side and replace the heading with an image.

- **Run-In Alert** shows how to run the alert's heading into the first line of the content.

- **Floating Alert** shows how to float an alert to the left or the right of the content with its heading on the left and its content on the right.

- **Left Marginal Alert** shows how to move an alert into the left margin using absolute positioning.

- **Right Marginal Alert** shows how to move an alert into the right margin using absolute positioning.

- **Form Validation** shows how to natively validate HTML5 forms and alert the user for wrong input.

JavaScript Alert

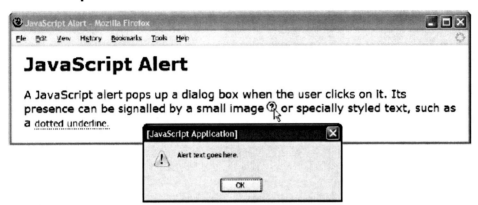

HTML

```
<h1>JavaScript Alert</h1>

<p>A JavaScript alert pops up a dialog box when the user clicks it.
  Its presence can be signalled by a small image<img class="alert-image"
  onclick="alert('Alert text goes here.');" src="help.gif" alt="alert" />

  or specially styled text, such as a
  <em class="alert" onclick="alert('Alert text goes here.');">
  dotted underline.</em>
</p>
```

CSS

```
*.alert-image { cursor:pointer; margin-left:3px; }

*.alert { cursor:pointer; border-bottom:1px dotted;
  font-style:normal; font-size:0.8em; }
```

JavaScript Alert

Problem	You want to insert helpful, yet nonessential messages into your document, such as tips or help. You do not want the alert to be visible unless the reader clicks it. You want an unobtrusive way to show the reader that the alert is present. You also want the alert to be accessible to nonsighted users.
Solution	To signal the presence of the alert, you can insert a small image following the text for which you want to supply extra information, or you can style the text. A dotted underline is the traditional signal that text has extra information associated with it. The image or styled text signals the presence of an alert. You can put the text of the alert in the JavaScript **alert()** function and put the alert function in the image's **onclick** attribute. A browser displays the alert in a pop-up dialog box when the user clicks the image. Screen readers recognize the **onclick** attribute and read its contents to the user.
| **Patterns**<br><br>HTML | ```html
<img class="alert-image" src="FILE.EXT"
  onclick="alert('ALERT TEXT');" alt="alert" />
```<br>*or*<br>```html
<em class="alert" onclick="alert('ALERT TEXT');"> TEXT </em>
``` |
| CSS | ```css
*.alert-image { cursor:pointer; }
*.alert { cursor:pointer; border-bottom:1px dotted; }
``` |
Location	This pattern works on any element.
Limitations	**onclick** is the only event that all major screen readers recognize and handle properly. Other events require testing for compatibility with screen readers.
Advantages	JavaScript alerts can contain several paragraphs of text and stay open as long as the user wants. This is a significant advantage over the Tooltip Alert design pattern.
Disadvantages	Normally putting JavaScript directly in markup is a poor practice. This case is an exception, because the script *is* content (a message to the user) and belongs in the content. For this reason, screen readers are designed to read the contents of **onclick** attributes. Pop-up dialog boxes annoy users because they interrupt the workflow. For example, the dialog box usually opens in the middle of the browser window, taking the user's eyes away from where he or she was reading. After having to click the OK button to close the dialog box, the user has to rescan the text to find the place where he or she was reading. The dialog box is unpleasant to look at. Its contents cannot be styled, and the dialog box cannot be styled. And unlike a web page, a user cannot zoom in to make the dialog box's small text easier to read.
Tip	Most popular JavaScript frameworks and toolkits have ways to create alerts. Since these usually have much more control over the styling of the alert box, they are more appropriate than simply using **alert()**. You can have a look at **http://plugins.jquery.com/plugin-tags/alert** for examples of alert plug-ins that work with the jQuery JavaScript toolkit. The W3C has been working on a new specification called "Web Notifications," which provides an API to display simple alerts to users outside of the web page. This spec does not specify exactly how a user agent should display these notifications, so presentation depends on the browser, e.g., it might appear at a corner of the user's display, or an area within the chrome of the user agent, etc. Although this functionality is supported at this time only in Google Chrome, it will probably become mainstream in the future.
Related to	Alert, Inline Alert; Image, Replaced Text (Chapter 14); Event Styling (Chapter 17)
```

Tooltip Alert

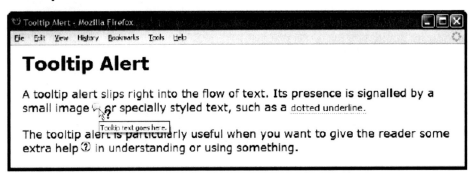

HTML

```
<h1>Tooltip Alert</h1>

<p>A tooltip alert slips right into the flow of text. It is usually signalled
  by a small image<img class="imagetip" src="alert.gif"
  title="Tooltip text goes here."
  alt="Tooltip text goes here." />

  or some type of text decoration, such as a
  <em class="texttip" title="Tooltip text goes here.">
  dotted underline<img src="invisible.gif" alt="Tooltip text goes here." />.</em>
</p>
```

CSS

```
*.tooltip-image { cursor:help; margin-left:3px; }

*.tooltip { cursor:help; border-bottom:1px dotted;
  font-style:normal; font-size:0.8em; }
```

Tooltip Alert

Problem	You want to insert brief, helpful, nonessential tips into your document. You do not want it to be visible unless the reader moves the mouse over it. You want an unobtrusive way to show the reader that the tip is present. You also want it to be accessible to nonsighted users. You do not want to use JavaScript in any way.
Solution	You can insert a small image following the text for which you want to supply extra information. This image signals the presence of a tip. You can put the tip in its **title** and **alt** attributes. A browser automatically displays the **title** text when the user mouses over the image, and a screen reader automatically reads the **alt** text of the image.
	If you do not want to use an image, you can style text to signal the presence of a tip. A dotted underline is the traditional signal that text has extra information. To make the tip accessible, you can insert a transparent, 1-pixel image with an **alt** tag set to the tip's text.
Patterns	

HTML	```<img class="tooltip-image" src="FILE.EXT"```
	  ```title="TOOLTIP TEXT" alt="TOOLTIP TEXT" />```
	
	or
	
	```<em class="tooltip" title="TOOLTIP TEXT">```
	  ```<img src="invisible.gif" alt="TOOLTIP TEXT." /> TEXT </em>```

CSS	```*.tooltip-image { cursor:help; }``` ```*.tooltip { cursor:help; border-bottom:1px dotted; }```
Location	This pattern works inline.
Limitations	Screen readers do not read **title** attributes, but they do read the **alt** attributes of images. That is why this design pattern requires the use of an image, even if you do not want sighted users to see it.
	Tooltips cannot be styled and displayed in tiny text, which can be hard to read. Tooltips are displayed after a one-second delay, which annoys users in a hurry, but appropriately prevents tips from popping up when the user unintentionally passes over them with the mouse. Lastly, tooltips disappear after six seconds, which limits the readable length to a brief sentence.
	Firefox 2 displays only the first 75 characters of the title in a tooltip. Other browsers display all the text in a title. Newer versions display beyond 75 characters.
Tips	The most natural and accessible place to put a tooltip image is after the text for which it provides help. Screen readers always read the image's **alt** text, and if the image cannot be displayed, a browser displays the **alt** text. It makes the most sense for the user to read or hear a tip after reading or hearing the text for which it provides extra information.
Related to	Alert, Inline Alert; Inline Elements (Chapter 2); Border (Chapter 6); Image, Replaced Text (Chapter 14)

Pop-Up Alert

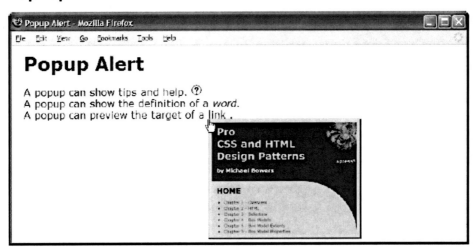

HTML

```
<h1>Popup Alert</h1>
<div>
  <p>A pop-up can show tips and help.
    <span class="popup-trigger" id="pt1"><img src="help.gif" alt="tip" />
    <span class="popup medium border">Pop-up help goes here.</span></span>
    <br />
    A pop-up can show the definition of a
    <dfn class="popup-trigger" id="pt2">word.
    <span class="popup medium border">Pop-up definition goes here.</span></dfn>
    <br />
    A pop-up can preview the target of a
    <a class="popup-trigger" id="pt3"
      href="http://www.cssdesignpatterns.com">link
      <img class="popup border" src="css-design-patterns-preview.jpg"
        alt="cssDesignPatterns.com preview" /></a>.</p></div>
```

CSS

```
*.popup-trigger { position:relative; }

*.popup { position:absolute; left:0; top:1em; z-index:1;
  padding:5px; text-align:center; }

*.popup-trigger *.popup { visibility:hidden; }

/* Nonessential rules are not shown */
```

Pop-Up Alert

Problem	You want to insert a pop-up to show helpful information to the reader. You want the pop-up to be hidden until the reader moves the mouse over it or clicks it. You want the browser to show the pop-up automatically like a tooltip, and you want it to remain showing until the user clicks it or moves the mouse away from it. You want an unobtrusive way to show the reader that the pop-up is present. You also want it to be accessible to nonsighted users. You want complete control over the style of the pop-up box, the position of the pop-up box, and the style of its contents. You do not want to insert any JavaScript into the document body.
Solution	You can insert an inline element with the **popup-trigger** class into your document. In the example, I used **\<span\>**, **\<dfn\>**, and **\<a\>** elements. When the user mouses over or clicks the contents of the pop-up-trigger element, this triggers the browser to display the pop-up. You can style the pop-up trigger with **position:relative** so you can position the pop-up relative to it.

Inside the pop-up-trigger element you can insert an inline element to hold the pop-up content. In the example, I use **\<span\>** and **\<img\>** elements. You can assign this element to the **popup** class. You can absolutely position the pop-up element to remove it out of the normal flow. You can use **left:0** and **top:1em** to position the pop-up immediately below the pop-up trigger. You can use **z-index:1** to make sure pop-ups are displayed in front of pop-up triggers.

You can use JavaScript libraries to dynamically assign events to pop-up-trigger elements. This keeps the markup in the body completely free from JavaScript, as described in the following sections. |

Pattern

| HTML | ```
<INLINE class="popup-trigger"> TRIGGER CONTENTS
   <INLINE class="popup"> POPUP CONTENT </INLINE>
</INLINE>
``` |
| CSS | ```
*.popup-trigger { position:relative; }
*.popup { position:absolute; left:0; top:1em; z-index:1; }
``` |
| **Location** | This pattern works inline. |
| **Limitations** | Internet Explorer 7 (and earlier versions) display pop-up triggers in front of pop-ups. You can solve this problem by laying out your page so that pop-up triggers are displayed on one side and pop-ups are displayed on the other. You can also solve this problem by assigning a unique ID to each pop-up trigger and styling each one so that it displays behind the previous one. In the example, I conditionally loaded a style sheet just for Internet Explorer, containing the following:

```
#pt1 { z-index:3; }
#pt2 { z-index:2; }
#pt3 { z-index:1; }
``` |

Pop-Up Alert

HTML Header

```
<head>
  <!-- only script elements are shown -->

  <script language="javascript" type="text/javascript" src="yahoo.js"></script>
  <script language="javascript" type="text/javascript" src="event.js"></script>
  <script language="javascript" type="text/javascript" src="chdp.js"></script>
  <script language="javascript" type="text/javascript" src="cssQuery-p.js"></script>
  <script language="javascript" type="text/javascript" src="page.js"></script>
</head>
```

page.js

```
function initPage() {
  assignEvent( 'click', '*.popup-trigger',
    applyToDescendants, '*.popup', toggleVisibility );

  assignEvent( 'mouseover', '*.popup-trigger',
    applyToDescendants, '*.popup', showElement );

  assignEvent( 'mouseout', '*.popup-trigger',
    applyToDescendants, '*.popup', hideElement );
}

addEvent(window, 'unload', purgeAllEvents);
addEvent(window, 'load', initPage);

//The functions addEvent() and assignEvents() are in chdp.js.
//Full documentation for each function is found in the source code.
```

Pop-Up Alert

Problem	To implement pop-ups, you need a way to attach events to HTML elements without coding them into the markup.
Solution	Using open source JavaScript libraries, you can dynamically attach events to elements. This eliminates event code within markup.
	There are several open source JavaScript libraries that you can use for this purpose. I chose two free libraries from Yahoo! that are licensed under a BSD license: **yahoo.js** and **event.js**. They are available at **http://developer.yahoo.com/yui/**.
	I also use an open source JavaScript library called **cssQuery.js** from Dean Edwards located at **http://dean.edwards.name/**. It is freely licensed under LGPL 2.1. It allows you to select elements in JavaScript using CSS selectors.
	I also provide an open source library called **chdp.js** freely licensed under a BSD license. It provides functions that integrate these other libraries.
	You can use these libraries by attaching each one to your document in the order shown in the example.
	You can attach your own JavaScript file to execute code specific to your document. The example names this file **page.js** and shows its code. The browser executes the two **addEvent()** functions first. The first **addEvent()** function attaches a generic function called **purgeAllEvents()** to the page's unload event. When the page unloads, **purgeAllEvents()** purges all attached events from memory. The second **addEvent()** function attaches **initPage()** to the page's load event. After the page loads, **initPage()** assigns events to elements using **assignEvent()**.
	It is easy to use **assignEvent()** to assign an event to elements. The name of the event goes in the first argument (without the "on" prefix). A CSS selector in the second argument determines which elements get assigned to the event. You can use any CSS 2.1 selector. **applyToDescendants()** goes in the third argument. The CSS selector in the fourth argument selects which descendants of the element that generated the event are affected by the helper function in the fifth argument. In the example, I use **showElement()**, **hideElement()**, and **toggleVisibility()** from **chdp.js** as helper functions to show, hide, and toggle the display of pop-up elements.
Tips	**This is a flexible framework.** You can use CSS selectors to apply any event to any element, and you can supply your own functions to handle events.
	You could use the Event Styling design pattern in Chapter 17 to change class names instead of using **showElement()**, **hideElement()**, and **toggleVisibility()**. Unfortunately, Opera 9 has trouble rendering *absolute* elements when you add and remove class names. To avoid this problem, this design pattern directly modifies an element's visibility using the DOM.
	You can build prettier alerts by using rounded corners with border-radius or shadow effects, as described in Chapter 6.
	You can combine this pattern with Transitions, Animations, and Transformations, as described in Chapter 1, to deliver a more stunning visual effect.
Example	The first **assignEvents()** function in the example assigns the **onclick** event to all pop-up-trigger elements. When the **onclick** event fires, **applyToDescendants()** applies **toggleVisibility()** to each pop-up descendant of the element that fired the event. **toggleVisibility()** hides an element when it is visible and shows it when it is hidden.
Related to	Alert, Inline Alert; Positioned, Closest Positioned Ancestor, Atomic, Absolute, Relative (Chapter 7); Left Offset, Top Offset (Chapter 9); Image, Replaced Text (Chapter 14); Event Styling, Rollup, Flyout Menu (Chapter 17)

Alert

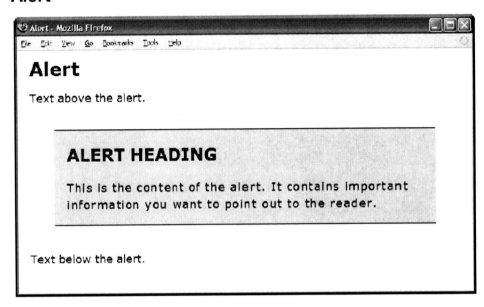

HTML

```
<h1>Alert</h1>
<p>Text above the alert.</p>

<div class="alert tip">
  <h3>Alert Heading</h3>
  <p>This is the content of the alert. It contains important information
    you want to point out to the reader.
  </p>
</div>

<p>Text below the alert.</p>
```

CSS

```
*.alert { margin:40px;
  padding-left:20px; padding-right:20px;
  border-top:1px solid black; border-bottom:1px solid black;
  background-color:gold; }
*.alert h3 { font-size:1.3em; }
*.alert p { letter-spacing:1.5px; line-height:1.5em; }
*.alert.tip h3 { text-transform:uppercase; }
```

Alert

Problem	You want to insert an alert into your document to point out important information to the reader. You want to separate the alert from surrounding text to make it stand out. You want to identify the purpose of the alert to the user and make the alert's purpose stand out in contrast to its content.
Solution	An alert consists of a heading and content packaged inside of a division. The heading identifies the purpose of the alert as a tip, note, caution, warning, and so forth. The content contains the alert's message. You can make the alert stand out by using whitespace, borders, backgrounds, and fonts.
	You can use **<div class="alert TYPE">** to identify the division as an alert and to identify the type of alert. For example, **<div class="alert tip">** identifies the division as an alert and identifies the type of alert as a tip. You can use any type of block element instead of the division. You can use ***.alert** to select the entire alert for styling. You can chain together class selectors to style specific types of alerts, such as ***.alert.tip{}**.
	You can use **<h3>** to identify the alert's heading. Since alerts are not as important as a main heading or topic headings, you may want to give them a low-level heading, such as **<h3>**. The heading signals to search engines that the alert's content is important. The heading typically contains one word, such as "Note," "Tip," or "Caution." You can use ***.alert h3{}** to select the heading for styling.
	You can use **<p>** to identify the alert's content. You can use ***.alert p{}** to select the content for styling.
Pattern	
HTML	``` <div class="alert TYPE"> <h3> ALERT HEADING </h3> <p> ALERT TEXT </p> </div> ```
CSS	``` *.alert { STYLES } *.alert h3 { STYLES } *.alert p { STYLES } *.alert.TYPE { STYLES } *.alert.TYPE h3 { STYLES } *.alert.TYPE p { STYLES } ```
Location	This pattern works anywhere you can use a block element.
Options	You can use other types of block elements to mark up the alert.
Tips	**If you want to add even more emphasis** to the alert, you can embed **<em>** or **<strong>** inside the paragraph or heading.
	You can build prettier alerts by using rounded corners with border-radius or shadow effects, as described in Chapter 6.
Related to	All design patterns in this chapter; Terminal Block Elements, Multi-purpose Block Elements (Chapter 2); Subclass Selector (Chapter 3); Margin, Border, Padding, Background (Chapter 6); Font (Chapter 10); Spacing, Inline Decoration (Chapter 11); Section (Chapter 13)

Inline Alert

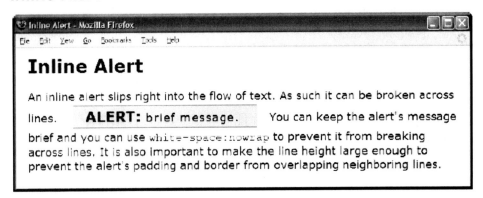

HTML

```
<h1>Inline Alert</h1>

<p>An inline alert slips right into the flow of text.
  As such it can be broken across lines.

  <span class="alert tip">
    <strong class="heading">Alert: </strong>
    <em class="content">brief message. </em>
  </span>

  You can keep the alert's message brief and you can use
  <code>white-space:nowrap</code> to prevent it from breaking across lines.
  It is also important to make the line height large enough to prevent the
  alert's padding and border from overlapping neighboring lines. </p>
```

CSS

```
*.alert { white-space:nowrap; line-height:2.3em;
  margin:0 20px; padding:8px 20px 5px 20px;
  border-top:1px solid black; border-bottom:1px solid black;
  background-color:gold; }

*.alert *.heading { font-weight:bold; font-size:1.3em; }

*.alert *.content { letter-spacing:1.5px; font-style:normal; }

*.alert.tip *.heading { text-transform:uppercase; }
```

Inline Alert

Problem	You want to insert an alert into the inline flow of your document. You also want the inline alert to work just like a block alert.
Solution	An inline alert consists of an inline heading and inline content packaged inside a span. The inline heading identifies the purpose of the alert as a tip, note, caution, warning, and so on. The inline content contains the alert's message. The inline alert works just like the Alert design pattern; the only difference is elements are inline. You can make the alert stand out by displaying it as a block, and using whitespace, borders, backgrounds, and fonts.
	You can use **`<span class="alert TYPE">`** to identify the span element as an alert and to identify the type of alert. For example, **`<span class="alert tip">`** identifies the span as an alert and identifies the type of alert as a tip. This works just like the Alert design pattern except we are using a span instead of a division. You can use **`*.alert`** to select the entire alert for styling. You can chain together class selectors to style specific types of alerts, such as **`*.alert.tip{}`**.
	You can use **`<strong class="heading">`** to identify the alert's heading. Heading elements cannot be used inline because they are block elements. **`<strong>`** is a good substitute because it indicates strongly emphasized text. The heading text is typically one word, such as "Note," "Tip," or "Caution." You can use **`*.alert *.heading{}`** to select the heading for styling.
	You can use **`<em class="content">`** to identify the alert's content. You can use **`*.alert *.content{}`** to select the heading for styling.
Pattern	
| HTML | ```
<span class="alert TYPE">
  <strong class="heading"> ALERT HEADING: </strong>
  <em class="content"> ALERT TEXT </em>
</span>
``` |
| CSS | ```
*.alert { white-space:nowrap; line-height:+VALUE; }
*.alert *.heading { STYLES }
*.alert *.content { STYLES }
*.alert.TYPE { STYLES }
*.alert.TYPE *.heading { STYLES }
*.alert.TYPE *.content { STYLES }
``` |
Location	This pattern works anywhere you can use an inline element, and it can be reliably floated and positioned.
Options	You can use **`display:block`** to render an inline alert exactly as if it were a block alert. This is useful when you have to mark up an alert within an inline context, but want it to look like a block alert.
Tip	**You can build prettier alerts by using rounded corners** with border-radius or shadow effects, as described in Chapter 6.
Related to	Alert, JavaScript Alert, Tooltip Alert, Pop-Up Alert; Inline Elements (Chapter 2); Subclass Selector (Chapter 3); Inline Box (Chapter 4); Spacing, Nowrap (Chapter 11)

Hanging Alert

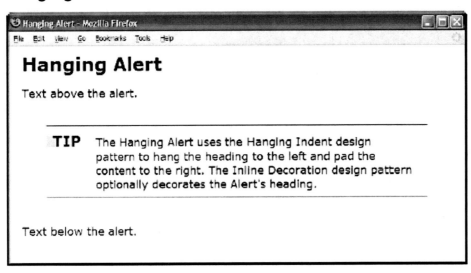

HTML

```
<h1>Hanging Alert</h1>
<p>Text above the alert.</p>

<div class="alert tip">
  <h3><span class="decoration"> </span>Tip</h3>
  <p>The Hanging Alert uses the Hanging Indent design pattern to hang the
    heading to the left and pad the content to the right. The Inline Decoration
    design pattern optionally decorates the Alert's heading.</p>
</div>
<p>Text below the alert.</p>
```

CSS

```
*.alert { padding-right:20px; padding-top:10px; padding-bottom:10px;
  border-top:1px solid black; border-bottom:1px solid black; margin:40px; }

*.alert h3 { display:inline; font-size:1.3em; text-transform:uppercase; }

*.alert.tip { text-indent:-80px; padding-left:80px; }
*.alert.note { text-indent:-110px; padding-left:110px; }
*.alert.caution { text-indent:-160px; padding-left:160px; }

*.alert.tip p { display:inline; margin-left:18px; }
*.alert.note p { display:inline; margin-left:20px; }
*.alert.caution p { display:inline; margin-left:20px; }

*.alert *.decoration { border-left:15px solid gold; margin-right:-10px;
  font-size:0.7em; vertical-align:2px; }
```

Hanging Alert

Problem	You want to insert a hanging alert into your document. You want its heading to be moved to the left and its content to the right. You want to adjust the indent to fit different types of alerts. You do not want to insert extra markup.
Solution	You can use the Alert design pattern to mark up the alert. You can style the alert using the Hanging Indent design pattern (Chapter 12). You can optionally use the Inline Decoration design pattern (Chapter 11) to decorate the alert's heading.
	To create a hanging indent, the alert's heading and paragraph need to be displayed as inline blocks. This puts them in the same inline formatting context. You can then use a positive value in **padding-left** to indent all the text in the heading and the paragraph to the right. You can use a negative value in **text-indent** to move the first line into the left padding area by an equal amount. For example, if you use **padding-left:100px**, you should use **text-indent:-100px**. Lastly, the first line of the paragraph needs to be moved to the right so that it lines up with the left indentation of the rest of its lines. You can select the paragraph and use **margin-left** to move the first line into alignment. Because the paragraph is displayed inline, **margin-left** affects only the beginning of the paragraph's first line.

Pattern

| HTML | ```
<div class="alert TYPE">
  <h3> ALERT HEADING </h3>
  <p>  ALERT TEXT </p>
</div>
``` |
| CSS | ```
*.alert { ANY_STYLES }
*.alert h3 { display:inline; }
*.alert.TYPE { display:inline;
  text-indent: -INDENT;
  padding-left:+INDENT; }
*.alert.TYPE p { display:inline; margin-left:+VALUE; }
``` |

Location	This pattern works anywhere you can use a block element, and it can be reliably floated and positioned.
Advantages	Because the properties used by this pattern are simple, they are well supported by every major browser.
Disadvantages	You have to play with **margin-left** until you are satisfied it aligns the paragraph's text. The exact value depends mainly on the heading's font.
Example	The example shows how you can use different selectors to adjust the hanging indent for different types of alerts. When you change the type of alert, the hanging indent changes too.
Tip	**You can build prettier alerts by using rounded corners** with border-radius or shadow effects, as described in Chapter 6.
Related to	Alert; Offset Static (Chapter 8); Inline Decoration (Chapter 11); Hanging Indent (Chapter 12); Inlined (Chapter 13)

Graphical Alert

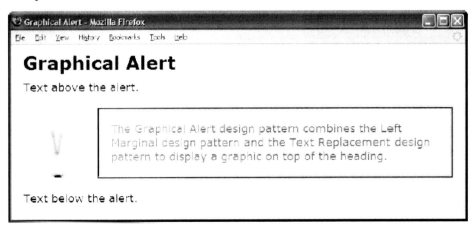

HTML

```
<h1>Graphical Alert</h1>
<p>Text above the alert.</p>

  <div class="alert tip">
    <h3><em>Tip</em><span></span></h3>
    <p>The Graphical Alert design pattern combines the Left Marginal design pattern
      and the Text Replacement design pattern to display a graphic
      on top of the heading.</p></div>

<p>Text below the alert.</p>
```

CSS

```
*.alert { position:relative; margin:20px 0 20px 120px; }
*.alert h3 { margin:10px 0; font-weight:bold; font-size:1.3em;
  text-transform:uppercase; }
*.alert p { margin:10px 0; }

*.alert.tip p { color:green; border:4px ridge green; padding:20px; }

*.alert.tip h3 { position:absolute; left:-100px; top:-15px;
  width:71px; height:117px; padding:0; overflow:hidden; }

*.alert.tip h3 em { position:absolute; left:20px; top:25px; }

*.alert.tip span { position:absolute; left:0; top:0; margin:0;
  width:71px; height:117px; background:url("tip.jpg") no-repeat; }
```

Graphical Alert

Problem	You want to insert an alert into your document with a graphical heading on the left and content on the right. You want the heading text to be shown in case the browser cannot display the image. You want screen readers to read the heading text. You do not want to embed an image in the HTML because the image is style, not content.
Solution	You can combine the Left Marginal design pattern with the Text Replacement design pattern (Chapter 10) to create the graphical alert.
	You can insert an empty span into the alert's heading. You can add the rules from the Text Replacement design pattern using the selectors shown in the pattern that follows. You can replace **TYPE** in the pattern with the class name that identifies the type of alert, such as tip, note, or caution. This allows you to use different images for different types of alerts. For example, you could use a star image for a tip and an exclamation image for a caution. You can replace **IMAGE_WIDTH** and **IMAGE_HEIGHT** in the pattern with the width and height of the image. You can replace **FILE.EXT** in the pattern with the file name of the image.
	You can optionally select the embedded **\<em\>** to position the heading. This allows you to control exactly where the heading is positioned independent from the graphic. If the graphic cannot be displayed, the heading will be right where you want it. You can choose any position as long as the graphic is large enough to cover up the heading in this position.
Pattern	
HTML	

```
<div class="alert TYPE">
  <h3><em> ALERT HEADING </em><span></span></h3>
  <p> ALERT TEXT </p>
</div>
```

CSS	Use the same selectors and styles as the Alert design pattern plus the following:

```
*.alert.TYPE h3 em { position:absolute; left:20px; top:25px; }
*.alert.TYPE h3 { position:absolute; left:-VALUE; top:±VALUE;
  width:IMAGE_WIDTH; height:IMAGE_HEIGHT;
  padding:0; overflow:hidden; }
*.alert.TYPE span { position:absolute; left:0; top:0; margin:0;
  width:IMAGE_WIDTH; height:IMAGE_HEIGHT;
  background:url("FILE.EXT") no-repeat; }
```

Location	This pattern works anywhere you can use a block element.
Tip	**You can build prettier alerts by using rounded corners** with border-radius or shadow effects, as described in Chapter 6.
Related to	Width, Height, Sized (Chapter 5); Margin, Border, Padding, Background, Overflow (Chapter 6); Positioned, Closest Positioned Ancestor, Absolute, Relative (Chapter 7); Text Replacement (Chapter 10); Left Marginal (Chapter 13)

Run-In Alert

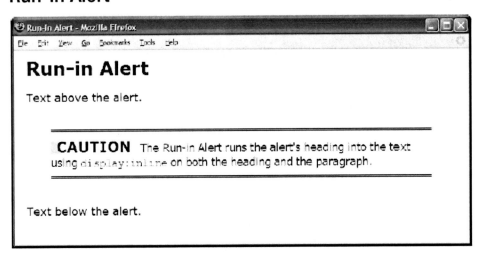

HTML

```
<h1>Run-In Alert</h1>
<p>Text above the alert.</p>

<div class="alert caution">
  <h3><span class="decoration"> </span>Caution</h3>
  <p>The Run-In Alert runs the alert's heading into the text using
    <code>display:inline</code> on both the heading and the paragraph.</p>
</div>

<p>Text below the alert.</p>
```

CSS

```
*.alert { padding-right:20px; padding-top:10px; padding-bottom:10px;
  border-top:1px solid black; border-bottom:1px solid black; margin:40px; }

*.alert h3 { display:inline; font-size:1.3em; text-transform:uppercase; }

*.alert p { display:inline; margin-left:10px; letter-spacing:-0.8px }

*.alert.caution { color:red;
  border-top:3px double red; border-bottom:3px double red; }

*.alert *.decoration { border-left:15px solid gold;
  margin-right:-11px; font-size:0.7em; vertical-align:2px; }
```

Run-In Alert

Problem	You want to insert an alert into your document where the alert's heading runs into the alert's paragraph.
Solution	You can use the Alert design pattern to mark up the alert. You can use the Run-In design pattern to get the heading to run into the paragraph by styling the heading and the paragraph with **display:inline**. As pointed out in the Run-In design pattern discussion in Chapter 13, CSS provides the rule **display:run-in** for this purpose, but only Opera, Safari, and Konquerer support it. Thus, we have to use the Run-In design pattern instead. Lastly, you can optionally use the Inline Decoration design pattern (Chapter 11) to decorate the alert's heading.
Pattern	
| HTML | ```
<div class="alert TYPE">
 <h3> ALERT HEADING </h3>
 <p>  ALERT TEXT </p>
</div>
``` |
| CSS | ```
*.alert { ANY_STYLES }
*.alert h3 { display:inline; }
*.alert p  { display:inline; }
``` |
Location	This pattern works anywhere you can use a block element, and it can be reliably floated and positioned.
Advantages	Because the properties used by this pattern are simple, they are well supported by every major browser.
	This pattern is closely related to the Inline Alert design pattern because it displays the heading and paragraph inline. If you want the Inline Alert design pattern to be styled like the Run-In pattern, simply do not assign **display:block** to its **<span class="heading">** and **<span class="content">** elements. The main advantage of the Run-In Alert over the Inline Alert design pattern is that **<h3>** and **<p>** have more semantic meaning than spans.
Example	In the example, I used the selector ***.alert.caution** to turn the text and borders red when the class of the alert is **caution**. I also inserted the Inline Decoration design pattern into the heading to give it more emphasis. In this case, the Inline Decoration consists of the **<span class="decoration"> </span>** styled with a gold left border.
Tip	**You can build prettier alerts by using rounded corners** with border-radius or shadow effects, as described in Chapter 6.
Related to	Inline Alert; Inline Decoration (Chapter 11); Inlined, Run-In (Chapter 13)

483

Floating Alert

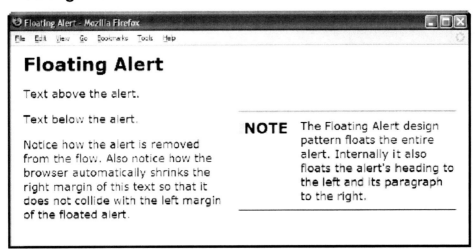

HTML

```
<h1>Floating Alert</h1>
<p>Text above the alert.</p>

<div class="alert note">
   <h3><span class="decoration"> </span>Note</h3>
   <p>The Floating Alert design pattern floats the entire alert. Internally it also
      floats the alert's heading to the left and its paragraph to the right.</p>
</div>
<p>Text below the alert.</p>
<p>Notice how the alert is removed from the flow. Also notice how the browser
   automatically shrinks the right margin of this text so that it does not
   collide with the left margin of the floated alert.</p>
```

CSS

```
*.alert { float:right; width:350px; margin-left:20px;
   border-top:1px solid black; border-bottom:1px solid black; }

*.alert h3 { float:left; width:50px; margin:10px 0;
   font-size:1.3em; text-transform:uppercase; }

*.alert p { float:right; width:250px; margin:10px 0; }

*.alert.note { color:blue;
   border-top:2px groove blue; border-bottom:2px ridge blue; }

*.alert *.decoration { border-left:15px solid gold;
   margin-right:-11px; font-size:0.7em; vertical-align:2px; }
```

Floating Alert

Problem	You want to insert a floating alert into your document.
Solution	You can use the Alert design pattern to mark up the alert. You can use the Float and Clear design pattern (Chapter 7) to float the alert. You can use the Opposing Floats design pattern (Chapter 17) to float the alert's heading to the left and its paragraph to the right.
Pattern	
| HTML | ```
<div class="alert TYPE">
  <h3> ALERT HEADING </h3>
  <p>  ALERT TEXT </p>
</div>
``` |
| CSS | ```
*.alert { float:LEFT_OR_RIGHT; width:+VALUE; margin:+VALUE; }
*.alert h3 { float:left; width:+VALUE; margin:+VALUE; }
*.alert p { float:right; width:+VALUE; margin:+VALUE; }
``` |
Location	This pattern works anywhere you can float a block element.
Advantages	The browser automatically calculates the positions of floats, dynamically sizes their height, and dynamically moves text and other floats out of the way. When the display is narrow, floats get pushed down. This makes the layout very flexible and adaptive to the user's environment. It is easy to control the general position of a float by floating it left or right and by placing margins around it. If you need finer control, you can also relatively position a float and offset it using **left**, **right**, **bottom**, and **top**.
Disadvantages	The main disadvantage to this design pattern is that you cannot float the heading and paragraph without floating the division as well. The browser removes floats from the normal flow. If you float a child, you also have to float its parent if you want to keep them together.
	Floats trigger bugs in browsers and are not well supported in minor browsers. It is difficult to control the precise position of a float. Its vertical position is roughly located at its nonfloated vertical position in the flow. Its horizontal position is the inner-left or inner-right side of its parent's container, or stacked next to or below a previously floated element.
Example	In the example, I used the selector ***.alert.note** to turn the text and borders blue when the class of the alert is **note**. I also inserted the Inline Decoration design pattern (Chapter 11) into the heading to give it more emphasis. In this case, the inline decoration consists of the **<span class="decoration"> </span>** styled with a gold left border.
Options	You can easily float an inline alert following these same techniques.
Tip	**You can build prettier alerts by using rounded corners** with border-radius or shadow effects, as described in Chapter 6.
Related to	Alert; Inline Alert; Float and Clear (Chapter 7); Offset Float (Chapter 8); Inline Decoration (Chapter 11); Opposing Floats (Chapter 17)

Left Marginal Alert

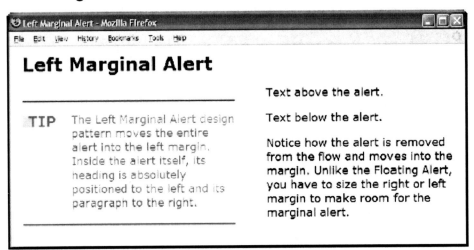

HTML

```
<h1>Left Marginal Alert</h1>

<div class="main">
  <p>Text above the alert.</p>
  <div class="alert tip">
    <h3><span class="decoration"> </span>Tip</h3>
    <p>The Left Marginal Alert design pattern moves the entire alert into the
        left margin. Inside the alert itself, its heading is absolutely positioned
        to the left and its paragraph to the right.</p>
  </div>
  <p>Text below the alert.</p>
  <p>Notice how the alert is removed from the flow and moves into the margin.
    Unlike the Floating Alert, you have to size the right or left margin
    to make room for the marginal alert.</p>
</div>
```

CSS

```
*.main { position:relative; margin-left:400px; }
*.alert { position:absolute; width:350px; left:-400px; height:190px;
  border-top:1px solid black; border-bottom:1px solid black; }
*.alert h3 { position:absolute; left:0; top:15px; margin:0;
  font-size:1.3em; text-transform:uppercase; }
*.alert p { position:absolute; left:80px; top:15px; margin:0; }
*.alert.tip { color:green;
  border-top:4px groove green; border-bottom:4px ridge green; }
*.alert *.decoration { border-left:15px solid gold;
  margin-right:-11px; font-size:0.7em; vertical-align:2px; }
```

Left Marginal Alert

Problem	You want to insert an alert into the left margin of your document.
Solution	You need to create a wide margin on the left in which to put the alert. You can use the Alert design pattern to mark up the alert. You can use the Left Marginal design pattern (Chapter 13) to move the alert into the margin. You can use the Offset Absolute and Offset Fixed design pattern (Chapter 8) to vertically position the alert and the Left Aligned design pattern (Chapter 9) to horizontally position the alert. You can use the Left Offset and Top Offset design patterns (Chapter 9) to position the heading and the paragraph.
| **Pattern**<br><br>HTML | ```html
<div class="main">
  <div class="alert TYPE">
    <h3> ALERT HEADING </h3>
    <p>  ALERT TEXT </p>
  </div>
</div>
``` |
| CSS | ```css
*.main { position:relative; margin-left:MARGIN; }
*.alert { position:absolute; width:+A_WIDTH; left:-A_WIDTH;
  height:+VALUE; }
*.alert h3 { position:absolute; left:0; top:TOP_OFFSET;
  margin:0; }
*.alert p { position:absolute; left:+VALUE top:TOP_OFFSET;
  margin:0; }
```

Use **margin-left:MARGIN** to create a left margin in the main block element that contains the alert, and use **position relative** to position it.

Set the alert, its heading, and its paragraph to **position:absolute**.

Set **width:A_WIDTH** to less than **MARGIN** so the alert will fit in the margin.

Optionally set **height:+VALUE** to the height you want the alert to be. This is necessary only if you are using **border-bottom** to render a bottom border.

Move the alert into the margin by setting **left** to the negative of **A_WIDTH**.

Use **left:0** to move the heading to the left side of the alert.

Use **left:+VALUE** to offset the paragraph to the right of the heading.

Use **top:TOP_OFFSET** to offset the top of the heading and paragraph from the top of the alert.

Use **margin:0** to clear the default heading and paragraph margins.

Note that the paragraph defaults to **width:auto**, which automatically sizes the paragraph to fit within the width of the alert. |
Location	This pattern works anywhere you have a wide left margin.
Advantages	You have complete control over the positioning of the alert. Also, the alert is placed outside the border of its parent. See Right Marginal Alert to place the alert inside the border.
Disadvantages	You need to ensure there is enough vertical space between marginal elements to prevent them from overlapping. Absolute positioning does not adapt as well to various devices as does the Fluid Layout design pattern (Chapter 17).
Tip	**You can build prettier alerts by using rounded corners** with border-radius or shadow effects, as described in Chapter 6.
Related to	Alert, Inline Alert, Right Marginal Alert; Offset Absolute and Offset Fixed (Chapter 8); Left Aligned, Left Offset, Top Offset (Chapter 9); Inline Decoration (Chapter 11); Left Marginal (Chapter 13)

Right Marginal Alert

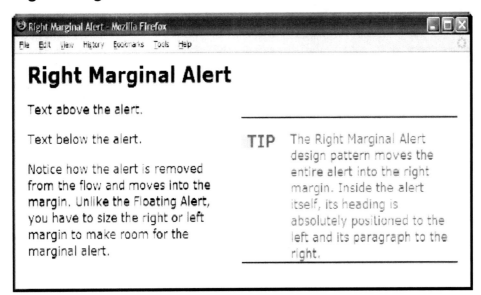

HTML

```
<div class="main">
  <p>Text above the alert.</p>

  <div class="alert tip">
    <h3><span class="decoration"> </span>Tip</h3>
    <p>The Right Marginal Alert design pattern moves the entire alert into the
       right margin. Inside the alert itself, its heading is absolutely positioned
       to the left and its paragraph to the right.</p>
  </div>

  <p>Text below the alert.</p>
  <p>Notice how the alert is removed from the flow and moves into the margin.
     Unlike the Floating Alert, you have to size the right or left margin
     to make room for the marginal alert.</p>
</div>
```

CSS

```
*.main { position:relative; padding-right:400px; }
*.alert { position:absolute; width:350px; right:0; height:190px;
  border-top:1px solid black; border-bottom:1px solid black; }
*.alert h3 { position:absolute; left:0; top:15px; margin:0;
  font-size:1.3em; text-transform:uppercase; }

*.alert p { position:absolute; left:80px; top:15px; margin:0; }
*.alert.tip { color:green;
  border-top:4px groove green; border-bottom:4px ridge green; }
*.alert *.decoration { border-left:15px solid gold;
  margin-right:-11px; font-size:0.7em; vertical-align:2px; }
```

Right Marginal Alert

Problem	You want to insert an alert into the right margin of your document.
Solution	You need to create a wide margin on the right in which to put the alert. You can use the Alert design pattern to mark up the alert. You can use the Right Marginal design pattern to move the alert into the right margin. You can use the Offset Absolute and Offset Fixed design pattern (Chapter 8) to vertically position the alert and the Right Aligned design pattern (Chapter 9) to horizontally position the alert. You can use the Left Offset and Top Offset design patterns (Chapter 9) to position the heading and the paragraph.
Pattern HTML	```<div class="main">
<div class="alert TYPE">
<h3> ALERT HEADING </h3>
<p> ALERT TEXT </p>
</div>
</div>```
CSS	```*.main { position:relative; padding-right:MARGIN; }
*.alert { position:absolute; width:A_WIDTH; right:0;
height:+VALUE; }
*.alert h3 { position:absolute; left:0; top:TOP_OFFSET;
margin:0; }
*.alert p { position:absolute; left:+VALUE top:TOP_OFFSET;
margin:0; }``` Use **padding-right:MARGIN** to create a right "margin" in the main block element that contains the alert, and use **position relative** to position it. **Set the alert**, its heading, and its paragraph to **position:absolute**. Set **width:A_WIDTH** to less than **MARGIN** so the alert will fit in the "margin." Optionally set **height:+VALUE** to the height you want the alert to be. This is necessary only if you are using **border-bottom** to render a bottom border. Use **right:0** to move the alert into the "margin" of the main block. Use **left:0** to move the heading to the left side of the alert. Use **left:+VALUE** to offset the paragraph to the right of the heading. Use **top:TOP_OFFSET** to offset the top of the heading and paragraph from the top of the alert. Use **margin:0** to clear the default heading and paragraph margins. Note that the paragraph defaults to **width:auto**, which automatically sizes the paragraph to fit within the width of the alert.
Location	This pattern works anywhere you have a wide right padding.
Advantages	You have complete control over the positioning of the alert. Also, the alert is placed within the border of its parent. See Left Marginal Alert to place the alert outside the border.
Disadvantages	You need to ensure there is enough vertical space between marginal elements to prevent them from overlapping. Absolute positioning does not adapt as well to various devices as does the Fluid Layout design pattern (Chapter 17).
Tip	**You can build prettier alerts by using rounded corners** with border-radius or shadow effects, as described in Chapter 6.
Related to	Alert, Inline Alert, Left Marginal Alert; Offset Absolute and Offset Fixed (Chapter 8); Left Offset, Right Aligned, Top Offset (Chapter 9); Inline Decoration (Chapter 11); Right Marginal (Chapter 13)

Form Validation

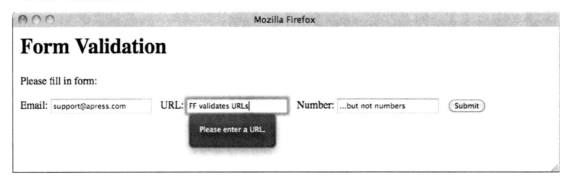

HTML

```
<h1>Form Validation</h1>
<p>Please fill in form:</p>
  <form method="post">
    <label>Email: <input type="email" required></label>
    <label>URL: <input type="url" required></label>
    <label>Number: <input type="number" max="100" min="0" step="2" required></label>
    <input type="submit" value="Submit"></form>
  </form>
```

CSS

```
input {margin-right: 10px;}
```

Form Validation

Problem	You want to validate user input in forms and display the necessary alerts.
Solution	Form validation has traditionally been done using JavaScript, e.g., there are several jQuery plug-ins that offer form validation at `http://plugins.jquery.com/projects/plugins?type=20`. HTML5 offers native validation for forms and also adds a number of useful input types like e-mail, web addresses, date pickers, and more. You can use this native validation mechanism to check user input and print alerts.
Pattern	
HTML	`<input id="INPUT ID" type="TYPE FOR VALIDATION" required>`
	Use `type="email"` **to validate e-mail addresses**, `type="url"` to validate web addresses, `type="number"` **to validate for e-mail addresses, etc.**
	Add the `required` **string inside the input element** to make it a required field.
	Add the `novalidate` **string inside the form element** to avoid native form validation.
	Use attributes `min`, `max`, `step` to fine-tune `type="number"`.
Advantages	Form validation is hard and error-prone, so having it performed natively by the browser and being RFC-compliant in cases like e-mail, etc., is very helpful.
Tips	**Some mobile devices that don't have a physical keyboard** can recognize several of the new HTML5 input types, and dynamically change the onscreen keyboard to optimize for that kind of input. For example, when you use an iPhone and focus an `input type="email"` element, you get an onscreen keyboard that contains a smaller-than-usual space bar, plus dedicated keys for the "@" and "." characters. Similarly for `input type="number"` you get a number scroller, etc.
	There are several more input types that the HTML5 specification defines, but browser support varies. Unless you are developing for a specific platform (e.g., iOS devices), it is probably wiser to continue using JavaScript validation and input widgets that are known to work with older browsers.
	Some forms of validations are notoriously hard to perform correctly even for browsers. For example, Chrome validates the string `foo@bar` as a correct e-mail address.
	Default validation alerts are ugly, but in the future it will be easy to add CSS style to them. Chrome and Safari have recently added support for pseudo-selectors like `::-webkit-validation-bubble{}`, `::-webkit-validation-bubble-top-outer-arrow{}`, `::-webkit-validation-bubble-top-inner-arrow{}`, and `::-webkit-validation-bubble-message{}`. At the time of this writing, Firefox has no way to style the error messages.
	Similarly you might want to change the text of the error messages. Firefox has support for the attribute `x-moz-errormessage`, which enables you to change the text of the error message. The same can be accomplished in Chrome using CSS and the `webkit-validation-bubble-message`.

INDEX

A

Alerts, 465
    dynamic alerts, 465
        JavaScript Alert, 466–467
        Pop-Up Alert, 470–473
        Tooltip Alert, 468–469
    form validation, 490–491
    static alerts, 465
        Floating Alert, 484–485
        Graphical Alert, 480–481
        Hanging Alert, 478–479
        Inline Alert, 476–477
        Left Marginal Alert, 486–487
        Right Marginal Alert, 488–489
        Run-In Alert, 482–483
Aligned
    Aligned-center Absolute
        CSS, 174
        explanation, 175
        horizontal/vertical center, 175
        HTML, 174
        limitations, 175
        location, 175
        patterns, 175
    Offset Absolute
        bottom-offset absolute element, 173
        CSS, 172
        HTML, 172
        left-offset absolute element, 173
        location, 173
        right-offset absolute element, 173
        styles, class/ID, 173
        top-offset absolute element, 173
    Offset Static Block
        center-aligned sized static block
          element, 169
        CSS, 168

        explanation, 169
        HTML, 168
        left-aligned sized static block
          element, 169
        limitations, 169
        location, 169
        margin-left:auto, 169
        margin-right:auto, 169
        right-aligned sized static block
          element, 169
    Offset Static Table
        block elements, 171
        CSS, 170, 171
        HTML, 170, 171
        inline elements, 171
        location, 171
    Outside
        absolute element, 177
        CSS, 176
        HTML, 176
        limitations, 177
        location, 177
        patterns, 177
        static blocks and floats, 177
    Static Inline
        CSS, 166
        horizontal patterns, 167
        HTML, 166
        terminal block container, 167
        vertical alignment, 167
        vertical center, 167
Aligned drop cap, 428–429

B

Block Quote, 458–459

Blocks, 265
   Background Bulleted, 274–275
   Block Spacer, 284–285
   Block Space Remover, 286–287
   Collapsed Margins
      CSS, 278
      HTML, 278
      padding and borders, 279
      sibling blocks, 279
   Horizontal Rule, 282–283
   Inlined, 276–277
   Left Marginal, 288–289
   Lists
      CSS, 272
      faux marker, 273
      HTML, 272–273
      indent lists, 273
      list-style-type property, 273
   Right Marginal, 290–291
   Run-in, 280–281
   Section, 270–271
   Structural Meaning, 266–267
   Visual Structure
      CSS, 268
      horizontal rule design pattern, 269
      positional styling, 268
      styling exceptions, 268
Box Models, 81
   Absolute Box
      absolute element, 95
      CSS, 94
      HTML coding, 94
      location, 95
      margin and border, 95
      Mozilla Firefox, 94
      selector, 95
      style, 95
      width, 95
   Block Box
      border and padding, 91
      CSS, 90
      HTML coding, 90
      location, 91
      margin-left and-right, 91
      margin-top and bottom push
        blocks, 91
      Mozilla Firefox, 90
      normal flow, 91

      overflow property, 91
      selector, 91
      styling, 91
      terminal block, 91
   Display
      block element, 83
      blocks, 83
      CSS, 82
      HTML coding, 82
      list item, 83
      Opera, 82
      property, 83
      types, 83
   division class HTML code, 84
   extents, 99
      Height, 102–103
      Shrinkwrapped, 106–108
      Sized, 104–105
      Stretched, 108–110
      Width, 100–101
   Floated Box, 96–97
   Inline Box
      border, 87
      CSS, 86
      inline formatting context, 87
      margin and line-height, 87
      Mozilla Firefox, 86
      padding, 87
      selector, 87
      span class coding, 86
   Inline–Block Box
      border and padding, 89
      image class, 88
      location, 89
      margin, 89
      Microsoft Internet Explorer, 88
      replaced-box, 88
      selector, 89
      span class, 88
      styling, 89
      width and height, 89
   properties, 85, 111
      background, 120–121
      border, 114–117
      margin, 112–113
      overflow, 122–123
      padding, 118–119

page break, 126–127
visibility, 124–125
selector, 85
Table Box
border, 93
border-collapse, 93
CSS, 92
flow, table, 93
HTML coding, 92
location, 93
margin, 93
properties, 93
style, 93
table cell, 92
width and height, 93

C

Callouts and Quotes, 447
Block Quote, 458–459
Center Callout, 452–453
Inline Block Quote, 460–461
Inline Quote, 462–463
Left Floating Callout, 448–449
Left Marginal Callout, 454–455
Right Floating Callout, 450–451
Right Marginal Callout, 456–457
Cascade order
competing rules, 14–15
guiding principles, 14
location groups, 15
rules sorted, 17
selector groups, 14
Center Callout, 452–453
Content alignment
Advanced Alignment Example
ac1 and ac2 classes, 263
CSS, 262
em measurements, 263
features, 263
font-size, 263
HTML, 262
inline elements, 263
MathML, 263
white-space:nowrap, 263
Hanging Indent
advantages, 251
CSS, 250

disadvantages, 251
HTML, 250
inline elements, 251
negative margin-left, 251
negative value, 251
padding-left, 251
pattern, 251
positive value, 251
structural block elements, 251
terminal block element, 251
Horizontal-aligned Content
CSS, 252
HTML, 252
inline elements, 253
justification algorithm, 253
patterns, 253
structural block elements, 253
terminal block elements, 253
text-align:center, 253
text-align:justify, 253
text-align:left, 253
text-align:right, 253
Nested Alignment
ac1, ac2, and ac3 classes, 261
CSS, 260
font-size values, 261
HTML, 260
inline elements, 261
Opera 11, 261
pattern, 261
Subscript and Superscript
Conditional Style Sheet design
pattern, 259
CSS, 258
em values, 259
Firefox 2, 259
HTML, 258
inline text elements, 259
Internet Explorer 7, 259
lle, 259
mademoiselle, 259
Opera 9, 259
patterns, 259
Text Indent
CSS, 248
HTML, 248
inline elements, 249
pattern, 249

positive margin-left, 249
positive value, 249
structural block elements, 249
terminal block elements, 249
Vertical-aligned Content
ÁMjx, 255
baseline, 255
CSS, 254
em height, 255
ex height, 255
fontlines, 255
HTML, 254
inline content, 255
inline elements, 255
paragraph, 255
pattern, 255
span, 255
Vertical-offset Content
ÁMjx, 257
baseline, 257
CSS, 256
ems, 257
HTML, 256
inline elements, 257
pattern, 257
pixels, 257
positive values, 257
subscript/superscript effect, 257
CSS syntax, 8
backslash, 9
case-sensitive, 8
constant values, 9
CSS comment, 9
element names, classes and IDs, 9
multiple classes, 9
property values, 10–13
right curly brace (}), 9
rulesets, 9
semicolon, 9
string, 9
Unicode UTF-8, 8
whitespaces, 10
Cufón, 217

D, E

Design patterns, 2
Absolute design patterns, 4

Alerts (*see* Alerts)
background property, 2–3
baseline style sheets, 30–31
CSS
Animations, 27
and HTML links, 18
properties and values, 19, 21–23
Transitions, 27
96 dpi
font-size values, 26
ratios between units of measure, 26
2D Transformations, 27
fixed units of measure, 25
flexible units of measure, 25
Left Marginal design pattern, 6
Marginal Graphic Dropcap design
pattern, 6
media queries, 24
pattern name, 2
problems, 2
selectors, 23
simplicity and power, 2
solutions, 2
Text Replacement design pattern, 5
trade-offs, 2
troubleshooting CSS, 28–29
using Cascade Order (*see* Cascade
order)
using CSS syntax (*see* CSS syntax)
using HTML (*see* HTML design
patterns)
using style sheets, 7–8
Drop Caps, 427
Aligned, 428–429
First-letter, 430–431
Floating
CSS, 436
HTML, 436
negative and positive values, 437
trigger bugs, 437
Floating Graphical
CSS, 438
HTML, 438
text dropcap style, 439
text replacement design pattern, 439
Hanging, 432–433
Marginal, 440–441
Marginal Graphical

CSS, 442
HTML, 442
image cannot be displayed, 444
text replacement design pattern, 443
top-offset sized absolute element
    design pattern, 443
+VALUE, 444
Padded Graphical
    background color/image, 435
    CSS, 434
    HTML, 434
    inline element, 435

F

First-letter Drop Cap, 430–431
Floating Alert, 484–85
Floating Drop Cap, 436–437
Floating Graphical Drop Cap, 438–439
Fluid Layout Overview, 382–383

G

Graphical Alert, 480–481

H

Hanging Alert, 478–479
Hanging Drop Cap, 432–433
Highlight white-on-firebrick, 209
Horizontal-aligned Content, 252–253
HTML design patterns, 33
    block elements, 35, 41
    Class and ID Attributes, 58–59
    Conditional Style Sheet, 48–49
    DOCTYPE, 44
        almost-standards mode, 45
        vs. content type, 44
        quirks and standards mode, 45
        strict and transitional, 45
    Header Elements, 46–47
    HTML Whitespace, 60–61
    Inline Elements, 35, 41, 56–57
    Multi-purpose Block Elements, 54–55
    Structural Block Elements, 50–51
    structural elements, 41
    Terminal Block Elements, 52–53
    XHTML, 41–43

HTML structure, design patterns
    block elements, 35, 41
    inline elements, 41
    structural elements, 41

I

Images, 293
    Basic Shadowed Image, 312–313
    Content over Background Image, 306–307
    Content over Image
        block element, 305
        CSS, 304
        HTML, 304
        inline decoration design pattern, 305
    Crater Lake pictures, 294
    CSS Sprite
        bitcons, 310
        CSS, 308
        Google Load Time Analyzer, 311
        history, 311
        HTML, 308
        HTTP and TCP/IP communications
            protocol, 311
        MSN home page, 311
        multiple background images, 309
        16•16 sprites offsets, 310
    decorative images, 295
    Fade-out
        CSS, 298
        gradient image and mask, 299
        gray gradients, Internet explorer 6, 299
        HTML, 298
    GIF format, 295
    Image Map
        HTML, 296
        map element, 297
        real-world map, 297
    JPG format, 295
    Northwest USA, 324–325
    PNG format, 295
    Replaced Text, 302–303
    Rounded Corners
        block and inline elements, 321
        CSS, 320

CSS3 multiple backgrounds, 321
HTML, 320
pad class, 323
rounded rectangle images, 322–323
Semi-transparent, 300–301
Shadowed
   background-position, 317
   block elements, 319
   CSS, 318
   HTML, 318
   image creation, 314, 315
   nested block elements, 315, 316
   shadow-lb.jpg indents, 314, 315
   shadow-rt.jpg and shadow-lb.jpg,
     314, 315
   shadow-rt.jpg indents, 314, 315
src attribute, 295
Inline Alert, 476–477
Inline Block Quote, 460–461
Inline Quote, 462–463

J, K

JavaScript Alert, 466–467

L

Layouts, 381
  Button
    client-side image map, 417
    CSS, 414
    HTML, 414, 416
    JavaScript events, 415
    page.js, 416
    server/reset form elements, 415
  Event Styling, 397
    CSS selector, 397
    HTML, 396
    jQuery, 397
    page.js, 396–397
    runtime elements, 396
  Float Divider, 390–391
  Floating Section
    CSS, 388
    HTML, 388
    Internet Explorer 7, 389
    section design pattern, 389
  Fluid Layout, 393

columns and rows, 383, 393
CSS, 382, 392
HTML, 382, 392
Flyout Menu
  add, remove and toggle functions,
    413
  CSS, 410
  drop-down menu, 413
  flyout-trigger class, 411
  HTML, 410, 412
  list-style-type, 413
  page.js, 412
Layout Example
  body and main section, 425
  CSS structural styles, 424
  design patterns, 425–426
  footer section, 425
  header section, 425
  HTML structural elements, 424
  nav and extra sections, 425
  postheader section, 425
  preheader section, 425
  title section, 425
Links, 418–419
Multi-column Layout, 420–421
Opposing Floats, 394–395
Outside-in Box
  CSS, 384
  HTML, 384
  vs. inside-out design, 386–388
  outer width, 385
Rollup
  CSS, 398
  HTML, 398, 400
  JavaScript, 401
  page.js, 400
  rollup-trigger class, 399
  screenreader-only design pattern,
    399
Tab Menu
  CSS, 402–404
  HTML, 402, 404
  list items, 405
  tab's box style, 405
Tabs, 409
  CSS, 406
  first click() function, 409
  HTML, 406, 408

mouseout() function, 409
mouseover() function, 409
page.js, 408
second click() function, 409
tab-content element, 407
Template Layout, 422–423
Left Floating Callout, 448–449
Left Marginal Alert, 486–487
Left Marginal Callout, 454–455

M

Marginal Drop Cap, 440–441
Marginal Graphical Drop Cap, 442–445
Multipart Internet Mail Extensions
    (MIME), 44

N

Negative margins outdent, 155
Nested Alignment, 260–261

O

Offset
    Absolute And Fixed
        advantages, 163
        CSS, 162
        HTML, 162
        margin-top and margin-left, 163
        shrinkwrapped-offset absolute
            element, 163
        sized-offset absolute element, 163
        tips, 163
    Float
        absolute and fixed elements, 161
        advantages, 161
        CSS, 160
        disadvantages, 161
        horizontal patterns, 161
        HTML, 160
        location, 161
        positive and negative margins, 161
        tips, 161
        vertical patterns, 161
    Indented Static Table
        CSS, 158, 159
        HTML, 158, 159

limitations, 159
location, 159
negative margin, 159
positive margin, 159
Relative
    atomic, 165
    CSS, 164
    HTML, 164
    limitations, 165
    location, 165
    normal/floating flow, 165
    patterns, 165
    z-index, 165
Static
    block elements, 157
    block patterns, 157
    CSS, 156
    HTML, 156
    inline element, 157
    inline patterns, 157
    location, 158
Ordered and unordered sets, 267

P, Q

Padded Graphical Drop Cap, 434–435
Pop-Up Alert, 470–473
Positioning, 153
    Aligned (see Aligned)
    Bottom Aligned
        CSS, 196
        HTML, 196
        limitations, 197
        location, 197
        patterns, 197
        shrinkwrapped absolute element,
            197
        sized element, 197
        static shrinkwrapped element, 197
        stretched element, 197
    Bottom Offset
        bottom-aligned element, 199
        CSS, 198
        HTML, 198
        limitations, 199
        location, 199
        margin-bottom, 199
        patterns, 199

Center Aligned
  CSS, 188
  horizontal center, 189
  HTML, 188
  limitations, 189
  location, 189
  patterns, 189
  sized element, 189
  stretched element, 189
  text-align:center, 189
  widths and margins, 189
Center Offset
  CSS, 190
  HTML, 190
  inline element, 191
  limitations, 191
  location, 191
  patterns, 191
  sized absolute element, 191
  stretched element, 191
Indented
  CSS, 154
  horizontally indented absolute
    element, 155
  horizontally indented static block
    element, 155
  HTML, 154
  limitations, 155
  location, 155
  margins, 155
  outdent, 155
  stretched absolute element, 155
  vertically indented absolute
    element, 155
Left Aligned
  CSS, 180
  HTML, 180
  limitations, 181
  location, 181
  patterns, 181
  shrinkwrapped element, 181
  sized element, 181
  stretched element, 181
  text-align:left, 181
Left Offset
  CSS, 182
  HTML, 182
  limitations, 183

location, 183
  margin-left, 183
  patterns, 183
Middle Aligned
  CSS, 200
  HTML, 200
  inline element, 201
  limitations, 201
  location, 201
  patterns, 201
  sized absolute element, 201
  stretched absolute element, 201
Middle Offset
  CSS, 202
  HTML, 202
  limitations, 203
  location, 203
  patterns, 203
  sized absolute element, 203
  stretched absolute element, 203
Offset (*see* Offset)
Right Aligned
  CSS, 184
  HTML, 184
  limitations, 185
  location, 185
  patterns, 185
  shrinkwrapped element, 185
  sized element, 185
  stretched element, 185
  text-align:right, 185
Right Offset
  CSS, 186
  HTML, 186
  limitations, 187
  location, 187
  margin-right, 187
  patterns, 187
Top Aligned
  CSS, 192
  HTML, 192
  limitations, 193
  location, 193
  patterns, 193
  shrinkwrapped element, 193
  sized element, 193
  stretched element, 193
Top Offset

CSS, 194
HTML, 194
limitations, 195
location, 195
margin-top, 195
patterns, 195
top-aligned element, 195
Positioning Models, 129
Absolute, 142
advantages, 143
CSS, 142
disadvantages, 143
HTML coding, 142
limitations, 143
Mozilla Firefox, 142
normal flow, 143
position ancestor, 143
selector, 143
Atomic
automatic rendering, 139
CSS, 138
HTML coding, 138
inline content, 139
Internet Explorer 6, 139
limitations, 139
Mozilla Firefox, 138
selector, 139
static blocks, 139
basic properties, 131
Closest Positioned Ancestor, 134
advantages, 135
CSS, 134
HTML coding, 134
limitaions and disadvantages, 135
location, 135
Mozilla Firefox, 134
pattern, 135
self-contained layout, 135
CSS, 130
Fixed
absolute size, 145
advantages and disadvantages, 145
CSS, 144
fixed elements, 145
HTML coding, 144
Internet Explorer 6, 145
Mozilla Firefox, 144
selector, 145

viewport, 145
Float and Clear, 148–149
HTML coding, 130
layouts, 131
Mozilla Firefox, 130
Positioned type, 132
ancestor, 133
CSS, 132
HTML coding, 132
left and right side element, 133
limitations, 133
location, 133
positive values, 133
selector, 133
Relative, 146
CSS, 146
float, 147
HTML coding, 146
Internet Explorer 7, 147
Mozilla Firefox, 146
normal flow, 147
offset, 147
selector, 147
Relative Float
advantages, 151
CSS, 150
HTML coding, 150
inline content, 151
Mozilla Firefox, 150
six types, 131
Stacking Context, 136
browser, 137
control, z-order, 137
CSS, 136
elements control, 137
Firefox, 137
HTML coding, 136
layer rendering, 137
numeric z-index, 137
Opera, 136
Static
block element, 141
CSS, 140
HTML coding, 140
inline element, 141
Mozilla Firefox, 140
normal flow, 141
top and bottom margin, 141

Positive margins indent, 155
Pull quotes, 447

R

Right Floating Callout, 450–451
Right Marginal Alert, 488–489
Right Marginal Callout, 456–457
Run-In Alert, 482–483

S

Selectors design patterns, 63
  Attribute Selectors
    case-sensitive match, 69
    CSS, 68
    element selection, 69
    existence selector, 69
    HTML, 68
    language, 69
    Mozilla Firefox, 68
    name spacing, 69
    value selector, 69
    word selector, 69
  Inheritance, 76
    CSS, 76
    HTML, 76
    limitations, 77
    not inherited properties, 77
    properties, 77
    visual (*see* Visual inheritance)
  Position and Group Selectors
    child elements, 67
    CSS, 66
    descendant elements, 67
    element position, 67
    first-child elements, 67
    HTML, 66
    Internet Explorer 7, 67
    list item, 67
    multiple selectors, 67
    sibling elements, 67
  Pseudo-class Selector, 72
    browser, 73
    CSS, 72
    HTML, 72
    hyperlink, 73
    Internet Explorer 6, 73

    visual indicator, underline, 73
  Pseudo-element Selector
    bugs, browsers, 71
    CSS, 70
    element selection, 71
    first-letter and-line, 71
    font and text properties, 71
    HTML, 70
    Mozilla Firefox, 70
  Subclass Selector, 74
    base class, 75
    class attribute, 75
    class of elements styling, 75
    CSS, 74
    HTML, 74
    paragraphs, 75
  Type, Class and ID
    case-sensitive, 65
    CSS, 64
    HTML, 64
    namespace, 65
    override, 65
    style, 65
Spacing content, 225–227
  Blocked
    CSS, 228
    HTML, 228
    inline element, 229
  Code
    CSS, 234
    HTML, 234
    inline elements, 235
    search engines and document
      processor, 235
  Inline Decoration, 240–241
  Inline Horizontal Rule, 244–245
  Inline Spacer
    CSS, 238
    emphasizing/deemphasizing space,
      239
    HTML, 238
  Line Break, 242–243
  Nowrap, 230–231
  Padded Content
    background-color/-image, 237
    blocked, 237
    CSS, 236
    HTML, 236

inline, 237
Preserved
  CSS, 232
  HTML, 232
  white-space:pre assignment, 233
terminal block element, 227
text-indent, 227
Style sheet, 7
Styling text
  Decoration
    background-image property, 211
    border property, 211
    CSS, 210
    HTML, 210
    line-throughs, 211
    location, 211
    overlines, 211
    padding-top/-bottom, 211
    patterns, 211
    transparent GIFs, 211
    underlines, 211
  Font
    color and case, 207
    CSS, 206
    embedding, 218–19
    family, 207
    HTML, 206
    location, 207
    pattern, 207
    size, 207
  Highlight
    background color, 209
    CSS, 208
    em measurements, 209
    forecolor, 209
    highlight-alert, 209
    HTML, 208
    location, 209
    padding distance, 209
    pattern, 209
    tiled image, 209
  Invisible Text
    CSS, 220
    HTML, 220
    limitations, 221
    pattern, 221
    terminal block element, 221
    text-align, 221

    text-indent, 221
    width and height, 221
  Replacement with Canvas and VML
    Cufón, 217
    cufon-yui.js, 217
    font converter, 217
    HTML, 216
    JavaScript, 217
    JSON data format, 217
    location, 217
    UTF-8 encoded, 217
  Replacement with Image
    absolute element, 215
    block element, 215
    CSS, 214
    fixed element, 215
    float element, 215
    HTML, 214
    pattern, 215
    span, 215
  Screenreader-only
    CSS, 222
    disadvantages, 223
    HTML, 222
    location, 223
    nonsighted users, 223
    pattern, 223
    pixel height and width, 223
    sighted users, 223
  Shadow
    background-color, 213
    block elements, 213
    CSS, 212
    filter:shadow, 213
    HTML, 212
    Internet Explorer 6, 212, 213
    pattern, 213
    Safari, 213
    zoom:1 triggers, 213

T, U

Table column layout, 353
  auto width, 354
  Column Width
    CSS, 356
    fixed-width cell, 357
    HTML, 356

minimum and maximum content
width, 357
types and values, 357
Content-proportioned Columns
CSS, 362
HTML, 362
sized and stretched tables, 363
VALUE_OR_PERCENT, 363
Equal Content-sized Columns
CSS, 370
design pattern, 371
HTML, 370
PERCENT, 371
Equal-sized Columns, 372–373
fixed tables, 353
fixed width, 354
Flex Columns
auto-layout tables, 377
CSS, 376
fixed-width and percentage-width
column, 377
HTML, 376
Inverse-proportioned Columns, 368–
369
Mixed Column Layouts
CSS, 378
design pattern, 379
HTML, 378
percentage width, 354
Percentage-proportioned Columns,
366–367
Shrinkwrapped Columns
content-proportioned columns
design pattern, 359
CSS, 358
HTML, 358
shrinkwrapped tables, 353
sized and stretched tables, 353
Sized Columns, 360–361
Size-Proportioned Columns, 364–365
Undersized Columns, 374–375
Tables, 327–329
border-collapse and table-layout, 329
Collapsed Borders, 336–337
Hidden and Removed Cells
CSS, 340
hidden tables and rows, 341
HTML, 340

removed tables and rows, 341
text-indent, 341
Layout, 350–351
Removed and Hidden Rows and
Columns, 342–343
Row and Column Groups, 331
CSS, 330
HTML, 330
table headers and footers, 331
Separated Borders
border-collapse:separate property,
335
CSS, 334
HTML, 334
nonbreaking space, 335
Striped Tables
background colors, 347
CSS, 346
HTML, 346
style border and padding, 347
Styled Collapsed Borders, 338–339
Table Selectors
column cells selector, 333
CSS, 332
HTML, 332
row cells selector, 333
row group selector, 333
style cells, 333
Tabled, Rowed And Celled, 348–349
Vertical-aligned Data, 344–345
TEXT DECORATION, 210–211
TEXT SHADOW, 212–213
Tooltip Alert, 468–469
Vertical-aligned Content, 254–255
Vertical-offset Content, 256–257
Visual Inheritance, 78
background property, 79
CSS, 78
design patterns, 79
HTML, 78
Mozilla Firefox, 78

CPSIA information can be obtained at www.ICGtesting.com
Printed in the USA
LVOW052258181111

255710LV00006B/2/P